Eastland

Legacy
of the
Titanic

GEORGE W. HILTON

Stanford University Press
Stanford, California

Stanford University Press
Stanford, California
© 1995 by the Board of Trustees of the
Leland Stanford Junior University

Printed in the United States of America

CIP data are at the end of the book

Stanford University Press publications
are distributed exclusively by Stanford
University Press within the United States,
Canada, Mexico, and Central America;
they are distributed exclusively by
Cambridge University Press throughout
the rest of the world.

Facing title page: The *Eastland* when all went well. The ship is shown steaming down the Chicago River in 1903, her first year of service. Her bow bears both the diamond and the shield logos of the Michigan Steamship Company painted on the hull. Her lettering, in contrast, was embossed. Note that it was common from the outset to operate with the gangway doors open. The forward gangway has an openwork guard across the lower half, but the second is entirely open. (Gordon Potter collection)

To Karen
because she,
too, habitually
asked the
reasons why

Preface

IN 1971, wishing to read dissertations in my department more intelligently, I resolved to audit econometrics, but because the mists of time lay heavy on my elementary statistics course, I decided to audit that first. The course was taught by my colleague Larry J. Kimbell, then assistant professor of economics, but long since risen in rank and distinction to professor of business economics and director of the business forecasting section of UCLA's Anderson Graduate School of Management. When he came to the list of statistical fallacies in the textbook—a list of the sort that appears in every beginning statistics text—he dutifully reeled them off, but then stopped and remarked that the worst statistical fallacy was not in the list. The worst fallacy, he said, was the reevaluation of prior probability on the basis of a single observation. He expatiated on the theme for a few minutes and passed on to the next topic. I went up to him immediately after the class and pointed out that the *Titanic* disaster had provided an extreme example of revision of the prior probability on the basis of a single observation. First, it resulted in an effort to design the partitions, bulkheads, and framing of ships so as to protect them against exactly the sort of impact the *Titanic* had suffered. Second, and more to the point, the disaster appeared to demonstrate that existing calculations on the lifeboat and life raft capacity required relative to licensed passenger capacity was erroneous. Drawing on some long-forgotten source, I said that it had previously been thought that if boat and raft space—boatage and raftage—were provided for about two-thirds of the passengers, this was adequate protection, for if an accident were so severe that the ship was lost, a third of the passengers would be lost in any event. Because the *Titanic*'s striking an iceberg caused the loss of the ship but left all of the passengers in a condition in which they might have been saved, that calculation appeared erroneous, and a movement for boats-for-all swept the earth. That movement, I said, made ships more top-heavy and increased the probability of their capsizing in harbor collisions, which are much more common than impacts with icebergs. I should add parenthetically that my statement now appears to me at best imprecise. I have found no substantiation for my citation of the two-thirds figure in the calculations of the time, and the reasons why naval architects accepted a smaller boat capacity relative to licensed passenger capacity were considerably more complicated than I reported to Professor Kimbell.

That evening I visualized a scene familiar to virtually anyone who had spent his formative years in Chicago in the first half of the twentieth century, the passenger steamer *Eastland* lying on her port side, approximately half submerged in the Chicago River. Could there be a causal relation between this scene and the *Titanic* disaster? The *Titanic* hit the iceberg on April 14, 1912, and the *Eastland* capsized on July 24, 1915, immediately after loading and while casting off her lines. Three and a quarter years should have been long enough for the boats-for-all movement to affect the *Eastland*. Was there a relation, or had I merely engaged in *post hoc ergo propter hoc* reasoning? It was clearly a problem that warranted investigation. Even apart from that specific hypothesis, the disaster presents an intellectual problem. The ordinary incentives of management to provide safety along with comfort and dispatch have protected millions of passengers since time immemorial, but those incentives did not protect the approximately 844 persons who died on the *Eastland*. Similarly, steamboat inspection has been practiced in one form or another in the United States since 1838. Its purpose has been to prevent wrongful deaths of exactly this character. Steamboat inspection has protected large numbers of Americans, but it did not protect these 844. Inevitably, under the circumstances, some casual explanations of the disaster have survived popularly, even though they have no foundation. Yet no qualified researcher—historian, naval architect, admiralty lawyer, or specialist in economic regulation—has previously seriously investigated the disaster. I confess being mystified at this professional and scholarly neglect, which persisted for over 75 years; it is in itself a phenomenon warranting explanation.

Although I began gathering material immediately after my discussion with Professor Kimbell, it was to be many years before I began drafting a manuscript. In part, I had a large project in railroading to be completed. More important, I was not satisfied by the state of my knowledge of the ship and of the disaster. Gradually I realized that much of what I did not

know about the ship the people who operated the ship also did not know. Then in 1990 archivist Thomas Kruski of the National Archives, Great Lakes Center, Chicago, found a copy of the transcript of testimony in the criminal trial of 1916 that the staff of the center had not previously realized it held. As I trust is apparent from my documentation, this proved by far the most informative source on the disaster, and allowed the study to be undertaken at book length.

Because I do not pretend to competence in naval architecture or marine engineering, I am necessarily indebted to several naval architects for their professional judgments. Harry Benford, professor emeritus of naval architecture and marine engineering at the University of Michigan, was encouraging from the outset and read the manuscript, as did practicing naval architects Walter C. Cowles and William duBarry Thomas, and Captain John F. Kalina, United States Navy, retired, formerly officer in charge of senior engineering courses at the United States Naval Academy. I solicited their comments on Professor Herbert Charles Sadler's evaluation of the *Eastland* in the criminal trial (Appendix C, below), partly because there are serious discrepancies between Sadler's assumptions and the historical evidence and partly because they could use their comments as a means for discussing the physics of the ship more generally. It should be stated at the outset that, although these men were most helpful and saved me from various errors, they did not entirely agree with all of my judgments, nor entirely agree with each other. This is inevitable. The historical record on the disaster has survived but poorly, given the disaster's magnitude. It is difficult to imagine who, in considering the contents of the file of the criminal case that followed the disaster, could have decided that the plans of the *Eastland* could be destroyed without loss, but someone did. Similarly, someone decided that the most important plans of the *Wilmette*, the naval training vessel that the *Eastland* became following the disaster, could be destroyed. The report of the commissioner on which the decision in the civil case was based was not retained, nor was the transcript of testimony that the commissioner took. The files on the Illinois criminal action were destroyed. Many of the observations of degrees of list of the ship were made by laymen with no pretension to technical competence. Such observers tend to overstate the actual degrees of list. Estimates of the time sequence of the disaster are not wholly consistent. Most important, of the three estimates of the metacentric height of the ship—the measure of initial transverse stability—cited in the present study, none, as far as is known, derives from any rigorous engineering calculation. No fully credible estimates of the metacentric height were made until the United States Navy converted the ship to its own use.

Following a suggestion from John Teichmoeller, Leonidas Polemis, graduate student in naval architecture at the University of Michigan, undertook an inboard profile from literary evidence and a reconstruction of the body plan of the ship by computer-assisted drafting from photographs of the wreck. He worked on this with Professor Peter Beier, who was most helpful. John P. Eaton and Charles A. Haas shared with me some of the results of their ongoing research on the *Titanic*, beyond what is published in their *"Titanic": Triumph and Tragedy* of 1986. Wyn Craig Wade commented on the prologue in light of the research for his *The Titanic: End of a Dream*.

Reverend Edward J. Dowling, S.J., professor emeritus of engineering graphics at the University of Detroit, allowed me to draw upon his unequaled antiquarian knowledge of the disaster. He was also helpful beyond what he could have expected when he alerted me to the fact that the Detroit *News* had provided excellent coverage of the disaster. When he proved correct, I extended my search to out-of-city newspapers that might reasonably have maintained bureaus in Chicago in 1915, and found a great deal of information not published locally. Reverend Peter J. Van der Linden of Port Huron shared his knowledge of the Jenks shipyard, and was particularly helpful in clarifying the priestly function of the Catholic clergy during the rescue operation. Gordon Wendt of Sandusky, Gordon Potter of St. Joseph, and several other members of the Steamship Historical Society of America, as well as the staff of the society's library at the University of Baltimore, provided valuable assistance. In particular, Randolph W. Chalfant of Baltimore located a description of the Ellis and Eaves system of induced draft when I had almost despaired of finding one, and otherwise drew on his accumulated knowledge as a marine enthusiast and professional architect. James Konas of Berwyn, who died as the book was nearing completion, provided help from his long acquaintance with the Czech community of Chicago's western suburbs. Raymond E. Short of Ludington shared with me his biographical research on the major figures in the *Eastland*'s history, and drew upon his experience with large twin-screw ships from his career as a crewman on the Pere Marquette car ferries. Paul Demmitt simulated the *Eastland*'s lettering for the book jacket. Oscar Dahl of Albert Lea, Minnesota, verified the burial of Svend Bothun with a degree of conscientiousness that one rarely encounters. Barry Zerbe of the National Archives in Washington showed a mastery of the arcane filing system the Navy used before 1925 that only long familiarity with the material could give. Ross D. Eckert read the manuscript with particular attention to the regulatory issues involved. Robert W. Gabler read the manuscript both early and late in its drafting and made many useful comments on the exposition. Eric C. Gabler assisted with various com-

puter problems. My wife, Connie, and my stepdaughter, Karen Smith
Adams, raised important questions and provided their usual support and
encouragement.

I found dealing with the forensic aspects of the disaster extremely unpleasant. In particular, in the course of the research I found a large number of photographs of removal of the bodies of the victims, scenes in the central morgue, and the like, but I have no desire to publish them. I have included in this book only two photographs of this aspect of the history, both of which have been widely published previously. Those so minded will find a large number of unpublished prints in the photographic department of the Chicago Historical Society and in the marine collection of the Milwaukee Public Library.

In the manuscript I have endeavored to be consistent with correct maritime usage as between "she," "it," and "he." An active ship is properly known as "she" or "her." The practice, which dates at least from the Romans, is thought to represent the ship's role as a mother to her crew, although there are rival explanations. A ship becomes "it" as a wreck, a museum piece, or other nonfunctioning entity. A ship in a menacing situation is known as "he" in reference to the officer who is making the menacing decisions.

Finally, I would counsel the reader against making the error that the world made concerning the *Titanic* disaster, namely, excessive generalization from a single observation. In the *Eastland* disaster essentially nothing went right. Entrepreneurial decision-making was carried on in deadly ignorance of the ship's history. Steamboat inspection not only failed to prevent the catastrophe but helped to produce it by mandating additions to the ship's top hamper without requiring a test of the effect on the ship's stability. Steamboat inspection over a long period protected managements against the well-grounded fears of the passengers. The captain's behavior was negligent, but the criminal action initiated by the State of Illinois against him was not pursued. He perjured himself, but was not detected. The civil action placed the blame on a chief engineer whose behavior, given what he had been told, had been exemplary, and denied damages to heirs of the deceased who were thoroughly entitled to compensation. One should not condemn entrepreneurial decision-making, steamboat inspection, the competence of merchant marine officers, or the procedures of criminal and civil justice on the basis of this case alone. One should not even condemn the boats-for-all movement on the basis of this disaster. I will not conceal my view that great popular outcries such as the boats-for-all movement are typically counterproductive. In economic jargon, they are usually efforts to minimize or maximize a single function as distinct from optimizing among several. They typically manifest no effort to equate costs and benefits at the margin. The objections to the La Follette Seamen's Act seem to me to be based on more than the *Eastland* episode alone, but the boats-for-all movement had the indisputable benefit that passengers in boat drills could be shown exactly where they should go in the event of a disaster. Lives may have been saved in avoidance of confusion on this point in subsequent disasters—but not in this one. In this book I seek only to explain some 844 wrongful deaths, and to argue that from whatever benefits the boats-for-all movement may have produced, these deaths should be subtracted.

In the first printing of this book I stated on page 42 that revisions to the *Eastland* between the 1903 and 1904 seasons probably did not extend to moving the engines. I based this statement on the fact that the ship was not drydocked. The four naval architects who assisted me (see pp. 271-81) all believe this was an invalid inference. They told me that the engines could have been moved fore or aft without drydocking, and that, because the ship's engine room was so simple, any changes major enough to affect the draft would almost certainly have entailed this. In this printing I have rewritten the passage on page 42 accordingly. It remains true that we have no direct evidence of what the revisions were.

G.W.H.

Contents

Major
Figures
in the
History

George T. Arnold—General manager, Chicago–South Haven Line, 1906;
 president, St. Joseph–Chicago Steamship Company, 1913–15.
James F. Bishop—Administrator of estates of the deceased, appointed by
 the State of Illinois.
Robert R. Blacker—Second president, Michigan Steamship Company.
Charles F. Clyne—U.S. District Attorney, Chicago.
Ray W. Davis—Assistant to William H. Hull, St. Joseph–Chicago Steam-
 ship Company.
Charles M. Dibbell—Radio officer of the *Eastland*, 1915.
Grant Donaldson—Chief Engineer of the *Eastland* on Lake Erie,
 1907–13.
Frank A. Dority—Second captain of the *Eastland*, 1903–6.
Charles C. Eckliff—Inspector of boilers and hulls, Grand Haven,
 Michigan.
William P. Eeles—Chief engineer of the *Eastland*, 1903–5.
Claude M. Ennes—Captain of the *Eastland* on Lake Erie, 1912–13.
Joseph M. Erickson—Chief engineer of the *Eastland*, 1915.
William A. Evans, M.D.—Foreman, coroner's jury, Chicago.

Edward A. Evers—Captain, Illinois Naval Reserve, master of the *Wilmette.*

Del Fisher—First mate of the *Eastland,* 1915.

Peter Fisher—Second mate of the *Eastland,* 1915.

Martin Flatow—Port agent at Chicago for the St. Joseph–Chicago Steamship Company.

Andrew Furuseth—President of the International Seamen's Union of America.

Walter K. Greenebaum—General manager of the Indiana Transportation Company.

Peter M. Hoffman—Coroner, Cook County.

Maclay Hoyne—State's Attorney, Chicago.

William H. Hull—Vice president and general manager of the St. Joseph–Chicago Steamship Company.

Sidney G. Jenks—Designer of the *Eastland.*

Kenesaw Mountain Landis—Judge, U.S. District Court, Chicago.

Charles Lasser—Baggageman of the Chicago & South Haven Steamship Company, 1915.

Luman A. Lobdell, Jr.—Employee of the collector of customs who counted passengers aboard the *Eastland,* 1915.

Joseph R. Lynn—Assistant harbormaster, City of Chicago, 1915.

Arthur D. MacDonald—Chief engineer of the *Kenosha,* 1915.

Lewis F. Mason—Attorney, commissioner in the federal civil action.

Robert H. McCreary—Deputy collector of customs, Chicago, in charge of counting passengers onto the *Eastland.*

George R. McDermott—Professor of naval architecture, Cornell University.

George W. Monger—Purser of the *Eastland,* 1915.

William L. Nack—Assistant engineer, *Eastland,* 1903–5; chief engineer, 1906.

Curtis J. Oakley—Employee of the collector of customs who assisted in counting passengers aboard the *Eastland,* 1915.

John H. O'Meara—Captain of the *Kenosha,* 1915.

Harry Pedersen—Captain of the *Eastland,* 1914–15.

John C. Pereue—Founder and secretary, Michigan Steamship Company; first captain of the *Eastland.*

William C. Redfield—Secretary of commerce of the United States, 1913–19.

Robert Reid—Steamboat inspector at Grand Haven, Michigan, in charge of licensure of the *Eastland,* 1914–15.

Helen Repa—Nurse, Western Electric Company, first nurse to arrive at the scene of the disaster.

T. W. Richards—Lieutenant, U.S. Navy, supervising constructor of the *Wilmette.*

Herbert Charles Sadler—Professor of naval architecture and marine engineering, University of Michigan.

A. A. Schantz—General manager, Detroit & Cleveland Navigation Company.

Walter Scott—Harbormaster, City of Chicago, 1910–11; consultant to steamship companies thereafter.

Clarence W. Sessions—Judge, U.S. District Court, Grand Rapids, Michigan.

Charles F. Silvernail—First assistant engineer, *Eastland,* 1915.

E. W. Sladkey—Head, printing department, Western Electric, the last passenger to board the *Eastland.*

Fred G. Snow—Second assistant engineer, *Eastland,* 1915.

Walter C. Steele—Secretary-treasurer, St. Joseph–Chicago Steamship Company.

David W. Taylor—Rear admiral, U.S. Navy, chief of the Bureau of Construction and Repair, 1917–18.

Merwin S. Thompson—Captain of the *Eastland* on Lake Erie, 1909–11.

George Uhler—Supervising inspector, Steamboat Inspection Service.

H. B. Vehstedt—Naval architect engaged by the City of Chicago to survey the wreck.

Adam F. Weckler—Harbormaster, City of Chicago, 1915.

William J. Wood—Naval architect in charge of revisions to the *Eastland* between the 1903 and 1904 seasons.

Eastland

Legacy
of the
Titanic

Prologue

THE *Eastland* disaster had its proximate cause in the *Titanic*'s striking of an iceberg on April 14, 1912—or more precisely, in the world's response to the *Titanic*'s accident. That response was, perhaps inevitably, highly emotional and, in retrospect, excessive. More important, that response was poorly related to the causes of the disaster. The actual cause of the accident was the juxtaposition of an extremely odd design feature of the *Titanic* with a deeply lamentable command given by the officer of the watch when confronted with an iceberg dead ahead. The ship had triple screws, with the outboard powered by quadruple-expansion reciprocating steam engines and the center by a low-pressure turbine utilizing the exhaust from the outboard engines. The rudder, immediately aft of the center screw, had a simple hinged design; it was not a balanced rudder with surfaces both fore and aft of the stock. Colin Carmichael has argued persuasively that such a rudder was inappropriate for so large a vessel.[1]

When the officer in command, William M. Murdoch, was alerted to the iceberg lying an estimated 1,500 feet dead ahead, he ordered his rudder hard left and all his engines full speed astern. He also ordered the watertight doors in the engine and boiler rooms closed. It is difficult to be very critical of him, for his situation demanded a split-second decision. Equally important, the ship was on her maiden voyage, so that her handling properties were not well known. The consequences of the command could not have been worse, however. The turbine could not reverse, and no gearing was provided to enable the center propeller to do so; only the outboard engines could be reversed. The center propeller simply stopped. Accordingly, any stream of water, ahead or astern, ceased to flow to the rudder from the center propeller. The outboard propellers did not flow onto it. Because the effectiveness of a rudder increases in proportion to the square of the speed of flow of water upon it, the effect was to slow the response of the ship in a fashion that proved lethal. She is estimated to have deviated from her course only about 2 points, or about 22 degrees, to port before the impact, when a 40-degree turn was required.[2] To achieve the change of course he sought, Murdoch should have not only ordered the rudder hard left, as he did, but gone full speed astern on the port screw only, continuing full speed ahead on the center and starboard engines.[3] As we now know from examination of the wreck, the ship grazed the iceberg, bursting and tearing plates longitudinally over a distance sufficient to flood her six forward compartments on the starboard side. This was enough to allow water to spill over her bulkheads—just as water fills an ice cube tray when poured from one end—causing the ship to sink over the course of somewhat more than two hours.[4] If Murdoch had instead simply ordered all his engines full speed astern and not altered course, he could have justified his action as following the general principle that when a collision is inevitable,

This view of the *Titanic* abuilding at Belfast taken from the stern shows the ship's unbalanced hinged rudder, argued to be inadequate for a ship of this size. (Steamship Historical Society of America)

one should strike at as fine an angle as possible. Such an action would have been interpreted as poor seamanship and would undoubtedly have ruined his career, but would also have limited damage to the bow of the ship, limited the loss of life to whoever was in the bow, and incidentally saved his own life, which was lost.

The magnitude of the disaster, which killed 829 passengers and 694 members of the crew, produced a popular outcry for reform of marine practices worldwide. Unfortunately, the outcry was not directed to the ship's very real design flaws—her archaic rudder and a center screw that could not be reversed, both of which went almost unnoticed—nor even to Murdoch's disastrous command. Rather, the censure fell upon aspects of the situation that measured up fully to maritime standards. One such aspect was the practice of running at full speed in an ice field, as the *Titanic* was doing. Maritime professionals did not consider this particularly risky, for icebergs, the above-water portions of which turn from blue to white from exposure to air and from draining of water, were typically visible at least three miles away. The one the *Titanic* hit, however, had just turned over and was still blue, an enormously unlikely circumstance that nonetheless convinced the public of the rashness of the established practice. The other aspects targeted by the popular outcry were the design of the *Titanic*'s bulkheads and her ratio of lifeboat capacity to passenger capacity, neither of which was unusual or deficient by the regulations of the time. The *Titanic* was built with bulkheads extending 2'-6" to 3'-0" above the waterline, which was about double the minimum required.[5] The compartments were not watertight from above, however. The *Titanic*'s boatage and flotation equipment were also well above minimum requirements. She carried 3,560 life belts; 48 life buoys; 14 30-foot lifeboats; 2 emergency cutters; and 4 Englehardt collapsible rafts. The boats, cutters, and rafts had an aggregate capacity of 1,178 persons. The *Titanic*'s licensed capacity was 2,603 passengers. On her maiden and only voyage she carried, in addition to 908 crewmen, just 1,320 passengers; she was barely more than half full. The applicable regulation of the British Board of Trade under the 1894 revisions to the Merchant Shipping Act of 1854 required passenger vessels of 10,000 gross tons and upward to have 16 boats under davits with capacity for about 550 persons. If immigrants were carried, boatage for an additional 400 persons was required, but the total might be reduced if inspectors believed the subdivision of the hull was adequate. The *Titanic*'s boat capacity exceeded the Board of Trade's minimum relative to passenger capacity by about 23 percent.[6]

In the years prior to the *Titanic* disaster it had been widely argued that the regulations of 1894 were based on a tonnage that had become an obsolete criterion with the introduction of steamers of the size of the *Lusi-*

tania and *Mauretania* of 1906. Early in 1911 the Board of Trade asked its Merchant Shipping Advisory Committee to consider revision of the requirements for larger vessels. The committee recommended in July 1911 that for vessels of about 45,000 tons, the range in which the *Titanic* fell, 16 boats should be carried under davits and 8 more should be kept readily available for attachment, with a capacity for about 830 passengers, and space for an additional 620 should be added if immigrants were carried. The boatage might be reduced by half if the subdivision of the ship's hull was adequate; the committee proposed a maximum boat capacity of 1,140 for a ship with a properly subdivided hull.[7] Accordingly, the *Titanic*'s boat capacity exceeded not only existing requirements but also the proposed requirements of 1911.

Why the regulatory authorities and the professionals in the field believed it was not necessary to provide boats for all passengers is important. Sir Westcott Abell argued that on a 600-foot vessel of 2,500 passenger capacity, only 400 linear feet could be used for boats. With a boat deck 60 feet above the water, and 20 boats to be launched from 10 sets of davits, it would require 10 minutes to ascertain that the ship would sink and 5 minutes to make the boats ready for loading after the order was given. Even if 20 boats containing 2,000 persons were gotten away from the ship in 30 minutes from the time the order was given, 500 persons would remain on board the ship waiting for additional boats or rafts to be launched.[8] *The Marine Engineer and Naval Architect* observed editorially that on troop ships under military discipline, the maximum rate at which boats could be loaded was 1,000 to 1,100 per hour. With ordinary passengers, it argued, the experience could only be worse.[9] There was no assurance that even with boats for all, all passengers could be gotten off in the time available to the crew. In an accident so severe as to cause loss of the ship, some passengers were likely to be killed or severely disabled on impact. In most disasters, rescue vessels are readily at hand, so that the ship's own boats may make more than one trip with survivors, and the rescue vessels' boats can also be used.

There was a further problem that loading lifeboats at a distance of 60 feet above the water was a risky business, as the experience on the *Titanic* itself demonstrated. Charles H. Lightoller, the highest officer of the *Titanic* to survive, defended his sending down lifeboats that were not full on the ground that fully loaded boats might not be sturdy enough to take the lowering over such a distance. The passengers were reported to be fearful of such a descent. He hoped to lower the boats to gangways on lower decks to be filled, but some of the gangways were under water, and many of the crew ordered to open the doors had not survived. Indeed, the *Titanic* disaster might have been used to demonstrate that boats-for-all was a very arbitrary criterion. The vessel was manned by officers of excellent formal credentials, who had nearly three hours in a calm sea to get the passengers off the ship. The *Titanic*, to the credit of her designers, did not list seriously in either direction in the course of sinking. Thus, the boats on both sides could be used; there was no presumption this would be true in another disaster. Even with all of these considerations operating in favor of the officers, they were able to save only 705 passengers and crew of the 2,228 persons aboard—fully 473 fewer than the 1,178 that the *Titanic*'s above-standard boatage could theoretically accommodate.[10] Abell drew from this the implication that a margin of an additional 50 percent in boatage would have been required to save all the passengers.[11]

Such considerations led the professionals in the field to look skeptically at the boats-for-all criterion. As Abell said, on the basis of a favorable experience in passenger safety since the turn of the century "the seamen's opinion was good, . . . all that was necessary was a reasonable number of boats."[12]

The *Titanic* was lost, but none of the passengers was even injured on impact, and all of them were left dependent on a supply of boats that, although it might have saved more of them than it did, could not possibly have saved all of them. The nearest ship did not respond, and the passengers were wholly dependent on the *Titanic*'s own boats. Thus this single disaster appeared to indicate that the traditional calculation for boat space was erroneous, and the cry "Boats for all!" spread the world over. Actually, the probability of a ship's hitting an iceberg did not differ after the *Titanic* disaster from what it had been before—1 in 1,000,000, in the evaluation of the *Titanic*'s underwriters in writing her insurance contract.[13] Such a suggestion would have been highly unpopular, however—about as unpopular as the comment that most ships run no risk of hitting icebergs at all. Similarly, it went unremarked in popular discussion that many marine disasters are of such a character that no boats can be launched.

More generally, the *Titanic* disaster provoked a thoroughly erroneous evaluation of the risks of sea travel. In fact, the introduction of the generation of large steel steamers of the character of the *Titanic*, coupled with the inauguration in 1901 of wireless communication and refinements in navigation devices, had greatly improved marine safety. Between 1892 and 1901, of the 3.25 million people who crossed the Atlantic, mainly in British ships, 73 died in accidents. Between 1902 and 1911, however, over 6 million crossed, only 9 of whom had been killed.[14] In the British inquiry into the *Titanic* disaster, Lord Alfred Chalmers, who had been nautical adviser to the Board of Trade from 1896 to 1911, expressed the view that the disaster had been so extraordinary that no changes in policy should be based on it. "The Board of Trade, the Marine Department," he said, "guards against ordinary occurrences, not extraordinary."[15] He remained an advocate of traditional calculations with respect to boatage and recommended that extensions in the scale of boatage relative to passenger capacity be left to the shipowners.[16] The British trade journal *Syren & Shipping Illustrated* essentially agreed with the *Titanic*'s underwriters in its evaluation of the probability of a recurrence of the disaster: "The odds against such an event would be almost a million to one."[17]

One of the best demonstrations of the effect of the popular outcry was the changes required in the *Olympic*, the *Titanic*'s running mate and near sister. After the *Titanic* disaster the *Olympic* was brought back to the builder, Harland & Wolff, and, over the course of five months, modified by raising and increasing the number of her watertight bulkheads and adding an inner skin up to a point well above the waterline, all in an effort to protect her from exactly the impact the *Titanic* had suffered.[18]

The outcry manifested itself in the calling of an International Conference on Safety of Life at Sea, which met in London late in 1913 and early in 1914. The United States was represented by a delegation that included two men who in very different ways were to be involved in the history of the *Eastland*. As its representative of the Great Lakes region the delegation included Herbert Charles Sadler, professor of naval architecture and marine engineering at the University of Michigan,[19] who in 1916 was to make the evaluation of the *Eastland* in the criminal action that followed the disaster.

As its labor representative, the delegation included Andrew Furuseth, president of the International Seamen's Union of America. Since the mid-1890's Furuseth had served as a lobbyist for seamen's unions, first for the Pacific Seamen's Union, of which he became secretary, and then for the International. He had sought an act that would give seamen greater freedom to collect wages, in whole or in part, in foreign or domestic ports short of completion of the voyages for which they had signed on, and then to quit their ships. He also sought the sort of improvements in working conditions one expects of a conscientious union executive: more ample living space, more opportunity to protest against food service, limitation of work in ports on Sundays, and the like. Replacement of commercial sailing vessels with steamships had reduced the demand for deckhands relative to firemen, oilers, stewards, and other personnel. The country had demonstrated a lack of comparative advantage for the operation of steamships, so that American shipping lines had declined relative to British, German, Japanese, and other foreign operators. In addition, American operators widely made use of foreign seamen, especially Chinese and Japanese on transpacific steamers. Furuseth had sought to deal with the decline by a variety of political measures to increase the demand for American seamen. He had more success in his efforts in the House of Representatives, but in December 1909 he interested the populist senator from Wisconsin, Robert M. La Follette, in his cause.[20] This was still not enough for Furuseth to secure a measure such as he wanted, but he immediately recognized the boats-for-all movement as his opportunity. As early as May 15, 1912, Representative William B. Wilson of Pennsylvania introduced a version of his bill.[21] It contained Furuseth's long-sought provisions for leaving ships short of the termination of the voyage, and had several provisions designed to increase the demand for American seamen. The percentage of seamen required to understand the orders of the officers— which is to say, be English-speaking—was set at 75 percent. The number required to be able-bodied seamen was established at 40 percent of the crew in the first year, rising to 65 percent in the fifth year after passage. In the most important of these provisions, the bill required boats for all, and two able-bodied seamen for each boat. No person was to be considered an able-bodied seaman unless he had reached the age of nineteen and had three years of experience. The bill passed the House of Representatives on August 3, 1912. It was introduced into the Senate by Thomas E. Burton of Ohio on August 5, 1912, but was not acted upon. Rather, on October 16, 1913, La Follette presented an alternative of approximately the same content, which as Senate Bill 136 passed the Senate on October 23.[22] The bills had not been reconciled, but by the time the International Conference on Safety of Life at Sea opened, Furuseth was in sight of victory.

On January 20, 1914, the conference issued its International Convention Relating to Safety of Life at Sea, which was a straightforward effort to protect ships from exactly the sort of accident the *Titanic* had encountered. When ice was reported, masters were required to proceed at night at moderate speeds. An international ice patrol was to be established, which the United States was invited to join. Regulations for construction of new ships after July 1, 1915, were to require bulkheads, watertight doors, and weathertight decks. Double bottoms were required in at least the forward portions of all ships of over 200 feet in length. Radiotelegraphy was to be required. Article 40, entitled "Fundamental Principle," stated, "At no moment on its voyage may a vessel have on board a total number of persons greater than that for whom accommodation is provided in the lifeboats and liferafts on board." Article 52 specifically applied the Fundamental Principle to existing vessels, but stated that individual countries might grant exemptions. In the only major provision of the convention unrelated to the *Titanic* disaster, governments were exhorted to remove wrecks and derelicts.[23]

The outbreak of World War I later in 1914 prevented any immediate implementation of the articles of the convention, but a movement to conform to some of its provisions spread to major maritime nations. Notably, the British Board of Trade on January 17, 1913, issued a directive effective March 1, 1913, that Furuseth interpreted as requiring that boats be provided for three-fourths of all persons on board British ships.[24] Furuseth, in anticipation of the content of the convention and in protest against the British enactment, resigned from the American delegation to the conference by cable to President Woodrow Wilson on December 22, 1913. Subscribing fully to the principle of boats-for-all, he argued that anything less might produce panic in seeking places on the boats or rafts.[25] On his arrival in New York, he told reporters that another *Titanic* disaster might occur at any moment because of the unfitness of vessels to deal with such an emergency and the use of stewards and other incompetents to handle boats.[26]

The possible negative effects of the boats-for-all movement were, of course, noted. On April 18, 1912, in the debate in Parliament immediately following the *Titanic* disaster, Sydney Charles Buxton, president of the Board of Trade, warned against legislating in a panic, saying "if you overload the vessel with boats, the real danger in the case of emergency would be that the very number of boats themselves might lead to disaster."[27] *Syren & Shipping Illustrated*, which was sympathetic to the boats-for-all movement, noted that the public rejected arguments such as Buxton's, citing as evidence that lifeboat builders were being inundated with orders from the major steamship companies.[28] *The Marine Engineer and Naval Architect* of July 1912 also noted a market-demand element in the boats-for-all movement, but pointed out its hazards:

> But owners seem frankly to admit that they are adding to their boats, not necessarily because they think it essential or even advisable to do so, but simply because the public wishes it, and it is the public whose custom they want and whose wishes must therefore be gratified. Against an excessive provision of boats it is argued that there is a danger of making ships too tender if extra weights are placed on the boat decks, whilst it is also pointed out that it is possible to so cumber the space that hindrances may be put in the way of them in time of emergency.[29]

The years shortly following the *Titanic* disaster produced two disasters involving transatlantic passenger steamers of similar magnitude, which might have been used as a test of the efficacy of the boats-for-all movement—but were not. At 1:55 A.M. on May 29, 1914, the Canadian Pacific Railway's *Empress of Ireland*, outbound from Quebec, was struck on the starboard side by the Norwegian collier *Storstad*, which penetrated about 18 feet into the hull at an angle of about 80 degrees, causing a gash about 28 feet wide. Water poured into the *Empress of Ireland* at a rate of about 500 tons per second. The captain, Henry George Kendall, ordered her full speed ahead toward the south bank of the St. Lawrence River, but the ship was too badly damaged to respond, and sank in 14 minutes. The *Empress of Ireland* carried 16 steel lifeboats, 7 on each side of

the boat deck and another pair aft. Following the *Titanic* disaster, the Canadian Pacific raised the davits and placed under each boat an Englehardt
collapsible lifeboat. The ship also carried 4 Berthon collapsible boats. The
total boat capacity was 2,000, well in excess of the 1,477 persons aboard.
The disaster occurred so quickly that it is unclear how many boats were
launched, but the most authoritative estimate is 5 or 6 of the boats on the
starboard side plus 1 of the Englehardt collapsibles. The ship capsized to
starboard, but the damage to the hull was so severe that it is unlikely the
weight of the additional lifeboats was significant. Because of the list, the
boats on the port side could not be launched. One boat was believed to
have been lost as the ship capsized onto it. The disaster killed 840 of the
1,057 passengers and 172 of the crew of 420. Of the 465 survivors, 217
were passengers and 248 members of the crew.[30] *Syren & Shipping Illustrated* observed:

> The *Empress of Ireland* catastrophe . . . almost rivals that of the *Titanic*, but there
> is at least the consolation of knowing that the loss of life was not due to any laxity
> in regard to the vessel's lifesaving equipment. Had the ship had double the number
> of boats, and had the arrangements for lowering those boats been ideal, the bill of
> mortality would have been just as heavy as it actually was.[31]

On May 7, 1915, the Cunard liner *Lusitania* was torpedoed by a German submarine off the Irish coast. The ship had 22 lifeboats, which had
been hung out on their davits as a precaution in light of wartime risks.
Twenty-six collapsible boats had been placed below the lifeboats. With
additional life rafts, there was boatage for 2,605 persons, more than 600
places in excess of the 1,257 passengers and crew of 702 that the ship was
carrying. The ship took the torpedo from starboard, listed seriously to port,
righted herself to within 5 degrees of even keel, and sank bow-first in
about 18 minutes. It is unclear how many boats were launched, but 6 were
found afloat after the ship sank. Of the 1,959 persons aboard, 1,198 died,
785 passengers and 413 members of the crew.[32] Because the ship was a
wartime loss, it is questionable how relevant this disaster is for the issue
of safety at sea in peacetime, but no less than on the *Empress of Ireland*,
the passengers lost their lives despite boat capacity well in excess of their
numbers.

The boats-for-all movement was unaffected by these observations. By
1914 the effort to reconcile La Follette's Senate Bill 136 with the House
bill, which was now identified with Representative Joshua W. Alexander
of Missouri, was in progress. The bills had passed both houses of Congress
over the strenuous objections of American operators. The general manag-
ers of the four largest excursion lines out of Detroit sent a joint telegram

to the Senate Commerce Committee protesting that the light construction of their steamers obliged them to carry boats and rafts of only 10- to 20-passenger capacity, and that hiring crews adequate to satisfy the law for the number of boats in prospect would drive them all out of business.[33] Captain J. A. White of the Hudson River Day Line said that Senate Bill 136, as drafted, would require one of his steamers of 3,000 capacity to have 100 boats and 200 seamen, many of whom might have nothing to do for 25 years before even a single passenger so much as fell overboard.[34] The New York *Times* observed editorially that the bill would mandate three times the number of men required and promote idleness and lack of discipline, "[b]ut the bill is written for the Seamen's Union and to make jobs."[35]

A. A. Schantz, general manager of the Detroit & Cleveland Navigation Company, the dominant operator of overnight steamers on Lake Erie, appeared before the committee on September 14, 1914, as spokesman for the independent Great Lakes operators—the lines not captive to steel companies or other industrial firms—to seek an exemption from the act for Great Lakes ships. He treated the bills as an application of the proposals by the London conference of the previous fall, pointed out that these recommended policies were formulated in the context of ocean-going steamers, and argued that they were inappropriate for Great Lakes vessels. He estimated that D&C ships passed other vessels at intervals of about three minutes in the Detroit River, eleven minutes in Lake Erie, and fourteen minutes in Lake Huron; the prospect of one of the company's ships sinking in isolation from other vessels, as the *Titanic* did, was absurd. He thought that, as the proposals stood, they would drive 90 percent of pack-

A. A. Schantz, general manager of the Detroit & Cleveland Navigation Company, in a photograph taken about 1901. Although he recommended the *Eastland* to the group that bought her early in 1914, he predicted the disaster—though not specifically to the *Eastland*—in his testimony to Congress on the La Follette Seamen's Act later in the year. (Library of Congress)

age freighters and passenger ships on the Great Lakes out of business. He

then recognized a general problem with regulation of economic activity:
the government cannot regulate a single variable in isolation from others
related to it.[36] He alerted the committee to a serious safety risk in the prospective addition of boats and rafts to existing Great Lakes passenger
ships:

We have shallow water to contend with on the lakes and in the harbors, therefore
we build boats of shallow draft. All of the lake line boats and equipment have been
built according to the regulations made by the supervising inspectors and approved
by the Secretary of Commerce, and are second to none. The boats now operated
could not comply with the requirements of the bill, on account of the light draft
and the construction of the cabins and upper works. The extra weight of lifeboats
and rafts would make them top-heavy and unseaworthy, and in our judgment, we
believe some of them would turn turtle if you attempted to navigate them with this
additional weight on the upper decks.[37]

There were considerable objections to the bill, even apart from the subject at hand. Because its provisions applied to foreign ships in American
ports, it amounted to a regulation of major maritime nations by a country
that no longer had pretensions of being among their number.[38] Britain particularly protested requirements that would increase the manning of its
ships under wartime conditions.[39] Congressman Halvor Steenarson of
Minnesota, an advocate of the bill, recognized that such provisions were
an effort to increase the costs of foreign operators, and to reduce the adverse effect of the act on American shipping lines.[40] Foreign governments
found offensive a provision giving Congress the right to abrogate treaties
for the return of deserting seamen. Furuseth was very eager for this and,
when the Senate ratified the convention from the London conference,
managed to secure a provision reserving to the United States the right to
abrogate treaties and agreements as required to impose higher standards of
comfort, safety, and health for all vessels in its waters to conform to
American regulations.[41]

In spite of the objections to Furuseth's bill, it passed the House of Representatives unanimously on August 27, 1914, as the Alexander Seamen's
Relief Bill. As the La Follette Seamen's Act, it passed the Senate on February 27, 1915, and was signed into law by President Wilson on March 4,
1915.[42] The law contained Furuseth's provision for English-speaking
crews, granted freedom to draw a part of accrued wages in order to leave
the ship short of completion of a voyage, specified the percentage of able-
bodied seamen required, and defined an able-bodied seaman as a man at
least nineteen years of age with at least three years' experience. Strangely,
the act prohibited flogging, a practice that had died out before the Civil
War and that was already illegal under existing statutes. The provisions for

lifeboats were modified from the strict boats-for-all rule with two able-bodied seamen per boat that Furuseth had sought. Rather, Section 14 of the act, which amounted to more than half the statute, was devoted to a very specific set of regulations for boats, including provisions for their sheer, cubic capacity, lettering, materials, and equipment. Davits were required to be such that boats could be fully loaded and launched manually at a 15-degree list; all boats had to be strong enough to be lowered into the water fully loaded. The secretary of commerce might grant exemption from this requirement to existing ships. The mandated numbers of davits were set forth in a table, the requirements ranging from 2 sets for ships of 100 to 120 feet in length to 30 sets for ships of 995 to 1,030 feet. Similarly, a ratio was established between the number of certified lifeboatmen and the capacity of boats, ranging from 1 such crewman for boats of up to 25-passenger capacity to 7 for boats of 161- to 210-passenger capacity. The ratio of number of davits to length and the requirement that boats be capable of hand-launching were to assure that boats would be relatively small and, therefore, numerous. Even so, this was a defeat for Furuseth, relative to the rule of boats-for-all and a fixed ratio of two seamen to a boat that he had sought. In particular, the act did not require that all certified lifeboatmen be able-bodied seamen. Furuseth's hostility to the use of stewards as lifeboatmen was written into the act, however, in a provision that limited stewards to calling and warning passengers, directing them to the boats, and maintaining order. Firemen, oilers, and others were not specifically excluded.

Instead of boats for all, the act required that boats be provided for 75 percent of passengers, with the rest to be put on collapsible or rigid-side boats, or on pontoon rafts. The boats and rafts had to be capable of manual launching. The requirement for boats and rafts was to apply to Great Lakes passenger vessels that operated over three miles offshore, but an exemption was provided for them between May 15 and September 15, when only 40 percent had to be accommodated in boats and 60 percent in collapsibles or rafts. For ships the keels of which were laid after July 1, 1915, on the Great Lakes and elsewhere, boats had to be provided for 75 percent of persons aboard, and rafts for 25 percent. The act did not immediately become effective. Rather, the text stipulated that it should become effective for American operators on November 4, 1915, eight months after Wilson signed it. It was to apply to foreign operators in American waters on March 4, 1916. This arrangement meant that seasonal operators, such as the Great Lakes excursion lines, would have a full year to adapt their operations to the new law. The transitional problems promised to be severe. The New York *Times* estimated that the act would increase the costs of operating a large Long Island Sound steamer by about

$2,000 per month.[43] Predictions that the act would wipe out American ships in the transpacific trade were quickly verified. The Pacific Mail Steamship Company, the dominant American operator, announced that it would go out of business after its departure from San Francisco on November 2, two days before the act was to come into effect. President R. P. Schwerin stated that act would raise the company's costs by $800,000 per year, although it had never made more than $200,000 in any year in its history, which dated from 1848. The management considered it useless to compete with Japanese operators under the new law.[44] The announcement was consistent with the *Times*'s view that the act would be counterproductive: rather than generating jobs in the American merchant marine, it would annihilate them by raising the costs of American operators to the point that they would be driven from the seas.[45]

The American trade magazine *Marine Journal* in its issue dated July 24, 1915—the day of the *Eastland* disaster—published an editorial arguing that the recent efforts to prevent disaster at sea had become "ludicrous." It stated that the changes in policy had given an incentive to continue to operate older ships in preference to new ones that would have to meet boats-for-all requirements. It considered previous laws adequate, and concluded, "the *Titanic* disaster was a miracle. In the seventy-five years that ocean-going steamers have been afloat no parallel disaster ever occurred, and it would not be possible to cause a similar one if the experiment were attempted. . . . [T]he disaster, notwithstanding the great loss of life, should never have caused the irreparable damage that it has to the marine industry through the inimical measures that Congress and the Administration have favored."[46]

This, then, was the framework of policy within which the *Eastland* disaster occurred. A movement to increase the boat capacity of ships relative to their passenger capacities was essentially ubiquitous, affecting the inspection and certification procedures of every major maritime nation. The American manifestation of the movement, the La Follette Seamen's Act, had been passed but was not yet in effect. The problem at hand is to ascertain, given what we can discover of the *Eastland*'s history, why she should have been the ship to verify A. A. Schantz's prediction that the La Follette Seamen's Act would cause a Great Lakes ship to capsize.

CHAPTER ONE

The Michigan Steamship Company

THE *Eastland* was built in 1903 for the Michigan Steamship Company as what was known in steamboating as an "opposition boat," a rival to the established operator between Chicago and South Haven, Michigan.

The route of 77 miles had been served by two independent operators, the Dunkley Company of S. J. Dunkley, which did business as the South Haven Line, and the H. W. Williams Transportation Company. The two merged before the 1902 season into the Dunkley-Williams Company. Dunkley-Williams planned to provide a service that had become standard among the cross-lake operators. The basic service was a round trip on which the company's largest vessel left Chicago in mid-morning on weekdays and Sundays, allowing passengers to reach the wharves along the Chicago River by streetcar. Because of the then-customary half day of work on Saturdays, the departure on that day was scheduled for about 2:00 P.M.

The Graham & Morton Transportation Company provided service on a similar schedule on the 60-mile route from Chicago to the twin cities of St. Joseph and Benton Harbor, about 25 miles to the south of South Haven.

After a trip of four to five hours, the steamer discharged her passengers and began loading fruit for the return trip to Chicago. The passengers had about four hours to enjoy the resort developments that sprang up at South Haven and St. Joseph before the steamer reloaded them for a late afternoon or dinnertime departure. St. Joseph proved the more successful of the two resorts, partly because the trip from Chicago was shorter, partly because South Haven had a Sunday blue law that made it a dull destination for weekend passengers. On Sundays, when no fruit was handled, the steamers provided, either once or twice, what was called the "peanut excursion," a short trip out into the lake and back into port for ten cents. On either the weekday or the Sunday schedule, the ship was back in Chicago by late evening.

The city's produce market grew up along South Water Street immediately adjacent to the wharves on the south bank of the river. It was an effective arrangement, providing the city with one of its principal forms of amusement in the pre-automobile era while allowing Michigan fruit to reach the city's grocery stores within 24 hours of harvesting. The basic mid-morning departure was insufficient, especially for Graham & Morton, the largest of the cross-lake operators, because of demands for trips at other hours, notably overnight crossings from Chicago on weekends. The basic schedule was also not well suited to the demands of residents of the Michigan towns. Second only to the demand for the basic schedule was a

Southern Lake Michigan. (James A. Bier, cartographer)

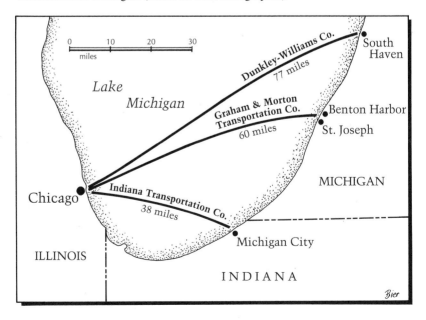

The *City of Kalamazoo*, of the H. W. Williams Transportation Company, was typical of the small wooden propeller steamers that served the Chicago–South Haven route before the introduction of the *City of South Haven* and the *Eastland*. (R. W. Appleyard collection)

demand for overnight fruit movements with early arrival at the market. This coincided with demands for trips to Chicago by Michigan residents who wanted to spend a full day in the city to transact business; inevitably, much of this business was with the produce merchants and brokers. A departure from Chicago about 5:00 P.M. was useful to allow passengers to return to Michigan without spending a night in a hotel in the city. Accordingly, the demands required one large steamer to handle the basic schedule and some smaller steamers to provide the off-hours trips. The trade had a big summer peak for about ten to twelve weeks ending in early to mid-September, for which a large steamer was necessary; the smaller ships could ordinarily handle the earlier and later trips.

Dunkley-Williams began operation with four steamers suitable to the off-peak trips: the *City of Kalamazoo, H. W. Williams,* and *Glenn,* all of the Williams line, and the *Petoskey* of the Dunkley company. A fifth vessel, Williams's *Easton,* was put up for sale.[1] Integral to the Dunkley-

Williams merger was a plan to order a large steel ship for the basic mid-morning departure.

The Michigan Steamship Company had its inception simultaneously in Captain John C. Pereue's approaching some local fruit shippers who had become dissatisfied with the rates and service they had received from Dunkley and Williams. Pereue was an experienced Great Lakes master, who had been in command of the *Hattie B. Pereue* and the *J. D. Marshall.*

R. R. Blacker, one of the organizers of the Michigan Steamship Company, from the volume *American Lumbermen.* (Library of Congress)

His principal associates were Robert R. Blacker and Patrick Noud, both of Manistee, and Captain J. J. McKean of Chicago. Blacker was a Canadian, born in Brantford, Ontario, in 1845, who had emigrated to Michigan at the age of nineteen. After a few years he settled at Manistee, where he quickly became a dominant figure in the local lumber business. Noud was his partner in the State Lumber Company, which succeeded some of Blacker's earlier enterprises in 1887. Blacker also dealt in the salt industry and was an active Democratic politician. By the turn of the century he had been mayor of Manistee, a state representative, and the secretary of state of Michigan.[2] Although the company's immediate intention was only to enter the Chicago–South Haven trade, in the longer run it planned to operate more widely on Lake Michigan, and in particular to serve Manistee.

For the initial service to South Haven, Pereue proposed building a steamer in a range of about 300 feet—widely interpreted—and designed chiefly to carry fruit to Chicago. The novelty of his conception was to provide the basic morning round trip out of Chicago and the westbound overnight voyage with the same vessel. He proposed running the first round trip from Chicago at 9:00 A.M. and the second at 5:00 P.M.[3] Because the overnight departure from South Haven was basic to Pereue's plan, the service would require not only a fast ship but one with a large number of cabins for sleeping accommodation. The design would also be influenced by the configuration of the harbor at South Haven. The ship would have to load in the Black River, which was normally about 12 feet deep; proceed out a dredged channel between piers into deeper water; and then cross a bar beginning about 1.25 miles out, where the depth was typically 12 to 13 feet.

Pereue succeeded in generating some local interest, and on October 9,

1902, Blacker filed articles of incorporation for the Michigan Steamship

Company in Indiana.[4] Captain L. A. Leighton, who was appointed general
manager, bought what was called the Joe Smith dock on the north side
of the Black River for the terminal at South Haven.[5] Efforts at securing
the steamer began at once. Both the Dunkley-Williams management and
Pereue's group wanted to christen their vessels "City of South Haven,"
but the one whose ship was launched first would secure the name. The
ships were ordered almost simultaneously in October 1902. The Michigan
Steamship Company management placed its contract with the Jenks Ship
Building Company of Port Huron, Michigan, on Tuesday, October 7. The
directors of Dunkley-Williams met in South Haven on Saturday, October 11; approved plans worked out with the Craig Ship Building Company
of Toledo, Ohio; and wired Craig to begin construction on their steamer.
Dunkley and Williams went to Toledo and made final arrangements on
October 13.[6] Progress on the Dunkley-Williams steamer proved much
more rapid. By January the framing for the hull and some of the deck
beams were in place, along with some of the plates on the hull.[7] It was
clear that she would be launched the earlier of the two—as she was on
March 23, 1903.[8] This assured Dunkley-Williams the rights to the name
"City of South Haven" and obliged Pereue to seek another name. At the
Michigan Steamship Company's first annual meeting, on January 20,
1903, the company announced a popular contest for a name, with a prize
of ten dollars in cash and a season pass on the steamer. Entries were limited to names of eight letters, either of American Indian origin or "sugges-
tive of speed, comfort and beauty."[9] No fewer than 565 submissions were
received before the closing date of the contest early in February, including
10 submissions of the name "Michigan," 22 of "Hiawatha," 8 of "Poka-
gon," and 13 of "Majestic," but these were rejected for duplicating names
of existing ships. Names of officers of the company were also rejected.
Late in April, as the ship was approaching completion in Port Huron,
the management chose the name "Eastland," submitted by Mrs. David
Reid of South Haven.[10] Because of Michigan Steamship's incorporation in
Indiana, the ship would be registered in Michigan City.

The *Eastland* was designed as a twin-screw ship with high-rising steel
sides and a fender strake, as distinct from a steamboat with overhanging
guards and a wooden superstructure. Professor Sadler in his evaluation
of the ship following the disaster characterized her as in type an English
Channel steamer.[11] Pereue specified twin screws in an effort to make her
easier to berth, to reduce vibration, to make her steadier in a rolling sea,
and, most important, to allow her to operate even after the failure of one
engine. He sought a ship with a service speed of 20 miles per hour, a
forced-draft speed of 24 miles per hour, and an emergency capability of

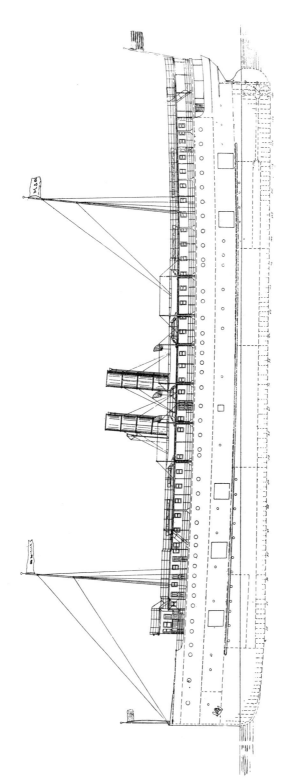

The only surviving plan of the *Eastland* is this port outboard profile, issued by Jenks before the ship was given her name. The illustration is reproduced from the *Marine Review*, but it also appeared in the Port Huron *Times*. (Library of Congress)

17 miles per hour on a single screw.[12] The twin screws, as designed, had
detachable blades and were mounted on shafts about 10 inches in diameter
and over 30 feet long, with brass sleeves.[13]

When the placing of the contract was announced, the ship was said to
be intended for 2,000 passengers, with sleeping accommodations for 500.
The plan was unusual for a Great Lakes ship in providing for two classes
of passengers, first and steerage. For the steerage class, the company reported that there would be sleeping accommodations for 150 men in the
area below the main deck forward of the engines and for a similar number
of women aft the engines. In fact, the area aft the engine rooms was used
as dormitory space for the firemen, oilers, and coal passers.

The ship was designed with a fairly orthodox configuration of four
decks. The main deck had five gangways, the first, extending from the
bow, to be used normally for loading and unloading baggage; the second,
fourth, and fifth for passengers; and the third for freight. These gangways
were relatively low, with the bottoms about four feet above the waterline
when unloaded and twenty inches to two feet when loaded. The aft gangway when fully loaded descended as low as one foot to eighteen inches
above the water.[14] The passenger gangways had half doors, the tops of
which were typically left open. The gangways were also fitted with openwork gates that could be put in place across the lower portion so as to
operate with the doors open. On the basis of photographic evidence, the
ship frequently operated in this fashion. The half doors as installed were
intended to be watertight, but there is evidence that they were not. After
the disaster, naval architect William J. Wood, in describing his experiences
on the ship's trial run, reported specifically that they leaked.[15] This was, in
fact, one of the problems Wood had been brought in to correct.

Because the gangways were so low, the ship from the outset had a very
small range of lateral stability. Professor Sadler, in his evaluation of the
ship in 1916 (printed below in Appendix C), estimated that a list of only
15 degrees would bring water over the closed half doors of the gangways.
This is an overly favorable evaluation, for the half doors were not watertight and were frequently left open. When the aft gangways were 18 inches
above the waterline, a list of only some 7.5 to 10 degrees was enough to
bring water onto the main deck.

The main deck had a bar aft, with a refrigerator for bottled beer. No
doubt the refrigerator was looked upon as a trivial part of the ship's design,
but it was to prove significant in the disaster. There was an area of only
about 30 linear feet on the main deck for cargo, expected to be only fruit.
Forward was a galley, connected by a dumbwaiter to what was called the
steam room, a facility for steam tables for the dining room, which was
immediately aft on the cabin deck, one deck higher. There was an officers'

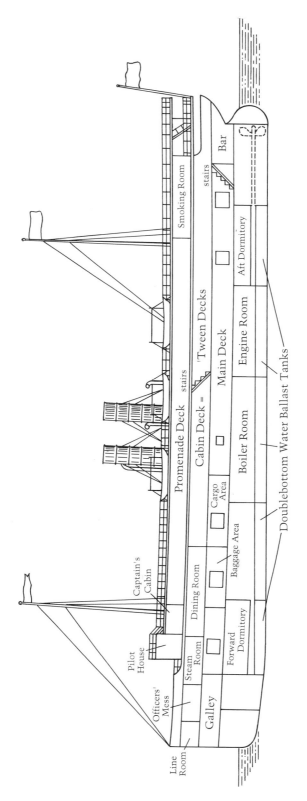

An inboard profile of the *Eastland* drawn by Leonidas Polemis on the basis of literary evidence of the placing of the ship's arrangements. Provided to assist the reader in following the text, it does not purport to be wholly accurate. It is also not complete, owing to a lack of information on the crew's mess and other important facilities.

mess forward of the steam room. One staircase led up aft from the main deck to the cabin deck. The ship had 2 parlor rooms with private baths and 86 ordinary cabins, arranged about the cabin deck and the promenade deck immediately above it. As was standard, a broad staircase connected these decks, and a balcony wrapped around the inside of the promenade deck, forming a grand saloon. There was a nursery on the cabin deck amidships, taking up the space of four cabins. Aft on the promenade deck was a smoking room, which housed the console of a steam calliope—an unusual fitting for a Great Lakes steamer. The calliope was intended to call attention to the ship in Chicago, but the city government disliked the devices and, after one was placed on the *City of South Haven* in 1907, prohibited the playing of calliopes in the Chicago River or for three miles out into the lake.[16]

The promenade deck extended forward beyond the pilot house. The promenade area of open deck outside the cabins was 7 to 8 feet wide. The hurricane deck carried 3 pairs of Lane & De Groot lifeboats, each measuring 22′ × 6′ × 2.6′, with 200-cubic-foot capacity, for 20 persons.[17] This deck was open to passengers; awnings could be stretched over the aft portion and also the exposed area of the promenade deck forward of the pilot house, to shield passengers from the sun.[18]

The *City of South Haven* was a similar vessel, being also a steel-hulled ship as distinct from a steamboat with guards and wooden superstructure, and having four decks. Both ships had two stacks, set in a fore-and-aft configuration. The *Eastland*'s were closely spaced and set rather far aft; the *City of South Haven*'s were thicker and placed farther forward. The two ships were easily distinguished at a distance. The *Eastland* was thought to have a profile more closely approximating a deep-seas craft and to express speed when viewed from a distance. The principal difference between the two ships was in the placement of the staterooms on the cabin deck. On the *Eastland* the cabins were brought out to the side of the ship, with portholes in the steel plating. On the *City of South Haven*, the cabins were set in, allowing a promenade around the cabin deck. This meant that the *Eastland*'s plating was carried one deck higher than the *City of South Haven*'s, giving the former a degree of protection against the seas ordinarily provided for propeller steamers intended for Lake Superior but not thought necessary for such vessels on the calmer Lake Michigan. This also meant that passengers wishing to be out on deck, as for example in waving to friends while departing or arriving, had to go one deck higher on the *Eastland* than on the *City of South Haven*. Accordingly, the *City of South Haven* lent herself better to pleasure travel, and the distribution of passengers was more consistent with stability. The *City of South Haven* was a single-screw vessel. The *Eastland* required a larger engine-room crew and,

One of a series of advertisements the Jenks Ship Building Company ran in the annual *Beeson's Marine Directory* in the early years of the century. The ship shown is the bulk freighter *Captain Thomas Wilson* of 1900. At 4,917 gross tons, she was the largest ship Jenks ever built. (Library of Congress)

as was determined from her later experience on Lake Erie, burned coal heavily and was relatively expensive to operate.[19]

The contract signed by Pereue and the Jenks firm on October 7, 1902, provided for a passenger steamer meeting the standards of the Great Lakes Register and the Bureau Veritas. The ship was to be 265'-0" between perpendiculars and 275'-0" overall, with a 38'-0" beam and molded depth of 22'-8". As built, however, she was reported in the American registries to have a depth of only 19'-6". She was to have four Scotch—that is, fire tube—boilers, 13'-4" × 12'-0", with two triple-expansion engines of 20" + 33" + 55" × 30".

This was an incentive contract. The ship was to run at twenty miles per hour for four consecutive hours between South Haven and Chicago with a panel of three experts aboard, one chosen by the steamship company, one by the builder, and a third by the first two experts. If in the panel's judgment the *Eastland* failed to make this target, Jenks reserved the right to make such repairs and changes at its own expense as would bring the ship up to speed. If the ship, even after such changes, proved unable to make twenty miles per hour, the purchase price of $250,000, of which $117,000 was to be in the bonds of the steamship company, was to be reduced by $2,500 per quarter mile per hour of shortfall. If the ship could not attain nineteen miles per hour, the company would have the right to reject her. In parallel fashion, if the ship could exceed twenty miles per hour, the builder was to receive an additional $2,500 per quarter mile per hour.[20]

The *Eastland* was the first passenger ship ever built by the Jenks Ship Building Company and, as it proved, the last one. The fact that the *Eastland* was the only passenger ship ever built by Jenks inevitably led some commentators after the disaster to conclude that the ship was amateurishly designed and unstable from the outset.[21] This does not appear to be correct. The shipyard had a short but generally successful history, and the process of designing the *Eastland* was thoroughly professional. The firm had been founded by William S. Jenks, who was born in Elmira, New York, on July 7, 1818. He had been brought to Birmingham, Michigan, as a child, but moved to Port Huron in 1858. There he established a machine shop in 1859, but after suffering a fire in 1861, he established the Phoenix Iron Works jointly with his son, Orrin L. Jenks. In 1890 William S. and Orrin Jenks, along with William G. Jenks and Angus M. Carpenter, incorporated the Jenks Ship Building Company, and opened a small shipyard on the site of Carpenter's coal yard on the north bank of the Black River just east of the Seventh Street bridge in Port Huron. The Jenks Ship Building Company absorbed the Phoenix Iron Works in 1899. The shipyard had been at least moderately successful in building bulk freighters for the trade in iron and copper ores from Lake Superior to the lower Great Lakes. As shown in the company's hull list in Appendix B, below, the earlier steamers were wood, but the firm shifted to steel with the *Ravenscraig* of 1900. With the conversion to steel ships, the firm moved its operations to a new and larger yard on the north bank of the Black River immediately downstream from the bridge of the Grand Trunk Western's old main line, which ran from Tappan, on the southwest edge of the Port Huron metropolitan area, to Fort Gratiot, on the St. Clair River opposite Point Edward, Ontario. The yard was a rather Spartan plant, with few permanent facilities. The narrowness of the Black River required side-launching of the ships in the usual Great Lakes fashion. Because William S. Jenks, the founder, had died on December 12, 1902, his son Orrin was head of the firm at the time the *Eastland* was built. Prior to the *Eastland* commission, the firm had built 23 ships and a fleet of barges. This did not make it a major shipbuilder, but the firm's output up to that time had passed $2 million, and the payroll for its work force of 400 employees was about $8,000 per week.[22] The company was nearing the end of its history, however. After the *Eastland* it produced only one more ship, the bulk freighter *F. B. Squire*, before suffering a serious fire in 1905 and leaving the industry in 1906.

The Jenks Ship Building Company opened the yard at which the *Eastland* was built when it converted to steel shipbuilding in 1900. The first product of the new yard was the bulk freighter *Ravenscraig*, shown here immediately after her side-launching. The photograph shows the constrictions imposed by the narrowness of the Black River. (Rev. Peter J. Van der Linden collection)

The only ship the Jenks Ship Building Company built after the *Eastland* was the bulk freighter *F. B. Squire* of 1903. She is shown in the St. Clair River running for the Jenkins Steamship Company. Jenks's bulk freighters were not particularly attractive. (Rev. Peter J. Van der Linden collection)

The commission for designing the *Eastland* was given to Sidney Grant Jenks, grandson of the founder. Preparing for a career in the family firm, Sidney Jenks had enrolled in engineering at Cornell University and taken his bachelor's degree in 1897. He began his calculations for the *Eastland* by consulting his former professor of naval architecture, George R. McDermott. The general design features of the ship described up to this point were not exceptional and were not issues in the criminal and civil actions that followed the disaster. Rather, the legal issues concerned the ship's metacentric height and the handling of her system of water ballast. Working within the design constraints of a twin-screw steamer with a draft of only ten to twelve feet, McDermott proposed a ship with a metacentric height of eighteen inches fully loaded.[23]

The metacentric height of a ship is the measure of her transverse stability. Be-

Sidney Grant Jenks, designer of the *Eastland*. (Rev. Peter J. Van der Linden collection)

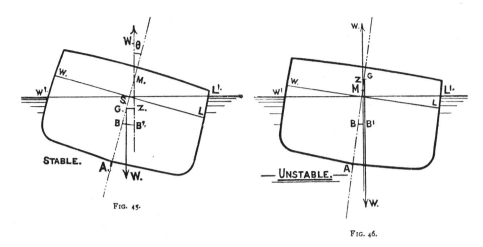

FIG. 45.

FIG. 46.

Diagrams of metacentric height from Edward L. Attwood, O.B.E., *Theoretical Naval Architecture* (London: Longmans, Green & Co., 1922), pp. 94, 96. A = center line of ship at keel. B = center of buoyancy. B′ = point to which center of buoyancy swings out at small angles of inclination. G = center of gravity. GM = metacentric height. G − Z or Z − G = righting lever. M = metacenter. O = angle of list or heel. S = center line at waterline. W = weight. W − L = waterline of ship. W′ − L′ = surface of water.

cause the *Eastland* eventually capsized, her metacentric height over the course of her history is of first importance. In figure 45 from Attwood's *Theoretical Naval Architecture*, B represents the ship's center of buoyancy, which is to say the center of forces pushing upward. G represents the center of gravity. W–L is the ship's waterline, and W′L′ the actual surface of the water. When the ship lists or is heeled—heel being list intentionally induced by the officers—the center of buoyancy swings out to B′. The metacenter, M, is the point on the center line of the ship at which the vertical line up from B′ intersects the center line at small degrees of list or heel, usually interpreted as less than 10 degrees. The parallel vertical lines running up from B′ and down from G are known as the couple. If the metacentric height (G–M) is positive, which is to say that M is above G on the center line, the couple is a righting moment and the horizontal line G–Z from the center of gravity to the point Z directly opposite it represents a righting lever. The ship will then tend to right herself from small degrees of inclination, shown by the theta symbol. If the metacentric height is zero, the ship is in a neutral equilibrium, such that she will tend not to right herself but to remain in an inclined position. If the metacentric height is negative, with G above M as in Attwood's figure 46, the ship is in an unstable position such that the forces acting upon her will tend to make her capsize.[24] As was stated in connection with the *Eastland*, if one stood with a five-pound weight on the center line of a ship with a zero metacentric height, the ship would begin to list in whichever direction one threw the weight, and if one partially filled a ballast tank to compensate, the ship would capsize from the slightest touch.[25]

It is not clear whether the *Eastland* was built with the metacentric height proposed by McDermott. The ship he envisioned was 60 feet longer than the *Eastland* as built; the 60 feet were removed from the center of the plan, presumably because of a shortage of funds.[26] H. H. Evans, one of the naval architects invited by the Chicago *Tribune* to comment on the *Eastland* following the disaster, observed that the removal of the 60 feet from the plan probably reduced the ship's metacentric height by taking out her "fullness at the waist."[27] By McDermott's recollection after the disaster, the ship he had discussed with Jenks had one deck less than the *Eastland*.[28] If the *Eastland* had an initial metacentric height of eighteen inches fully loaded, she was about average for a Great Lakes ship of the time.[29] McDermott, however, visualized the ship as primarily a freighter, for which such a metacentric height would have been satisfactory, but the *Eastland* from the outset served primarily as a passenger vessel, and by the time of the disaster was wholly a passenger excursion ship that did not carry freight at all. For such a ship, where the distribution of passengers was highly variable, normal practice would have been to provide a metacentric height of two to four feet, fully loaded.

Metacentric height may be ascertained by a process of shifting a weight laterally across the deck of the ship. One or two plumb lines are hung at the ship's center line, and readings are taken with inclinations of 5 to 6 degrees. By a simple arithmetical and trigonometric calculation, the metacentric height is determined.[30] Standard practice is to take the metacentric height of a new ship in this fashion, but not to take it thereafter. As far as can be determined, the metacentric height of the *Eastland* was never taken by an inclining test at any time in her history as a commercial vessel, although the United States Navy made such tests after acquiring her subsequent to the disaster. Jenks testified in the criminal trial following the disaster that no inclining test had been done on her when she was new, although he admitted under cross-examination that such a test would have been desirable.[31]

The *Eastland* was side-launched at 2:30 P.M. on May 6, 1903, into the Black River at Port Huron.[32] She was christened by Captain Pereue's wife, the former Frances Elizabeth Stufflebeam. The occasion was festive, if only because it represented expansion of the Jenks firm into building of passengers ships. No passenger steamer had been built at Port Huron since the ferry *Omar D. Conger* in 1882. Bunting was put out and school children were given a partial day free to attend the ceremony. The crowd was

Jenks issued two photographs of the *Eastland* on the ways at Port Huron, taken before and after the propellers were attached. (Collections of Harry Benford and R. W. Appleyard)

estimated at about 6,000.[33] The *Eastland* was launched fully fitted out except for her engines and boilers. Sidney Jenks observed that she went about two and a half feet into the river, rolled to a 45-degree angle, and righted herself "just as nice and steady as a church."[34] He allowed 200 tons for her boilers, 80 tons for boiler water, and about 190 tons for her machinery, expecting that she would be ordinarily stable.[35] Jenks was apparently correct. In the ship's original configuration in the season of 1903, she had no serious problems of instability of the sort that came later to characterize her.

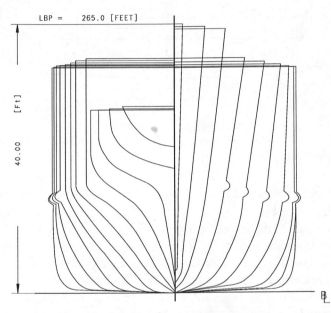

LBP = 265.0 [FEET]

[Ft]

40.00

B L

Above, a body plan of the *Eastland*'s hull, a reconstruction by computer-assisted drafting by Leonidas Polemis from photographs. As with the other reconstructions, it cannot be considered entirely accurate. The lines at right delineate the hull from the bow, the lines at left from the stern. Below, a simplified presentation of the waterlines of the hull, derived from the same data by Peter Beier, Professor of Naval Architecture at the University of Michigan. Professor Beier estimates that the prismatic coefficient of fineness, a measure of the fullness of the hull, was between .67 and .685, with a best estimate of .68. The prismatic coefficient of fineness measures the displacement of the hull relative to an imaginary prism of a volume given by the area of an underwater cross-section of the hull amidships multiplied by the length of the ship at the waterline. For a more rigorous definition, see note 2 to Walter C. Cowles's comment on Professor Sadler's testimony in Appendix C, below. The estimate of .68 implies the *Eastland* was not exceptional in fineness or fullness of her hull.

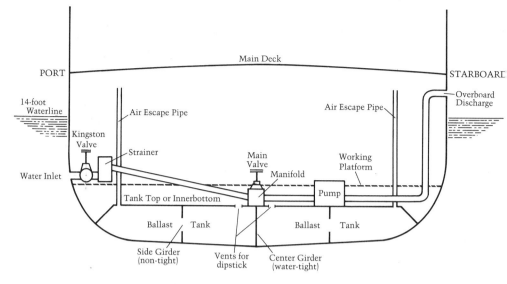

A cross section of the *Eastland*'s ballast system by Leonidas Polemis. This diagram is also reconstructed from literary evidence and should not be considered wholly accurate.

To deal with the problem of the shallowness of the Black River at South Haven and the bar offshore, Jenks had equipped the ship with a system of ballast tanks, or more specifically, of watertight compartments in a double bottom 48 inches high, fed by a manifold. The initial intent for this system was to allow the ship to shift quickly between a draft of 10'-6"—which was considered the low-water condition in the Black River—to her normal draft, which was about 14'-0".[36] The system had twelve tanks. A single compartment at the bow called the fore peak tank could be filled from the manifold, but none of the ship's various operators made a practice of using it. A single tank at the rear was not connected to the manifold, but could be filled with a hose; this tank also was never reportedly used for stabilizing the ship. The system, as a chief engineer viewed it, consisted of ten tanks, symmetrical between port and starboard, divided by a metal partition fixed to the keelson. Each tank had a longitudinal gridiron partition or girder to prevent water from moving unimpeded laterally. This arrangement was intended to give the water in the ballast tanks the properties of a viscous liquid. The ballast system, which ran the length of the ship, was fed by a pipe about ten inches in diameter, located amidships on the port side by the engine room, with an intake six to eight feet below water level, depending on load. The intake was described as a Kingston valve, a type of conical valve in which, in the closed position, the pressure of the sea forces the valve onto its seat, keeping it tight. The valve had a screw con-

trol. Immediately inboard from the valve was a strainer. The Kingston
valve was normally kept open, and was closed only to service the strainer;
it was not used for stabilization of the ship.[37]

Water was ingested through the pipe by gravity into a manifold, a con-
duit of square cross-section of about 14 inches in each dimension, connected to each of the tanks by a pipe 6 inches in diameter. Because of the
relative diameters of the pipes leading into the manifold and out of it into
the tanks, two tanks could be filled as rapidly as one. The angle of descent
of the pipe from the intake to the manifold is unrecorded, but after the
disaster the chief engineer testified that the seavalve, or intake, was at approximately the same level as the manifold, or slightly lower.[38] On the
basis of known dimensions of the ship, the intake appears to have been
slightly higher than the manifold, with a pipe descending about 2'-2" over
the course of a lateral distance of 19 feet, which implies an angle of about
6.5 degrees.[39] The valves from the intake and to the pipes into the tanks
were arranged longitudinally along the manifold over a linear distance of
10 to 12 feet. The manifold was paralleled by a metal walkway. The valves
were all normally controlled by a detachable 16-inch wheel that was
moved from valve to valve as required. Alternatively, the valves could be
turned with wrenches. Consequently, the system was not well suited to
immediate responses. The tanks, to prevent overfilling, were equipped
with vertical vent pipes extending up about 10 feet to a point above water
level. Use of the hull as the bottom of the tanks had the incidental advantage, given the fact the ship was expected to hit bottom frequently in the
Black River or on the bar offshore, that if the hull were punctured, only a
single watertight compartment would be flooded. The ship was never to
suffer such an accident, however.

The fact that the tanks followed the contours of the hull meant that the
tanks were of greatly different capacities. The largest were the two No. 3
tanks, each of which was approximately 64 feet long and 19 feet wide.
These tanks were amidships, beneath the boiler room, and were nearly
rectangular. Each of them could hold approximately 82.5 tons. The entire system, including the fore and aft peak tanks, was filled experimentally after
the ship was raised following the disaster and found to have a capacity of
647 tons. Filling both No. 3 tanks added about 18 inches to the ship's draft.
Reports of the relative size of the other tanks are not consistent, but the
No. 2 tanks were second largest, capable of holding about 53 tons each.
The No. 4 tanks were located under the engine room. They were reportedly
smaller than the No. 2's, with a capacity of over 40 tons each. The No. 1
tanks and No. 5 tanks held the rest, a total of about 80 tons between the
four, but they were not used by most chief engineers for heeling the ship
because of fore-and-aft trimming problems. It took about 25 minutes to

fill either or both No. 3 tanks, or 10 to 12 minutes to fill either the No. 2 tanks or the No. 4's. To fill the entire system required about an hour. The system had no meters. The chief engineer had to estimate the content of a tank on the basis of the length of time the water had flowed. This was one reason why chief engineers customarily pumped out the tanks entirely before loading passengers; they could then estimate the content of the tanks more accurately than if they began with the tanks partly filled. Each tank had a vent from which air exhausted as the tank was filled; when water flowed from this vent, or when it ceased to give off a characteristic whistling sound, the chief knew the tank was full. He could ascertain the water level in a partly filled tank by inserting through the vent a rod in the nature of a dipstick painted with one-inch gradations, but this was too time-consuming for short-term calculations. The vents for the dipstick were at the aft portion of tanks Nos. 1 through 4, but on the forward edge of tanks No. 5, all located for ready access along the center line of the ship. The vents were simply holes, not valves. They had covers, which were closed when the tank was to be filled completely, but they were normally left open for use of the dipstick when the tanks were only partly filled. This arrangement had the obvious disadvantage that momentary inattention could cause a tank to overflow, discharging water about the hull. It was estimated that a 22-degree list would cause water to flow over the center longitudinal bulkhead from one side to the other. Because of this, but also for more general reasons, the hull was fitted with both port and starboard bilge pumps. If the vents for the dipstick were open, the system was not watertight from the top. This fact proved important in the evaluation of what had happened in the disaster, and was a major consideration in the civil case.

Communication between the bridge and the engine room was by a Chadburn telegraph, but it contained only the standard Great Lakes engine commands, none concerning the ballast system. Such communications could be made by a voice tube. Actually, all masters of the ship habitually left management of the system to the chief engineer, in normal circumstances giving only general directives to keep the ship stable, with specific orders only for regulating the degree of heel to adjust the angle of the gangplank for loading or unloading. The system was emptied by means of a reciprocating duplex pump, 18″ × 24″, discharging through a port forward of the engine room on the starboard side about 2′-6″ to 3′-0″ above the waterline when the ship was on even keel. The system could be pumped out at about the same rate as it could be filled, or possibly slightly more rapidly. Because the system was pumped out through the same manifold by which it was filled, the system could not ingest water into the tanks on one side and discharge it from the tanks on the other side simultaneously—another characteristic that proved important in the disaster. It was also impossible to pump water from one side to the other directly. The chief engineer was guided in management of the system by an inclinometer consisting of an arrow-shaped metal pendulum about 18 inches long mounted on the forward bulkhead of the engine room. Deviation from vertical was shown in inches, not degrees; the chief engineer made his own estimate of degrees of list or heel.[40]

The *City of South Haven* had no water ballast system of this sort for lateral stability, although she did have tanks in her collision compartments for fore-and-aft trimming.[41]

The *Eastland*'s boilers and engines had been installed by early July, and the fitting-out process was shortly completed. On Monday, July 13, she was shown to the owners, and on the following day she was opened from 2:00 to 4:00 P.M. at her berth at the foot of Griswold Street for public inspection. The ship made an excellent impression. Her main public room had been finished in mahogany, the cabins with cream paint. The dining room was faced with quarter-sawed oak with blue panels ornamented with clusters of fruit. The ship had a dark hull, probably dark green in conformity with the Jenks firm's practice on its bulk freighters. The lettering was in large raised letters with heavy serifs, also consistent with Jenks's practice on its freighters. Pereue, his wife, Leighton, and most of the other principal figures in the Michigan Steamship Company had come over to Port Huron on the 13th and expressed themselves pleased with the steamer.[42] Departure was delayed until the anchors arrived, but she left

The *Eastland* in one of her most engaging portraits, taken off South Haven in 1903 by the local professional photographer A. A. Appleyard. The ship was thought to have a deep-seas appearance that conveyed an impression of speed in the open lake. (R. W. Appleyard collection)

Port Huron about 2:30 A.M. on July 16 with Pereue in command.[43] Title to the ship remained in the hands of the Jenks firm pending the speed trial provided for in the contract. Robert Close of the Jenks staff served as chief engineer, with A. J. Wilson as his assistant and Edward Moore as steam-fitter.[44] Sidney Jenks and his wife and Mrs. Pereue were also in the company. Leighton had offered that anyone from South Haven who was willing to come to Port Huron by train at his or her own expense could make the trip back on the steamer without charge.[45] There were about 250 persons aboard. The *Eastland* called at Mackinac Island about 2:00 A.M. on the 17th and put into Manistee about 3:00 P.M. for a public inspection. She left about 7:30 P.M. and arrived in South Haven on July 18 about 4:00 A.M. The trip had been calm, mainly in pale moonlight, and the ship had behaved perfectly. She was welcomed with the fire whistle on the local pumping station. Although the original plan had been to call for only an hour to discharge the passengers returning to South Haven, the ship had to take coal, and there was considerable local interest in seeing the interior. Several hundred people inspected her. There was a short ceremony at which Mrs. L. G. Rhodes read a poem composed by E. L. Keasey in honor of the occasion:

> Ho! Friends of the *Eastland*'s Passengers,
>   We hail this happy day.
> This bracing breeze from the rippling seas
>   Drives trifling cares away.
> We sail for a land where a happy band
>   Looks out with an anxious eye,
> And warm hearts leap as their watch they keep
>   For our ship gainst the sky.
> Let us look with cheer for those friends so dear
>   And have on our hearts engraven
> A loyal thought for the *Eastland*'s crew
>   And a hope for our home in Haven.[46]

The ship was to leave on her first regular trip to Chicago at 10:00 P.M., but in what was to be premonitory of her troubles in the Black River, she fouled one of her lines in a propeller and could not leave the harbor until 10:30.

If the *Eastland* in 1903 had no problems of instability, she developed plenty of others. Notably, she could not meet her target speed under the incentive contract. The original plan of having her run two round trips per day proved impractical immediately upon her entering service on July 18, 1903; on July 21 the company announced an orthodox schedule of departure from Chicago at 9:30 A.M. and from South Haven at 5:00 P.M., exactly duplicating the *City of South Haven*'s timetable.[47] The *Eastland* was scheduled for only two night crossings per week, from Chicago on

Fridays and Saturdays. When she had the test provided for in the contract, whereby three judges, one of whom was the Chicago naval architect William J. Wood, were to ascertain her ability to cross the lake at twenty miles per hour, she failed.[48] The ballast system proved unable to provide the change in draft originally envisioned. The ship frequently hit bottom in the Black River and on the bar off South Haven, once fouling her starboard screw with a steel cable picked up in the river, and in her first four weeks of operation requiring replacement of 22 of the detachable blades on her propellers.[49] The only reported problem of the ship that stemmed from her design features was a consequence of her low gangways. Backing out of South Haven on July 19, 1903, she was observed by personnel on duty at the Life-Saving Service station to be listing enough to bring water into several open ports. The surfman on duty pulled out of the station to notify the captain, and the problem was resolved with no serious consequences.[50]

Toward the end of the 1903 season the *Eastland* had a minor accident that caused the replacement of Pereue as her master. On the morning of July 23 she was putting about in the Chicago River off the Michigan Steamship Company's berth on the south bank immediately west of the Wells Street bridge. Her stern struck the tug *George W. Gardner* at the wharf of the Dunham Towing & Wrecking Company on the north bank. The tug rolled over and was swamped, convincing Blacker that his associate Pereue, who had never commanded a twin-screw ship before, was unqualified to handle the *Eastland*. On August 27, apparently by Blacker's decision, Pereue was replaced as master of the ship by Frank A. Dority, first mate of the Goodrich Line's *Iowa*. This was a sound choice, for Dority had extensive experience as master of the early Great Lakes car ferries, which were large twin-screw ships of the character of the *Eastland*.[51] Because the car ferries put into their slips without tugs, their masters developed excellent reputations for berthing by the handling of twin screws.

Blacker emerged from being the principal financier of the firm to become its actual head, replacing Patrick Noud as president on December 10, 1903.[52] Angus M. Carpenter of Jenks Ship Building was made vice president because Jenks, in the course of the settlement on the *Eastland*, had retained an equity of $75,000 in

Angus M. Carpenter, who represented Jenks as vice president of the Michigan Steamship Company. (Rev. Peter J. Van der Linden collection)

The Michigan Steamship Company's second ship was the wooden *Soo City*. Her design was quite orthodox for a Lake Michigan propeller steamer, with a single deck for freight and another for passengers. Boilers and engines were placed fairly far aft to allow a large unbroken area for package freight. The ship was built in 1888 by F. W. Wheeler of West Bay City for the Arnold Line's service between the Straits of Mackinac and Sault Ste. Marie, but she ran for many operators. She was being taken to the Atlantic in 1908 when she foundered in the Gulf of St. Lawrence. (Drawing by Samuel Ward Stanton)

Both of the Michigan Steamship Company's vessels in South Haven in the summer of 1904, the *Soo City* in the foreground and the *Eastland* to her stern. (R. W. Appleyard collection)

Michigan Steamship. This was not an unusual arrangement; Jenks had re-

tained equities in several of the freighters it had built. At Michigan Steamship's meeting of December 10, the directors voted to buy or lease a second ship, probably intending a large steel steamer for service from
Chicago and Milwaukee to Ludington and Manistee, a project that had
been noted in the local press in September.[53] Actually, for 1904 the company merely leased the small wooden propeller-steamer *Soo City* as a second ship for early-season and off-hours service on the existing South Haven line.

Over the course of three days in September 1903, Michigan Steamship
and Jenks Ship Building worked out an arrangement to deal with the *Eastland*'s problems by speeding her up and reducing her draft. Michigan
Steamship agreed to accept the ship as being able to operate at nineteen
miles per hour, thereby gaining a refund of $10,000. The company agreed
to devote the $10,000 to some revisions in the ship at the builder's yard,
and Jenks agreed to contribute $25,000 to the project.[54] Because of Jenks's
equity in Michigan Steamship, the agreement was apparently amicable.
The *Eastland* returned to Port Huron on September 22 and spent the entire
winter of 1903–4 at the foot of Griswold Street. The changes were made
at that point mainly in April and early May 1904, under Wood's direction.
The ship was not drydocked.

The effort to speed up the ship was implemented by installation of the
Ellis and Eaves system of induced draft. The other major change agreed
upon was adding the McCreery system of air-conditioning.[55] The design
of the ship in which the plating was brought one deck higher than on the
City of South Haven must have produced a stuffy interior, which the management felt it necessary to relieve. The induced-draft system was a British invention, patented in 1895 by J. D. Ellis and William Eaves of John
Brown & Company, and produced by the firm in Sheffield. Brown marketed the device as a suction-draft system "producing the greatest amount
of evaporation combined with economy and comfort."[56] To judge from
surviving advertisements, it was not marketed as a means of increasing

William J. Wood, the naval architect who superintended the revisions in the *Eastland* between
the 1903 and 1904 seasons, from a series of
sketches of witnesses before the coroner's jury
on July 27, 1915, done by an artist for the Chicago *Tribune*. (Chicago *Tribune*, July 28, 1915,
p. 2, from UCLA Libraries)

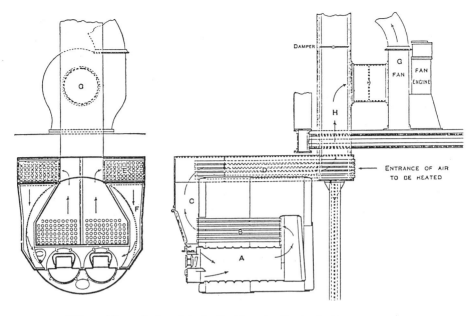

Ellis and Eaves induced draft. (Smithsonian Institution)

speed. It is illustrated in the cross section and side elevation from *The Marine Engineer* of August 1, 1898.[57] The device was based on two heat exchangers, D, which warmed air being fed to a Scotch boiler in the fashion that a feedwater heater warms water being fed into a steam locomotive. Air entered the pipes of the heat exchangers at ambient air temperature, as indicated in the side elevation, and was raised to 320 degrees Fahrenheit as it moved to the left. It then descended through a housing, F in the cross section, built around the boiler. The warmed air entered the firebox, A, and proceeded as hot gas through the firetubes, B, up through the housing C to E, through the heat exchangers at a temperature of 450 degrees, up the uptake H, and through the fan G, whence it exhausted through the stack. Most installations had a fan for each boiler, but some used one fan for two boilers. There is no evidence on the number of fans installed on the *Eastland*. There is also no surviving information on what weight was added by retrofitting this device on an existing boiler. It presumably lowered metacentric height by placing the additional weight of the heat exchangers above the boiler and placing the fans on the main deck.[58]

The McCreery system was an American device, one of several airconditioning systems patented by Joseph McCreery of Toledo between 1888 and 1902, all of which entailed cleansing a stream of air by forcing it through a cascade or spray of running water. Some of his devices also made use of ice. There is no direct evidence as to which of McCreery's patents was used for the *Eastland*, but it was probably a system of processing air through a cascade that descended by gravity over a series of inclined planes, with return of the water to the top of the machine by buckets on a chain. McCreery specifically designed this system for use in ships, railroad cars, and other locations where a free-flowing, readily replenished supply of water was not available.[59] Whichever McCreery device was used, Wood was pleased with it, declaring that it produced the best distribution of cold, clean, dry air that he ever experienced.[60] Again, there is no evidence on the weight of the system as installed, but because it moved air downward through the mechanism into a series of overhead ducts, there is a presumption that it was mounted on the hurricane deck, and thus reduced metacentric height.

Whatever may have been the additional weight from the induced-draft

The modifications to the *Eastland* in the spring of 1904 included the McCreery system of ventilation. Joseph McCreery's air-conditioning device specifically intended for ships is shown in his patent no. 586,363 of 1897. Air from intakes above the hurricane deck enters at the port lettered *a* at the upper left. *R′* is one of a pair of wings that may be opened and closed to regulate the admission of air. The flow of air turns the fan (*N*), which drives a chain of buckets (*P*) that raise water from the sump at the bottom. The water is discharged onto the top inclined plane, from which it cascades over the lower inclined planes back to the sump. The stream of air passing through the falling water is cooled and cleansed before escaping through the vent (*a2*, at lower left) into overhead ducts on the decks below. The device was not notably original. (Smithsonian Institution)

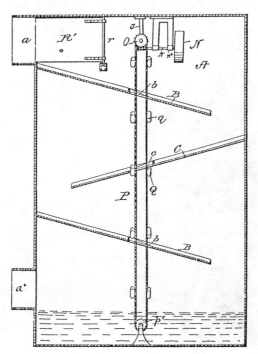

and air-conditioning systems, it was enough to cause the ship to squat when under way, promising to aggravate her chronic problem of striking bottom. To deal with the problem Wood undertook to relocate some of the ship's machinery.[61] The exact nature of the repositioning was never stated, either at the time or after the disaster. Because the ship's machinery was quite limited, this probably meant some forward or aft movement of the engines and incidentally moving the condensers. Although such changes might have been facilitated by drydocking, they could have been made with the ship afloat at Griswold Street. We know only what the Port Huron *Times* reported: the changes were extensive and time-consuming.[62]

Although leakage of water through the gangways was recognized as one of the ship's problems—admittedly a lesser one—Wood did not correct it. Albert R. Jefferson, the ship's first officer in 1904, testified in the criminal trial following the disaster that the gangways were not watertight during his tenure on the ship.[63]

The *City of South Haven* was similar in size and outline to the *Eastland*, but differed in several respects. Her plating was carried to a deck lower, and her gangways were perceptibly higher. The ship ran to South Haven until she was requisitioned by the War Shipping Board in 1918. After the war, she became the *City of Miami* of the Miami-Havana Navigation Company. Her impressive appearance was ruined by bringing her plating at the bow one deck higher to protect her from the high seas. After two years of operation to Cuba, she was sold back to the Great Lakes to run as the second *E. G. Crosby* between Milwaukee, Muskegon, and Grand Haven. She operated until the early 1930's, but was then laid up at Sturgeon Bay, where she was nearly destroyed by fire on December 3, 1935. Efforts to rebuild her failed, and she was scrapped in the early 1940's. (T. H. Franklin collection, Steamship Historical Society of America)

(Gordon Wendt collection)

The changes were in one respect a success. In 1903 the *Eastland* had, in general, been slower than the *City of South Haven*, but in 1904 she was typically faster.[64] She made her best reported crossing that season at 22.25 miles per hour.[65] The new induced-draft and air-conditioning systems, combined with Wood's repositioning of machinery to reduce her draft, however, produced a ship that was to prove chronically top-heavy. The Chicago *Tribune* reported immediately after the disaster that the changes of 1904 had reduced her metacentric height, fully loaded, to only four inches.[66] By contrast, in an inclining test conducted just after the disaster in 1915, the metacentric height of the *City of South Haven* in unloaded condition was found to be 4'-10".[67] This test was conducted just after the disaster in 1915, which generated a wave of interest in metacentric heights of the Chicago excursion ships.

Whatever the accuracy of the *Tribune*'s statement regarding the *Eastland*'s measurement, after the changes she manifested the characteristics of a ship with a short metacentric height. Such a ship has a slow easy roll, making her comfortable for passengers and relatively stable in a rolling sea. William P. Eeles, Michigan Steamship's chief engineer, testified that when he brought the ship back from Port Huron on May 8–9, 1904, he used no ballast, but although she took a pounding from a southwest sea on Lake Michigan, "she was as steady as could be."[68] Dority, who continued as the ship's master through the 1906 season, characterized her as the best sea boat he had ever sailed.[69] One of the *Eastland*'s later masters, Merwin S. Thompson, was an avid defender of the ship's reputation on the ground that in his experience with her on Lake Erie she handled well in bad weather, specifically in returning from Cedar Point to Cleveland with a heavy sea behind her.[70] However, the late Captain Frank E. Hamilton stated in his notes on the ship that she had difficulty with easterly winds from the bow, both on Lake Erie and on Lake Michigan. He reported that while running to Cedar Point, she occasionally returned late to Cleveland because of difficulty making progress into easterly winds. After her return to Lake Michigan in 1914, he said that she had problems with northerly or easterly winds on her outbound trips from Chicago, frequently causing her passengers to be seasick.[71] If both Thompson and Hamilton were correct, the ship was most unusual in performing better with winds from astern than from the bow.

An undesirable consequence of a short metacentric height is that the ship must be loaded and unloaded with great care to prevent the metacentric height from becoming negative. This problem was aggravated in the *Eastland*'s case by the practice of all of her chief engineers of admitting small amounts of water to the ballast system for stabilization at the wharf and when approaching or leaving it. From the outset, all of the *Eastland*'s chief engineers regularly admitted water to the ballast tanks opposite the wharf to compensate for the tendency of passengers to congregate on the side adjacent to the wharf to wave to friends on shore. A partly filled tank creates what is called a free-surface effect, which affects the stability of a ship like a variable weight higher in the ship, irregularly and unpredictably acting to reduce metacentric height. The effect is worst with small amounts of water in the tanks and disappears when the tank is full. Professor Herbert Charles Sadler in his evaluation of the *Eastland* in the criminal trial following the disaster, reproduced below in Appendix C, has an excellent explanation of the fashion in which the free-surface effect operates.

Without a single exception the *Eastland*'s reported difficulties occurred during or immediately after loading or preparatory to unloading. It was said of her that she behaved like a bicycle, being unstable when loading or unloading but stable when under way.[72] This was attributed to the effect of the twin screws in stabilizing her,[73] but alternatively, one presumes that as she went out into the lake, her passengers probably tended to move downward from the open deck space, increasing her metacentric height, and her chief engineers adjusted the ballast tanks as required. Her stability problems in loading and unloading caused her to be popularly known as a "cranky boat," a phrase that was to some extent a solecism. The term, it was argued by several officers, was more properly applied to a ship that did not hold her course well, and the *Eastland* was reportedly exemplary in that respect.[74] "Tender" would have a been a more accurate term for her.

The first manifestation of the *Eastland*'s instability after her alterations of 1903–4 occurred on Sunday, July 17, 1904. All of the cross-lake lines had heavy peaks of traffic westbound on Sunday evenings, when they carried not only day-trippers who had left Chicago that morning but also passengers who had gone east on Friday or Saturday or on the previous weekend. In 1904 William P. Eeles, the chief engineer, and his assistant, William L. Nack, regularly used tanks No. 2 and No. 4 for lateral stabilization. They also filled the No. 1 tanks in conjunction with the No. 2's to raise her stern to protect her propellers when crossing the bar after departure from South Haven. Because the ship had been built without tanks specifically designated for potable water, the No. 3 tanks were used at that time to hold the ship's water for drinking and cooking. Fourteen inches of potable water provided all the supply required, and the pipes through which this water was pumped out ended eight inches above the bottom of each tank.[75] Consequently, the No. 3 tanks typically carried between eight and fourteen inches of water, evenly divided between the two, which is to say they were ordinarily no more than approximately one-third filled.

The *Eastland*'s main bunkers were in the shape of a horizontal "H." The crossbar ran athwartship above the No. 3 tanks. It was 38 feet from side to side, 8 feet fore-and-aft, and 15 feet deep, all below the waterline except for the top 15 to 18 inches. The smaller bunkers at the sides ran fore and aft, extending out to the hull. Professor Sadler, in his examination of the ship after the disaster, determined the size of the bunkers at 5,050 cubic feet, which he thought capable of holding 126 tons of coal.[76] It was

While running for the Michigan Steamship Company between 1903 and 1905, the *Eastland* used a wharf on the south bank of the Chicago River immediately west of the Wells Street bridge. The berth is shown in a postcard view. (Rev. Peter J. Van der Linden collection)

customary to leave Chicago with the bunkers filled, putting the vessel down by about a foot. The ship burned about three tons per hour or about 25 tons in the course of a round trip. The usual practice was to use coal from the athwartship bunker eastbound and from the side bunkers as required returning. Leaving South Haven on July 17, 1904, she carried an estimated 100 tons.[77]

Consistently with the season, July 17 was extremely hot. The ship loaded a crowd that Dority estimated at about 3,000 people.[78] Captain Ira B. Mansfield, federal hull inspector at Chicago, who was aboard the ship, stated that the load was 2,142 adults and an unspecified number of children.[79] The purser, George Hale, testified that he received 2,370 tickets from the collector.[80] The load, in any case, was well short of the *Eastland*'s licensed capacity of 3,300. The largest group of passengers was what remained of a party of Chicago postal workers that had crossed to South Haven on the previous day. Because the interior of the ship had become uncomfortably hot—the McCreery air-conditioning system notwithstanding—an exceptionally large number of passengers, which Dority estimated at 1,000 to 1,200, went to the hurricane deck.[81] William H. Cochrane, general passenger agent of the company, estimated the concentration on the upper deck at over 1,200 passengers.[82] If their average weight was between 150 and 160 pounds, 1,000 to 1,200 passengers amounted to a concentration of 75 to 96 tons at the top of the vessel. If the 6 lifeboats weighed 3.62 tons each, the combined weight of passengers and boats on the hurricane deck was about 97 to 118 tons.[83] The ship left South Haven with water in her No. 1 and 2 ballast tanks to raise her propellers to clear the bar. There was relatively little potable water in tanks No. 3. Chief engineer Eeles planned to take in additional ballast water after clearing the bar and then to take in potable water in mid-lake.[84]

After about 5 minutes of running at full speed, or approximately 1.5 miles out into the lake, shortly after clearing the bar, the ship for no obvious reason began listing to port by about 12 to 15 degrees. Eeles ordered Nack to pump the water out of tanks No. 1 and 2 and then to begin admitting water to the starboard No. 4 tank. Nack let water into the starboard No. 4 tank for about 5 minutes. The ship straightened up in somewhat under 10 minutes from the beginning of the list to port, but immediately began to list more severely to starboard.[85] Dority ordered his engines into check—a term unique to the Great Lakes system of commands, meaning approximately half speed ahead—put the bridge in command of his first mate and went below to talk with Eeles. Eeles told him that he had been unable to get the water ballast into the right place, but assured him that he could do so. Dority went to the hurricane deck to urge the passengers to go below to the main deck. The list had reached a reported 20 to

25 degrees to starboard. Water came through the two aft starboard gangways and partly flooded the main deck. Henry J. Welch, a member of the postal workers' party, estimated that the water on the main deck reached 18 inches deep.[86] The movement to starboard had stopped; the ship may have reached a new equilibrium position.[87] Dority assured the passengers that the list would grow no worse, but told them that they could speed its correction by going below.[88] They were at that time concentrated on the starboard side of the hurricane deck, where they added to the instability. The press reported that the crew threatened the passengers with a fire hose, but Dority denied this.[89] Eeles ordered Nack to handle the engines and took charge of the ballast system himself.[90] He put water into the port No. 4 and 5 tanks and in the course of about 25 minutes righted the ship. The entire episode had occupied somewhat more than half an hour.[91] A large number of passenger had panicked, and many put on life jackets. The head of the postal workers' group urged Dority to return to South Haven, but he rang "ahead strong," the Great Lakes equivalent of "full speed ahead," and continued to Chicago, where the ship arrived about 40 minutes late.[92]

This episode has a relatively unambiguous explanation. The ship's metacentric height had been reduced to a low figure at best by the alterations of the previous winter. It was a Sunday, so that she carried a large number of passengers but no fruit. She carried only a small amount of ballast water in her forward tanks and a low supply of potable water in tanks No. 3. The heat of the day caused an abnormally large percentage of the passengers, at least a third, to congregate on the hurricane deck. The combination reduced the ship's metacentric height to negative, and she had a strong free-surface effect from the potable water in tanks No. 3. Eeles and Nack, presuming the metacentric height to be positive, as in Attwood's diagram of stability (see page 28, to be visualized as the *Eastland* viewed from the bow), sought to correct the list to port by admitting water to the starboard ballast tanks. The ship was actually as in Attwood's diagram of instability (also page 28). Admission of water to the starboard ballast tanks moved the center of gravity, G, to starboard and initiated a more severe list in that direction. The list to starboard of 20 to 25 degrees was only about half what would have been required to bring her seavalve above the waterline, and thus Eeles was able to ingest water into her No. 4 and No. 5 port tanks as he wished. In urging the passengers below, Dority lowered the center of gravity, but if the ship had capsized, they would have been in a more difficult position to escape. If Welch was correct that water on the main deck reached 18 inches deep, then it may be said on the basis of what we know about the inflow of water in the disaster of 1915 that the water would virtually immediately have begun running down into the engine and

The *Eastland*, at right, leading the *City of South Haven* out of South Haven in the late afternoon as they began their return to Chicago. (R. W. Appleyard collection)

boiler rooms, quickly worsening the distribution of weight to starboard. If the ship had reached a new equilibrium position when the degree of list to starboard stabilized at 20 to 25 degrees, it could have been only a very temporary condition, for the inflow of water would rapidly have undone it. Accordingly, Eeles must have had a very narrow margin of time to save the ship. As many of the passengers thought, the whole event was an extremely close call to a catastrophe. In the disaster of 1915 the ship was caught by the mud in the Chicago River approximately half submerged at what would not otherwise have been an equilibrium position, but in the event of 1904 she was in the open lake, where, if she had capsized, she would have continued over until she floated keel-up. If the event began when the ship was about a mile and a half out of South Haven, and she kept running at full speed for just under ten minutes before Dority ordered his engines into check, she was probably somewhat less than five miles out of port at the worst of the episode. Lifesaving personnel would not, as in 1915, have been immediately at hand; her load of passengers was probably greater; thus the loss of life would almost certainly have been heavier.

This episode had several consequences. First, it initiated the sinister reputation the ship developed among passengers. Predictably, this increased public preference for the *City of South Haven*, especially in South Haven itself. The event had occurred within full view of the spectators on the South Haven piers. Second, it caused the company immediately to restrict the maximum number of passengers on the hurricane deck to 500, and in 1905 to ban them from it completely.[93] Third, the event brought about some alterations in the handling of the ballast tanks, although there is conflicting evidence about the time sequence of the changes. Dority testified that he simply issued an order to keep the No. 3 ballast tanks filled at all times.[94] Nack testified that he and Eeles concluded in a conversation on the day following the event that their present use of tanks No. 3 was itself a force of instability from water sloshing about and that they should install a new galvanized tank for potable water above tanks No. 3 at the end of the season. The company actually installed a set of four longitudinal tanks 6 inches in diameter and 18 to 20 feet long, with an aggregate capacity of about 4,000 gallons of potable water.[95] Nack reported that the new potable-water tanks were usually kept filled. In spite of their addition, Nack testified that tanks No. 3 were left empty for all of 1905 and not kept filled until he replaced Eeles as chief engineer in 1906. He said tanks No. 4 and 5 were used for stabilization in the interim, both to weigh the ship down and to compensate for the tendency of passengers to congregate toward the wharf in loading and unloading, or toward the *City of South Haven* when the two steamers were in proximity in the lake.[96] In any case, the ship began leaving South Haven with one or more ballast tanks filled, so that the bow had to push through about 18 inches of sand and mud as she crossed the bar.[97] Finally, the company, either voluntarily or at the request of Captain Mansfield, applied for and received a reduction in her licensed capacity to 2,800 passengers, effective July 26, 1904.

During the 1904 season the Michigan Steamship Company painted out the shield logo from the *Eastland*'s bow and lettered a small "Chicago & South Haven Line" above her name. The company also adopted a yellow band on her stacks. (R. W. Appleyard collection)

The changes wrought in the aftermath of the near capsizing of July 17, 1904, prevented a recurrence of a serious incident, but the ship continued to have troubles. What was now her twice-daily scraping on the bar off South Haven damaged her hull, brought sand into her bearings, and continued to break blades on her propellers—28 blades had to be replaced in 1904.[98] To deal with this damage the ship was drydocked in late September at the yard of the Shipowners' Dry Dock Company at the southern tip of Goose Island in the North Branch of the Chicago River.[99] Michigan Steamship then arranged for her to be taken to the yard of the Chicago Ship Building Company in South Chicago for some major modifications. The work was projected to cost $50,000.[100] Because the ship was making only one night trip per week, she no longer needed her original comple-

TABLE I

Licensed Passenger Capacity of the Eastland, *with Reasons for Changes*

Date	Capacity	Reason for change
July 19, 1903	2,800	Initial licensed capacity
June 24, 1904	3,300	Application of Capt. Dority, followed by inspection
July 26, 1904	2,800	Near-capsizing of July 17, 1904
June 23, 1905	2,907	Removal of 49 cabins from promenade deck
June 18, 1906	3,000	Application of W. H. Cochrane for higher capacity
May 29, 1907	2,400	Severe listing of August 5, 1906
June 13, 1908	1,950	First certification at Cleveland; poor life preservers cited
June 26, 1908	2,200	Replacement of poor life preservers
July 2, 1908	2,400	Capacity corrected to include babes in arms
June 12, 1909	2,000	Poor life preservers cited
June 26, 1909	2,200	Addition of life preservers
June 17, 1910	2,200	No change; removal of remaining staterooms noted
June 4, 1913	2,000	Circular letter following *Titanic* disaster
June 10, 1914	2,045	Addition of all or most of 31 life rafts
June 7, 1915	2,183	Application of W. H. Hull
July 2, 1915	2,500	Addition of 3 boats and 6 rafts

SOURCES: Data through 1913 from letter of Ira B. Mansfield and William Nicholas (n.d.), Bureau of Marine Inspection and Navigation, Steamboat Inspection Service, Numerical Correspondence, 1905–23, box 549, no. 71330, part 3, National Archives, Washington, D.C. Later data from letter of Robert Reid and Charles C. Eckliff to Supervising Inspector, 8th District, Detroit, August 16, 1915, ibid. The June 7, 1915, datum in the document shows capacity as 2,253, which includes crew. It is corrected here on the basis of Reid's testimony in the criminal transcript, p. 766.

ment of cabins. The 49 cabins aft the stacks on the promenade deck were removed in favor of an expanded social room. Some toilets were added. A second staircase was added, connecting the main deck with the forward portion of the cabin deck. A lunch counter was relocated from the cabin deck to the main deck aft.[101] Her hull was repainted white, and a fourth pair of lifeboats was added.[102] The boats, produced by the firm of David Kahnweiler's Sons in New York, were 20′ × 6′ × 2.5′, of 180-cubic-foot capacity, for 18 persons each.[103] There is no evidence whether the management added the boats voluntarily or under regulatory directive. The ship had no reported safety problems in 1905, but the management proved unable to pay either bill, and she was libeled by both Shipowners' Dry Dock and Chicago Ship Building. She was also libeled by the Armstrong Cork Company for a bill of $1,691.50 for life preservers.[104] To deal with the first of these, which was a bill of only $1,000, the company made a special assessment of $25 per share.[105] Reconciliation of the dispute with Chicago Ship Building required reorganization of the company; the ship was sold in December 1905, for $100,000 to Robert R. Blacker, who was still serving as president of the Michigan Steamship Company.[106]

The Chicago–South Haven Line

Robert Blacker reorganized the company as the Michigan Transportation Company, again in Indiana, on December 21, 1905,[107] but he made no attempt to operate independently in 1906. Rather, he arranged a copart-

The *Eastland* fitting out at Manistee for the 1905 season. The ship received a fourth pair of lifeboats and a coat of white paint for her hull. (Captain Frank E. Hamilton collection, Rutherford B. Hayes Memorial Library)

nership with Dunkley-Williams to consolidate the two operations as the Chicago–South Haven Line. The two firms chose as general manager George T. Arnold of Mackinac Island, the principal operator of local steamers in the Straits of Mackinac area. Nominally, this brought Arnold into his first contact with the *Eastland*, but in actuality he served only as an adjudicator of disputes between the two firms.[108] He continued his residence on Mackinac Island and took no active role in the management of the *Eastland*. He testified after the disaster that he had heard nothing unfavorable about her stability, either from her earlier history or during her operation under his nominal management.[109] If his testimony was honest, it demonstrated how exceedingly nominal his association was, for the *Eastland* had her second serious listing during the year of the copartnership.

On Sunday, August 5, 1906, the *Eastland* was returning from South Haven with 2,530 passengers. All of the Chicago passenger lines followed the usual, but not invariable, practice of positioning their ships for the trip out in the morning. This required the *Eastland* to put about upstream from the Chicago–South Haven Line berth on the south bank of the Chicago River just west of the Clark Street bridge. Concentration of passengers

CHIGAGO-SOUTH HAVEN LINE
STEAMSHIPS

"EASTLAND"
AND
City of South Haven
$1 SOUTH HAVEN and RETURN

Safest, fastest and best equipped excursion steamships on fresh water.

Docks: North End Rush Street Bridge, CHICAGO

Phone, Main 4711   W. H. COCHRANE, Gen'l Mgr.

The *Eastland* coming into South Haven in 1906, lettered for the Chicago–South Haven Line. (R. W. Appleyard collection)

on her starboard side caused her to list by an unspecified amount as she passed over the streetcar tunnel below La Salle Street approaching the berth. The ship was righted, but the incident resulted in an official complaint. There was a division in regulatory authority between the Steamboat Inspection Service in the U.S. Department of Commerce, which established licensed capacities, and the U.S. Bureau of Customs of the Treasury Department, which counted passengers onto ships to assure compliance. The officials who had counted the passengers onto the *Eastland* at South Haven and then crossed with the ship reported the listing to the Treasury, which sent out Special Agent George E. Foulkes to investigate. On the basis of that event and also an alleged overcrowding on July 23, 1905, he concluded, "I am of [the] opinion that prudence and a reasonable degree of comfort require that the number permitted to be carried be reduced." [110]

Otherwise, the *Eastland*'s safety experience in 1906 was satisfactory. After the disaster Nack testified in considerable detail on what his practices as chief engineer for that season had been. He regularly kept both tanks No. 3 filled for stability and used the No. 4 tanks to compensate for lists, usually using only 15 to 20 tons of water. He occasionally also used tanks No. 5 for trimming. He followed the usual practice on the ship of pumping out the tanks at night, and he customarily left the covers to the vent holes open. His crew took soundings through them with the dipstick half-hourly and posted the readings on a blackboard in the engine room. Nack took handling of the ballast system very seriously, and did not entrust the decisions to any subordinates.[111] Nonetheless, as a consequence of the event of August 5, 1906, the *Eastland*'s licensed capacity was reduced to 2,400 for the 1907 season.

CHAPTER TWO

The
Lake Shore
Navigation
Company

THE *Eastland* was sent at the end of the 1906 season to Manistee for winter lay-up. Blacker agreed to continue the copartnership for the 1907 season. The *Eastland* had carried about 150,000 passengers in 1906, as compared with 105,000 in 1904 and 121,000 in 1905; the demand clearly warranted two large steamers in the service. Blacker, however, received an offer reportedly of $150,000[1] from a group in Cleveland that sought the ship for service to the Cedar Point amusement park at Sandusky and to Toledo. He accepted the offer and paid $20,000 to Dunkley-Williams to get out of the copartnership.[2] The Dunkley-Williams management reorganized its service as the Chicago & South Haven Steamship Company.

The Cleveland group, which organized itself as the Lake Shore Navigation Company, was headed by Charles B. Shanks of the Winton Automobile Company. A. E. Thompson was appointed general manager.[3] A. H. McLachlan was hired as captain and Grant Donaldson as chief engineer. The group's plan was to have the *Eastland* leave Cleveland at 8:00 A.M., discharge at Cedar Point (53 miles) at 11:00 A.M., and proceed to Toledo. Returning, the ship was to load at Cedar Point at 6:40 P.M. and arrive in

Cleveland at 9:30 P.M. This schedule proved impractical, either because of time constraints or because of problems in turning the ship in the Maumee River.[4] Accordingly, the *Eastland* throughout her operation on Lake Erie ran a simple round-trip from Cleveland to Cedar Point, with some moonlight excursions from Cleveland.

The ship had another ownership change before the 1909 season. A group headed by Peter Witt, a populist politician who was one of the principal figures in the Cleveland street railway, assumed ownership and reorganized the operation as the Eastland Navigation Company. The new firm was capitalized at $270,000, of which $140,000 was paid in and $130,000 borrowed from the Depositors Savings & Trust Company. D. J. Collver of the firm of Collver & Miller, steamship agents in Cleveland, reported after the disaster that he had been the only director of the bank to vote against the loan, believing on the basis of the ship's reputation that she was not seaworthy.[5] They hired as captain Merwin S. Thompson, but continued to employ Donaldson as chief engineer. After the 1909 season they removed the remaining 39 cabins, possibly to lighten the ship, but more probably simply because the ship no longer made any night trips. Thereafter what had been known as the cabin deck was called the 'tween decks.[6]

The operating history of the ship on Lake Erie is not well documented, but several accidents were reported. On her first trip into Sandusky Bay, June 8, 1907, she broke rudder chains backing away from Cedar Point pier.[7] She had serious groundings in Sandusky Bay on September 4,

The *Eastland* loading passengers in 1908 at Cedar Point for her return to Cleveland. Adjacent is the sidewheeler *State of Ohio* loading for Toledo. (Captain Frank E. Hamilton collection, Rutherford B. Hayes Center)

This postcard was sold to passengers during the *Eastland*'s period on Lake Erie. The lettering of the lowest pennant, "Future: that you'll remember me," has always been thought prophetic. (Rev. Peter J. Van der Linden collection)

1909, and July 18, 1912.[8] She struck a breakwater when approaching Cleveland on a moonlight excursion on July 25, 1912, through an error in navigation.[9] All of these were accidents of the sort that may befall any ship; none appears to have stemmed from the *Eastland*'s individual characteristics. Frank Lee Stevenson, the author of a pamphlet on the ship issued after the disaster, stated that she listed so seriously to port at Cleveland while loading 1,900 Sherwin-Williams employees for an excursion that capsizing was averted only when the passengers moved to the starboard side. He did not state a date, and the event has not been identified in Cleveland newspapers.[10] Similarly, the Chicago *Evening Post* reported immediately after the disaster that condemnation proceedings had been threatened after she listed and nearly overturned just before berthing in Cleveland, but again no date was provided.[11] Robert O. Moyer of Cleveland, a compositor, testified after the disaster that he had been a passenger on an outing of the Maccabees, a fraternal organization, aboard the *Eastland* on July 1, 1912. Leaving Cleveland the ship listed first to port by what he estimated to be 25 degrees and then to starboard by 30 degrees, but was then righted. He was alarmed enough by the experience that he left the ship at Cedar Point and returned to Cleveland by interurban.[12] The event was apparently not noted in Cleveland newspapers, but Moyer's ac-

$5,000 REWARD

The Steamer Eastland was launched in 1903. She is built entirely of steel and is ocean type in construction. Her water compartments when filled carry 800 tons of ballast. She is 269 feet long, beam 36 feet and draws 14 feet of water. She has twin screws, driven by two powerful triple expansion engines, supplied with steam from four Scotch boilers.

The material she is built of, the type of her construction, together with the power in her hold, makes her the stanchest, fastest and safest boat devoted to pleasure on the Great Lakes

All this is well known to the people acquainted with marine matters. But there are thousands of people who know absolutely nothing about boats, the rules and regulations for their running, and inspection and licensing of the same by the U. S. Government. In the hope of influencing this class of people there have been put into circulation stories to the effect that the Steamer Eastland is not safe.

Unfortunately, we do not know who the persons are that have caused to be put in circulation these scandalous stories. Their motives, however, are easily guessed. Therefore, in justice to ourselves and in fairness to the 400,000 people that have enjoyed themselves during the past four seasons on this palatial craft (and that without a single mishap), we offer the above reward to any person that will bring forth a naval engineer, a marine architect, a shipbuilder, or any one qualified to pass on the merits of a ship who will say that the Steamer Eastland is not a seaworthy ship, or that she would not ride out any storm or weather any condition that can arise on either lake or ocean.

THE EASTLAND NAVIGATION CO.

count was corroborated by a fellow passenger, J. Grant Snyder.[13] Grant Donaldson, the *Eastland*'s chief engineer at the time, did not mention the event in any of his testimony. Moyer's testimony suggests that the event was similar to that of July 17, 1904. In both instances, the initial list was to port and the second and more serious list to starboard. Nothing in the ship's history to date had tested whether a chief engineer could as readily deal with an event in which the initial list was to starboard and the second to port. Because the ballast system was asymmetrical—admitting water by gravity from port and pumping it out to starboard—it was a question to be faced.

In the general dearth of information on the ship's performance on Lake Erie, one piece of documentation is conspicuous. The Eastland Navigation Company placed a half-page advertisement on Tuesday, August 9, 1910, in both the Cleveland *Plain Dealer* and the Cleveland *Leader*, offering $5,000 to anyone who could substantiate rumors that the *Eastland* was unsafe.[14] The advertisement implied that such rumors were circulated by rival operators. As far as is known, no one came forth with an analysis of the ship by a naval architect or otherwise to claim the award. This advertisement has usually been construed as showing that the ship's passengers correctly interpreted her habitual careening while loading and unloading as symptomatic of a dangerous instability. Merwin S. Thompson, consistently with his habitual defense of the ship's reputation, denied this explanation, and treated the advertisement as only an effort to deal with rumors that had followed the steamer from Lake Michigan.[15] Nils B. Nelson, the federal hull-inspector at Cleveland who inspected her throughout her career on Lake Erie, testified after the disaster that when people would come to him to say, "I rode on the *Eastland*, and is she safe?" he would respond that she was. He considered her dependent on her water ballast system, and told the ship's captain on several occasions to watch it carefully, but Nelson, too, thought the *Eastland* a fine sea boat that rolled easily and without jerks.[16] From the event of July 17, 1904, until the disaster, there was an unusual asymmetry in information: the passengers appeared to recognize the potential dangers of the ship better than the managements or the inspectors did. The passengers were frightened by the ship's instability in loading and unloading, whereas the officers were reassured by her stability at sea, although both were symptomatic of her short metacentric height.

The experience of the *Eastland* on Lake Erie demonstrates a counterproductive aspect of safety regulation of the character of steamboat inspection. Even if it is successful in weeding out unsafe vessels and prohibiting unsafe practices, the regulation gives the public the impression that all ships are equally safe because they have all satisfied the same inspec-

These two views of the *East-land* departing Cleveland for Cedar Point were taken by the Detroit Photographic Company in 1911. They show her in the last year of her stacks at full height. (Library of Congress)

Below, the *Eastland* loading at her berth in the Cuyahoga River in 1912. The reduced height of her stacks is apparent. Note that the ship carried no life rafts on Lake Erie. (Detroit Photographic Company collection, Library of Congress)

tion requirements. Robert W. Poole, Jr., has pointed out that the procedures of the Federal Aviation Administration in certifying aircraft as airworthy give the public the incentive to consider all aircraft equally safe and thus not to inquire into the relative safety of various types, which actually differ significantly in accident experience.[17] Here, as evidenced by the Eastland Navigation Company's advertisement of 1910, or by the queries put to Nelson, the public had a perfectly well grounded fear that the *Eastland* was unsafe, but was reassured alike by the managements and by the inspectors that the fears were baseless. The regulation served to protect the managements in a situation in which the managements should have had no protection.

Photographic evidence shows that her Lake Erie operators reduced her stacks by one ring—about a third—after the 1911 season. This change, which can hardly have served any purpose but to decrease her topheaviness, apparently indicates that the management recognized the ship had a stability problem. The advertisement of the previous year probably stemmed from this recognition, rather than, as Thompson believed, from an effort to deal with the reputation that followed the ship from Lake Michigan.

The *Eastland* had already been certificated for the 1912 season when the *Titanic* disaster occurred. A circular letter advising conservatism in licensing procedures with respect to passenger capacity relative to lifeboat capacity was issued by the supervising inspector general of the Steamboat Inspection Service on April 27, 1912.[18] This letter, in conformity with British practice, resulted in a change from gross tonnage to passenger capacity as the criterion for determining required boat space. The *Eastland*'s capacity for the 1913 season was reduced from 2,200 to 2,000, or 1,381 passengers when the ship was to travel more than five miles from the shore.[19] Her course between Cleveland and Cedar Point could readily be set so as not to take her more than five miles from the Ohio coast; hence the more stringent limitation was not a serious handicap. She had, however, accumulated losses of $175,000 to $200,000 on Lake Erie, so her operators were under pressure from their bank, the Depositors Savings & Trust Company, to dispose of her.[20] They offered her for sale at the end of the 1913 season.

CHAPTER THREE

The
St. Joseph–
Chicago
Steamship
Company

BACK on Lake Michigan was a group looking for a steamer. The Graham & Morton Transportation Company, as mentioned above, was the dominant operator from Chicago to the twin cities of St. Joseph and Benton Harbor. At the outset of the 1913 season Graham & Morton dropped St. Joseph from its schedule and consolidated its facilities in Benton Harbor, in a new terminal on the streetcar line that ran between the two cities.[1] Benton Harbor, being the more industrial of the two, accorded with Graham & Morton's incentives with respect to freight, and it also provided more direct access for passengers to the House of David, the principal single tourist attraction of the area. Adversely, the change left St. Joseph, which had the resort development of the two cities, without direct service to Chicago. The project of a specific St. Joseph–Chicago steamer line was developed by Mrs. E. A. Graham, of the family that had long dominated Graham & Morton; William H. Hull, her son-in-law; Walter C. Steele; and several fruit growers in the area. Hull had been manager of Graham & Morton's wharf in St. Joseph and had been secretary of the local street railway for thirteen years. He quickly became the principal figure in the new firm and remained so throughout its short history. He was elected vice president and appointed general manager.[2] Steele served as secretary and treasurer.

Hull's first duty was to locate a ship for the 1913 season. He arranged to buy for $25,000 from George T. Arnold a wooden steamer of only 525 gross tons, the *Eugene C. Hart.* The terms agreed upon were for Arnold to accept payment of $16,700 in cash and $8,300 in stock of the company, about $1,600 to $1,700 vested in him as an individual and the rest transferred to his Arnold Transit Company.[3] This made him a major shareholder in the new firm and caused him to become its president.[4] As in his general managership of the Chicago–South Haven Line in 1906, he was a nominal head of the firm who continued his residence on Mackinac Island, and took no role in actual administration.

The *Eugene C. Hart* proved too small for the trade, and Hull began to seek a larger ship. A. A. Schantz, general manager of the Detroit & Cleveland Navigation Company, in February 1913 recommended the *Eastland,* clearly never anticipating that she would verify his warning to the Senate Commerce Committee the following year that the La Follette Seamen's Act might cause a Great Lakes ship to capsize. Hull first saw her in late August 1913, when he made the Cleveland–Cedar Point trip.[5] He recommended purchase of her to Arnold in October. At the meeting of December 30, 1913, at which the company decided to pursue the purchase, there was no discussion of the ship's stability problems. Neither Hull nor Arnold had heard of such problems, and specifically had no knowledge of the events of July 17, 1904, and August 5, 1906—even though Arnold was nominally manager of the firm that had operated her in 1906.[6] Steele was

Running mate of the *Eastland* for the St. Joseph–Chicago Steamship Company was the *Eugene C. Hart*, an orthodox Lake Michigan propeller steamer. The ship is shown in winter lay-up at Green Bay earlier in her career. (T. H. Franklin collection, Steamship Historical Society of America)

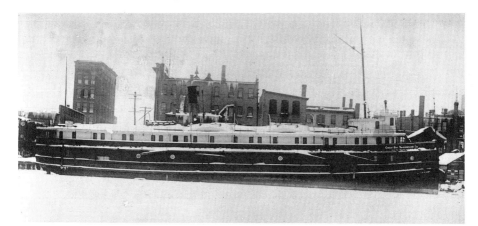

particularly explicit that he had learned nothing of the ship's stability problems. He testified at the coroner's inquest following the disaster: "I didn't know much about the boat except that we got it at a bargain. All I do is to sign blank checks." [7] Hull negotiated with the Witt group's general manager, J. F. Mulholland, throughout the winter and in February 1914 made a trip to Cleveland to inspect her in winter layup, accompanied by Steele and Captain Walter Scott, a former Chicago harbormaster who had later acted as consultant to Graham & Morton. Scott wrote a favorable report on the ship, which was submitted to the directors.[8] The St. Joseph–Chicago Steamship Company bought the *Eastland* on June 1, 1914, for $150,000, contingent upon her passing her federal inspection.[9]

Walter C. Steele, secretary-treasurer of the St. Joseph–Chicago Steamship Company.

The *Eastland* was brought back to Lake Michigan by Claude M. Ennes, who had been her captain on Lake Erie in 1912 and 1913, with Donaldson as chief engineer. On June 4 the ship called for coal for about two hours at Mackinac Island, where Arnold came down to visit her. He spent five to ten minutes walking about her alone; this proved the only time he ever set foot on the *Eastland*. He and Ennes testified after the disaster that at this time they discussed coaling the ship, but both were explicit that they discussed neither her stability nor her physical properties more generally.[10] Ennes brought the *Eastland* up to the former Graham & Morton wharf in St. Joseph about 11:30 A.M. on June 5. The Graham family still controlled the wharf and had arranged to use it for the *Eastland*. The arrival proved a festive occasion. About 300 people had come down to welcome her, and as she came up to the wharf a local musician, Tony Lessing, played on the calliope "Somebody's Coming to Our House," "Home, Sweet Home," and "Auld Lang Syne." Graham & Morton's *City of Benton Harbor* gave her a long blast of welcome from the Benton Harbor side of the harbor. Because the *Eastland*'s interior was cluttered, it had not been planned to open her for inspection, but the demand was so great that Hull admitted anyone who wished. The St. Joseph *Daily Press* called her "Queen of the Lakes." [11]

The *Eastland* was then taken to Benton Harbor, where her federal inspection was performed on June 7–10, 1914. Her inspectors were Robert Reid, federal inspector of hulls for the district from Les Cheneaux Islands northeast of Mackinac Island to St. Joseph, and Charles C. Eckliff, federal inspector of boilers for the same district. Both were based at Grand Haven, Michigan. Reid had sailed the Great Lakes for 37 years and had been inspector at Grand Haven since 1908. Both men had some degree of previous experience with the *Eastland*. Reid had been inspector at Chicago in

Graham & Morton put its most modern steamer, the *City of Grand Rapids*, on the morning departure out of Chicago to Benton Harbor when the *Eastland* went into service from Chicago to St. Joseph. The *City of Grand Rapids* is shown here on her way up the St. Clair River on the trip from her builder, the Great Lakes Shipbuilding Company, in Cleveland to Lake Michigan. The ship had been built for Graham & Morton's Chicago-Holland overnight service, which had an interurban connection for Grand Rapids. (Rev. Peter J. Van der Linden collection)

1906, and there had measured the *Eastland*'s deck space for consistency with her licensed capacity of 3,000.[12] Eckliff had counted passengers onto the ship at Chicago on six occasions in 1906, observing her to list no more than 4 to 6 degrees, even with her full load of 3,000 passengers. He had also inspected her in 1907.[13]

As a consequence of the inspection of June 1914, Reid certificated the *Eastland* for 2,045 passengers for the season. He reasoned that if the ship had safely carried 3,000 passengers in 1906, the removal of her cabins, which gave her an estimated 3,500 square feet of additional deck space, would allow her to handle 2,045 without difficulty.[14] In the 1914 season the *Eastland* carried 8 lifeboats, 31 life rafts, and a workboat.[15] Hull testified that he spent $3,200 on additional equipment to raise her capacity after coming from Cleveland; this equipment was presumably the life rafts.[16] Ennes testified that he put 20-odd life rafts on her on arrival in

---

Opposite: The *Eastland* at her berth in St. Joseph. Hull's management restored a painted diamond to the bow, similar to the one the ship had carried in her earlier service on Lake Michigan. It was apparently only an ornament rather than a company logo, as it had been for the Michigan Steamship Company. (Chicago Historical Society)

Chicago.[17] According to literary and photographic evidence, she carried only her 8 lifeboats on Lake Erie. There is no record of when the workboat was added. The ballast system was within Eckliff's jurisdiction, but he required no changes in it in 1914, nor for 1915.

With the inspection out of the way, the *Eastland* was ready for service. The management held a reception on her on the evening of June 12, and at 9:00 the following morning she left for Chicago.[18] She went into service on June 14 with an orthodox schedule of departures from Chicago at midmorning on weekdays and at 2:00 P.M. on Saturdays. Graham & Morton responded to the new rival by shifting its most modern ship, the *City of Grand Rapids* of 1912, from the Chicago-Holland night line for which she had been built to the morning trip out of Chicago to Benton Harbor.

The *Eastland* went into service with Ennes and Donaldson still in charge, even though both were eager to go back to Cleveland. Hull was already actively seeking a captain. He chose Harry Pedersen, whom he had known for five or six years. Pedersen was born in Norway in 1860, and had passed the Board of Navigation there in 1879. He had emigrated to the United States in 1885, secured his pilot's license in 1896, and taken his master's license three or four years later. He had previously been master of the *Bay State* of the Boutell Steel Barge Company, and the *Nortown* of the Northwestern Steamship Company. In 1913 he had commanded the yacht *Natoma*.[19] Pedersen, who lived on a farm near Millburg, just east of Benton Harbor, applied for the position on the *Eastland*, although he had never before commanded an excursion vessel. Hull inquired about him among Graham & Morton captains, for whom Pedersen had adjusted compasses as a consultant. Hull found Pedersen well recommended and hired him, effective June 26, 1914.[20] Pedersen talked with Ennes and Donaldson before they left for Cleveland. Ennes told Pedersen that he had left handling of the ballast tanks to Donaldson, and suggested that Pedersen do the same with his chief engineer.[21] Pedersen complied so fully that, as he testified after the disaster, he never even went down to look at the tanks.[22] He told the state's attorney at that time that he also knew very little about the machinery of the ship.[23] In sum, he dissociated himself from the duties of the chief engineer about as thoroughly as a master could have done. Before leaving, Donaldson recommended as chief engineer Peter Robertson, who served only for the 1914 season.[24] The unlicensed personnel were recruited mainly from St. Joseph, Benton Harbor, and other ports on the west coast of Michigan. Except for one or two firemen, it was a non-union crew.

The management arranged for the *Eastland* to load in Chicago from the wharf of the Northern Michigan Transportation Company on the north bank of the Chicago River immediately east of the Rush Street bridge, on a site now occupied by the Wrigley Building. In 1913 the company for the

Eugene C. Hart had used a wharf at Kinzie Street on the North Branch for freight and when outbound called at La Salle Street for passengers.[25] The new facility was much preferable, both in consolidating passenger and freight operations and in accessibility. Northern Michigan was the principal operator from Chicago to Mackinac Island and to intermediate points far north along the Michigan coast. Because this company's arrivals and departures were less frequent than those of Goodrich or Graham & Morton, a cross-lake operator could easily be accommodated at the wharf. The *Eastland* now served exclusively as a passenger steamer; the management handled the fruit on the *Eugene C. Hart* on overnight trips on weeknights. The *Hart* also made the line's one overnight passenger trip from Chicago on Saturday at 11:00 P.M. The *Eastland* handled between 158 and 788 persons on ordinary weekday departures, going over 1,000 only on weekends and on some moonlight charters.[26] Her service seems to have been satisfactory in this period. Beyond Captain Hamilton's observation noted in Chapter I that she had difficulty with northerly and easterly winds on her eastbound trips, there are no reported complaints about her ordinary performance for the St. Joseph–Chicago Steamship Company.

Only once in the 1914 season did the *Eastland* carry her full licensed capacity, on Saturday, July 25, for a charter by the Indiana Transportation Company for an annual picnic in Washington Park at Michigan City, Indiana, for employees of the Western Electric Company's Hawthorne plant in Cicero, on the west edge of Chicago. Because a year later she capsized on a repeat of this charter, her experience is instructive, partly by way of contrast, partly because her performance in 1914 influenced the terms of the charter party for the 1915 excursion.

The picnic at Michigan City had been an annual event since 1911. It was organized by the Hawthorne Club, a social body of Western Electric employees that was encouraged by the management though not literally a Western Electric organization.[27] The club arranged for the excursion each year with Walter K. Greenebaum, president and general manager of the Indiana Transportation Company, the regular operator on the Chicago–Michigan City route. The excursion required movement of several thousand people, far beyond the capacity of Indiana Transportation's own ships. Accordingly, Greenebaum regularly contracted for vessels from other Lake Michigan lines on the basis of a single-trip charter, using the owning line's officers and crew. The arrangement was ideal for the Hawthorne Club in providing it with economical movement of a large but not

Walter K. Greenebaum, general manager of the Indiana Transportation Company.

entirely predictable number of people. The ships discharged the picnickers at Indiana Transportation's wharf on the north bank of Trail Creek just west of the Franklin Street bridge, from which they had immediate access to Washington Park. The park was an ample facility with a bathing beach to the north and the central business district of Michigan City across Trail Creek to the south.

Greenebaum's 1914 charter party with the St. Joseph–Chicago Steamship Company provided for a single round trip by the *Eastland* for $500.[28] A tug was to be provided to assist the *Eastland* into the Chicago & South Haven Steamship Company's wharf immediately west of the Clark Street bridge—the berth the *Eastland* had used for the 1906 season—and also to take her out to Lake Michigan. The Chicago & South Haven berth had the attraction of being immediately west of the Indiana Transportation Company's own wharf between Clark and Dearborn streets. The *Eastland* regularly used no tug to depart, for her berth at Rush Street gave her a straight course into Lake Michigan of about three-fourths of a mile. In berthing, the *Eastland* typically put about near the mouth of the river and was pulled by a tug, frequently the Dunham Towing & Wrecking Company's *Kenosha*, stern first into the Northern Michigan Transportation Company's wharf. The *Kenosha*, her chief engineer estimated, berthed the *Eastland* some 40 to 60 times in this fashion.[29] Departing from the Chicago & South Haven wharf without a tug was impractical because of a reverse curve in the river between State and Rush streets. More to the point, city ordinances required a tug for passing through any bridge that opened, or for backing movements.[30] By plan, the *Eastland* was to be the second steamer out after Indiana Transportation's own *Theodore Roosevelt*; she was to proceed directly to Michigan City, discharge the excursionists, and return empty to Chicago for her scheduled 2:00 P.M. departure for St. Joseph. She was to leave St. Joseph at 6:00 P.M. as usual, but call at Michigan City, 36 miles to the southwest, at 7:45 on her way back to Chicago. The call at Michigan City added only 14 miles to her trip.

On the evening of July 24, 1914, the *Eastland* arrived as usual from St. Joseph and discharged from her starboard side. She did not take coal, in spite of the fact that she was to run 210 miles instead of her usual 120. Towed by an unidentified tug, she proceeded west up the Chicago River to the confluence of the North and South branches, turned, and was towed to the Chicago & South Haven wharf, where she spent the night. She loaded in the morning from two starboard gangways and was then towed past the reverse curve in the river and through the Rush Street bridge. She then proceeded to Michigan City, where she arrived punctually about 10:00 A.M. The charter party also provided for a tug at Michigan City. The *Eastland* had difficulty unloading, however, because her gangways were

The *Eastland* putting about in Trail Creek at Michigan City on July 25, 1914. The photograph was taken by a Western Electric employee, C. W. Robbins. After the disaster the picture was published in both Western Electric's and the Bell System's employee magazines. (New York Public Library)

too low for the Indiana Transportation Company's wharf. This delayed her empty return to Chicago.[31] As a consequence, she was late for the departure at 2:00 P.M. for St. Joseph and her 6:00 P.M. departure from there. She returned to Chicago, as planned, via Michigan City, where she picked up the last 1,395 passengers from the picnic, whom she discharged at her own berth at Rush Street. This experience had been satisfactory enough that the parties were willing to have the same arrangement in 1915, but Hull remembered the *Eastland*'s failure to meet her schedule, and was to insist on a change in the contract to deal with the problem.

For the 1915 season several changes were made on the *Eastland*. Some boiler tubes were replaced; the bar was extended into the dormitory space aft the engine room, presumably for storage; and the firemen's bunk room was shifted to the area originally planned for male steerage passengers. In addition, concrete was put on the decks at two points. First, in the dining room on the 'tween decks, where spillage of liquids had caused some rot to the wood underneath the linoleum, about two inches of concrete were put down and covered by new linoleum. Pedersen reported that about two tons of gravel were brought up to the 'tween decks for this.[32] In inspecting the steamer for the 1915 season, Reid noted the addition, and estimated that the concrete covered 30 to 40 linear feet, running the full width of the ship.[33] He did not estimate its weight, but on the basis of the reported dimensions and the weight of concrete of 150 pounds per cubic foot usually assumed by architects or structural engineers, the weight would be between 14.25 and 19 tons.[34] Second, the company proceeded to lay concrete over a larger area on the main deck where passengers entered, presumably from the aft gangways. No one provided data with which to establish the weight of the concrete laid on the main deck, but Pedersen testified, "of course, that is a good deal heavier."[35] He went on to estimate under interrogation that it was about twice as heavy. Because the weight of the concrete per cubic foot and the area covered are both in doubt, an estimate of the weight of the application must be in a very wide range. If the reported area and depth of the application on the 'tween decks are accurate, the total weight of the concrete on the two decks could hardly have been less than 30 tons and may have been as high as 57 tons. If, as Professor Sadler estimated in his evaluation of the ship after the disaster, her metacenter was approximately 16 feet above her keel, it was below the main deck, and the center of gravity was a short distance below the waterline. Accordingly, the concrete, being distributed between the main deck and the 'tween decks, reduced her metacentric height. We know that Reid observed the concrete, but he took no action. He did not suggest that the effect of the added weight be ascertained by an inclining test. Yet, the

The *Eastland* in her penultimate state, with eight lifeboats and 31 rafts piled onto her hurricane deck. The ship is awaiting departure for St. Joseph from the Northern Michigan Transportation Company's wharf immediately east of the Rush Street bridge. (Chicago Historical Society)

addition of the concrete added to a menacing situation. As the *Eastland*'s earlier history abundantly demonstrated, her stability was already poor; the addition of this much concrete must have made it very marginal indeed.

There was a change made in regulation for the 1915 season: in 1914, 2.5 cubic feet of air had been required per person on the life rafts for buoyancy; for 1915 this requirement was raised to 3.0 cubic feet. Reid also wrote to Pedersen that life rafts would have to provide 4 square feet of space per person. The two directives reduced the capacity of a life raft by about one-fifth.[36] Nonetheless, upon Hull's request Reid certificated the ship for 2,183 passengers and a crew of 70.[37]

The other change for the 1915 season was the hiring of a new chief engineer, Joseph M. Erickson. Like Pedersen, Erickson was a Norwegian by birth. He had been born in Christiania, Norway, 32 years earlier and emigrated to the United States in 1902. He had been sailing since the age of 15. He came to the Great Lakes in June 1905, and took his license as an engineer by an examination of seven days' duration administered by Reid and Eckliff in July 1909. With this credential, he became second assistant engineer on the railroad car ferry *Ashtabula* on Lake Erie in May 1911. He took his examination to qualify for first assistant engineer from Reid and Eckliff in the spring of 1912 in Grand Haven. He returned to the *Ashtabula* for the season, and in March 1913, took his examination again from Reid and Eckliff for a chief engineer's license, which he received on April 2, 1913. He sailed as chief engineer on the freighter *C. W. Watson* of the Tomlinson Line in 1913 and on the same line's *Sultana* in 1914.[38] Meanwhile, he had met Reid's daughter Florence in December 1913, and married her on Christmas Day, 1914.[39] Mainly in response to her desire that he take a position in which he would be home more frequently, he applied for the chief engineer's position on the *Eastland*.[40] Reid wrote to Hull, recommending Erickson to the extent of stating that he had passed his examinations in satisfactory fashion and had served for a season on the *Sultana*.[41] Given the fact that all of his certification had come from Reid and Eckliff, and that he had married Reid's daughter, Erickson could not have avoided allegations of nepotism when his professional competence was questioned after the disaster. He aggravated the problem when he hired his 19-year-old brother, Peter Erickson, as oiler on the *Eastland* after his appointment.[42] Actually, Joseph Erickson's credentials were quite satisfactory. He had served on four ships with water ballast systems.[43] The Great Lakes car ferries were large twin-screw ships that used ballast tanks to correct for the heavy, variable loads of railroad cars. In particular, trimming of them is quite delicate during loading and unloading. They typically have long metacentric heights, however.[44]

Hull hired Erickson on April 1, 1915, and thought him very competent in fitting the ship out for the season.[45] Hull was to question Erickson's competence early in the season, however. The *Eastland* proved to be steaming so poorly that she was having difficulty meeting her schedule. Hull brought Donaldson back from Cleveland on Sunday, July 18, 1915, to offer him the chief engineer's position, stating that he considered Erickson destitute of ability, that Erickson lacked system, and that the job was too big for him.[46] Erickson also had some friction with his first assistant, Clarence Rexford, who had served under Robertson in 1914. Erickson, in anticipation of being fired, wired his resignation to Hull on July 15, effective July 19.[47] Donaldson, however, declined the job, but worked with Erickson for the next three days as first assistant engineer, replacing Rexford, who quit on July 19. The company then promoted the second assistant engineer, Charles F. Silvernail of Manistee—the name was apparently an anglicization of Carl Silbernagel—to first and hired as second assistant engineer Fred G. Snow of Ludington, whose experience was with the Pere Marquette car ferries.[48] Hull, on Donaldson's advice, declined to accept Erickson's resignation, and specifically asked him to stay on.[49] Erickson blamed the problem of poor steaming on low-quality coal and had apparently dealt with it already by switching to the coal of the Pittsburgh Coal Company. The switch was quite successful; he reported that with the new coal the ship had made her fastest eastbound crossing, 2 hours and 54 minutes.[50]

It is notable that in this questioning of Erickson's competence, his handling of the ballast tanks was not an issue. He was doing what Donaldson, Robertson, and the previous engineers had done: admitting and pumping out small amounts of water to compensate for the distribution of passengers.[51] This was considered satisfactory and noncontroversial.

In June and at the beginning of July 1915, two related sequences of events occurred. In the first, the Hawthorne Club began its preparations for the annual Western Electric picnic in the same fashion as in 1914. It negotiated with Greenebaum, telling him that about 7,000 passengers would move on the excursion, and left to him the charters of ships from operators other than his Indiana Transportation Company. Greenebaum accepted the proposal, offering to handle the passengers at a reduced rate of 50 cents each to be charged to the Hawthorne Club if the number exceeded 4,000.[52] Greenebaum chartered the *Eastland* on the same terms as in 1914: $500 for a morning trip to Michigan City, an empty return to Chicago, and a call at Michigan City on her evening return from St. Joseph. Indiana Transportation was to pay for tugs at both ports, and the *Eastland* would again load from the Chicago & South Haven wharf on the south side of the river between Clark and La Salle streets. The charter party was drafted with only one change—but that one could hardly have

been more important. Because Hull remembered the *Eastland*'s delay in
unloading at Michigan City in 1914, and her consequent inability to meet
the rest of the day's schedule, he insisted upon an additional clause providing that she should be the first ship out on the excursion, leaving no later
than 8:15 A.M.[53] If the trip had been made, the Hawthorne Club would have
realized $625 from the excursion, the St. Joseph–Chicago Steamship
Company $500 plus concession revenues, and the Indiana Transportation
Company $730.[54] Western Electric and the Hawthorne Club promoted the
excursion vigorously, staging two parades to advertise it on the plant
grounds, posting signs, and exhorting employees to take early sailings to
enjoy a full day at the picnic. Foremen were issued tickets, which they sold
for 75 cents each to their subordinates. In the immediate aftermath of the
disaster, some survivors claimed that the foremen had used excessive sua-
sion, to the point that some employees thought that they risked layoffs by
not making the trip.[55] The composition of Western Electric's labor force
assured that the crowd would be predominately of young people, mainly
single and in the dating age. The dating relation brought onto the excursion
a large number of people who were unaffiliated with Western Electric. The
Indiana Transportation Company also reserved the right to sell tickets for
the trip to the general public from its own offices, but it sold only a small
number.

In the second sequence of events, which occurred simultaneously, the
St. Joseph–Chicago Steamship Company undertook an effort further to
increase the *Eastland*'s licensed capacity. The immediate motivation was
to deal with expected peak loads on the July 4 weekend and on the Western
Electric excursion, for the ship was doing very poorly in regular service—quite a bit worse than in 1914. In June 1915 her biggest load was
634 people, and she handled over 200 only three times.[56] Consequently,
we cannot know whether the *Eastland* would have encountered stability
problems following the addition of the concrete to her decks if loaded to
her licensed capacity of 2,183, for her passenger counts never approached
that level. The season was considered a poor one by all the Lake Michigan
operators because of bad weather. In addition, the trade was in the early
years of a secular decline that would virtually extinguish it by the 1930's,
although that was not yet recognized. The more important motivation was
the impending imposition of the La Follette Seamen's Act on November 4.
As stated above in the Prologue, the act had been passed but was not to be
effective for the 1915 season. It was variously expected to reduce the *Eastland*'s licensed capacity to 1,028,[57] 1,470,[58] 1,492,[59] or 1,552.[60] Given the
framework of policy in effect, it was clear that the company would have to
increase boat and raft capacity in order to raise her licensed capacity, either
immediately or after the act came into force.

The effort to increase licensed capacity over the 2,183 authorized by

Reid at the outset of the 1915 season was carried on by Hull and Pedersen, although their accounts at the federal criminal trial differ markedly. Hull testified that after the spring inspection, Pedersen came to him to say, "Mr. Hull, if we get three rafts of 25 person capacity and one of 50, we can get a license for 2570 people." Hull replied that he would have to think it over because rafts cost considerable money. Pedersen responded that the more capacity she had in the 1915 season, the less would be the cut when the La Follette Seamen's Act came into effect. Hull said he then learned nothing further of the effort to increase capacity until he noted some boats being shifted from the *Eugene C. Hart* to the *Eastland* at St. Joseph.[61]

Pedersen's version of the events began with Hull's approaching him in the spring of 1915, stating without assigning a reason that he wanted an increase in capacity over the recent authorization. Pedersen responded that he thought the ship could take it.[62] Pedersen then approached Reid with this request, but left to Reid the calculation of what additional lifesaving capacity would be required and what the new licensed capacity would be. Pedersen testified that he considered Reid "a careful man," adding, "he would not give me any more than was right."[63] Pedersen stated that he himself had made none of the calculations and would have been incapable of doing so.[64]

Of the two versions of how the effort to increase licensed capacity was initiated, Hull's is the more credible. Pedersen's testimony in the criminal trial and more especially in the civil trial contained strong elements of self-exculpation, eventually reaching, in the civil case (as will be discussed in Chapter VII), a statement that can hardly be interpreted other than as perjury. There is a further consideration that Hull showed some recognition that the ship was nearing a limit in the amount of lifesaving equipment that she could safely carry, but Pedersen at no time gave any indication that he considered this a problem. Hull wrote to Secretary of Commerce William C. Redfield on June 30, 1915, to protest the prospective reduction of the *Eastland*'s licensed capacity under the La Follette Seamen's Act, stating explicitly that the ship could not take much more weight of lifesaving equipment. With respect to adding enough boat and raft capacity to maintain her passenger capacity under the new law, he wrote, "This is a physical impossibility. If it were possible to put this amount of equipment on the *Eastland* the weight that would be added to its upper deck would make the boat difficult to handle."[65] Accordingly, Hull was probably correct in testifying that the increase in licensed capacity originated in an effort of Pedersen to increase the allowed number of passengers once the Seamen's Act came into force. There appears to be no reason to question Pedersen's testimony that he left the actual calculations to Reid, however.

Reid's computations were entirely concerned with the ratio of lifeboat and life raft space to passenger capacity. He testified in the federal criminal

action that he never determined the ship's center of gravity, and did not
think it necessary for fixing her capacity. He considered the center of buoyancy variable and impossible to determine.[66] He stated explicitly, "the
number of people that can be carried is governed by the percentage of the
boats and rafts and the life preservers for each person carried." [67] In reject-
ing the option of a capacity of 3,000 he specifically cited the effect of the
changes wrought by the *Titanic* disaster: "As near as I recollect, [from]
the reasons that were brought out, we wanted to comply with the instruc-
tions sent out by the Bureau after the *Titanic* disaster; we were trying to
have a safe figure when we reduced her from 3000 to 2500." [68]

On the basis of Reid's calculations, Pedersen concluded that he would
have to provide boat and raft space for 30 percent of the additional passengers, and proceeded to shift 3 lifeboats and 2 life rafts from the *Eugene C.
Hart* to the *Eastland*. This was inadequate for the capacity of 2,500 Reid
was willing to allow. Accordingly, the company ordered 4 additional life
rafts weighing 1,100 pounds each from David Kahnweiler's Sons at a price
of $135 each.[69] Of the 3 lifeboats added, 2 were 18.2′ × 5.1′ × 2.7′, of
163-cubic-foot capacity, for 16 persons each. One was reportedly a product of Thomas Drum & Son, and the other was presumably from the same
source. The third lifeboat was 18.2′ × 5.8′ × 2.5′, of 146-cubic-foot
capacity, for 14 persons.[70] All of this equipment was placed on the hurricane deck, raising the count to 11 lifeboats, 37 rafts, and a workboat. The
size of the workboat is not recorded. The accompanying photograph of the
ship at her wharf at Rush Street in her final state shows 2 additional boats
with a single davit each at the sides abaft the previous 4 pairs, the third
boat on the ship's center line aft the stacks between the fourth pair of boats,
and the workboat on the center line immediately forward of the stacks.[71]
The rafts were piled at the stern. The ship, which, it should be remembered, was designed with 6 lifeboats with a total of 120 seats for an initial
licensed capacity of 2,800 passengers, now carried 11 lifeboats and 37 life
rafts with an aggregate capacity of 776 places for 2,500 passengers—a
good demonstration of what the changes in inspection requirements since
the *Titanic* disaster had accomplished. Life jackets weighing about 5.5
to 6 pounds each were provided for all passengers and crew, 400 to 600
on the hurricane deck, the rest on the promenade deck or in the crew's
quarters.[72]

When the changes were completed on July 2, 1915, Pedersen, who was
in St. Joseph, phoned Reid in Grand Haven to notify him that the job had
been finished by installation of the four new life rafts from Kahnweiler.
On the same day, Reid issued an amendment to the *Eastland*'s certificate
stating that the steamer was equipped with boatage and raftage for 776

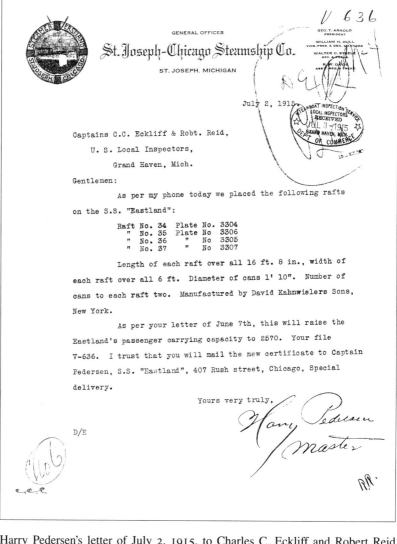

GENERAL OFFICES

St. Joseph-Chicago Steamship Co.

ST. JOSEPH, MICHIGAN

GEO. T. ARNOLD
PRESIDENT
WILLIAM H. HULL
VICE-PRES. & GEN. MANAGER
WALTER C. STEELE
SEC. & TREAS.
R. W. DAVIS
ASST. SEC. & TREAS.

V 636

July 2, 1915.

Captains C.C. Eckliff & Robt. Reid,

  U. S. Local Inspectors,

    Grand Haven, Mich.

Gentlemen:

    As per my phone today we placed the following rafts

on the S.S. "Eastland":

      Raft No. 34 Plate No. 3304
       " No. 35 Plate No 3306
       " No. 36   "   No 3305
       " No. 37   "   No 3307

    Length of each raft over all 16 ft. 8 in., width of

each raft over all 6 ft. Diameter of cans 1' 10". Number of

cans to each raft two. Manufactured by David Kahnwielers Sons,

New York.

    As per your letter of June 7th, this will raise the

Eastland's passenger carrying capacity to 2570. Your file

V-636. I trust that you will mail the new certificate to Captain

Pedersen, S.S. "Eastland", 407 Rush street, Chicago, Special

delivery.

             Yours very truly,

                     Harry Pedersen

                     Master

D/E

Harry Pedersen's letter of July 2, 1915, to Charles C. Eckliff and Robert Reid confirming that he had completed the additions of life rafts necessary to raise the *Eastland*'s licensed capacity to 2,500 passengers and a crew of 70. (National Archives and Records Administration, Chicago)

persons and life preservers for 2,570, allowing her to carry 2,500 passengers and a crew of 70 between May 15 and October 15.[73] Reid followed his usual practice of accepting the captain's word for changes and then inspecting the ship for compliance at his earliest opportunity.[74] In this instance, he inspected the ship over the July 4 weekend in Chicago. Nothing

in this sequence of events differed from normal practice except that a
phone call rather than a letter was the means of notification of the inspector. Reid noted that railings of gas pipe had been erected on the hurricane
deck to keep passengers away from the boats and rafts, which now occupied most of this deck. The railings left the passengers with two connected
areas fore and aft, each capable of accommodating about 100 to 150 per-

The certificate issued by Eckliff and Reid on July 2, 1915, granting Pedersen's
request for an increase of the *Eastland*'s capacity to 2,570. (National Archives and
Records Administration, Chicago)

Form 858

FILE No. V **636**

**'ERTIFICATE AMENDING CERTIFICATE OF INSPECTION BY CHANGING CHARACTER
OF VESSEL, ROUTE, EQUIPMENT, ETC.**

DEPARTMENT OF COMMERCE
STEAMBOAT-INSPECTION SERVICE

OFFICE OF U. S. LOCAL INSPECTORS

PORT OF **Grand Haven, Mich.**

DATE, **July 2, 1915**

This certifies, *That the following-described amendments are hereby authorized
in the certificate of inspection expiring on* **June 7,** *, 1916, issued*
to the **steam** *vessel named* " **EASTLAND**"
(Steam, motor, sail, or barge.)
classed as **Passenger** *, built at* **Port Huron**
(Passenger, freight, etc.)
in the State of **Michigan** *, in the year* **1903** *, and last inspected in the*
local district of **Michigan** *, in the State of* **Michigan**
on the **7th** *day of* **June** *, 191* **5** *, namely:*

This steamer being equipt with boatage and raftage for seven hundred and
seventy six (776) persons, and life preservers for twenty five hundred and seventy
(2570) persons, may carry from May 15th to October 15th, both dates inclusive, 2570
persons, viz: Twenty Five hundred passengers and crew of S eventy.

U. S. Local Inspectors.

The *original* of this certificate must be transmitted by the local inspectors to the chief officer of customs where the original
certificate of inspection was filed, or where a copy of the certificate of inspection or examination of the vessel was filed, to be filed
by the chief officer of customs with the original certificate of inspection, or with the copy of certificate of inspection or examination;
and a *duplicate* of this certificate must be furnished by the local inspectors to the vessel, which copy must be framed under glass and
posted on board near the certificate of inspection, if the certificate of inspection is required to be posted, or kept on board with the
original certificate of inspection or examination, if the certificate of inspection or examination is not required to be posted, to be shown
on demand.
Local inspectors issuing this certificate will keep a copy thereof on file in their office, with the copy of the certificate of inspection
or examination that it amends.
Any additional equipments required must be stated in full herein.

11—4199

sons.[75] Walter Scott, who said he had put up the railings, estimated the space aft as capable of holding 100 people and the space forward as capable of 200.[76]

The company made no reported tests of the operation of the *Eastland* under the new circumstances. It certainly made no inclining test to determine her metacentric height. Even if one accepts Hull's rather than Pedersen's account of the origin of the changes of July 2, Hull was negligent in making no effort to ascertain the effect of the changes on the stability and handling of the *Eastland*—particularly in view of his letter to Redfield of only three days earlier recognizing that the ship was limited in the additional safety equipment she could handle. The Detroit & Cleveland Navigation Company in the same period and for the same reason, preparation for the imposition of the La Follette Seamen's Act, placed two additional boats each on its *City of Alpena II* and *City of Mackinac II*. It made no reported inclining test, but A. A. Schantz brought Professor Sadler to Detroit from Ann Arbor to observe what Schantz described as "all sorts of maneuvers" of the two ships in the Detroit River to determine if there had been any loss of stability.[77] Hull made no similar attempt.

The *Eastland* in her final state, with eleven lifeboats, approaching St. Joseph in July 1915. Note that the ship is operating with her aft starboard gangway entirely open, even though she will discharge at St. Joseph from the port side. (A. A. Appleyard photograph, Gordon Potter collection)

The *Eastland* in her final state, with 11 lifeboats, a workboat, and 37 rafts. She is shown awaiting departure from the Rush Street wharf on Sunday, July 18, 1915, six days before the disaster. There were no known alterations to the ship in the interim. (Mariners Museum)

After the changes of July 2, 1915, the *Eastland* capsized on the first occasion that she was loaded with her new licensed capacity of 2,500 passengers. The explanation of the disaster presented here is that the changes of July 2 reduced the *Eastland*'s metacentric height to an insignificantly positive figure. The figure remained positive until the first time she was fully loaded, July 24. At some time during loading on that date, her metacentric height turned negative and the ship capsized. For various reasons, it is impossible to make a more definite statement on the causes of the disaster than this. As noted earlier, the metacentric height of the ship was never taken by an inclining test at any time in her history as a commercial vessel. We cannot know what it was on the eve of the changes of July 2, 1915. But we can be sure, on the basis of William J. Wood's estimate of the metacentric height at four inches after the changes of early 1904 and in light of the addition of a great deal of concrete before the 1915 season, that it was quite low. Similarly, we do not know the weight of all the additional equipment, but a rough estimate can be made. The weight of lifeboats and rafts removed from the top deck of the wreck was 62 tons.[78] If all of the rafts had the same weight of 1,100 pounds as each of the 4 added on July 2, and if the workboat weighed half as much as a lifeboat, then

each lifeboat weighed between 3.62 and 3.96 tons. On this calculation the
weight of the 3 boats and 6 rafts added on July 2 was, then, about 14 to
15 tons.[79] But this estimate overstates their weight, as is evident from the
fact that the lifeboats added on July 2 were smaller than the original 6 and
the pair added for the 1905 season. In the federal criminal action Reid
estimated the weight of all the rafts at about 20 tons, which is consistent
with the foregoing computation. Although he said he had made an estimate of the weight of the 3 additional boats in his calculations, he ada-
mantly refused to state this in cross-examination, saying, "I am not qualified to answer that."[80] After the disaster A. A. Schantz made a casual
estimate from Detroit that the additional weight of the added boats and
rafts was only 8 tons.[81] This is more consistent with one's expectations
concerning the weight of lifeboats. If one takes Schantz's estimate as a
lower bound, the additional weight added on July 2 was between 8 and
15 tons. This was considerably less than the weight of the concrete added
before the 1915 season, but the added weight was placed on the highest
deck of the ship. The additional 317 passengers allowed after the additions
of July 2, weighing an estimated 140 to 150 pounds each, including baggage, added about 22 to 24 tons. The estimates of the average weight of
passengers in the disaster are lower than in the event of July 17, 1904,
because of the higher proportion of young women aboard the ship. In addition, because the trip was purely a day excursion, there is a presumption
that the passengers carried less baggage. We have no way of knowing the
exact effect of the additions on metacentric height. Reid, when asked
whether he ever made tests of metacentric height, responded that he never
did, that such tests were not required, and that in his opinion the lack of
such tests was "one place where the [Steamboat Inspection] service was
lame."[82]

On July 6, soon after Reid's inspection of the *Eastland* over the July 4
weekend, she was drydocked for a hull inspection by Ira B. Mansfield and
William Nicholas.[83] She missed three days of service for this inspection,
but there is no indication that it concerned anything but the soundness of
the hull.

It was observed above that the government cannot regulate a single
variable. Here it should be observed that the government cannot regulate
every variable. It would simply be too costly to attempt to regulate every
variable concerning a ship, as in this instance to make an inclining test to
take metacentric heights before and after the addition of lifesaving equipment. Pedersen, as stated, made a casual judgment that the ship could take
the equipment and left the determination to Reid. Hull, his letter of June 30
to Redfield notwithstanding, testified that it had never occurred to him

that the additional equipment might add to the ship's problem of top-heaviness.[84]

In the decision to add the three boats and six rafts, Erickson was not consulted. More important, Erickson was never told that the passenger capacity had been increased, or that the handling of the ship required any alteration. In preparation for the trip on which the disaster occurred, he was told to expect a full load, but he was not told what that load would be.[85] Not to tell him that the changes in the ship might have reduced the metacentric height to negative was another act of serious negligence on the part of the management. As noted in connection with the event of July 17, 1904, what a chief engineer does in handling water ballast on a ship of positive metacentric height is inappropriate on a ship of negative metacentric height, possibly causing her to capsize in the direction to which he has admitted water. If Erickson had known that the *Eastland*'s metacentric height might turn negative in the course of loading, he might not have observed the company's practice of beginning loading with the ballast tanks empty, and might have made his subsequent decisions differently. Following the disaster, James P. McAllister, head of the New York towing firm McAllister Brothers, wrote to Redfield that there was nothing unusual about a ship's having a negative metacentric height with her ballast tanks empty, and that the majority of ships with water ballast systems that his firm towed would not be stable unless the tanks were completely full. He wrote, "It is a well known fact that few of our ships will stand up without their ballast unless all top hamper has been removed."[86] Even if this is an over-statement, as seems likely, the *Eastland* was not unique if she had a negative metacentric height with her tanks empty. If this line of argument is valid, the failure to alert Erickson of the possibility that her metacentric height might now become negative in the course of loading was a more immediate cause of the disaster than the increase in top hamper itself.

There is a question whether the changes of July 2 aggravated the movements of the ship in loading and unloading that for several years had frightened

many of her passengers and at least some of her crew. There is some evidence that the changes did so. Martin Collins, a law student at Northwestern University, quit a job on the *Eastland* on July 20 out of worries about the ship's stability. Chester Adams, a watchman, tried to quit early in July expressly because he considered the ship a freak and unsafe. A man named Harry Brown arrived from Syracuse to replace him, but when Brown, out of fear, refused to take the job, Adams stayed on until payday, quitting a few days before Collins. Dr. S. Myres Hubbard, an intern with the Chicago & North Western Railway's hospital service in Chicago, worked as an attendant at a refreshment stand on the main deck of the *Eastland* for three weeks in July, and felt "things were not right by the very action of the ship." He did not quit, but remained wary, and after the disaster told a reporter for the *Examiner*, "I beat it up the stairs at the first twitch of the ship."[87]

Nonetheless, the ship operated for just over three weeks between the changes of July 2 and the disaster without having any problems of stability. On her regular trips, as Table 2 shows, she was carrying well under a thousand people out of Chicago, except for a peak load of 1,062 passengers on Sunday, July 18.[88] Her largest load of any kind was 1,123 passengers on a moonlight excursion of the Peerless Chapter of the Masonic Order on Friday, July 23. There were no listing problems. Erickson reported that the most severe list in the week before the disaster was 10 to 15 degrees, or 20 degrees at most, leaving St. Joseph on Monday, July 19, but the ship had righted herself without difficulty.[89] In the course of dis-

TABLE 2

Passenger Loads on the Eastland, *July 2–24, 1915*

Date	Load	Date	Load	Date	Load
July 2	214	July 10	213	July 18	1,062
July 3	854	July 11	542	July 19	205
July 4	580	July 12	235	July 20	914
July 5	493[a]	July 13	198	July 21	314
July 6	0[a]	July 14	87	July 22	298
July 7	0[a]	July 15	205	July 23	294[b]
July 8	0	July 16	189	July 23	1,123[c]
July 9	161	July 17	525	July 24	2,501

SOURCE: Certified list of passengers carried out of Chicago by the steamer *Eastland*, 1915, by Robert H. McCreary, file of U.S. v. Hull et al., National Archives, Great Lakes Region, Chicago, Record Group 21, CR 1628, file 358,803 (3 boxes). Figure for July 24 corrected for boarding of E. W. Sladkey. See Chapter IV.

[a] Did not operate—drydocked.
[b] At 9:35 A.M.
[c] At 8:50 P.M.

charging the Masonic excursion, Pedersen asked Erickson to heel the ship slightly to starboard to raise the port gangway to facilitate unloading, but she responded normally.[90]

The period of grace was over, however. On the morning following the Masonic excursion, the *Eastland* would take out the Western Electric excursion. The charter party, by providing that she should be the first ship out, assured that she would be loaded to her new licensed capacity, and the disaster was at hand.

CHAPTER FOUR

The
Disaster

THE events of the disaster will be presented chronologically. The basic element in the chronology is chief engineer Joseph M. Erickson's engine room log, which he provided to federal inspectors in the form of a manuscript letter on the day following the disaster. The log was published in Secretary of Commerce Redfield's volume of hearings on the event, *Investigation of Accident to the Steamer "Eastland."*[1] The bridge's log was lost in the accident.[2] As will be set forth below, during the disaster Captain Pedersen suffered a blow on the head that temporarily disoriented him; it may also have affected his memory of the events immediately earlier. In addition, his testimony, as noted in the previous chapter, contained strong elements of self-exculpation. The times, especially if based on Pedersen's testimony, should be considered approximate. Erickson reported watching the clock in the engine room closely only after 7:10 A.M.[3]

11:50 to 11:55 P.M., Friday, July 23. The *Eastland* returned to Chicago with the Masonic excursion. Hull had directed Pedersen to discharge to starboard and to proceed with a tug to the turning basin at the confluence of the two branches of the Chicago River, to turn there, and to approach the Chicago & South Haven wharf as in 1914,[4] but Pedersen chose not to do so and discharged as usual to port at Rush Street after putting about in the river and being towed to the Northern Michigan Transportation Company's wharf.

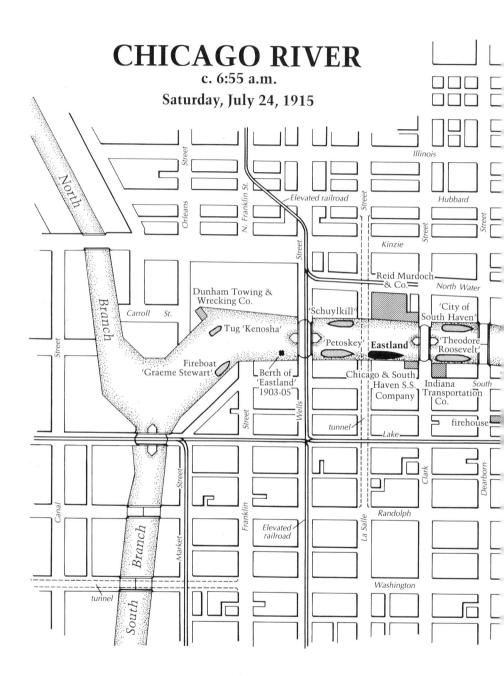

Hill Steamboat Co.

'Maywood'

Michigan Canal

Street

Cass

Rush

Pine

Street

Northern Michigan Transportation Co.

Water Street

'Illinois,' 'Missouri,' 'Rochester' (relative position uncertain)

⟹ *Lake Michigan* 1200 feet

Street

Street

Street

ater Street

Chicago

'Christopher Columbus'

River

North

Street

Slip A

Slip B

Slip C

'Racine'

Puritan'

River

'Indiana,' 'Georgia,' 'Alabama' (relative position uncertain)

Goodrich Transit Co.

Avenue

Graham & Morton Transportation Company

'United States'

South tion

Water Street

Street

house

Michigan

Dearborn

State

Avenue

Wabash

Street

Street

Street

0   400   800   1200   1600

feet

12:30 A.M., Saturday, July 24. Pedersen returned to the ship after taking his report of passengers handled to the customs house. He passed Erickson and told him to "Fill her up." The ship was scheduled not only to take the Western Electric excursion and her regular Saturday departure to St. Joseph, but also to make an additional round trip for an unspecified purpose to St. Joseph leaving Chicago at midnight. Pedersen anticipated running over 400 miles before having time to take coal again.[5] Erickson arranged for the *Eastland* to be coaled from a barge of the Pittsburgh Coal Company. This firm operated out of a yard on the north bank of the Chicago River near its mouth, from which it could make quick deliveries to any of the Chicago passenger lines. Pedersen, who considered the coal desirable ballast, estimated that about 25 tons were put aboard and that the ship had 60 to 70 tons in total.[6] Erickson estimated that bunkers held 110 tons after the Masonic excursion, and that an additional 55 tons were loaded.[7] Erickson's estimate was probably too high, but Pedersen's was unquestionably too low. H. B. Vehstedt estimated on the basis of examination of the wreck that the bunkers could hold 125 tons if carefully packed, but estimated 110 tons as a practical maximum.[8] Coal passers on the ship testified before the federal grand jury that she had 104 tons aboard, about 79 on the port side and 25 on the starboard.[9] Seventy-five to 80 tons of coal were removed from the hulk after it was raised, but some had fallen into the river.[10]

3:00 to 3:30 A.M. The coaling being completed, the ship proceeded upriver to the Chicago & South Haven wharf. She did so in an unusual fashion, by backing—as a twin-screw ship could do—with an unidentified tug on her bow.[11] This movement required her to back through swing-span bridges at Rush Street and Clark Street. Chicago was in the process of converting such bridges to its characteristic double-bascule type; the conversion had been made for State and Dearborn streets. The backing movement was probably completed about 3:55.[12]

5:30 A.M. Martin Flatow, port agent for the St. Joseph–Chicago Steamship Company, who had slept for the night in his office at the Rush Street wharf, walked to the *Eastland*'s berth at Clark Street.[13] The river was 0.1 foot below normal; the sky was overcast with a slight northwest wind.[14] The temperature was 70 degrees and remained so. The river had by this time been reversed so that it flowed, as at present, upstream from Lake Michigan into the South Branch. The current was about 1 to 1.5 miles per hour; Pedersen considered this no factor in his calculations.[15] Because the river was slightly lower than in 1914 and the ship considerably heavier, she had to be loaded differently. She was placed with her aft gangway approximately at the east building line of La Salle Street because the wharf was several feet lower in this area than to the east. By loading here, the angle of the gangplank descending into the gangway could be minimized. It was considered impractical to load from the higher portions of the wharf into the forward gangways.[16] Joseph R. Lynn, the assistant harbormaster, estimated that the stern of the ship projected about 30 feet west of the east building line,[17] but judged on the basis of the location of the aft gangway on the outboard profile of the ship, the distance was about 38 to 40 feet. In either case, the stern extended over the La Salle Street tunnel. This position required the ship to be moored so that her aft gangway was a short distance—variously reported as 2′-9″ and 4′-0″ off the wharf.[18] The gangway was about 18 inches below the wharf. Immediately forward was a rope fender about

Martin Flatow, port agent for Chicago of the St. Joseph–Chicago Steamship Company.

5 feet wide and as thick as a human body.[19] The gangplank was 8 to 10 feet long and 3.5 feet wide.[20] The bow of the ship was 21 to 22 feet out from the wharf, about 60 feet west of the Clark Street bridge.[21] This was not a position from which she could have sailed directly, for her starboard screw would have fouled the wharf.

The *Eastland* was moored with 5 lines. Forward, she had a breast line

The area from which the *Eastland* loaded, photographed from the wreck. According to reports, the gangplank was approximately at the building line. The Chicago & South Haven Line's baggage room is at the right. The aft breast line was placed on the cleat in front of it. This area was chosen because the wharf is perceptibly lower here. The stairs down from La Salle Street also gave immediate access to the ship. (National Archives and Records Administration, Chicago)

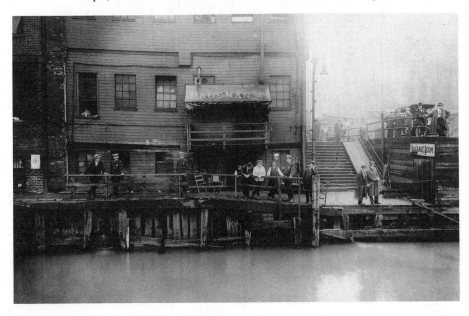

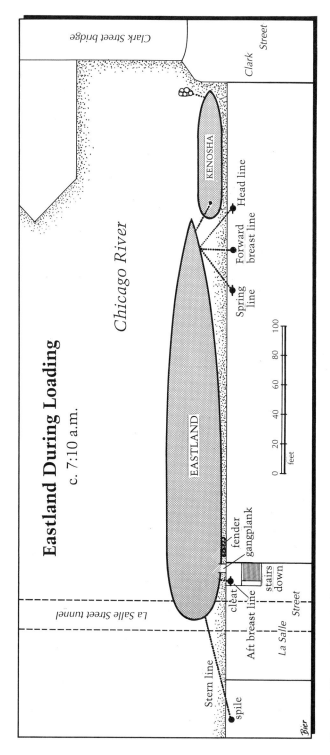

Eastland During Loading
c. 7:10 a.m.

Clark Street bridge

Clark Street

Chicago River

KENOSHA

Head line

Forward
breast line

Spring
line

EASTLAND

fender
gangplank

stairs
down

cleat

Aft breast line

La Salle Street tunnel

La Salle Street

Stern line

spile

feet
0   20   40   60   80   100

Bier

(James A. Bier, cartographer)

that extended at a right angle from the ship's center line to a spile. This was a new Manila line of 3.5 to 4.5 inches in diameter. From the same chock, about 21 feet from the bow, ran a head line forward and a spring line aft. Both were made fast to wooden cleats on the wharf; these lines were intended to keep the ship from moving forward or aft. At the stern were only two lines, an aft breast line and a stern line. The stern line extended out from the 'tween decks about 75 to 100 feet west of the ship to what was variously reported as a cleat or spile, probably the latter. The aft breast line ran from a chock on the main deck abaft the gangway through which the ship was loading to a cleat immediately west of the gangplank. Normal practice would have entailed a line forward from the stern, but in this instance it would have fouled the boarding area.[22] The ship drew about 9'-0" forward and between 12'-0" and 14'-0" aft; her bottom cleared any obstructions beneath her by about 4 feet.[23]

Forward of the *Eastland* on the south bank of the river across the Clark Street bridge at the Indiana Transportation Company's wharf lay the company's own *Theodore Roosevelt*, which was to load for the picnic's second departure at 8:00 A.M. The company's *United States*, which was on charter for the season to the Chicago & South Haven Steamship Company, was moored on the south bank east of the Dearborn Street bridge. To the *Eastland*'s stern, west of La Salle Street, lay the *Petoskey*, a wooden propeller steamer of 1888 chartered for the excursion from Chicago & South Haven and scheduled for the 8:30 departure. Although the ship had established a good reputation for dependability, the *Petoskey* was neither large nor modern, nor had she been designed as an excursion ship. Inevitably, she was less attractive to the passengers to the picnic than the *Eastland* and *Theodore Roosevelt*. There were to be three other departures. The small steamer *Maywood* of the Hill Steamboat Company of Kenosha was to leave after the *Theodore Roosevelt* but before the *Petoskey*.[24] The *Racine*, chartered for the excursion from the Chicago, Racine & Milwaukee Line, was to leave at 10:00. The *Rochester*, a steamer that Indiana Transportation had chartered for the entire season of 1915 from a subsidiary of Canada Steamship Lines, was to leave at 2:30 P.M.[25] The *Rochester* was at the Rush Street wharf. The *Maywood* was not reported in the area, and may still have been at Hill's wharf at the head of the Michigan Canal, an artificial harbor later known as the Ogden Slip, immediately north of the river. No ship was moored at the Reid-Murdoch building on the north bank of the river opposite the *Eastland*, but opposite the *Petoskey* on the north bank was the big package freighter *Schuylkill* of the Pennsylvania Railroad's Anchor Line moored with her bow pointed west just short of the Wells Street bridge. The *City of South Haven*, which, like the *United States*, was not chartered for the excursion, was moored on the north bank opposite the *Theodore Roosevelt* in the expectation of moving into the Chicago & South Haven wharf for her regular departure once the *Eastland* had vacated it. The *Racine* was already in the area, probably on the north bank opposite the *United States*.[26]

6:15 A.M. Fred G. Snow came on duty. He and Charles Silvernail pumped out the ballast tanks, consistently with the long-standing policy on the ship of starting a voyage with the tanks empty.[27]

6:20 A.M. Erickson finished breakfast and went to duty in the engine room.[28] Pedersen's chronology here, as for more important events, is different. Pedersen testified that he arose at 6:30, went out onto the deck for one or two minutes, and returned to the cabin to consult his chart to ascertain the course to Michigan City. He said he then had to calculate the variation from the magnetic compass to determine the true course. He stated that he then went down to breakfast, returned to his cabin about 7:00, smoked a cigar, and went to the bridge.[29] While entering the mess, he passed Erickson, who was going to duty. Because Erickson places his coming out of the mess about 6:20, it seems more likely that Pedersen arose earlier than he stated, went first to breakfast, and then returned to the captain's cabin, ostensibly to consult his chart. It is difficult to see why he had to calculate the variation from the magnetic compass, for charts of the U.S. Lake Survey, then as now, show this. He may have intended to calculate the decline in variation since the most recent charts were issued in 1909. Alternatively, he may have meant that he intended to calculate the deviation, which is to say the additional difference from the compass reading characteristic of an individual ship. Pedersen, as he passed Erickson, asked him to keep the ship stable during the voyage because the steel pendulum that served as the indicator of list in the engine room biased his magnetic compass.[30] This is also a strange observation, for the indicator, only eighteen inches long, was not large enough to have a significant effect on a steel ship, and was at a considerable distance from the bridge in any case. This may have been a facetious comment. Pedersen was, however, to follow an unfamiliar course on a day that he expected to be foggy. It had already begun to drizzle.[31] Wheelsmen Albert Webber and William Gordon were on the bridge with him.[32]

6:30 A.M. Preparations began for loading for a 7:30 departure. Two weeks previously Greenebaum had notified Robert H. McCreary, deputy collector of customs in charge of the Marine Department, of the excursion. On the presumption that, as in 1914, the ship would load from two gangways, McCreary assigned two of his subordinates, Luman A. Lobdell, Jr., and Curtis J. Oakley, to count passengers aboard. Lobdell had worked the Masonic excursion on the previous evening and spent the night aboard. He arose at 6:00, had a cup of coffee, and went to the gangplank at 6:30. Oakley arrived at 6:30 expecting to be stationed at a forward gangway, but upon seeing that only the aft gangway was to be used, joined Lobdell there. Flatow, purser George W. Monger, assistant purser James Stenson, and Lobdell began loading passengers at 6:40.[33] McCreary arrived about 6:45.[34]

About 5,000 people had already arrived for the excursion, double what could be accommodated on the *Eastland*. People had not been assigned to specific ships, and there were no passenger lists, either for *Eastland* or for the excursion as a whole. The passengers boarded with considerable enthusiasm. According to the Red Cross's classification of the victims, about 57 percent of the passengers were Western Electric employees, and the rest not.[35] About 56 percent were women.[36] The picnic was, after all, the one great social outing of the year for what were mainly young people otherwise engaged in the repetitive activities of telephone manufacture and assembly. It was to them what the annual Christmas party has been to employees of many firms in recent years, and they behaved accordingly.

6:41 A.M. The *Eastland* began to list to starboard from the usual concentration of passengers toward the wharf. This was almost immediate and probably more severe than in the ship's ordinary operations, simply because in an affinity excursion of this character the people aboard necessarily knew large numbers of the people on the wharf. Del Fisher,[37] the first mate, who was on the promenade deck forward of the pilot house prepa-

The Indiana Transportation Company's flagship, *Theodore Roosevelt*, had been built by the Toledo Shipbuilding Company in 1906. She was big, well proportioned, fast, and well suited to the company's short trips. Generally considered the best designed of the purely day steamers that operated out of Chicago, she was active until 1946 and was scrapped at Milwaukee in 1950. (T. H. Franklin collection, Steamship Historical Society of America)

At the time of the disaster the Indiana Transportation Company's *United States* was east of the Dearborn Street bridge. She was not scheduled to depart on the excursion; newspaper advertisements indicate she was on charter to the Chicago & South Haven Line. In the photograph she is shown on the north bank of the Chicago River with Graham & Morton's *Puritan* in the background. (T. H. Franklin collection, Steamship Historical Society of America)

ratory to casting off her forward lines, estimated the list to starboard at 10 degrees for 6 to 10 minutes.[38] Relative to the ship's habitual behavior, this was not exceptional, but the list brought the starboard side down enough that the gangplank rose to within three to four feet of the top of the aft gangway, halting loading for about 15 to 30 seconds at an unspecified time before boarding could be resumed.[39] Oakley estimated that the starboard list brought the aft gangway within 18 inches of the water.[40]

6:48 A.M. Erickson noted the list to starboard and, according to his gauge tender John V. Elbert, said to the engine room crew, "Boys, steady her up a little."[41] The men began correcting for the starboard list by admitting water to the No. 2 and 3 port ballast tanks for 2 to 3 minutes.[42] Because of the absence of meters on the system, it is impossible to know how much they admitted, but if, as stated in the description of the ballast system in Chapter I, it took 25 minutes to fill either or both No. 3 ballast tanks and 10 to 12 minutes to fill No. 2, what Erickson ordered admitted must have been well under a quarter of the capacity of the tanks. It was at this point that the management's failure to tell Erickson that the *Eastland*'s metacentric height might now be negative with a heavy load became important. Admitting the water to the No. 2 and 3 tanks for stabilization on the side opposite to the wharf was consistent with the ship's practice of many years, but this was based on a presumption of positive metacentric

height. Now the metacentric height was probably slightly negative, or if
not, it shortly became so as the passengers continued to board. Under the
circumstances, the admission of water to two large port ballast tanks was
extremely dangerous, both in shifting the list to port and in creating a
strong free-surface effect. The problem of shifting the list to port was aggravated by the distribution of the coal, which if the coal passers were
correct, was more than three-fourths on the port side. Distributing a relatively small amount of water over two such large tanks produced a free-
surface effect considerably greater than what the same amount of water
could have done in a single tank. As noted in Chapter I, the free-surface
effect of water in partly filled ballast tanks acts on the stability of a ship
like a randomly moving weight several decks above. If the metacentric
height was negative, or shortly became negative, what Erickson did would
have initiated the sequence of events that, in fact, ensued. The short-run
effect was what was desired, however, and the ship had straightened up by
6:51.[43] By what he had done, Erickson had probably brought the ship to
even keel at a neutral or unstable equilibrium with a metacentric height in
the vicinity of zero. As passengers continued to load, it was not a situation
that could have persisted.

6:53 A.M. The ship began to list slightly to port. Fred M. Reed, a Western Electric official who was on the hurricane deck, estimated on the basis
of movement of the masts that this list reached about 10 degrees.[44] Erickson testified that he ordered open the valve from the intake to the manifold
and the valve into the No. 2 starboard tank for four to five minutes. This
put the ship again on an even keel.[45] Snow testified that Erickson ordered
water into the No. 2 and 3 starboard tanks, but agreed that this righted the
vessel. Erickson had brought the *Eastland* to a second unstable equilibrium. Snow estimated that the ship was on even keel for five to ten minutes.[46] Reed estimated she was on even keel at this time for not more than
a minute.[47]

6:55 A.M. A phone call was made to the Dunham Towing & Wrecking
Company for a tug. The company's *Kenosha* had been up the North
Branch of the Chicago River. At 6:00 A.M., when the tug's chief engineer,
Arthur D. MacDonald, reported for work, he found the tug at a point off
Clybourn Avenue, where she was being used in salvage operations on a
sunken steamboat. She had then come directly down the North Branch and
by 6:55 was lying off the towing company's dispatching office on the north
bank just west of the Wells Street bridge, awaiting orders. The dispatcher
shouted to the tug's captain, John H. O'Meara, that he was to take out the
Eastland, which was only about two blocks to the east. The tug responded
immediately, and took her place at the *Eastland*'s bow about 7:00.[48] With
her own line the *Kenosha* made her bow fast to the south side of the pilings

that protected the south abutment of the Clark Street bridge. The tug's cook asked O'Meara whether there was time to serve breakfast. O'Meara responded that there was. During breakfast, which occupied 15 to 20 minutes, deckhand William Flannigan, who was in charge of the line to the tug, called down from the *Eastland*'s promenade deck to the *Kenosha* to take the line. The tug's deckhand who handled lines and her fireman went out to the deck aft; took the line, a steel cable extending out about 25 feet; and made it fast to the tug's towing bit.[49] Photographs of the wreck show that the *Eastland*'s towing line was payed out through a chock on the 'tween decks on the starboard side about 7 feet from the bow. The deckhand and the fireman returned to their mess, and the tug's crew finished breakfast. Flannigan went below to the *Eastland*'s line room at the bow on the 'tween decks to await the order to take in the cable when the tug was whistled off.[50]

7:00 A.M. McCreary notified Greenebaum that the passenger count had reached 1,600 shortly after 7:00.[51] Lobdell and Oakley both reported lower counts, that the load was 1,026 at 7:00 and 1,700 at 7:15.[52] The passengers were loading at a rate of about 50 per minute.[53] A light port list resumed as they loaded, and Erickson, who could not observe the loaded passengers from his position in the engine room, supposed that they were congregating on the port side.[54] They had, in fact, not moved in any large numbers from the starboard rail.

7:05 A.M. Erickson started the engines to dissipate the condensation in the cylinders, starboard astern, port ahead, presumably dead slow.[55]

7:07 A.M. Erickson pumped out the port No. 3 ballast tank.[56] He did not pump out the port No. 2 tank, believing there was little water in it. This course of action retained some weight below the center of gravity, but reduced the free-surface effect. Snow testified that the port No. 3 tank was entirely pumped out, or at least cleared to the point that the pump would eject no more.[57] Richard J. Moore, a salesman for the Murphy Varnish Company, stated after the disaster that the exhaust port on the starboard side had been disgorging tons of water as he boarded about 7:10.[58] It should be borne in mind that, as stated in Chapter I, water was admitted by gravity from the port side and pumped out to starboard through the same manifold, so that it was impossible to admit water to the tanks on one side and pump it out from the tanks on the other side simultaneously. Nor could water be pumped from one side to the other. Accordingly, Erickson was confronted throughout the event with a choice whether to admit water to one set of tanks or to pump it out of the other. This was greatly to restrict his options. He could have admitted water to both sides simultaneously, or pumped it out from both sides simultaneously, but neither of these alternatives was apparently attractive to him.

7:10 A.M. Harbormaster Adam F. Weckler arrived at the Clark Street bridge, believing it was his obligation to attend the loading of such a large number of passengers. He estimated the *Eastland*'s list at 7 degrees to port.[59] At this time or immediately thereafter he noted that passengers were being rejected and directed to the *Theodore Roosevelt* on the east side of the bridge. He deduced from this that loading of passengers had ended.[60] Flatow also reported that loading ended about 7:10, and that preparations for taking in the gangplank began immediately.[61] Lobdell, counting passengers in at the gangplank, notified McCreary at 2,400, 2,450, and 2,475, and announced "That is all" at 2,495,

Adam F. Weckler, harbormaster of the City of Chicago.

admitting only 5 more.[62] McCreary denied admission to passengers when the count reached 2,500, but he admitted one female washroom attendant.[63] Because the passengers had loaded at a relatively rapid rate, it is questionable whether the count could have been perfectly correct. There is no reason to believe that it was highly inaccurate, however. McCreary, as soon as the 2,500 passengers were loaded, left Lobdell in charge and walked across La Salle Street to the *Petoskey*, which was beginning to load for the 8:30 departure.[64]

Radio officer Charles M. Dibbell noted the list and walked over to the *Eastland*'s starboard rail to look down upon the wharf. A watchman there shouted up to him to attempt to move the passengers to starboard. He did so, but reported after the disaster that they showed no inclination to follow his directive.[65]

7:13 A.M. Pedersen came out of his cabin at 7:11 or 7:12, and proceeded to the bridge, arriving at 7:13. He estimated the list as slightly to starboard.[66] Either this was a gross error in judgment, or he actually came to the bridge considerably earlier. It is presumably an error in judgment, for as noted below, his estimate of the time of his order to "Stand by" differs from Erickson's by only a minute. He observed that, because of the rain, there were relatively few passengers on the hurricane deck; he estimated only about 125 abaft the pilot house and 50 at the stern, where second mate Peter Fisher—who was unrelated to Del Fisher—stood awaiting the order to cast off the aft lines.[67] George Haber, an employee of one of the South Water Street commission houses who observed the disaster from the wharf between the *Eastland* and the *Petoskey*, estimated the number on the hurricane deck at 150.[68] If Pedersen was correct in his estimate of the number of passengers on the hurricane deck, as he appears to have been, the total weight of passengers, boats, and rafts on that deck was about 74 to 75 tons, significantly less than the 97 to 118.5 tons previously estimated as the weight there during the event of July 17, 1904. Del Fisher noted that there were few passengers on the promenade deck forward of the pilot house.[69] Dancing had begun inside the cabin on the promenade deck aft, attracting many of the passengers. Bradfield's Orchestra, a five-piece violin and mandolin group, provided the music.[70]

7:15 A.M. David Durand, an employee of the Watson Warehouse diagonally across the river from the *Eastland*, looked out of a third-story window and noted that the ship was listing badly to port. He called to Walter Perry, a fellow worker, to come to the window. This produced two witnesses who observed the rest of the event from the north at a relatively high angle.

Del Fisher observed that loading had ended and went into the pilot house for his rain gear. He noted the ship was listing to port, but felt no alarm.[71] He returned to his position on the promenade deck near the bow.

7:16 A.M. The list to port had worsened to what Erickson estimated at 10 to 15 degrees by the period 7:10 to 7:15.[72] At 7:16 he ordered the valves opened from the intake to the manifold and from the manifold to the No. 2 and 3 starboard ballast tanks.[73] He himself opened the valve for the No. 3 starboard tank, and Peter Erickson the valve for No. 2. Snow opened the valve from the intake, giving it eight to ten revolutions.[74] Although the valve would take twelve to fourteen revolutions, ten were normally sufficient to admit the maximum amount of water. Examination of these valves on the wreck confirmed that they were open.[75] Nonetheless, Erickson endeavored to bring water into his No. 2 and 3 starboard tanks for at least seven minutes without being able to do so.[76] This was, as it remains, one

The Chicago & South Haven Line's *Petoskey*, which loaded to the west of the *Eastland* for the excursion, was a wooden propeller steamer similar in size and configuration to the *Eastland*'s old running mate, *Soo City*. (Drawing by Samuel Ward Stanton)

of the mysteries of the disaster. Literary evidence indicates that all of the

ship's chief engineers, including Erickson, had been able to deal with lists
of this magnitude by admitting water. The coroner's jury heard evidence
that the valve from the intake to the manifold had frozen during the previous winter, damaging the valve and causing some of the tanks to flood.[77]
It had been repaired, however; Erickson had reported no difficulty with it
earlier in the season, and in particular he had no difficulty taking water
into the port tanks at 6:48 and the starboard tanks at 6:53. The strainer immediately inboard from the Kingston valve might possibly have become
clogged. Pedersen testified in 1932 that, when the ship did not respond, he
presumed there was some paper over the strainer.[78] Yet there is no evidence
that he knew Erickson was attempting to admit water at this time; none of
the testimony on the disaster indicates that there was voice communication
between the bridge and the engine room at any time. Similarly, none of the
evidence from examination of the wreck suggests any clogging of the intake. This element had not been a source of difficulty in the ship's operation previously. Nack testified that it was easily kept clean by quickly closing and opening the valve.[79] Peter Erickson testified that he had never
known the intake valve to fail.[80] Because the entire system was below water level, even if the intake dipped from the 6.5 degrees estimated earlier
to some negative figure, water should still have flowed into the tanks. Because Erickson was attempting to admit water into the starboard ballast
tanks, he would have been unable to attempt to pump out whatever remained in the port No. 2 tank, but he gave no indication in his testimony
that he wanted to do this. Indisputably working against the officers was the
fixity of the weight on the hurricane deck. In the event of July 17, 1904,
the excessive weight on the hurricane deck was mainly a load of passengers, whom Dority could direct to go below. Now the excessive weight on
the hurricane deck was the newly added set of boats and rafts, which could
not be moved in the short compass of time available.

Erickson's inability to admit water to the ballast system after his order
of 7:16 was regarded at the time as one of the major contributors to the
disaster, but in retrospect this appears very unlikely. Because the ship was
now fully loaded and her metacentric height almost certainly negative,
there is no presumption that he could have saved the ship even if he had
been able to admit water into the starboard tanks as he sought. Nack testified on the basis of his experience on the ship from 1904 to 1906 that with
2,500 passengers, a list, and relatively little water in the ballast tanks, the
Eastland could not have been stabilized and should have been evacuated.[81]
This implies that the ship was doomed by 7:10 and that Erickson could not
have dealt with the problem with the water he sought to admit to the starboard tanks at 7:16. With a negative metacentric height, the best he could

have done by what he was attempting was to return her briefly to even keel in a third unstable equilibrium. To judge from his actions and his later testimony, at no time did Erickson recognize that he was dealing with a negative metacentric height. If he had come to this conclusion after 7:16 and attempted to fill all of the tanks on both sides, he could not have stabilized the ship in the time remaining even if the blockage had not occurred, given the speed at which the ballast tanks could be filled.

7:17 A.M. Ray W. Davis, Hull's assistant, became concerned about the list, went to the engine room, and asked Erickson if an effort was being made to straighten the ship. Erickson told him what he was doing and asked Davis to talk with the first mate, but also asked him to assure that the ship's starboard fender strake was not hanging on the wharf.[82] That problem was common at the Rush Street wharf, though it had not entailed serious consequences.[83]

7:18 A.M. The ship righted herself very perceptibly over the course of about two minutes.[84] This was noted by all observers, on the ship and off. Lynn testified in 1932, on the basis of his observations from the Clark Street bridge, "she got up, say around 18 to 20 inches, possibly more, possibly less." [85] Because this testimony came more than seventeen years after the event, it is open to question. The Red Cross stated in its report of 1918 that this second reversal brought the ship almost back to an even keel.[86] No one estimated it in degrees. The reversal was probably caused by the free-surface effect from the water in her port No. 2 and starboard No. 2 and 3 tanks, but there may have been other counterforces at work.

The reversal in the movement to port had several consequences. On the basis of the movement of the pendulum, Erickson thought very briefly that the danger had passed, and said to Snow, "I believe we are getting her," or "We have got her." [87] Pedersen was reassured that the ship was righting herself. Lynn, who had been deputed by Weckler to get the ships due out on the excursion through the bridges with dispatch, called up to Pedersen, "Hello, Cap, when you are ready you can have the bridge any time you want it." [88] Hearing this, O'Meara began his preparations for departure. He ordered the *Kenosha*'s line cast off from the south side of the pilings just short of the Clark Street bridge. He maneuvered the tug out into the river and cast her line onto the north side of the pilings so as to position her towing bit to the north of the *Eastland*'s bow.[89]

At approximately 7:18 the gangplank was drawn in. Lynn testified that the gangplank was being taken in when he arrived at that time—although some of his observations already cited appear to date from a few minutes earlier.[90] McCreary estimated only that the gangplank was taken in five to ten minutes before the disaster, which would place it in the period from 7:17 to 7:25, depending on his definition of the instant of capsizing.[91] One

The *Maywood* was to follow the *Theodore Roosevelt* out on the excursion. The ship was a strange choice. Only 130 feet long, she added little capacity to the movement. Built for local service between Escanaba, Gladstone, and other points on northern Lake Michigan, she was in her first year of service for the Hill Steamboat Company of Kenosha. (Rev. Peter J. Van der Linden collection)

additional passenger came aboard at this time. E. W. Sladkey, head of Western Electric's printing department, arrived as the gangplank was being drawn in. He noted that the *Eastland* was listing to port, and thought fleetingly that she might have some trouble before she got far out into the lake. He decided to go to one of the other steamers, but he then saw some of the people who worked in his department waving to him from the promenade deck of the *Eastland* near the bow, urging him to join them. He decided to do so, and jumped over the water to the aft gangway, raising the passenger count to 2,501. He immediately went up to the promenade deck to join his subordinates, and thought it odd that the ship, on the basis of the angle of the deck, was listing perceptibly to port even though there was no large number of passengers there. Most of the passengers were, like the people he had come up to see, along the starboard rail. He remained there, talking with his group.[92] His observation of the list, which dates from about 7:19, implies that the Red Cross overstated the reversal of 7:18 when it concluded that the ship returned almost to an even keel.

With Sladkey's jumping aboard, the number of people on the ship reached 2,573, of whom 72 constituted the crew. McCreary had ordered the counting of all passengers, including children and babes in arms.[93] Greenebaum reported that 2,408 tickets were collected,[94] implying that

93 non–fare-paying children had boarded. The number of tickets collected indicates that the counting of passengers aboard was approximately accurate, even if not wholly so.

Lobdell testified that when loading ceased and the gangplank was taken aboard, Flatow ordered that the aft breast line be cast off and taken in.[95] Sladkey stated explicitly that the line was being taken in along with the gangplank when he arrived.[96] This is the most specific evidence on the casting off of this line, but some observers—including Flatow—spoke in their testimony as though the line had stayed in place but gone slack later, when the process of casting off the ship's lines generally began.[97] There is no presumption Flatow had the authority to order the line cast off, but he may have done so. The preponderance of evidence is that the line was cast off at 7:18 by Charles Lasser, the baggageman of the Chicago & South Haven line, who later told a reporter that he cast off one stern line and stood by to throw off the other.[98] The stern line running to a point farther west on the wharf remained in place, but it was hand-held by deckhand William Barrett in the expectation of allowing it to go slack when it was cast off a few minutes hence.[99]

7:20 A.M. The list to port resumed. Erickson noticed water coming onto the main deck through a scupper on the port side. He stopped the engines, fearing that they were a source of instability.[100] Richard J. Moore, who had boarded about ten minutes earlier, started up the staircases toward the hurricane deck. When he reached the 'tween decks, he heard a crash below him and, looking back down, saw beer bottles and shards rolling over the main deck. He believed the crash had been caused by the falling over of the refrigerator behind the bar, and estimated the event at eight to ten minutes before the capsizing, which is to say no later than 7:22. He testified that this event did not create panic among the passengers. He was probably wrong that what he heard was the refrigerator falling over, but almost certainly correct in the opinion he expressed that this marked approximately the final moment that an orderly evacuation of passengers could have been attempted.[101] David Durand, from his position on the third story on the north bank, saw the resumption of the list, and observed that it caused a major movement of passengers away from the port rail to starboard, but noted that this did not affect the movement of the ship to port. He was quoted by a reporter as saying, "She was listing way over by 7:20 and the crowd on the decks swarmed over to the dock side, but it was too late." [102]

7:21 to 7:22 A.M. Pedersen observed that loading had been completed and that passengers were being turned away. He began his preparations for immediate departure.[103]

McCreary returned from the *Petoskey* to the *Eastland* to talk with Lobdell, who was standing in the gangway from which the gangplank had been drawn in. Lobdell was to accompany the ship and to count passengers on her later calls; he had been assigned to her for two to three weeks.[104] McCreary noted that the *Eastland* was listing to port as he talked with Lobdell, but he continued to expect the ship to right herself.[105]

7:23 A.M. The list to port became so heavy that Erickson directed Silvernail to tell the passengers forward on the main deck to move to the starboard side. He made the same request to the passengers immediately abaft the engine room and asked Monger to spread the message more widely.[106] Frederick W. Willard of Western Electric stated that the passengers complied without panic.[107]

Water began coming in through the port gangways onto the deck. Joe Conrad, a fireman and oiler on the ship who stood smoking in the forward starboard gangway, looked over to the port gangway opposite him and noted that it was leaking water onto the main deck.[108] Lobdell testified in Secretary of Commerce Redfield's inquiry that he heard a girl shout, "The water is coming in." He stood up on the sill of the starboard gangway so that he could see the aft port gangway and observed that all four sections of the doors were open.[109] When asked if a wire screen were in place over the lower portion, he replied that he could not recollect seeing it, but one presumes the openwork gate was in place.

As the water ran down into the engine room, Snow opened a warning signal known as a Modoc whistle, but in his letter to his wife assuring her that he had survived the disaster, he said that it went unheeded.[110]

> The Chicago, Racine & Milwaukee Line's *Racine* was chartered for the excursion and due to depart at 10:00 A.M. The ship was the former Graham & Morton steamer *Argo*. The CR&M Line had bought her in 1910 from underwriters to whom Graham & Morton had abandoned her after a severe accident at Holland late in 1905. (Rev. Peter J. Van der Linden collection)

7:24 A.M. Pedersen rang "Stand by" on his engine room telegraph. Erickson responded immediately. Erickson assigned this occurrence to 7:24,[111] Pedersen to 7:25.[112] Pedersen thought that the list to port was still only a "trifle"; he testified in 1916, "Well I wasn't excited at all when I rung up the stand by."[113] He also called for opening the Clark Street bridge. Lynn, after telling Pedersen at 7:18 that he could have the bridge any time he wanted it, had walked off the bridge to the wharf, where with his foot he tested the three forward lines from the ship and found them taut.[114] Consequently, Pedersen, standing on the *Eastland*'s starboard flying bridge, requested of Weckler, rather than of Lynn, that the Clark Street bridge be opened for him. Weckler refused on the ground the ship was listing too heavily, and directed Pedersen to trim her.[115] Pedersen, in one of his earliest but most conspicuous violations of the truth, later in the day told newspaper reporters that Weckler had told him to throw the lines off, but he had refused.[116] Lynn, meanwhile, braced his back against a building on the south bank to sight the *Eastland* against the Reid-Murdoch building across the river, estimated the list at 20 to 25 degrees, concluded the ship's situation was now hopeless, and walked back up to the Clark Street bridge to tell Weckler that the vessel was going over, probably taking the wharf with her.[117]

Upon ringing "Stand by" on his telegraph, Pedersen also pressed a button to actuate a buzzer at the stern, where second mate Peter Fisher was awaiting the order to cast off. Pedersen stated immediately after the disaster that he had intended the buzzer as a directive to cast off,[118] but in 1916 he testified that he had intended it only as "Stand by."[119] Peter Fisher, consistently with the ship's practice, interpreted the signal as the order to cast off. Lasser threw off the stern line, and apparently ran directly up the wharf to the bow to await orders from Del Fisher to throw off the three forward lines.[120] Weckler shouted down, however, ordering him not to cast off any of the lines because of the list. Pedersen issued no order to Del Fisher to cast off any of the forward lines, and all remained in place and taut.[121] The stern began to swing out from the wharf, as intended, and the bow swung in slightly toward the wharf. It should be stressed that the ship capsized while moving. As the ship moved out, passengers on the upper decks drifted away from the starboard rail—their first substantiated movement to port. Theodore Soderstrom, a survivor, estimated that several hundred people who had been waving to friends on the wharf moved toward the port rail, where people were already ten to twenty deep.[122] Dibbell reported that the majority of the passengers were at the port rail by the time of the capsizing.[123]

Knowing what Pedersen planned to do is important to understanding the orders he gave. He intended next to blow one short blast on the *East-*

land's whistle as a directive to the second mate to let go the lines aft—this is consistent with his statement that his buzzer signal had indicated only "Stand by." He expected the second mate to respond with a buzzer. He then planned to blow an unspecified blast for the *Kenosha* to stand by to take the bow out into the river. He assumed it would take O'Meara two minutes to get the tug into position. In the interim, Pedersen would have ordered the *Eastland*'s forward breast line and the head line let go. He wanted to get "a little twist on her" by leaving the spring line in place. He would then have ordered left rudder and gone ahead on the port engine to move the bow to port. As soon as the starboard screw was free of the wharf, he would have ordered the starboard engine astern, and ordered the spring line let go. O'Meara, on the *Kenosha*, would have blown for the Clark Street bridge to be opened. Pedersen would presumably then have ordered both engines ahead slow. He planned to whistle off the tug when the *Eastland* cleared the Rush Street bridge, and to proceed out into the lake in his usual fashion.[124]

O'Meara stood on the deck of the tug, waiting for five to seven minutes for the order to pull. He quickly became uneasy when the order failed to come. He planned to let go the *Kenosha*'s line on the pilings when the bridge opened.[125] Weckler called to him directing him neither to pull on the line from the *Eastland* nor to blow for the bridge on the ground that the bridge would not be opened until the ship had righted herself.[126] The directive, which Arthur MacDonald placed at only 30 seconds before the capsizing, was unnecessary. Being in an excellent position to observe the list, and having towed the ship on many previous occasions, O'Meara was one of the first figures in the event to recognize that a disaster was impending.

7:25 A.M. The *Eastland* made her third and last reversal of direction in the list to port.[127] There is no direct evidence of the magnitude, but it was considerably less than the second. Erickson stated that it lasted for about a minute,[128] but Pedersen estimated that it was only of a few seconds' duration.[129] Pedersen, who was confirmed by this in his view that the ship was recovering, left the flying bridge and walked back along the starboard side to supervise the casting off of the lines.[130] Erickson, who was by this time desperate in his efforts to right the ship, ordered Snow to start the port bilge pump to deal with the water coming in through the scuppers and gangways.[131]

7:27 A.M. The ship resumed her list to port, reaching an angle that Erickson estimated at 25 to 30 degrees. When she reached 20 degrees, the stokers and oilers in the boiler room and lower engine room concluded, partly from the list and partly from the water coming down from the deck above, that the ship was now doomed and went quickly up to the main

The ungainly package freighter *Schuylkill* of the Pennsylvania Railroad's Anchor Line was berthed opposite the *Petoskey* at the time of the disaster. Her crew was active in the rescue effort. The ships of this line were named after rivers in Pennsylvania. (Rev. Peter J. Van der Linden collection)

deck by the steel ladder running straight above them.[132] She stayed at the angle of 25 to 30 degrees for somewhat over a minute before the list continued.[133] When the list reached an estimated 33 degrees Peter Fisher asked the passengers on the hurricane deck to move to starboard, but the angle was too great and the deck too wet from the rain for them to comply.[134]

Oakley, who had left the *Eastland* when her passenger count reached 2,470, had counted approximately 120 passengers aboard the *Petoskey* when he noticed that the flow of people had slackened. Sensing what was happening, he went to a point from which he could see the *Eastland*. She had been listing to port by about 10 degrees when he left her, but he now estimated she was listing by 30 to 40 degrees.[135]

Still there was no general panic. The band on the *Theodore Roosevelt*, playing "I'm on My Way to Dear Old Dublin Bay," could be heard on the open decks. The crowd had so encroached on the *Eastland*'s dance floor that dancing had become impossible and Bradfield's Orchestra simply played ragtime to amuse the throng. The musicians dug in their heels to brace themselves against the list so as to keep playing. Ever since loading began, the passengers had treated the ship's listing as a joke, partly because of the convivial atmosphere of the excursion, partly because some of them were familiar with the *Eastland*'s habitual careening during loading and unloading. A survivor, George Olinger, told the Chicago *Evening Post* with respect to the list: "The people paid little attention to it at first,

but after it had rolled from side to side several times the boys and girls
began to make fun of it. When it would go over first on one side and then
on the other they would laugh and shout: 'All together, hey!' " [136]

7:28 A.M. The angle of list reached 45 degrees. The dishes began
slipping off the shelves and racks in the pantry, rousing in pantryman
Charles J. Ramond his first fears of what was impending.[137] In the dining
area chief steward Albert Wycoff saw his dishes fall out of the rack and
reported, "a scene of wild excitement followed." [138] The piano slid from
its position on the platform on the promenade deck, almost crushing two
women as it rolled to the port wall.[139] Bradfield's Orchestra stopped playing in the middle of a bar. It was probably at this time that the refrigerator behind the bar toppled over, producing a crash that could be heard
throughout the ship and thereby alerting the passengers generally that the
disaster was upon them.[140] As the refrigerator slid to port, it pinned a
woman or possibly two women beneath it.[141] Water poured in through the
aft port gangway and through the portholes on the main deck, most of
which were open. The passengers on the main deck were in a state of
panic, especially in attempting to go up the staircases to the 'tween decks.
Bodies on the wreck were found highly concentrated on the main deck
around the bottom of the main staircase. Early reports to the contrary notwithstanding, the staircase did not collapse, but the rush to it proved the
worst single trap for the passengers in the hull.[142] Erickson sent his brother
Peter to see once again if the ship's fender strake was hanging on the
wharf, but the young man was unable to make his way among the frantic
passengers to reach the starboard gangways.[143]

The panic was now universal. Pedersen finally recognized the condition
was hopeless and shouted down from the rail to Flatow on the wharf, "For
God's sake, open up your gangway." Flatow tried to comply, but there was
no time remaining.[144] Some passengers escaped through the open gangways or over the half doors, but as Pedersen recognized, his order to Flatow and the flight of passengers through the gangways added to the panic
inside the ship.[145] As passengers and members of the crew, plus Lobdell,
jumped off the ship to starboard, either onto the wharf or into the river,
they contributed to the problem by lightening the starboard side. By this
time the passengers on the port sides of the main and 'tween decks, in
particular, had virtually no chance to escape. The inflow of water and the
worsening distribution of the weight of the passengers accelerated the
movement of the ship to port, and she went into the river quickly, in not
more than two minutes. She went in quite gently. Fred G. Fischer, one of
two traffic policemen who had been assigned to watch the loading process,
said that she "just turned over like an egg in the water" and made no
splash.[146] The three forward lines were still in place. The spring line and

the head line ruptured, but the breast line, being new, held and pulled over the spile to which it was fastened until the loop at the end of the line came free.[147] Contrary to Lynn's fears, the wharf held.

7:30 A.M. The *Eastland* came to rest in the mud, with her bow 19.2 feet from the wharf in about 20 feet of water. The stern at the rudder was 37 feet out in water 23.5 feet deep, and at the farthest point of the 'tween decks 64.6 feet out in a depth of 22.9 feet. The hurricane deck was in about 24 feet of water fore and aft, with a maximum depth of 27.5 feet intermediate. The stern extended about 41.7 feet west of the east building line of La Salle Street, just over half of the way across the street.[148] Lynn estimated that the ship moved three to four feet upstream in the course of casting off her lines and capsizing.[149] As the wreck lay, the surface of the water coincided closely with the center line of the ship. The bow lay about two feet above the surface, but the stern slightly below it.[150] Because the vents from the ballast tanks were open, the port tanks filled with water and the starboard tanks drained in the capsizing—a point that was to be important in the civil trial.

O'Meara ordered the *Kenosha*'s line off the pilings and had it put onto the wharf as quickly as possible so that passengers who had crawled onto the starboard side of the wreck could use the tug as a bridge to the wharf.[151] This was considered one of the principal single acts in holding down loss of life. It is notable that no attempt was made to launch any of the *Eastland*'s own boats and rafts, nor to break out any of the life jackets or other lifesaving gear. The time interval from the deck officers' realizing the ship was doomed to the final capsizing was too short. There is no evidence that any of the officers even considered launching the boats and rafts. One of the *Eastland*'s boats floated free from its davit on the wreck and a six-year-old boy climbed into it.[152]

As the ship was sinking into her final position, Pedersen endeavored to pull himself into the pilot house with his right arm, but fell, hitting his head, incurring a headache, and, in his retrospective view, putting himself out of his head for the period immediately after the disaster.[153] Erickson, fearing an explosion when the cold water from the river hit the hot boiler shells, turned on the injectors to bring cold water into the boilers and reduce the temperature of the steel.[154] He stayed at his post until the water

---

Opposite: The wreck almost immediately after the disaster, as survivors attempt to find their way off the stern. Passengers standing on the propeller shaft are making use of the aft breast line as well as some lighter lines run out by the fire department. If Lobdell and Sladkey were correct that the aft breast line was cast off about 7:18, it was probably restored by the firemen in the foreground with the aid of the ladder at the edge of the wharf. (Chicago Historical Society)

reached his neck, but then made his way to the steering cable under the main deck on the starboard side and dragged himself up onto an air duct to a porthole, through which watchman Robert Brooks pulled him to safety.[155] Conrad grabbed a clamp at the top of the starboard forward gangway in which he was standing, hoisted himself up as the ship went over, and found safety on top of the hull.[156] Dibbell stayed by the starboard rail and climbed over it onto the hull as the ship turned beneath him.[157] Sailors knew what to do on a capsizing ship; the passengers, typically, did not.

CHAPTER FIVE

The
Immediate
Aftermath

Rescue

Efforts to rescue the passengers began even before the *East-land* settled into her final position in the mud. As related in Chapter IV, Joseph R. Lynn, the assistant harbormaster, went down about 7:24 A.M. from the Clark Street bridge to the wharf to test the three forward lines with his foot, estimated the *Eastland*'s list by sighting her against the vertical elements in the Reid-Murdoch building across the river, and then went up the stairway to tell harbormaster Adam F. Weckler that the ship was now in a hopeless position. Lynn then proceeded to a public telephone near the south abutment of the bridge and phoned to the fire department for assistance. By the clock on the Reid-Murdoch building, the time was 7:29.[1] The closest firehouse was—where it remains—on the east side of Dearborn between South Water and Lake streets, barely more than a block from the scene. When John Lescher, the policeman who had stood with Fred Fischer at the gangplank during loading, saw the ship go into her final plunge, he ran up the stairs to Clark Street to a police call box, where he turned in his alarm, probably not more than a minute after Lynn alerted the fire department.[2] The Coast Guard estimated that its men arrived within ten minutes of receiving notification of the disaster.[3] Consequently, trained rescue personnel were at hand almost immediately upon the ship's coming to rest at 7:30.

The first nurse arrived almost simultaneously. Western Electric had planned a hospital tent on the picnic grounds at Michigan City, to be staffed by three nurses from the medical facility at the Hawthorne plant. The three had agreed to cross on the *Theodore Roosevelt* at 8:00. One of the nurses, Helen Repa, in full uniform, was approaching the wharf area on a streetcar on Lake Street when she heard the sound of screams above the noise of the streetcar and over the roar of traffic. A mounted policeman stopped traffic, including the streetcar, explaining that an excursion boat had been upset. Because the accident had occurred at the Chicago & South Haven wharf, there were some immediate rumors that the ship was the *City of South Haven*. Ms. Repa correctly concluded the ship was one of the vessels for the picnic, got off the streetcar, climbed onto the back step of one of the first ambulances reporting to the scene, went to the wharf, and made her way against the flow of survivors onto the exposed starboard side of the *Eastland*. She reported:

> I shall never be able to forget what I saw. People were struggling in the water, clustered so thickly that they literally covered the surface of the river. A few were swimming; the rest were floundering about, some clinging to a life raft that had floated free, others clutching at anything that they could reach—at bits of wood, at each other, grabbing each other, pulling each other down, and screaming! The screaming was the most horrible of all.[4]

Ms. Repa began her ministrations with an effort at resuscitation of the unconscious, and later tried to deal with cuts and bruises. Survivors from the decks or the interior of the ship were typically badly cut because chairs and benches had slid down on top of them.

One of the first physicians to arrive was Dr. Thomas A. Carter of the Chicago Health Department, who served as head police ambulance surgeon for the city. He began examining unconscious victims as they were brought to the wharf, attempting to find a pulse in the neck. If he did so, he called for a pulmotor. If he could find no signs of life, he merely said, "Gone," and proceeded to the next person.[5]

Rescue efforts from the river side of the wreck came more slowly. The fireboat *Graeme Stewart* was only two blocks away, but her response was slow. A passerby, John Parotto, testified in a statement of 1919 that he had been on the Wells Street bridge when he observed both the initial list to starboard and the early list to port. He had run over to the *Graeme Stewart* at her berth at the foot of Franklin Street and told a crew member that the *Eastland* was going to tip over. The crew member responded that Parotto was crazy, that the *Eastland* was not turning over, and that the crew of the fireboat was at breakfast.[6] Frank Actobowski, an employee of the produce firm of Edward McFadden at South Water and Wells streets, claimed to have notified the crew of the *Graeme Stewart* immediately after the capsizing.[7] Even then, the fireboat did not approach the scene of the disaster quickly. The captain, Patrick Lyons, was accused of delaying on the west side of the Wells Street bridge for about ten minutes out of fear of a boiler explosion on the wreck.[8] Lyons denied this, stating that the river was too clogged with people for him initially to approach more closely than Wells Street.[9] Helen Repa's account appears to bear him out.

The police were accused of a similar reluctance to go aboard the wreck. Charles Smith, a teamster who threw some ropes to survivors in the river, reported that firemen went aboard at once, but he saw no police on the hull for about half an hour, because, he thought, of fear of an explosion. He thought they could have saved 25 to 50 people by going onto the wreck immediately.[10]

Proximity to the South Water Street produce market was an essentially unmixed benefit. In spite of the early hour, practically all of the labor force was already at work, and news of the disaster spread almost instantaneously. A produce market inevitably has at hand a large number of wooden crates and cases, which quickly became the principal lifesaving devices in the disaster. In particular, the firm of Cougel Brothers at La Salle and South Water streets was a specialist in poultry with a big supply of empty chicken coops and egg crates, which quickly went into the river. One employee said he threw at least 25 chicken coops into the water, and estimated that 200 or more were thrown in by others.[11] William P. Kearney estimated that 250 to 300 were thrown in and that 20 to 30 passengers survived by clutching the coops that he alone had thrown in.[12] Sherwood S. Mattocks, who arrived almost at the instant of capsizing, found a gangplank and two loose planks, threw them into the river, and then pushed a flat-bottomed boat into the stream, from which he saved an estimated seven passengers.[13] Charles Nicholas Klein, an employee of the firm of Alex Getz on South Water Street, took off his coat, vest, hat, and shoes, jumped into the river, and assisted fifteen girls and one man to safety. He then went aboard the wreck and pulled four people out of a gangway and a girl through a porthole. He tried to pull a woman through a porthole, but she proved too large to pass through it, sank back in, and died.[14] William Raphael, manager of one of the produce houses, dove into the river and was pulling two women to safety when someone he described only as a fat man clutched the dress of one of the women. Raphael kicked him in the face, but the woman, along with the fat man, was drowned. A. W. Perkins, an express driver who had just come off duty, was wearing his bathing suit under his suit, preparing to go to the beach. He stripped down to it, dove in, saved one woman, lost another, and returned to save two girls. Edward

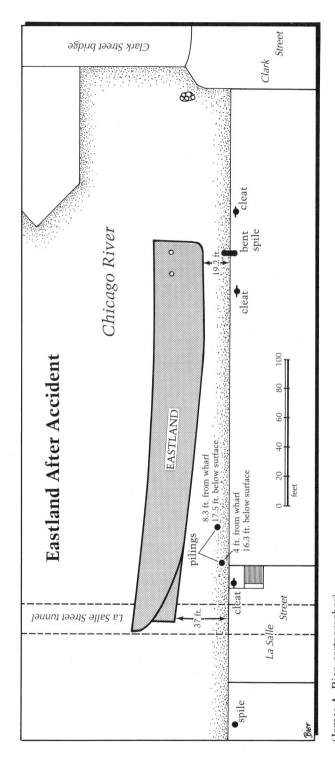

Eastland After Accident

Clark Street bridge

Clark Street

Chicago River

cleat

cleat

bent spile

cleat

EASTLAND

8.3 ft. from wharf
17.5 ft. below surface

4 ft. from wharf
16.3 ft. below surface

19.2 ft.

pilings

0   20   40   60   80   100
feet

cleat

La Salle Street tunnel

37 ft.

cleat

La Salle Street

spile

Bier

(James A. Bier, cartographer)

Atkin found a small boat under the Clark Street bridge and rescued what he estimated at 20 people.[15] An unidentified man who had been lurking in the area, contemplating suicide in the river, instead jumped in, pulled out nine people, and was himself dragged out exhausted.[16] The produce market was scoured for ropes, which were thrown into the river to assist the people clutching the crates and boxes to reach the shore.

The efforts of volunteers to assist survivors were to bulk large in the later legal history of the disaster. By their exertions they gained legal status at admiralty law as life salvors, who then had a claim against the owner of the ship, or as it proved, against the value of the hulk. They would appear as an organized group in the civil trial that followed the disaster, as will be discussed below.

Boats quickly arrived on the scene. Although the *Eastland* had launched none, the *Theodore Roosevelt, Petoskey*, and *Racine* did so within minutes. The crew of the *Schuylkill* began throwing out lines almost immediately. Edward Johnson and Frank Kehoe, who were in the river with the workboat *Siren*, brought the craft to the stern of the *East-*

A scene relatively early in the rescue operation. The *Petoskey* in the background had not yet been moved past the wreck to the Rush Street wharf. (Chicago Historical Society)

land. Because of the *Siren*'s origins as a yacht, she had a graceful clipper bow that allowed her to extend well over the *Eastland*'s hull, making her easy to board. Johnson jumped into the river and assisted about 30 people into the craft. He then climbed into a boat from the *Petoskey*, which he found half-filled with water. He was afraid it would sink, but pulled about 15 survivors into it.[17] The *Kenosha*, thanks to O'Meara's early recognition of the impending disaster and his positioning of her as a bridge from the wreck to the wharf, assisted several hundred survivors to land. Dunham's tugs *Racine, Waukegan, Indiana,* and *Rita McDonald* shortly responded. When the *Graeme Stewart* arrived, she pulled up to the partly submerged hurricane deck of the *Eastland* and, having a strong and deep hull, inflicted considerable damage on the deck, rigging, and stacks. The disaster per se, however appalling in loss of life, did little damage to the *Eastland*, but the rescue and salvage efforts were to do a great deal. The City of Chicago also responded with the fireboat *D. J. Swenie*, the tug *Chicago Harbor No. 4*, and the police patrol vessel *Carter H. Harrison*, which became the city's central authority for direction of the rescue efforts. The Erie Railroad's harbor tug *Alice Stafford* proved one of the most useful vessels, taking about 50 survivors to safety. The Merchant's Lighterage Company's *Commerce* also assisted in the rescue.[18] The operation was quick and thorough. Marie Chudik, who walked by the site at 8:00 A.M. on her way to board the *Christopher Columbus* for Milwaukee, reported that virtually all of the survivors had been pulled out of the river by the time she passed.[19]

Meanwhile, Captain William T. Bright had brought the Northern Michigan Transportation Company's *Missouri* into the berth that the company shared with the *Eastland* just east of the Rush Street bridge. He heard of the disaster almost immediately and took a cab to the Clark Street wharf. He went to the second floor of one of the produce houses and observed that the survivors coming out of the hull were having great difficulty climbing off the exposed starboard side onto the *Kenosha*. He shouted from the window that ashes should be taken from the fireboxes of the three tugs that were then on the scene and distributed on the *Eastland*'s bow to give the survivors better traction.[20] The ashes were spread about quickly, and became conspicuous in photographs of the wreck.

The experiences of the survivors demonstrate a consistent pattern. Those who were on deck or in proximity to gangways on the starboard side mainly survived; those who were deep in the hull and on the port side in general did not. People in intermediate situations had mixed prospects of survival. The most favorably situated were passengers on the open decks on the starboard side, who could crawl over the rail onto the hull as the ship capsized. E. W. Sladkey was still talking with his subordinates

One of the holes cut in the hull to facilitate rescue operations is visible in this photograph taken while bodies were still being removed from the wreck. The spile pulled over by the forward breast line is evident, along with the line itself. The other ships shown are the large city fireboat *Graeme Stewart* and the smaller tug *J. W. Taylor*. (Chicago Historical Society)

along the starboard rail forward on the promenade deck when the ship began going over. He held tightly onto the rail until the port rail went into the water, then climbed over the starboard rail and onto the hull. From there he jumped onto the deck of the *Kenosha* and walked to safety without even wetting his feet.[21] Most of the people in his area had nothing to hold onto and were swept into the water. The *Examiner* reported that several hundred passengers survived by reaching the starboard rail and climbing over it as Sladkey did.[22] Many of the people on the covered portion of the promenade deck assisted themselves over the rail with short lines of rope hanging down from the overhead. Of the approximately 150 passengers on the hurricane deck, George Haber estimated from his vantage point on the wharf that 12 jumped, probably to starboard to reach the exposed hull or the wharf, and the rest were pitched into the river.[23] Henry Vantak, who was on the ship, made exactly the same estimate.[24] Anyone in the river, owing to the immediate response of rescue personnel and the life salvors, plus a large amount of floating furniture from the ship, had a good chance of surviving.

Although the event was actually of 50 minutes' duration, the capsizing as the passengers perceived it occurred abruptly at 7:28. The virtually instantaneous nature of the disaster in the passengers' perception constituted a very random element in their survival. This, in turn, explains one of the worst aspects of the disaster, the extent to which it knifed through families and groups of friends, quickly killing some members while leaving others with physical injuries no worse than bruises—plus psychological trauma to be borne for life. Harry Evenhouse stood talking with his sisters, Anna and Jennie, on the main deck, starboard side, when the plunge came. His sisters were swept down to port by gravity with the rest of passengers, but his own foot caught in something he could not identify, and he was held back. He extricated himself and climbed out of a gangway onto the hull. His sisters had no chance of survival and were killed.[25] Joseph Brozak was saved when his coat caught on a nail, but his four companions were all lost.[26] Mrs. Albert Pierson was sitting on the starboard side on an open deck—probably the promenade deck—with her husband, when he excused himself to go to the smoking room. The ship capsized almost immediately, Pierson was killed, and his widow escaped with nothing worse than a severe gash on her left arm.[27] In the same fashion, Joseph Valchar left his wife, Mary, on deck to go below to search for friends. Mary survived, but he did not.[28] Henry H. Thyer, his wife, Helen, and their two children, Harry and Helen, stood together on deck, and were all pitched into the river. Mrs. Thyer endeavored to hold onto both her children, but lost her grip on her daughter, who was lost along with her husband. A Chicago city fireman rescued Mrs. Thyer and her son.[29] Mildred Anderson, a member of the Hawthorne Club's organizing committee for the excursion, stood talking with her sister, Lottie, and eight other young women in a parlor engaged by the club. Like most of the rest of the passengers, they paid no attention to the swaying until the ship suddenly began to turn over. Mildred Anderson kept her position on the ship, but Lottie was plunged into the river. Lottie was initially said to have died, but was later reported to have been saved from the river by use of ropes.[30]

However irrelevant the prospect may have been to the calculations of Hull and Greenebaum when they wrote into the charter party contract that the *Eastland* should be the first ship out on the excursion, that provision exacerbated the problem of the disaster's killing randomly through families. This provision, by assuring that the steamer would be filled, caused people randomly to be sent to the *Theodore Roosevelt* or the *Petoskey* after the loading of the *Eastland* ended, about 7:10. Marie Krebel, a Western

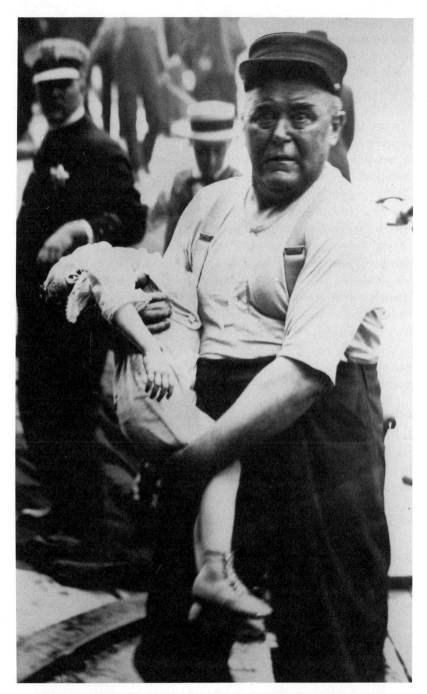

This famous photograph by Jun Fujita shows one of the men who worked around the wharves carrying the body of a drowned child. The horror in his face symbolized the tragedy to newspaper readers nationwide. (Chicago Historical Society)

Electric employee, boarded the *Eastland*, but her brother Andrew Krebel and his wife took the *Theodore Roosevelt*. The couple stood on the open deck watching the *Eastland* go over, having the harrowing experience of fearing that Marie was dying before their eyes, followed by verifying that she had, indeed, done so.[31] Margaret Smith boarded the *Eastland*, planning to rendezvous there with her brother Harry, who had worked for Western Electric for five years. Simply by mistake, Harry boarded one of the later steamers. Margaret, who was twenty and single, was killed.[32] Loss of friends and working associates owing to separation between steamers was common.

Hundreds of people could report that they had only narrowly escaped boarding the *Eastland*. Frank Collias of Flint, Michigan, who was in Chicago to buy equipment for his projected shoe-shining parlor, had planned to take the excursion with some friends. Approaching the wharf, he encountered some people whom he had not seen since his youth in Greece. He decided to have a round of drinks with them, and to take the *Theodore Roosevelt* instead of the *Eastland*.[33] E. T. Clippert of Detroit stopped in a barber shop for a shave, and arrived at the *Eastland* about three minutes after the gangplank had been drawn in.[34]

As a consequence of the abruptness of the capsizing, there were few examples of laborious or prolonged escapes. Such as there were occurred mainly among people in the hull who worked their way straight up from the port side of the wreck to the starboard to escape through a porthole or by one of the apertures cut in the hull by the rescue squads. Crew members, partly because they were in a less crowded part of the hull, partly because they were familiar with the ship, were in a better position to do this than the passengers. Charles Silvernail reported that he fought against the water for 30 minutes before he could escape out the starboard side.[35] Jay Fisher, an oiler, went up the ladder from the lower engine room when he heard Snow's warning whistle, then after the ship had capsized, climbed up to a porthole, through which he emerged onto the hull to await rescue.[36] Ray Davis, who had been a football player at the University of Michigan, worked his way out of the wreck into the river, and rather easily swam to safety.[37] Not all the tortuous escapes were accomplished by crew members, however. A passenger, Annette Jarolin, jumped from the port rail just as the ship was going into the water, sank deeply, and came up through a port window into Pedersen's cabin, from which she climbed out a starboard window to safety.[38]

Similarly, the ship's capsizing was so abrupt that there were few tales of courtesy or heroism demonstrated in the course of the plunge itself, but there were some. Agnes Summit, who was picked up from the water by the *Kenosha*'s crew, told reporters that she had seen men give women the first chance to escape.[39] Albert Turek, a passenger, saved seven people from the river before an eighth dragged him to his own death.[40] Such stories were the exception, however. Most survivors and observers reported that almost everyone pursued only his or her own survival, and that on the whole the women acquitted themselves better than the men. The *Tribune* reported:

In the crisis the women were the stronger. While men fought madly for their lives the women and girls, after the first panic, quickly recovered. Either they clung patiently to rails and bits of wreckage, or, if trapped in the hull, they waited calmly for rescue or death. Rescued, their thoughts for the most part were of those not so fortunate. With the men it was different. They dragged the women from places of temporary safety in order that they might be saved. They struggled madly to save life, not for others, but for themselves. And some, when rescued, stood stunned and helpless watching others at work.[41]

Some specific evidence is consistent with this. Anna Goldnick, who lost her friend Eleanor Doneske, reported seeing men tear clothing, lifesaving equipment, and chairs from women in their efforts to survive.[42]

The abruptness of the disaster also affected the role of the clergy. Because the great majority of passengers were Roman Catholics, the priestly function in the rescue was extremely important. Seven priests were reported in the press to have served. The first to arrive was Father Thomas Kelly of the Precious Blood parish on the near West Side; he reached the scene at about 7:50. His first act was to administer conditional absolution to all aboard. Four priests came from the Holy Name Cathedral shortly afterward, led by Father M. J. Fitzsimmons, administrator of the archdiocese. Father John O'Hearn went immediately into the hull, where he heard confession from about a dozen men and women. Fathers Herman Wolff and D. J. Dunne stood on the hull to anoint the foreheads of both the living and the dead as they were brought out on stretchers.[43] Fathers Edward Mullaley and P. J. O'Callaghan of St. Mary's parish were also reported at the scene by the Chicago *Daily Journal*. The *Journal*, ignoring that the priestly function applies also to the dead, made a valid point—albeit in offensive terminology—that the disaster, by producing few lingering deaths, limited what the priests could accomplish among the living: "There was little work for them. The result of the *Eastland*'s somersault could be phrased in two words—living or dead." [44]

Inevitably, stories arose of premonitions of the disaster. Had the accident never occurred, such presentiments would quickly have been forgotten or dismissed as neurotic fears. In retrospect, they appear as part of the rational evaluation of the ship by her passengers. Mamie Ponicki, 18, an employee of Sears, Roebuck, who was to go on the trip as a date, left home Saturday morning saying, "Good-bye, Mother; I may never see you again."[45] In the best-documented example, Paul Jahnke, an electrician at Western Electric, and his wife, Louise, who had been married only six weeks, were explicitly afraid of the *Eastland*. As they left for the excursion, Jahnke left his keys with their landlady, Mrs. Paul Altman, with $50 to be given to his mother if they did not return. His wife told her mother, Josie Markowska, that something awful was going to happen, such that she did not want to make the trip. Mrs. Markowska told her to go, have a good time, and not think about an accident lest she bring it on.[46] Miss Ponicki and Mr. and Mrs. Jahnke were all killed.

The *Eastland*'s situation required a field hospital and, inevitably, a very great deal of morgue space. The American Red Cross was alerted immediately, and only about half an hour later its local director, John J. O'Connor, was formulating plans for relief.[47] By coincidence, the employees of Reid-Murdoch, a wholesale grocery firm, were also having their annual picnic on July 24, leaving a large, modern building virtually empty immediately across the river from the wreck. A receiving facility for the survivors who required medical attention was established on the ground floor. Reid-Murdoch authorized the Red Cross to make use of any food on the shelves that might be of help to the survivors. The Sherman and La Salle hotels along with the Weeghman and Thompson restaurant chains sent sandwiches, and the major Loop department stores sent blankets and cots. Survivors who were in good condition were mainly housed under awnings of the produce firms to protect them from the rain until they felt able to leave. Nurse Repa thought that such survivors were better off with their families as soon as possible, and endeavored to send them home quickly. She simply hailed the first passing motorist, loaded his car with survivors and asked him to take them home. She reported that not a single motorist refused.[48] The American Express Company put its entire fleet of trucks at the disposal of the rescue workers.[49] About 150 survivors who required emergency treatment or bed rest were taken, depending on their condition, either to the Sherman Hotel, to the Franklin Emergency Hospital, or to the Iroquois Memorial Hospital, a facility on Market Street that had been established in honor of the victims of the Iroquois Theatre fire of 1903—previously the city's worst disaster—specifically to treat emergencies.

The first ten bodies recovered were brought to the *Theodore Roosevelt*, the passengers of which were evacuated, but then a morgue was established in the basement of the Reid-Murdoch building. From the outset some of the bodies were taken directly to mortuaries in the immediate area.[50] A central morgue was established on Saturday afternoon at the Second Regiment Armory on Washington Boulevard at Curtis Street, to which bodies were brought throughout the day. They were laid in rows of 85. Most could not be immediately identified, and were simply assigned numbers. Their possessions were placed in large envelopes marked with their respective numbers.

People who had reason to believe that their relatives were among the victims at the Armory were admitted shortly before midnight, twenty at a time, to begin identification. A telephone line was run to a taxicab placed immediately outside the Armory. People in the queue were interrogated there to spare them the ordeal of search if the bodies had already been identified or if the person being sought had been found among the survivors. This process was also an attempt to screen out the morbidly curious, who were unfortunately numerous—considerably more numerous than the people seeking to identify victims. The screening effort was unsuccessful, and by the end of the day anyone who wished was admitted. Nonetheless, the identification process went off generally quietly until the early hours of Sunday morning, when a mixture of emotional strain and lack of sleep caused several people to break down, and a few to lapse into deranged laughter. As the Red Cross report correctly concluded, "The heartrending scenes of the Armory had better be left undescribed."[51] By 7:00 A.M. on Sunday, Red Cross nurses had cared for 30 hysterical and exhausted women.

Identification of the victims was a depressing and impersonal process. This morgue was set up in the Second Regiment Armory the afternoon of the disaster. (Chicago Historical Society)

When a body was identified, one of the volunteers from Western Electric who manned the morgue would shout "Identified," and the body would be taken to an enclave established by the coroner for the death certificate to be made out. On the basis of early examinations, Coroner's Office physician Joseph Springer concluded from the presence or absence of water in lungs that most of the victims recovered from the wreck had died of suffocation rather than drowning.[52] The Coroner's Office, however, bought a rubber stamp reading, "Drowned, July 24, 1915, from steamer EASTLAND, Chicago River at Clark Street," with which it imprinted the death certificates, ending any inquiry as to suffocation versus drowning.

Municipal authorities threw wire nets across the river at La Salle Street and at the Randolph and Harrison Street bridges to prevent bodies from moving up the South Branch.[53] A phone call was made to Lockport to close a bear-trap dam to stop the flow in the river. The current had stopped by about 10:00 A.M. Saturday.[54] In the expectation that stopping the current might cause some bodies to move east, an additional net was placed under the Clark Street bridge.

Rescue efforts continued throughout the day. Charles Klein estimated that he brought 42 bodies out of the hull, and as late as 3:30 P.M. found a woman alive in it, wedged between a barrel and some rubbish.[55] After rescuing her, he collapsed from ingesting a great deal of river water, and was taken to Iroquois Hospital, where he was kept until midnight. In his case and more generally among the survivors, public health authorities worried about exposure in the river to typhoid and other diarrheal infections. The river was apparently cleared enough to allow ships to pass the site of the disaster, for the *Petoskey*, along with the *Rochester*, was reported to be taking the Indiana Transportation Company's regular departures for Michigan City from the Rush Street wharf later in the day.[56]

The officers of the ship were engaged in rescue operations until about 10:00 A.M Saturday.[57] At that point there arose a conflict between Pedersen and the police who were superintending the rescue. The police proposed to cut with acetylene torches into the exposed portion of the hull for access to passengers who might still be alive. Pedersen, along with Del Fisher, objected, according to Pedersen's detractors because he wanted to preserve the structural integrity of his ship, but according to him because the police were about to cut into the coal bunker.[58] Pedersen proposed to cut in above the soda counter on the 'tween decks. The police appear to have been correct. The cut that Pedersen had sought to prevent was made, and about 40 people were led to safety through the opening. As a result of this episode Pedersen and a reported 14 others from the officers, crew, and management were arrested for interference with the rescue effort. Pedersen gave his oilcloth coat to a survivor, a Mrs. Ralson, and went off to City

Hall for arraignment. On the way a man broke through Pedersen's police guard to hit him in the face.[59] The view that his behavior had been negligent was already widespread.

Thereafter the rescue effort was conducted or at least supervised almost unilaterally by the police. They had already put an end to the independent efforts of the life salvors. Otto J. Blaha, an employee of the Waskow Butter Company on South Water Street, had thrown some egg cases and chicken coops into the river and then threw out some ropes to survivors. He claimed to have saved a girl, age nine, and a boy, fourteen. After a few more rescue attempts, the police ordered him off the wharf.[60] Daniel P. Brazill, who worked at 111 South Water Street, cut ropes from some fifteen wagons and threw them into the river to assist survivors to shore until the police ordered him to stop.[61] Inevitably, the disaster attracted a huge crowd of onlookers. The police cordoned off the streets for a block in each direction from the river. So many onlookers crowded onto the Clark Street bridge that there was a real danger of its collapsing, but the police shortly ordered the public off it. There was, in fact, a secondary accident, although not a major one. Twenty-one of the bodies had been taken to the P. J. Gavin & Sons mortuary at 642 North Clark Street. A small crowd seeking identification of the deceased gathered outside on the sidewalk, which gave way, plunging the group into the basement, injuring seven people, two seriously.[62]

Placing the rescue efforts in the hands of the police and other professionals was probably desirable. Nurse Repa complained that at about 9:30 "A crowd of willing but ignorant volunteers kept getting in the way, and made our attempts at resuscitation almost useless." [63] By that time the rain was coming down heavily, further impeding the rescue efforts. Nonetheless, Ms. Repa reported that by noon bodies were being brought up from the interior of the ship. After that, almost all of the bodies recovered were of women and children; she speculated that mothers had taken their children into the cabins to escape the drizzle of the morning.[64] At 2:30 the Red Cross announced, apparently erroneously, that all of the bodies above water had been removed from the hull, and stated correctly that eight professional divers were at work in the portions of the wreck below water.[65]

Excluding the public had the additional attraction of getting rid of a criminal element, which took advantage of the situation for petty theft. Two men were arrested for picking the pockets of onlookers, and another for posing as a life salvor to steal wallets of the deceased. Farther away, some criminals, upon learning the identities of the deceased, robbed their homes. Later, others attempted confidence schemes on the heirs in connection with the prospect of a financial settlement.[66]

News of the disaster spread quickly about the city both by word of

This postcard shows the eight divers—seven in diving gear—who removed bodies from the submerged portion of the wreck immediately after the disaster. (Rev. Peter J. Van der Linden collection)

mouth and by extra editions of newspapers. The city had at that time three major league baseball teams, two of which had games scheduled for that afternoon. The White Sox were to play the New York Yankees at Comiskey Park and the Chicago Whales of the Federal League were scheduled against the Baltimore Terrapins at Weeghman Park—the present Wrigley Field—on a day promoted in honor of the Whales' manager, Joe Tinker. The Cubs were in Boston, but the *Tribune* had scheduled a scouting session for amateur and semi-professional players at their ball park on the West Side. All of these events were quickly called off in honor of the victims.[67] As it proved, the games would not have been played in any case, for the rain continued throughout the day. The weather served as a perfectly appropriate setting for what was rapidly developing as the worst day in loss of life in the city's entire history.

There was also no cheer in Michigan City. The excursion was immediately called off when the disaster occurred. An advance party of Western Electric workers had been there for two days. Bunting had been set in place along Franklin Street, the city's principal thoroughfare. Floats for a parade scheduled to proceed up the street from Washington Park at noon were at the ready in the Indiana Transportation Company's freight house on the wharf. Louise Radoll, who was to have been queen of the procession, had died on the *Eastland*.[68] Hotels and restaurants had reportedly doubled their supplies of provisions for the day.[69] A banquet had been arranged at the Vreeland Hotel.[70] The disaster ended the Western Electric picnic permanently; it was never attempted again.

One of the figures who would probably have been most prominent in the immediate aftermath of the disaster was not in the city. Mayor William Hale Thompson, along with the governor of Illinois, Edward F. Dunne, was in San Francisco for ceremonies at the Illinois pavilion at the Panama-Pacific Exposition, to be culminated with Chicago Day on the following Tuesday, July 27. The planned events were canceled in favor of a memorial service at the Exposition. Upon receiving news of the disaster Thompson immediately arranged for a special section of the Overland Limited to return the Illinois party to Chicago. In an interview in Omaha during the trip, he stated that he had once traveled on the *Eastland*, but had been afraid that she would capsize, and was never willing to ride her again.[71]

In Thompson's absence, Acting Mayor William R. Moorhouse executed the functions of the mayor quite decisively. Notably, he ordered wooden panels eight feet high put along the Clark Street and Wells Street bridges to screen out the morbidly curious.[72] A janitor at a local building admitted passengers to the roof for ten cents to watch removal of bodies, and on

A diver prepares to go down onto the submerged portion of the main deck of the *Eastland*, probably during the search for victims. (Chicago Historical Society)

Saturday owners of launches took viewers past the wreck for ten or fifteen cents. Such craft were ordered away on Sunday.[73] Inevitably, such prohibitions were only partly successful; an estimated 500,000 people came to the Loop to view the wreck on Sunday alone.

Retrospective views of the ship quickly became common in the press. The Chicago *Tribune* had about twenty hours following the disaster to prepare its coverage for the Sunday edition. The paper did a superb job, fully covering the events of the disaster itself, and digging into the ship's history. In particular, the *Tribune* interviewed William J. Wood and published an extensive account of his involvement with the *Eastland*'s trial under the incentive contract by which she was built, and his work on the revisions to her before the 1904 season.[74] It was not difficult for the *Tribune* to document the ship's stability problems in her earlier operation on Lake Michigan and also in her service on Lake Erie. The event of July 17, 1904, was particularly well documented and easy to use as an example of the ship's chronic problems. Unfortunately, her recent history went almost unnoted. The changes of July 2, 1915, were not mentioned.

However, on page 8 of the issue there appeared an inconspicuous short article entitled "Seamen's Law Blamed for Accident by Ship Owner: It Causes Boats to be Topheavy by Adding Unnecessary Equipment." It proved to be an interview not with a shipowner but rather with A. A. Schantz, general manager of the Detroit & Cleveland Navigation Company, whose recommendation had caused Hull and his associates to buy the *Eastland* in 1914 for return to Lake Michigan. Schantz was quoted as saying with respect to the La Follette Seamen's Act:

From what I have learned of the accident I am convinced it was due in part at least to the presence of life rafts and other heavy equipment required by this law. When the bill was before congress we argued that some such accident was likely to occur, but they laughed at us. The boat was simply top-heavy and turned turtle—an accident that couldn't possibly have occurred had it been properly trimmed.[75]

In wire dispatches Saturday evening the staff of the New York *Times* noted as a possible cause of the accident the installation of lifesaving equipment in preparation for imposition of the La Follette Seamen's Act. On the 25th it raised the question with Secretary of Commerce William C. Redfield, who was to undertake an inquiry into the disaster but had not yet done so. Reasoning a priori rather than bothering to ascertain what equipment the ship had, Redfield wired back to the *Times* that because the *Eastland* was used in summers only, and the act would not be in force until November, any changes in the ship would not be made until the following June. The *Times* concluded editorially from his response that the interpretation of the disaster as being caused by "changes [that] had lately been made in the equipment of the *Eastland* [was] founded on rumors which lack verification."[76] Accordingly, the correct explanation of the disaster was in print in Chicago on Sunday and elsewhere by Monday, but it was ignored or rejected and played no role in the efforts to assign blame, seek retribution, and assure equity in the financial settlement.

The *Tribune* followed the ship's history for several days, securing an evaluation of her by John Devereaux York, a local naval architect who had become suspicious of the ship during her earlier service out of Chicago. York argued that her virtual absence of a keel and her complete absence of bilge keels contributed to her instability.[77] Great Lakes ships generally have relatively flat bottoms with very little keel. Thus this explanation passed from notice quickly.

Claude M. Ennes, one of the *Eastland*'s captains during her service on Lake Erie, suggested that the disaster might have stemmed at least in part from portholes below the fender strake that had been left open.[78] Erickson testified that prior to loading on Saturday morning he had checked the deadlights—the Great Lakes term for the covers of portholes—and found that they had been closed by the watchman in the course of his regular duties, with the exception of one or two, which Erickson closed himself. Erickson believed that no water had come in from this source.[79] Diver Harry Halvorson, who examined the portholes below the fender strake on the wreck, found eleven closed and two at the bow open.[80] They were probably not a source of water until quite late in the capsizing. Unfortunately, other casual explanations of the disaster also arose quickly and persisted far longer. In particular, the *Tribune* published a statement by John V. Elbert, the gauge tender, that the capsizing had been caused by a rush of passengers to port to see a passing launch.[81] The management accepted the alleged rush to port as its initial explanation. By September Hull had combined this with a presumption that the ship had been resting on pilings near the wharf, such that the leverage pulled her over.[82] This explanation persisted throughout the legal actions and, even though thoroughly refuted in the testimony, has survived on a popular level to the present day.

The *Tribune*'s conclusion from its inquiries into the history of the ship is the most succinct that could have been drawn from the disaster: "The ugliest of facts is that not what was unexpected but what was expected and predicted happened."[83]

It is instructive parenthetically to contrast the *Tribune*'s view with Robert M. La Follette's. Oblivious to the fact that preparations for imposition of his act had been a proximate cause of the disaster, in an editorial in his weekly magazine entitled "A Sacrifice to Greed," he attributed the disaster to avarice on the part of Hull and to "loose inspection laws and lax regulations of the government." He argued that his Seamen's Act would have prevented the disaster by lowering the *Eastland*'s capacity to little more than 1,000 passengers.[84] In this, he may well have been right. If the ship had not been further modified, her capacity would probably have been reduced to some figure consistent with the 1,123 people she carried safely on the Masonic excursion of July 23. Andrew Furuseth, who interpreted the disaster as showing the hand of God in answer to those who sought repeal of the Seamen's Act, made the same argument as La Follette, estimating that the act would have limited the *Eastland* to 1,200 passengers.[85] Given the *Eastland*'s marginal stability, one cannot predict with certainty what would have happened to her after the act became effective for her 1916 season, but the disaster in the form it took could have occurred only when it did: on the one occasion when she was fully loaded in the transitional period between passage of the act and its effective date of November 4.

Efforts at notification of the families of the victims and the survivors began immediately after the disaster. The absence of a passenger list on the *Eastland* was to make identification—alike of victims and survivors—infinitely more difficult than it had been after the three major ocean disasters of the preceding years. Within fifteen minutes of the capsizing, Western Electric employees had begun collecting names of survivors and phoning relatives from the warehouse of the Sprague Warner Company, a wholesale grocery firm on the North Branch at Erie Street. An empty store was shortly located at 214 North Clark Street and simply broken into to serve as a headquarters. When the owner of the store was located, he declined compensation for its use. A functioning central information bureau had been established in the store by 9:30 A.M. By 10:00, Illinois Bell had installed a line to which it assigned a number that quickly developed local fame, Franklin 188. The owner of an adjacent store volunteered its use, and the telephone company expanded the number of phones to twenty. A system of alphabetical lists combined with index cards was set up to record information on death or survival, and to record the phone numbers of those who had called. At 2:30 Western Electric and the Red Cross opened a telephone station at the employment office of the Hawthorne plant to coordinate information with personnel records and to deal with inquiries.[86] A third inquiry office was set up on the bandstand gallery of the Armory on Sunday morning.

Western Electric's chief operator at the Hawthorne plant, Margaret Condon, had planned to go on the picnic, and arrived at the wharf at 7:30, exactly when the capsizing occurred. She recognized that she could do nothing there, and returned home. A call from Western Electric awaited her, requesting that she superintend the phone station at the plant. She complied and worked continuously for 34 hours, from about 1:00 P.M. on Saturday until late Sunday night. One of her subordinates, when notified of the loss of a sister, came in for three hours of volunteer work as a method of distracting herself from grief.[87]

The dissemination of information was necessarily imperfect. After Helen Repa was seen going onto the wreck, someone reported to the telephone station that she had climbed over the side and fallen into the river. After the misinformation was relayed to her home, her sister came down to search the morgues and emergency rooms. The sister found Ms. Repa working over a man in the emergency facility in the Reid-Murdoch building, shouted, "My God, it's Helen!" and fainted.[88]

In general, the identification process produced a consistent picture of the victims as being Western Electric employees, their families, friends, and especially their dates. Standing out from this was one anomaly, a man named John Hilles. As far as could be ascertained, he had come to Chicago specifically to take the excursion and had spent one night in Elsner's Hotel on Halsted Street, but left no record of where he lived and no evidence that he had any relation to Western Electric or to any of the other passengers.[89]

By the morning of Friday, July 30, all of the dead at the Armory had been identified except one, a seven-year-old boy who bore the number 396. Partly because he was so young, partly because his anonymity symbolized the depressing impersonality of the method of dealing with the deceased, his identification later that day as Willie Novotny of Cicero brought forth a particularly widespread outpouring of sympathy. Both of his parents and his older sister had been drowned; no one had been left from his immediate family to identify him. His funeral on the 31st at the Bohemian School, where he had been a pupil, was treated as a memorial to all the children who had died on the *Eastland*. Mayor Thompson and several other high city officials announced that they would attend.[90]

As would be expected, most of the victims had lived in Berwyn and Cicero or on the far West Side of Chicago within short distances of the Hawthorne plant. Some 30 to 40 funerals were scheduled in the area, mainly in Catholic churches, on the 28th alone.[91] Bishop Paul P. Rhode conducted a single service for 29 victims in St. Mary's Church in Cicero.[92] Some funerals were held in the homes of victims. When the service for Martha Peterson was held in the living room of her home in Austin, the floor of the adjacent room gave way under the weight of the mourners, injuring several people, none seriously.[93] The number of funerals far exceeded the number of hearses available. Marshall Field & Company made available 39 of its trucks, both as hearses and as buses for mourners.[94] Some morticians on the West Side were accused of doubling or tripling the prices of their coffins.[95] The cemeteries of the Catholic Archdiocese of Chicago, in which most of the victims were buried, were unprepared for the volume of burials. The Archdiocese's Resurrection Cemetery in the far southwest suburbs received 76 of the deceased and St. Adalbert's in the north suburbs 65. Inevitably, given the heavy concentration of Czechs among the victims, the Bohemian National Cemetery received the largest number of the deceased, at least 130. Interment there of Kate Dubek, her daughter, Katie, and her son, Jan, was delayed for an hour because the gravediggers were overburdened with earlier burials.[96] For the bodies of victims from the East whose families wanted them buried at home, Western Electric chartered baggage cars of the Pennsylvania Railroad to carry the remains to the New York area. A car with 10 coffins arrived at Pennsylvania Station on July 27 and another with 16 on the 28th.[97]

Western Electric made little attempt to operate the plant. It placed its trucks at the disposal of employees for use in funerals. Coming in to work was voluntary; only about 100 employees appeared Monday, and about 1,000 Tuesday. Wednesday, the day of the largest number of funerals, was made explicitly a day of mourning, with the plant largely empty and draped in black. Local residents, who recognized that the disaster had decimated the plant's work force, quickly came looking for jobs. Western Electric turned away some 500 on Monday and 300 on Tuesday.[98]

The *Tribune* initially reported that 919 bodies had been recovered, and that the final total was expected to reach 1,200 or even 1,800.[99] These figures were excessive, and the paper began reporting lower but escalating numbers that appear quite consistent with the list of victims shown in Appendix D of this volume. On the morning of July 27 it reported 826 bodies recovered, 819 of which had been identified, with 413 persons missing. Later on the 27th the Cook County coroner, Peter M. Hoffman, closed the morgue at the Armory, transferring the five bodies that remained unidentified to the Sheldon Mortuary on West Madison Street.[100] By July 30, the *Tribune* reported the total of deceased at 835, with only one unidentified—Willie Novotny—but stated that 519 people were missing.[101] The category of the missing was always ambiguous because only 687 of the approximately 1,700 survivors reported themselves to the police.[102] Others reported to the Red Cross, but neither organization published their names. A large number simply dried themselves off as best they could and went home.[103] Apart from the severe gap in documentation of the disaster that this created, it makes it impossible to know the precise number of people on the ship at the time of the capsizing. One can only accept the official total of people aboard as approximately correct.

On August 14 the *Tribune* reported that 844 bodies had been recovered, and that 8 people were still missing.[104] The Coast Guard, in its Wreck Report, stated that 836 lives were lost but reported that it was impossible to secure their names.[105] On September 2 the office of the Coroner of Cook

County issued an official total of 812 deceased.[106] The Red Cross accepted

this, and added its own estimate that there had been 2,337 survivors, 1,139 male and 1,198 female.[107] This entails a considerable statistical discrepancy, for it would require the total aboard the ship to have been 3,149, whereas the federal counting procedure, which could hardly have erred by 576 people, established the number at 2,573. The discrepancy probably implies some degree of freeloading on the Red Cross relief operations.

The actual total of dead was considerably larger than the official figure, and apparently approximated the *Tribune*'s final reported number. The microfilmed death records at the Church of Jesus Christ of Latter Day Saints Family History Library in Salt Lake City have 702 death certificates stamped as deceased on the *Eastland*, but the certificates are incomplete, especially in entirely lacking the documentation for victims whose names began with the letter S.[108] An additional 110 names can be found in the entry book of the Coroner of Cook County devoted to the disaster.[109] The file of the civil trial contains a partial list of estates for which the State of Illinois established a trustee, plus estates that had individual trustees.[110] The Chicago *Tribune* printed three lists of victims,[111] and Western Electric published in its house organ a list of employees and their families lost in the disaster.[112] Several newspapers in other cities published lists, which mainly but not entirely duplicated the early lists published in Chicago. Some of the deceased were covered in specific stories in various newspapers. Eliminating obvious redundancies or erroneous entries, the various sources show a total of somewhat under 1,000 deceased, as listed below in Appendix D. This undoubtedly overstates the actual number. The list probably contains some redundancies because discrepancies exist between the lists, and particularly because Slavic names may have been recorded in anglicized forms in some places and in original form in others. It also probably contains names of some people initially listed as dead who actually survived without identifying themselves to authorities. The incomplete list of estates in the file of the civil case contains 5 names that appear in no list of the deceased and cannot be substantiated. Because there is no surviving list of all of the 878 estates represented in the civil action, one cannot presume that the 5 names exhaust this category. Such names may represent variant names of actual victims, or heirs or assignees of the estates of victims, or merely persons who were fraudulently attempting to secure proceeds of the settlement. These names should be excluded from an estimate of the actual number, along with names appearing only in the early lists in newspapers, whose authenticity cannot be established from other sources. On the other hand, the absence of the death certificates for the letter S is a serious downward bias. Judging from analogy to other letters, it is unlikely that all of the deceased whose names began with S could be picked up from the other sources. Salomea Slominski has no death certificate in the microfilmed record, and was not picked up by the identification process at all. She is absent from the Coroner's Inquest Record, and is in no newspaper listing of victims. There is no presumption that she could have been counted either in the coroner's official total or in the *Tribune*'s estimates. She appears only in the list of estates for which the State of Illinois established a trustee, but her interment record at Resurrection Cemetery shows that she is a bona fide victim of the *Eastland*.[113] Similarly, Charles Jamieson appears only in the Chicago *Examiner*'s accounts of funerals of *Eastland* victims, but is verified in the records of Rosehill Cemetery.[114] Such search is hampered by the problem that our knowledge of the cemeteries of the victims is based almost entirely on the death certificates and the *Tribune*'s list of deceased of July 31, 1915, plus some individual accounts of funerals. The cemeteries of a large number of victims are not recorded; not all cemeteries open their interment records to search; and not all of the deceased were buried in the Chicago area. As noted, Western Electric sent the remains of victims from the East to New York, and as the list of deceased in Appendix D indicates, victims were buried widely over the Midwest. Svend Bothun, for example, was buried in a rural cemetery north of Albert Lea, Minnesota.[115]

To judge from what appear to be solid documentations of deaths, the disaster killed approximately the 844 people the *Tribune* reported. The reasons for the discrepancy between the coroner's estimate and the actual number of deaths are in doubt. The Red Cross, recognizing the problem, stated that some victims died subsequently,[116] but newspaper reports do not bear this out. The only later death reported was a suicide. John Salak, a janitor at Western Electric, survived the disaster, but his wife Fannie did not. Unable to bear his bereavement, he committed suicide so as to be buried with her.[117] The apparent explanation for the discrepancy is that the coroner's estimate is complete only for the bodies processed through the central morgue at the Armory, and misses a large number of deceased who were taken directly to various mortuaries. The highest number assigned to any of the bodies taken to the Armory was 749, but two more were taken to the Sheldon Mortuary after the identification operation was shifted there, bringing the total to 751.[118] This is well short of the totals reported in the press and even of the official total.

The total of approximately 844 dead should be considered from the perspective of the relative numbers of deaths shown in the accompanying table. In particular, the number of passengers killed, 841, exceeded the number of passengers lost on the *Titanic* by 12. A total of 844 was the third highest among disasters in the history of the American merchant marine, the highest—more than three times over—in the history of the Great

TABLE 3

137

The
Immediate
Aftermath

Estimated Deaths in Selected Major Disasters

Disaster, with cause and date	Total	Passengers	Crew
MAJOR MARINE DISASTERS, 1912 – 15			
Titanic, struck iceberg, April 14, 1912	1,523	829	694
Empress of Ireland, collision, May 29, 1914	1,012	840	172
Lusitania, torpedoed, May 7, 1915	1,198	785	413
Eastland, capsized, July 24, 1915	844	841	3[a]
AMERICAN MERCHANT MARINE DISASTERS			
Sultana, boiler explosion, above Memphis, Tenn., April 22, 1865	1,653		
General Slocum, fire, New York City, June 15, 1904	957		
Eastland	844		
CITY OF CHICAGO DISASTERS			
Eastland	844		
Iroquois Theatre fire, December 30, 1903	606		
Chicago fire, October 8–9, 1871	300–400		
GREAT LAKES DISASTERS			
Eastland	844		
Lady Elgin, collision, September 8, 1860	279		

SOURCES: Data for the *Titanic* from estimate of John P. Eaton, *A "Titanic" Time Line*, App. 3 (unpublished; copyright, John P. Eaton; all rights reserved). Data for the *Empress of Ireland* from James Croall, *Fourteen Minutes: The Last Voyage of the "Empress of Ireland"* (New York: Stein and Day, 1979), p. 147. Data for the *Lusitania* from A. A. Hoehling and Mary Hoehling, *The Last Voyage of the "Lusitania"* (New York: Henry Holt, 1956), p. 227. Data for the *Sultana* and the *General Slocum* from Charles Hocking, F.L.A., *Dictionary of Disasters at Sea During the Age of Steam* (London: Lloyd's Register, 1969), pp. 266–67, 671. Data for the Iroquois Theatre fire from Chicago *Tribune*, July 25, 1915, p. 6. Data for the *Lady Elgin* from Hocking, *Dictionary*, p. 409.

[a] Includes Peter Boyle, a crew member of the *Petoskey* who drowned in the rescue effort.

Lakes, and the highest of any disaster of any type in the history of Chicago. It has retained these unfortunate distinctions to the present day. And, as far as is known, the disaster is the worst ever to befall a ship that was still moored to her wharf.

Of all the deceased, only two proved to have been members of the crew. James Stenson, the *Eastland*'s assistant purser, who had taken tickets as the passengers boarded, was the only officer who died.[119] Joe Brennan, an ephemeral character of unknown age and marital status, was identified as a deckhand from New Haven, Michigan.[120] The *Petoskey* also lost a crew member when Peter Boyle dove into the river and died while attempting to rescue a woman from the *Eastland*.[121] Some of the deceased had worked aboard the *Eastland* without being literally members of the crew. Frank Tranckitella and Erich Krueger, musicians in Bradfield's Orchestra, were killed, along with Joseph Bertrand, who worked for a concessionaire on

The gravestone of Katerina Ivanecky in the Bohemian National Cemetery in Chicago. The stone, lettered in Czech, reads, "Here rests Katerina Ivanecky, died on the ship *Eastland*, 24 July 1915, at age 19 years. She sleeps in peace." Except that she was a Western Electric office employee, rather than a factory hand, she was representative of the victims: young, female, single, and Czech. The photograph on the stone conveys youth, attractiveness, and good nature through the years.

the ship. There were probably others classified as passengers who were actually working aboard the ship in similar capacities.

In 1918, in the course of writing the final report on its relief operations in the disaster, the Red Cross provided a breakdown of the deceased by sex, age, marital status, and other characteristics. Because the Red Cross based its estimates on the coroner's figure of 812 deaths, its data may seriously understate the magnitude of the catastrophe. Even so, the enormity of the event is overwhelming when one considers it in the light of the individuals involved. The disaster wiped out 22 whole families. The largest was George and Josephine Sindelar and their 5 children, along with Mrs. Sindelar's sister, Regina Dolezal.[122] The building at 2301 South Kolin Avenue, an ordinary residence with a basement apartment, was totally bereft of occupants when both of the families it housed—Julius Schroll with his wife, Emma, and Alfred Anderson with his wife, Anna, and son, Maurice—perished on the *Eastland*.[123] The accident widowed 175 women and killed 32 of their children. Mary Braitsch lost her husband, John, and all 5 of her children, who ranged in age from 17 years to 5 months.[124] Three of the widowed women were pregnant; three children never knew their fathers. Eighty-four men lost their wives, along with 35 children. In the largest single class of deaths, 262 couples lost a total of 290 children. There were 19 families in which the children alone survived. The most widely publicized such case was that of Charles W. and Kate Trogg, whose bodies were found in the hull in close embrace, as if in a final show of affection. Their 2 children had been left at home, and were now orphans.[125] A total of 24 young children were left dependent. Of the 56 percent of the deceased who were female, most were young single women who worked in the factory.[126] On one bench where 22 young women normally worked, only 2 reported for duty when the Hawthorne plant reopened on Thursday; the rest had died. One of the "twine rooms" where women worked on the wrapping material for telephone wires was reportedly entirely wiped out.[127] Deaths were highly concentrated among the young: 70 percent of the victims were between 15 and 30.

The deceased were heavily concentrated in the Czech, Hungarian, and Polish communities of Berwyn and Cicero, all groups that ranked low in the social structure of the time and, as a consequence, suffered some degree of discrimination. This fact proved important on several levels. First, it accounts for the widespread anglicization of names, with the attendant difficulty in identification of victims mentioned earlier. Second, the social standing of the victims was a disincentive to scholarship on the disaster. Although the death toll of passengers exceeded that on the *Titanic*, the disaster killed no one who by ordinary standards was a person of distinction. The *Titanic* killed Samuel Ward Stanton, a distinguished marine artist; Jacques Futrelle, an excellent writer of mystery stories; and a variety of people from the international financial community or the social world of the affluent whose names have become universally identified with the accident. The collision of the *Empress of Ireland* was fatal to the actor Laurence Irving and his wife. The torpedoing of the *Lusitania* killed the writer and anthologist Elbert Hubbard. The only victim of the *Eastland* with even a small claim to celebrity was Joseph Bertrand, who was said to have been bantamweight boxing champion of the West Coast.[128] The victims were, no less than the famous, very real persons, with satisfactions and prides, likes and dislikes, savings and debts, families or plans for families, and, most of all, ambitions that were snuffed out in an instant as they sought only a day's amusement. As Robert Burns wrote, "A man's a man for a' that."

Third and most important, the fact that the victims were predominately factory workers meant that the resources of the heirs were in almost all cases very limited. When Charles M. Hays, president of the Grand Trunk Railway of Canada, perished on the *Titanic*, his death may have been a serious administrative problem to the railway and a severe emotional blow to his family, but his heirs were almost by definition well prepared financially for the future. Particularly because the *Eastland* killed so many heads of families, the disaster was a crushing financial misfortune for hundreds of people. The widow of Charles Menges, a 40-year-old electrician at Western Electric, for example, was reported without resources except for Menges's accrued wages for the previous week.[129] Nicholas H. Suerth, 42, left a wife and 6 children, none of whom was employed, and only one of whom, his son, Joseph, 16, who survived the disaster, was of an age such that he could reasonably be expected to enter the labor force in the near future.[130] Boleslovas Sivickis, 40, was helping support his wife and two children on a farm in Lithuania through emigrant remittances.[131] Michael Tseuko, 42, had left his wife in Hungary a year and a half earlier, and was working as a laborer at Western Electric to save enough money to bring her to Chicago.[132] Even though the most common victim was an unmarried person under the age of 30, many of the young were major financial supporters of their families. Jacob Suchwalko, who was 19 and single, was the sole support of his mother.[133] Carl Knoff, also 19, supported both his parents and 2 sisters.[134] Frances Badalewska, 20, was the chief wage earner for a family of 8.[135] Vincent Hinczewski, 21, was the sole support of a widow and her 5 children.[136] In the most extreme example, Anna Comerford, 18, was the sole support of her mother and 8 siblings.[137]

The situation of the heirs presented both the immediate problem of meeting funeral expenses, or dealing with unpaid bills, and the longer-range problem of coping with life without the principal source of income in the family. There was a further problem that the White Star Line, the Canadian Pacific Railway, and the Cunard Line, operators of the *Titanic, Empress of Ireland*, and *Lusitania*, respectively, were all large and well-established companies, thoroughly insured, and viable even in the face of a serious loss, but the St. Joseph–Chicago Steamship Company, only two years old, had never been profitable, and showed no prospect of being able to survive the loss of its principal vessel. Hull announced on July 27 that the company would run the *Eugene C. Hart* until the end of the fruit season, but then liquidate.[138] The Indiana Transportation Company also ceased operation, putting its three ships into winter lay-up at Michigan

City on July 28, presumably in fear of having them libeled in Chicago in
the prospective civil case.[139] This company, too, never operated again. Accordingly, the only recourse of the heirs of the deceased would be against
the insurers, members of Lloyd's of London. The sum to be recovered for
each of the deceased was $10,000, the statutory compensation in the State
of Illinois for a wrongful death. By the standards of the heirs, this was a
very large sum. In real terms, it was to become larger, for the civil action
dragged on well over twenty years, into the mid-1930's, a period of serious
deflation. The files for probate of the estates of the victims typically state
that the deceased died intestate and lacked real assets except for the prospect of recovery of $10,000 from the St. Joseph–Chicago Steamship
Company.[140] Consequently, the civil case promised to be anything but an
abstract legal exercise.

Immediately, however, there was a pressing problem of short-term
relief.

Relief

On the day of the disaster Acting Mayor William R. Moorhouse scheduled
a conference of officials of the city, Western Electric, and the Red Cross
for 10:00 A.M. the following day, Sunday, July 25, at his office in City Hall.
Fifty people responded, who became known as the Mayor's Committee.
James Simpson, vice president of Marshall Field & Company, was appointed chairman, and Julius Rosenwald, head of Sears, Roebuck & Company, who was the city's most prominent philanthropist, was made treasurer and chairman of the finance committee. A decision was made to raise
$200,000 within 48 hours. In addition, Western Electric appropriated
$100,000. Both sums were quickly oversubscribed. The Mayor's Commit-
tee had raised $350,000 by the end of its second week of existence. West-
ern Electric's direct subvention was $100,601, to which were added
$78,518 from the company benefit plan and $2,271 from the funds of the
Employee Benevolent Association, a total of $181,390. The funds from
the benefit plan were mainly the company's standard death benefit of six
months' salary to heirs of employees with over five years of service and a
year's salary to heirs of employees with over ten years of service. Of the
additional $100,601, a reported $75,806 went for funeral expenses. Western Electric also made its medical, nursing, and welfare staffs available to
survivors and to families of victims, both at the plant and by house calls.
The medical staff at Hawthorne inoculated over 200 people against typhoid. The company adopted an explicit policy of favoring victims' relatives in applications for employment.[141]

The Red Cross, in preparing to disburse the anticipated $350,000, found itself confronted with more than 900 families with deaths or injuries. Deaths were spread among 661 families. The Red Cross adopted a short-run policy of "Give prompt relief. Ask questions later." [142] No less than Western Electric, it was largely concerned with burial expenses in the week immediately following the disaster. In the longer run, it adopted a basic scale granting $200 to survivors for each adult lost and $150 for every child. For the 24 children in 19 families who had lost both parents, the Red Cross allocated an income stream of $12 per month to the age of 16, which it considered normal working age. A widow received the basic benefits of $200 for a lost adult and $150 per child, plus a $500 compensation for her widowhood and a sum ranging from $500 for support of a child under the age of 7 to $100 for support of a 15-year-old. From these payments, sums were subtracted for widows who had working children over 16. Sorting out the various claims and determining the disbursements was a time-consuming process, not completed until 1918. Including $9,305 in grants the Red Cross received from Western Electric, which are double-counted because of inclusion in Western Electric's total, the Red Cross expended $379,415. The victims proved to hold life or injury insurance that paid them $267,160. [143]

At minimum the relief efforts of Western Electric and the Red Cross,

plus some small assistance from United Charities, managed to bury the
dead, grant some short-run help in dealing with the consequences of a
wholly unexpected catastrophe, and provide some minimal assistance in
the long-run problems of raising the orphans created by the ordeal. All of
this antedated federal disaster relief. In May 1916, Representative Adolph
J. Sabath of Illinois introduced a bill in the U.S. House of Representatives
investing the Court of Claims with jurisdiction over claims of survivors
and heirs against general U.S. Treasury funds, and waiving the statute of
limitations.[144] The bill made little progress; no hearings were held and it
did not pass. In February 1917, Sol F. Roderick, the state representative
from the area in which the victims were concentrated, introduced a bill in
the Illinois legislature to pay each of 358 heirs of the deceased $10,000
each from state funds on the grounds that the disaster had been caused by
the state's failure to remove a piling from the wharf area. The interpretation that the disaster had stemmed from the *Eastland*'s resting on pilings
had been refuted in the criminal trial in 1916, but it remained widespread
in popular discussion. The Committee on the Judiciary of the Illinois
House of Representatives found that the disaster presented no grounds for
a legal action against the State of Illinois. The state constitution provided
that the state should not be a defendant in any suit at law or equity, and the
committee concluded that this prohibition should apply to admiralty cases.
Under the circumstances, the committee recommended to the House that
the bill not be passed.[145] It was not.

The Chicago City Council appropriated $20,000 for essentially unres-
tricted use in connection with the disaster.[146] The city provided medical
facilities, policing, and services of the fire department, but the relief effort
was basically a private activity. The disaster evoked a benevolence, a self-
lessness, and a cooperation in the face of catastrophe that could not have
been maintained for any long period. It did, however, show the city and its
citizens at their best for the short compass of time required. If anything in
connection with the *Eastland* may be said to have been successful, it was
the relief effort that followed the disaster.

Salvage

Under the Rivers and Harbors Act of 1899, popularly known as the Wreck
Act, the owners of a vessel that had become a major obstruction to a navigable waterway were required to remove it within 30 days at their own
expense at penalty of loss of title to the ship.[147] The Chicago River was
225 to 250 feet wide in the immediate vicinity of the disaster, and because
the *Eastland* blocked about half of it, none would question the applicabil-
ity of the act. It is unclear, in light of the legal actions impending, why

the St. Joseph–Chicago Steamship Company at that stage thought it useful to retain title to the hulk. Only two operators, as Hull viewed the company's options, could do the job of righting the hulk so that it could be removed from the area: the Great Lakes Towing Company, of which Captain Alexander Cunning was wrecking master, and the Great Lakes Dredge & Dock Company, for which Captain William Reid of Port Huron undertook wrecking jobs. The Great Lakes Towing Company was the more attractive because it owned a specialized salvage vessel, the *Favorite*, with Cunning as her master. The *Favorite* was a 181-foot steel steamship built by the Buffalo Dry Dock Company in 1907, equipped with wrecking beams, hydraulic jacks, hawsers, steam pumps, a machine shop, a small sawmill, and a blacksmith shop. Her basic device for a job such as the one in prospect was a set of large ballast tanks that could be filled to bring the vessel down, and then pumped out to provide buoyancy for the hulk moored to her. The ship, which exemplified the term "state-of-the-art," had an excellent reputation based on a large number of salvage assignments. In particular, she had performed masterfully in salvaging the railroad steamer *Ann Arbor No. 4*, which had capsized on May 29, 1909, in the Manistique & Lake Superior Railroad's slip in Manistique, Michigan, after being ineptly loaded with cars of iron ore. The salvage job had been particularly difficult because the iron ore—the heaviest cargo commonly handled—had inflicted comprehensive damage to the interior of ship. Nonetheless, Cunning had righted the ship by June 25, and towed her off on the following day. The *Ann Arbor No. 4* was approximately the same size as the *Eastland*.[148] All of these considerations, plus the fact that Great Lakes Towing had a large submersible pontoon barge at its disposal, persuaded the St. Joseph–Chicago management to choose it for the job. On the day following the disaster St. Joseph–Chicago secretary and treasurer Walter C. Steele wrote to Captain Robert Young of the Dunham Towing & Wrecking Company, Great Lakes Towing's local affiliate, soliciting a

While its berth was blocked by the wreck of the *Eastland*, the Chicago & South Haven Steamship Company moved its operations to the *Eastland*'s former terminal at the Rush Street bridge. (UCLA Libraries)

South Haven

Until further notice South Haven Steamers will arrive and depart on regular schedule from

North End of Rush St. Bridge

Daily 9:30 A. M. and 9 P. M., except Saturday and Sunday. Saturday 2:00 P. M., 10:30 P. M. and 11:00 P. M. Sunday at 10:00 A. M.

Fare on day boat **$1.25** Round-trip

Telephone Franklin 814.

The wreck relatively early in the salvage operation. Ashes from the fireboxes of tugs were spread about at the suggestion of Captain William T. Bright to give the survivors traction as they walked off the hull. Note also the spile pulled over by the forward breast line as the ship capsized. (National Archives and Records Administration, Chicago)

bid for a no-cure-no-pay agreement to right the *Eastland*. In response, Cunning offered to raise the *Eastland* for $34,500, provided that Great Lakes Towing be made exempt from all claims of damage to the hull or loss of time of the ship. Hull wrote his lawyer in Chicago asking him to represent the company and to sign the contract on Cunning's terms.[149]

The *Favorite* was based at St. Ignace, Michigan, a central location on the Great Lakes, but she proved to be in Duluth at the time. Cunning set out with her immediately and arrived in Chicago on July 28.[150] The pontoon was in Cleveland, but Great Lakes Towing's tug *T. C. Lutz* towed it to Port Huron and the *Michigan* towed it to Chicago.[151] The pontoon was 100′ × 10′ × 12′, displaced 1,200 tons of water, and was divided into 13 watertight compartments, each with a 9-inch suction pipe, connected to 12-inch pumps. The pontoon took about a week to arrive, but this did not delay the salvage operation, for a great deal of preparation had to be done before the pontoon could be put to use.

Cunning might have looked upon the job as routine—if anything in his business was—except that the position of the wreck made it difficult to work on. The wreck was too close to the wharf for the *Favorite* to ap-

Captain Alexander Cunning's wrecking steamer *Favorite* was necessarily among the most familiar ships on the Great Lakes. She worked on wrecks in all parts of the Lakes above Niagara Falls. She is shown upbound in the St. Clair River. (Rev. Peter J. Van der Linden collection)

proach it from the south, and neither the wharf nor the adjacent buildings were strong enough for Cunning to fasten any tackle in the area. The stacks, masts, and boats of the *Eastland* were removed to reduce interference with navigation on the river, and also to facilitate the salvage operation. The wreck was held in place throughout the operation by lines fore and aft in the same locations that the breast lines had been during loading. Cunning began his work on the hull by sealing all of the openings below water. He had divers place two one-inch steel cables under the hull, one forward to be handled by the *Favorite*, and the other aft to be made fast to the pontoon barge once it arrived—as it did on August 8. The barge was equipped with a crane, which Cunning also used in the stern area of the wreck. He used a crew of 32 men, who worked 12 to 14 hours a day for 16 days. They worked nights for 3 to 4 days toward the end of the procedure. Commonwealth Edison had strung 125 tungsten-nitrogen lights on the *Eastland* during the removal of the victims; the *Favorite* had both sealed lights underwater to assist the divers and searchlights on her superstructure. Ten floodlights had been placed on the Reid-Murdoch building to illuminate the entire working area. Cunning placed four pumps aboard the wreck, each of which could issue a stream of water about a foot in diameter. Pumping began August 4, but had to be abandoned when some of the holes in the hull were found not to have been closed, and when

Opposite: This night scene during the salvage operation illustrates how closely the submersion of the wreck coincided with the center line of the ship. (Chicago Historical Society)

Pumping the Eastland Light for Raising Today.

The Chicago *Tribune* published this diagram of the salvage operation on Friday, August 13, the day Captain Alexander Cunning began raising the *Eastland*. The hulk proved more intractable than anticipated, and the job could not be completed until the following day. (UCLA Libraries)

By the close of work on August 13, the *Eastland* had been raised to an angle of 73 degrees, but would still not float. The *Favorite* is in the foreground. (Chicago Historical Society)

The hulk of the *Eastland*, probably on August 14, immediately after being re-floated by the Great Lakes Towing Company's *Favorite*. The company's tug *Michigan* and its pontoon barge are at the stern. (Chicago Historical Society)

the main deck collapsed from the weight of water against it as the hull was emptied. These problems were dealt with, and the hull was pumped out mainly on August 11. Cunning used three tugs, the *Michigan, Rita McDonald,* and *Kenosha,* both to move his equipment about and to provide steam for the pumps.

Preparations had been completed by 9:00 P.M. on August 12, and the raising of the hulk began on the following morning. This proved a more difficult operation than Cunning had anticipated, partly because the *Eastland* had sunk about two feet into the mud since the disaster and partly because his crew had sealed the openings imperfectly. Cunning began pumping out the *Favorite*'s tanks to raise his own ship and to increase the angle of the hulk attached to her by cable. He expected the hulk to right itself when the angle reached 45 degrees above horizontal, but it did not do so, mainly because the coal in the bunkers had shifted heavily to port in the course of the disaster. Mud, in places three to four feet deep, had accumulated on the port side also. On August 13 Cunning got the hulk up to an angle of 73 degrees, but still it would not right itself or float. The job continued until shortly before noon on the 14th, when the hulk reached 80

The *Eastland* immediately after raising on August 14. The *Favorite* is moored to the wharf at the stern. (Rev. Peter J. Van der Linden collection)

Photographed from the Clark Street bridge, the hulk of the *Eastland* shortly after being raised on August 14. (Rev. Peter J. Van der Linden collection)

degrees and floated, albeit with a serious list to port because of the coal and mud. There had been some fears that because the wreck had extended out over the La Salle Street tunnel the port propeller might penetrate the roof of the tunnel while the ship was being lifted, but no such problem arose. Harbormaster Weckler suspended navigation on the river for about twelve hours while the hulk was raised. Because it was widely anticipated that additional bodies would be found in the river beneath the hulk, the city had a barge with coffins at hand. No additional victims were discovered, however.[152]

With his job completed, Cunning turned the hulk over to the owners. It remained moored to the Chicago & South Haven wharf for three days—according to the Chicago *Daily News* because Flatow could find no one willing to serve on it while it was moved.[153] At about 1:30 P.M. on August 17 the *Kenosha* and *Indiana* slowly towed the hulk away through the Wells Street bridge and up the North Branch to the former facility of the Shipowners' Dry Dock Company on Goose Island, which since 1912 had been a yard of the Chicago Ship Building Company. The American Ship Building Company, which had controlled both enterprises, was in the process of shutting down Shipowners' and shifting its activities to Chicago Ship Building's South Chicago yard. Hull had previously arranged to berth the hulk at the east wall of the unused dry dock No. 2 at Shipowners' for

The hulk of the *Eastland* was turned near the point of her capsizing and towed bow-forward to the berth arranged for her on the North Branch. The photograph above shows the hulk from the stern, taken from the Clark Street bridge; the one below shows it being maneuvered slowly through the Wells Street bridge by the Great Lakes Towing Company's *Kenosha*. (Rev. Peter J. Van der Linden collection)

A series of three separate photographs of the hulk of the *Eastland* at its mooring on the North Branch of the Chicago River. The photographs, commissioned by the federal government, appear to have been taken with an 8″ x 10″ view camera. (National Archives and Records Administration, Chicago)

$25 per month. It was still widely anticipated that the ship might be re-
paired for service out of another city.[154] With the hulk removed, the wharf
area at Clark Street was dredged out to a uniform depth of 21 feet between
August 24 and 28.[155]

The hulk was a ghastly sight. The white of its hull had become a sickly
gray, on the port side from the mud in the river and on the starboard from
the ashes spread to provide the survivors friction while they made their
escapes. Windows were broken in the pilot house, and the hurricane deck
was a shambles. The hulk remained at its new berth for over a year, clearly
visible through trees from passing streetcars on Halsted Street. The hulk
provided an ideal visual reminder of the catastrophe while the efforts com-
menced to resolve the legal problems it had engendered.

Initiation of the Legal Actions

The nature of the disaster was such as to divide responsibility for the legal
actions among every possible jurisdiction. It had taken place in Illinois,
and thus would be subject to the state's civil and criminal statutes, but it
occurred on a navigable waterway under federal authority. The immediate
area in which the wreck had come to rest was maintained by the City of
Chicago. Cook County was responsible for state grand jury actions. By
July 27 seven inquiries into the disaster had been announced by, respectively, State's Attorney Maclay Hoyne; Coroner Peter M. Hoffman; United
States District Attorney Charles F. Clyne; United States Secretary of Commerce William C. Redfield; General George Uhler, supervising inspector
of the Steamboat Inspection Service; the Harbors and Wharves Committee
of the Chicago City Council; and the Illinois Public Utilities Commission.

The first of the inquiries, that of Coroner Hoffman, began on the afternoon of the day of the disaster. Hoffman appointed a jury headed by
Dr. William A. Evans, a physician who had served as head of the city's
health department under the administration of Mayor Fred A. Busse, and
who had more recently achieved considerable fame in the Chicago area as
health editor of the *Tribune*. The other members were William F. Bode,
vice president of Reid-Murdoch; Colonel Henry F. Allen, a mechanical
engineer of the Department of Public Works; Harry Moir, manager of the
Morrison Hotel; J. S. Keough, general manager of W. F. McLaughlin &
Company, the dominant local coffee firm; and Eugene Beifeld, manager
of the College Inn, the nightclub of the Sherman Hotel. Evans was an ideal
choice, both because he had established himself as a trusted local figure
and because the *Tribune* was certain to publicize his findings. The jury
took evidence from July 24 to 29, and the city published a volume of hearings.[156] The *Tribune* published Evans's summary of the jury's findings in a

series of three articles.[157] Regarding the *Eastland* Evans concluded, "the

factor of safety was so low that skillful management was required." [158] He defended only Weckler, who, he said, "impressed me as the one man who saw his duty and did it." [159] Evans was particularly hostile to Pedersen for making no effort to take the passengers off while the ship listed seriously for what he thought was about fifteen minutes, and highly critical of the management for having hired him:

If a captain stands by and sees his boat go over slowly while tied to the dock and gives no command looking to the safety of his passengers, clearly he is not a man of decision and judgment. He was selected by the manager of the owning company. How far they could go in failing to select a clear headed man of decision as captain without being guilty of criminal carelessness remains to be seen.[160]

On July 29 the coroner's jury recommended that Hull, Pedersen, Erickson, Greenebaum, Reid, and Eckliff be held to the Illinois grand jury on the charges of manslaughter and such other offenses as the facts might warrant.[161] The jury followed this recommendation with the observation:

Nothing in the testimony offered before this jury indicated that the passengers were guilty of any unusual act that contributed to the disaster, and we are of the opinion that no act of the passengers was responsible for the disaster. In absence of evidence of undue acts on the part of the passengers or of violent physical causes, such as explosions, fire or collision, the fact that this vessel overturned is proof either that it was improperly constructed for the service employed or that it was improperly loaded, operated or maintained, or that several or all of the causes operated to bring about the serious result. It is our judgment that the steamship *Eastland* was both improperly constructed for the service employed and improperly loaded, operated and maintained, and that the parties named are responsible.

The Cook County grand jury was reconstituted monthly, but because this directive from the coroner's jury came at the end of the month, Judge George M. Kersten held over the July jury and assigned it the case. Its deliberations were not made public, but on August 11 it brought into Kersten's court indictments under Illinois statutes of Hull, Arnold, Steele, and Davis for manslaughter.[162] The four officers of the firm were indicted on five counts:

1. They knew the *Eastland* was unseaworthy and had no stability.
2. They permitted 2,500 passengers aboard, which was more than the ship's carrying capacity.
3. They were negligent in hiring an incompetent engineer, who because of his lack of skill was unable to control the ship properly.
4. There was not sufficient help on the ship to control her properly.
5. The ballast tanks were allowed to be out of repair and not filled with water.

Pedersen and Erickson were indicted on the charge of criminal care-lessness that Dr. Evans had seemed to feel was most appropriate.[163] The indictment of Pedersen was on five counts:

1. He permitted boarding of a larger number of passengers than the ship could safely carry.
2. He failed to warn the passengers to leave when it became apparent that the ship was about to overturn.
3. He was negligent in not seeing that the ballast tanks were properly filled.
4. He was negligent in not seeing that the tanks were in good condition and repair.
5. He was negligent in failing to keep the chock holes and gangways closed when the ship was boarded.

The indictment of Erickson charged three counts:

1. Negligence in filling the ballast tanks.
2. Negligence in keeping the ballast tanks in repair.
3. Negligence in failing to close the chock holes and gangways.[164]

Foreman George A. Hughes appended to the indictments a report to Kersten recommending several changes in policy. It proposed that the Steamboat Inspection Service be transferred from the Department of Commerce to the Navy Department and reorganized so as to avoid confusion in authority. The jury concluded, inevitably, that the partly filled ballast tanks had been more dangerous than empty ones, and stated that a fixed ballast system should have been required by the inspectors and the owners. It proposed that plans for ships be submitted for federal approval, that no passenger vessel be dependent on a water ballast system, and that completed ships should be subject to compulsory inclining tests. Ships, it recommended, should be required to have two interconnected seacocks, rigged so that one side could be pumped in while the other was being pumped out, and arranged so that water could be pumped from one tank to another.[165]

The July Cook County grand jury was reconvened on August 13 to consider additional indictments. It met for only an hour, and decided to defer action until the federal grand jury had acted, or as it proved, simply progressed in its deliberations. The jurors then went off to inspect the hulk, which was just about to be raised.[166] On August 27 the county grand jury brought in to Judge Lockwood Honore an indictment of Greenebaum for manslaughter on the ground of knowingly leasing an unseaworthy vessel and being responsible for the death of Kate Austin.[167] This initiated the use of the name of Kate Austin, a 47-year-old widow who worked as a cook in Western Electric's food service facilities, as proxy for the names of victims generally. Mrs. Austin's name was twentieth in alphabetical order among the well-documented victims; the choice of her name over Marya Adamkiewicz's, which was first, was a good indication of the social values of the time. Foreman Hughes told the press that the jury had also voted indictments of Oakley and Lobdell, and wanted to do so for Reid and Eckliff, but were instructed by a representative of State's Attorney Hoyne that state courts lacked jurisdiction over federal officials.[168]

Federal action began on the afternoon of July 24, when President Woodrow Wilson, from his summer retreat at Cornish, New Hampshire, wired Secretary of Commerce Redfield, who was in Syracuse, New York, to go to Chicago to undertake an inquiry into the disaster. Redfield complied immediately, and arrived in Chicago on the 28th.[169] His principal subordinate in this field, General George Uhler, supervising inspector of the Steamboat Inspection Service, proved to be in San Francisco. Uhler's deputy, Dickerson N. Hoover, Jr., was in Washington, D.C. Redfield first undertook a series of public hearings, which ran through the week of the 26th. Second, he ordered a Board of Inquiry consisting of Uhler; Hoover; James L. Ackerson, a naval architect who represented the U.S. Navy; E. C. Gillette, superintendent of marine construction of the U.S. Lighthouse Service; William A. Collins and Frank W. Van Patten, both local inspectors; Marvin B. Pool, a merchant; Harry A. Wheeler, a banker; Barratt O'Hara, lieutenant governor of Illinois; and Philip B. Foulke of St. Louis, chairman of the U.S. Chamber of Commerce's committee on the Steamboat Inspection Service.[170] A member to represent organized labor was sought without success.

Redfield's public hearings included extensive interrogations of the men who counted passengers onto the *Eastland* before the disaster, and the transcript is particularly rich in documenting the event of July 17, 1904, which was receiving considerable notoriety as a demonstration of the *Eastland*'s instability. Redfield invited Dority, Eeles, and Nack, who had been officers in that event, to testify on their experiences. He also solicited a letter from Professor George R. McDermott of Cornell University on the ship's design, and took testimony from various inspectors who had been concerned with the ship over her history. In particular, on July 26 he invited Reid and Eckliff from Grand Haven to testify on their certification of the *Eastland* in 1914 and 1915. Both inspectors came to Chicago voluntarily, but upon their arrival at his hearing on the 28th, they were arrested by Illinois authorities and taken to the county jail, even though no formal charges had been levied against them. The rationale of this action was that the coroner's jury was expected to recommend action against them to the Cook County grand jury—as it did the following day—and that being from Michigan, they should be apprehended while in Illinois. This course of action was at best highly questionable, and their lawyer sought a writ of *habeas corpus* from Judge Kenesaw Mountain Landis, to whose district court the federal criminal case had been assigned. The two inspectors were brought into his court in handcuffs on August 1, something that Reid in particular thought an affront, and that Redfield agreed was "unnecessarily harsh." [171] On August 3 Landis ordered their release on bond of $2,500 each. Pedersen, who was also named in the coroner's jury's recommendation, was reported free on bond of the same amount, but Erickson was said to be still in jail, unable to raise the money.[172]

Redfield convoked a session in the courtroom of Judge Christian A. Kohlsaat of the Federal Circuit Court of Appeals on July 29 for the twin purposes of initiating the deliberations of the Board of Inquiry and coordinating the proposed public investigations. William L. O'Connell, chairman of the Public Utilities Commission, had already announced that his organization would not undertake its projected inquiry.[173] As it proved, decisions concerning the future course of public inquiries were shortly to be undone. Landis, with a heavy-handedness only too characteristic of his later administration of baseball, on July 31 issued an injunction against persons subpoenaed to appear before the federal grand jury testifying in any other hearing.[174] This truncated the ongoing hearings of Coroner Hoffman and Secretary Redfield, and prevented the Chicago City Council's inquiry from being undertaken. Instead, the City Council appointed a committee on excursion boats generally, which took no actions on the *Eastland* per se but initiated a series of stability tests on the small steamers that ran from downtown Chicago to Jackson and Lincoln parks.[175] The federal grand jury never published its hearings, and they appear not to have survived. Transcripts of Hoffman's and Redfield's hearings were published, and are useful historical sources on the disaster, but because the hearings were limited to one week, they were necessarily incomplete, notably in having little testimony by Pedersen and Erickson. Both testified in Hoffman's inquiry, but said little because of their lawyers' fears of self-incrimination.[176] Neither testified before Redfield. The effect of Landis's order was to limit the historical documentation of the disaster seriously. The only thorough examination took place in the federal criminal trial, the transcript of which is an unpublished source so obscure that it lay unknown even to the archivists who held it.

The federal grand jury, which had 23 members, began its hearings on July 30.[177] It heard over 100 witnesses, including some, such as Charles Lasser, who did not testify in the other inquiries.[178] By August 10 the jury was reported as ready to hand down 15 to 20 indictments.[179] It adjourned on August 21, however, without taking action. It reconvened on September 21, and on the following day brought in indictments of Arnold, Hull,

Greenebaum, Pedersen, Erickson, Reid, Eckliff, Steele, the St. Joseph–
Chicago Steamship Company, and the Indiana Transportation Company
for conspiracy to defraud the federal government by preventing the execution of marine laws, and for criminal carelessness. Both charges carried the penalty of a prison term—two years for the conspiracy, ten years
for criminal carelessness—or a $10,000 fine, or both.[180] Steele appeared
before Landis on September 28 with St. Joseph–Chicago's lawyers to
request the federal government to relinquish jurisdiction over the defendants. None had posted the bond of $10,000 required, and all who were
residents of Michigan reported their intention to fight extradition. Governor Woodbridge N. Ferris of Michigan had already announced his willing-
ness to cooperate in extradition efforts. Clyne planned to begin extradition
actions at St. Ignace, Michigan, in proximity to Arnold's home on Mackinac Island.[181] Landis responded by issuing, on September 29, a federal
bench warrant for the arrest of Arnold, Hull, Reid, Eckliff, Pedersen, and
Erickson—but not Greenebaum, who was a resident of Chicago, or Steele,
who was in the city—on the charge of conspiracy to operate an unsafe
ship.[182] Strangely, the prosecution proceeded on the charge in the bench
warrant, conspiracy to operate an unsafe ship, rather than on the two
charges in the indictment. So was initiated the federal criminal case, which
proved to be the only criminal action the disaster brought forth.

Landis's order of July 31 ending testimony before rival inquiries also
prevented the Board of Inquiry from taking evidence. Its deliberations
seem not to have been recorded, but its report survives in the National
Archives in Washington, D.C., and its recommendations were published
at the end of the transcript of Redfield's hearings, which was printed as a
congressional document. The Board of Inquiry proposed that no passenger
vessel should depend on liquid ballast for stability, and that new plans or
changes in vessels over 100 tons be approved by a board of naval architects
to be established within the Department of Commerce. The proposed
board should serve as an appellate body for those contesting the decisions
of local inspectors. The Board of Inquiry recommended further that increases in passenger capacity be made only after personal examination by
an inspector of the Steamboat Inspection Service and creation of a written
record. Inspectors were to require owners of vessels the stability of which
they had reason to question to make inclining tests under the supervision
of naval architects to be provided by the Department of Commerce.[183]
The proposal for a board of naval architects for this purpose was embodied
in a bill, Senate 1221–House 4787, brought in by Senator Duncan U.
Fletcher of Florida and Representative Joshua W. Alexander of Missouri
in December 1915.[184] The bill, which would have represented a generali-

The multi-deck excursion steamer appeared to laymen as a type of ship that might present stability problems. Immediately after the *Eastland* disaster, suspicion was directed to the Ashley & Dustin Line's *Put-in-Bay*, shown here in 1940. The ship, built to a design by Frank E. Kirby, was well designed and very stable. (Charles Mensing photograph, Rev. Peter J. Van der Linden collection)

zation of the *Eastland*'s disaster about as thoroughly as the La Follette Seamen's Act did of the *Titanic*'s, did not progress to hearings and did not pass.

Without change in statutory authority, the Steamboat Inspection Service responded to the wave of interest in metacentric heights stirred by the disaster with some inquiries of its own. There were two types of vessel that looked casually as if they might present stability problems. One was the multi-deck excursion vessel with relatively little protection against the seas that was looked upon as a characteristically American type. Such ships were suitable only for relatively sheltered waters, and accordingly became particularly identified with the Hudson River and the Detroit and St. Clair rivers. Frank E. Kirby had designed several ships of this type for the Hudson River Day Line and the operators out of Detroit. The Ashley & Dustin Line's *Put-in-Bay*, the only one of the ships of this type based in Detroit that regularly operated far out from the shore into Lake Erie, looked to many lay observers as if she might present a problem. The Steamboat Inspection Service convoked a meeting of its supervising inspectors at Detroit from September 22 to October 5, which gathered extensive evidence on the design characteristics of the steamers that served the port and on the practices of the officers in handling ballast tanks. Captain Fred J. Nemo, local inspector of hulls at Detroit, testified that the large steamers of the Detroit & Cleveland Navigation Company used water ballast for trimming at the wharf, but were not dependent on such ballast for stability.[185] Arthur J. Fox, captain of the *Put-in-Bay*, testified that he used the ship's trim tanks only to heel her at the wharf to adjust the angle of the gangplanks. The ship had an anti-roll tank on her center line, used for potable water, which Fox felt provided stability. He reported that she regularly started her trips with her tanks empty but had no problems because of the practice.[186]

The other type of ship that looked casually as if it might present stability problems was the whaleback steamer. This was a design particularly identified with the Great Lakes, developed by Captain Alexander McDougall and built by his American Steel Barge Company in Superior, Wisconsin. Viewed from the bow, a whaleback had a nearly cylindrical hull with a long spoon-shaped prow that swept upward markedly. The design looked as if the hull were in something approaching a neutral equilibrium, from which it could turn over easily. Actually, the ships were very well designed, and had an ideal record for stability. The design passed out not from considerations of stability but principally because the hull, being entirely of curved plates, was expensive to construct. The question of the stability of whalebacks was particularly urgent in Chicago, because the city's most heavily utilized excursion steamer, the *Christopher Columbus*,

The Goodrich Line scheduled a highly publicized inclining test of its *Christopher Columbus* off Grant Park to deal with worries about the ship's stability. Her unusual hull shape conveyed no confidence, but she was actually entirely stable. The ship at right is the *United Shores*, a local steamer that ran from downtown Chicago to Jackson and Lincoln parks. (Chicago Historical Society)

was the only passenger vessel ever built to this design. She had been designed by McDougall and built at the yard in Superior in 1892. She had operated between the foot of Randolph Street and the World's Columbian Exposition in Jackson Park for the duration of the fair in 1893. She had then run a daily round trip to Milwaukee, first for independent operators, and after 1898 for the Goodrich Line. Goodrich's directors recognized immediately that the disaster to the *Eastland* would work to the disadvantage of the excursion trade generally and their strangely shaped *Christopher Columbus* in particular. They directed their general manager, Harry W. Thorp—who had long prided himself on a low opinion of the *Eastland*—to arrange a conspicuous inclining test on the *Christopher Columbus*. He scheduled it off Grant Park, Chicago, for August 5, and with newspaper advertisements invited the public to observe it. He had the ship loaded with 7,500 sandbags, which were the equivalent in weight to 4,687 passengers, and had them moved to starboard to produce a list of 10 to 12 degrees. The ship had no difficulty, and righted herself at the end of the test.[187] If any readings of metacentric height were taken, the results were not published. As noted in Chapter I, a formal stability test was done on the *City of South Haven* in this period, with the finding that her metacentric height was 4'-10" in unloaded condition.

Among Landis's immediate problems was disposition of the hulk of the *Eastland*. As noted earlier, Hull had arranged for the hulk to be raised and moored in a yard of the Chicago Ship Building Company on the North Branch of the Chicago River. To deal with the prospect that the ship might be rebuilt and restored to service out of another city, two Chicago aldermen, Robert M. Buck and Ellis Geiger, announced that they would seek a court order directing DeWitt C. Cregler, the city custodian, to seize the hulk as a deadly weapon, have it scrapped, and disburse the proceeds for relief of the victims.[188] Nonetheless, Landis issued an order on August 17 releasing the hulk to its owner.[189] Given that the St. Joseph–Chicago Steamship Company was about to liquidate and that the various legal actions in prospect assured damage claims amounting to many times the value of the hulk—as it proved, approximately 194 times—Hull could have had no conceivable interest in retaining title to it. On August 18 the company's lawyer, Charles E. Kremer, requested that a trustee be established for the hulk.[190] Landis complied, and on August 19 the company surrendered title to the hulk to U.S. Marshal John J. Bradley. On August 21 Landis issued an injunction against suits or legal actions of any nature against the *Eastland*, assuring that any efforts at recovery of damages be made within the framework he was establishing. Landis appointed as trustee for the hulk Captain Denis E. Sullivan, an experienced lake master who was acting as a steamship and insurance agent with an office in the Continental & Commercial Bank building.[191] Sullivan hired Milton Edwards, a licensed Great Lakes master, as custodian. On August 27 Landis issued a monition directing all claims against the hulk to be submitted to Sullivan by December, and on September 20 Landis ordered Sullivan to sell it. Sullivan announced that the hulk would be sold at auction at 11:00 A.M. on December 20 at Bradley's office in the federal building.

At the appointed hour only two bidders appeared. Captain Edward A. Evers of the Illinois Naval Reserve announced in advance of the sale that he intended to bid for the hulk to rebuild it as a naval training vessel. He was quoted as saying:

The boat will make a fine training ship for the reserve. I mean to bid on it and expect to get it. There is nothing radically wrong with the hull. We could remove the two upper decks, put proper ballast in the hold, and provide watertight bulkheads and the *Eastland* hoodoo would be broken, and the boat prove a speedy, serviceable craft. It's a question of feasibility—not sentiment.[192]

Evers was opposed by attorney O. A. Gilbert of Boston, who represented Charles W. Morse's Continental Steamship Company of New York. Morse had a checkered career as an operator of steamers on the Hudson River and the Atlantic coast; he had been a dominant figure in the trade in the early years of the century, but failed after the Panic of 1907 and went briefly to federal prison under a conviction of 1909 for his financial dealings.[193] Gilbert opened the bidding for the *Eastland* at $5,000, and Evers responded with $10,000. Gilbert's final bid was $45,000. Gilbert told reporters that if the auction had been held two months earlier, he would have bid higher. He stated that Morse had intended to bring the ship through the Welland Canal to modify her as a freighter for coastal or transatlantic use. Reflecting the short-run demands for shipping in the period before America's entry into World War I, he asserted that the ship would have paid for herself in a single voyage. That might have been so in the immediate time frame of late 1915; however, for Morse's purposes it would have been necessary to keep the hulk in Chicago under guard until spring, and there was no assurance what the traffic would be then.[194] Evers consulted briefly with Kremer, and bid $46,000, whereupon Sullivan declared him the purchaser. Sullivan turned title to the hulk over to Evers on December 28. Evers had bid for the ship without any appropriation for what he was doing. He had successfully solicited funds for the purchase from Chicagoans whom he declined to identify, of whom utilities operator Samuel Insull was rumored to be the principal figure.[195] Evers stated to reporters that he planned to remove and replace the superstructure and install a permanent ballast system. He estimated the cost of the conversion at $100,000, which he hoped to secure from an appropriation, presumably from federal funds.[196] In a trivial adjunct to the auction, the ship's radio apparatus, which was of the spark type, not capable of voice communication, was sold separately for $15. The proceeds of the auction were deposited with the court and invested in Liberty Bonds at 5 percent. Sullivan's duties being ended, he was reimbursed for expenses of $1,912.87 and discharged in January 1916.[197]

Not only did Landis have to dispose of the hulk, but also, more importantly, he had to set up some mechanism for initiation of the civil actions for recovery of damages against the *Eastland*'s insurers by the heirs of the deceased. On August 16 the St. Joseph–Chicago Steamship Company petitioned for limitation of liability to the value of the hulk plus revenues pending, less the cost of salvage and certain prior claims.[198] The eligibility of the company for this limitation is the subject matter of Chapter VII, but for the present it is sufficient to say that if it were found that the ship was seaworthy at the time of the disaster and that the disaster occurred because of the actions of the officers without the knowledge and privity of the management, the company would be entitled to such a limitation.[199] If it were found that the ship was not seaworthy, the owners would be ineligible for the limitation, and her insurers would be liable for the State of Illinois's statutory damages for a wrongful death, $10,000 in the instance of each of the deceased. The controversy on this point was certain to be in the courts for years, or as it proved, for decades.

On August 18, 1915, Landis named James F. Bishop as administrator of the estates of Kate Austin and the rest of the deceased, and appointed

ments.[200] Both were attorneys in private practice in Chicago. Bishop immediately instituted a suit in the name of the estate of Earl H. Dawson, an
18-year-old press feeder at Western Electric.[201] In the longer run, Bishop
had to arrange representation with the heirs of the deceased. His repre-
senting them was not automatic; they were free to hire individual attorneys or to represent themselves. Mason's first reported activity was acting
as U.S. commissioner in the sale of the hulk in December.[202] Both men
were to be prominent in the civil actions that would run for more than
twenty years.

Impact on the Industry

The disaster, in spite of its magnitude, caused little of the questioning of
social values and even of religious beliefs that the *Titanic*'s sinking had
produced. It also appears to have had only a minor impact on the Lake
Michigan passenger steamship industry. Initially, the *Tribune* reported that
on the day of the disaster Graham & Morton's steamers left with normal
loads.[203] Marie Chudik, who had walked past the site of the disaster on her
way to the *Christopher Columbus*, reported that the crowd on the trip to
Milwaukee was small and subdued.[204] On the following day, Sunday, traffic on the steamers out of Chicago was only about 20 percent of normal.[205]
Undeniably, the disaster caused some people to question the safety of lake
steamers, which, no less than British transatlantic liners, had proven themselves a very secure mode of travel. This may have been an incentive for
people to turn to automobiles, which especially in that period were much
inferior in their safety record.

The Lake Michigan passenger lines are usually thought to have peaked
about 1912. Graham & Morton's *City of Grand Rapids* of that year was
the last major investment in the industry before its decline. After 1915 the
La Follette Seamen's Act proved as costly as had been predicted. Goodrich, throughout its history the largest of the Lake Michigan operators,
suffered the most. The company's one big excursion steamer, the *Christopher Columbus*, had her capacity cut from 4,000 to about 2,200. Unlike
the cross-lake excursion operators, Goodrich operated its major routes—
Chicago to Racine-Milwaukee and Chicago to Grand Haven–Muskegon—all year around, but its passenger traffic was almost entirely limited
to the summer months. The company was not a specialized carrier of fruit.
Goodrich ships operated in the off-seasons essentially as freighters for
general cargo, with only handfuls of passengers. The manning requirements for passenger vessels under the La Follette Seamen's Act became so
onerous to the company in the off-season as to threaten its long-standing
mode of operation if not its very existence. It quickly dropped plans to

spend a half million dollars on a new passenger steamer, and instead built a smaller ice-breaking freighter, the *Nevada*, in 1915 to operate the off-season service on the Chicago–Grand Haven–Muskegon route more economically. Goodrich acquired some similar ships by absorbing two small Lake Michigan lines, the Benton Transit Company in 1929 and the West Ports Steamship Company in 1930.[206] As anticipated, the La Follette Seamen's Act contributed to the decline of domestic marine operations generally. The prediction that Great Lakes operators would stick with older vessels was verified. The Detroit & Cleveland Navigation Company's huge sidewheelers *Greater Detroit* and *Greater Buffalo* of 1924 were the only large passenger vessels built for the Great Lakes after the act went into effect.

The traffic of the Lake Michigan lines was all of a character to be prone to the competition of motor transport. The principal freight from Michigan, fruit, could move directly in trucks from farms or centralized shipping facilities to the Chicago market without transshipment. This was, in fact, one of the earliest trades to shift to trucking. By 1932, 90 percent of the traffic moved by truck, the rest by rail, and none at all by ship.[207] Passenger traffic was predominately pleasure travel, which shifted to the automobile over the course of the 1920's. Hard-surfaced highways, including an undivided four-lane road through Indiana, linked Chicago and the Michigan ports relatively early. The Chicago & South Haven Steamship Company gave up in 1927. Graham & Morton was merged into the Goodrich Line in 1924, but Goodrich itself became unprofitable in 1926 and was wound up in bankruptcy proceedings in 1932–33.[208] Independent operators served what was left of the demand for day excursions out of Chicago with the *Theodore Roosevelt* until World War II and with the *City of Grand Rapids* until 1950. The longest-lived operation, inevitably, was the Wisconsin & Michigan Steamship Company's cross-lake service between Milwaukee and Muskegon, which operated as an auto ferry rather than competing with the automobile. The company's *Milwaukee Clipper* operated until antipollution requirements laid her up after the 1970 season.

The industry conformed to a standard pattern of decline, going first quickly and then slowly, finally passing out of existence after a long period. The experience was entirely parallel to the declines of local steamboats on the other Great Lakes, on Chesapeake Bay, Long Island Sound, the Hudson River, Puget Sound, and elsewhere. The *Eastland* disaster could not have had a positive effect on the industry, but there is little reason to believe that it had any strongly negative influence relative to forces that would have caused the industry to decline and to be eliminated in any case.

CHAPTER SIX

The
Criminal
Actions

O N September 22, 1915, preliminary to announcement of the federal grand jury's indictments, State's Attorney Maclay Hoyne and federal District Attorney Charles F. Clyne met to coordinate the state and federal criminal actions. The Cook County grand jury, it will be remembered, had acted more quickly than its federal counterpart. Hoyne agreed to waive any priority the state had on that ground, and to allow the federal action to be disposed of before any state action was taken.[1]

The Federal Action

As mentioned in the previous chapter, on September 29, 1915, Judge Kenesaw Mountain Landis issued a federal bench warrant for the arrest of Arnold, Hull, Reid, Eckliff, Pedersen, and Erickson—but not Greenebaum, Steele, or Davis—on the charge of conspiracy to operate an unsafe ship.[2] Because the alleged conspiracy had taken place in Michigan, but also because of problems in extraditing residents of Michigan to Illinois, the case was assigned to Judge Clarence W. Sessions of the District Court at Grand Rapids, Michigan. Because of the technical nature of issues in admiralty, such cases are typically heard without a jury. By prearrange-

Clarence W. Sessions, the judge in Grand Rapids, Michigan, who early in 1916 heard the federal criminal action for conspiracy to operate an unsafe ship. (Grand Rapids Bar Association)

ment Sessions took evidence as a commissioner. His handling of the case was very adept; as should be evident from the documentation of the present book, the transcript of testimony in the case is by far the most complete surviving source on the disaster.

The prosecution was carried on by U.S. District Attorney Charles F. Clyne, assisted by Joseph B. Fleming of his own staff in Chicago and Oliver E. Pagin of the attorney general's office in Washington. Clyne, in his initial presentation, alleged that the *Eastland* was exceptionally top-heavy and cranky, inclined to list dangerously, and liable to capsize from sudden shifts of wind or sea, or from the shift of passengers on deck. Specifically, he argued that the ballast system was inadequate in having a single seacock of inadequate dimensions, lacking a metering system, and being unable to pump out one side while filling the other. He also charged that the officers were incompetent. Finally, he alleged that the defendants connived to send the ship forth in this unseaworthy condition in violation of the law.[3]

The defendants had individual attorneys, notably James J. Barbour for Pedersen and Clarence Darrow for Erickson. Barbour argued in his initial motion for dismissal that there was no evidence of a crime.[4] Darrow mainly organized his defense around an argument that the *Eastland*, though seaworthy and correctly handled, had been resting on some underwater obstruction. Such an interpretation had arisen almost immediately, partly because the actual reason for the disaster was quite technical, partly because the ship went into the river so abruptly after 7:27 that she gave the superficial impression of falling off something. Lynn, observing the ship rolling over, initially concluded that she must have been resting on the bottom, and so testified to the coroner's jury, but he later concluded on the basis of soundings around the wreck that he had been wrong.[5] This interpretation that she had been resting on something was necessarily coupled with a presumption that some other force acted on the ship to pull her over to port, such as the tug pulling on her,[6] or a sudden shift of passengers from starboard to port. The alleged shift of passengers to port has been variously attributed—either immediately or in subsequent interpretations—to their watching any of several happenings: the tug moving past preparatory to taking the *Eastland* out;[7] a launch passing with a motion picture camera;[8] a speedboat moving up the river at 40 miles per hour;[9] a whaleback steamer going past;[10] a fireboat passing down the river;[11] another steamer on the excursion pulling out of a berth to the west and passing the *Eastland*;[12] a troop of mounted policemen crossing the Clark Street bridge.[13] It has also been attributed simply to a desire of the passengers to watch the sights on the river generally.[14]

The question whether the *Eastland* was resting on an obstruction was of prime interest to the City of Chicago, for if Darrow could succeed with this line of argument, the city might be found in contributory negligence for dereliction of its obligation to keep the river free of obstruction. Accordingly, the obstructions in the river at the Chicago & South Haven wharf were thoroughly explored and carefully mapped. Weckler ordered Percy R. Hynes, junior engineer for the municipal Bureau of Rivers and Harbors, to take soundings in the immediate area of the disaster. Hynes did so on October 9, 1915, and found two pilings, both of which had been put in place to secure tackle for lowering sections of the La Salle Street tunnel when it was reconstructed for electric streetcars in 1911. The larger was about 4 feet out from the wharf approximately at the east line of La Salle Street, 16.1 feet below the surface with the water 0.2 feet below normal, or 16.3 feet below datum. The smaller was 8.3 feet out, 26.2 feet east of the east line of La Salle Street, 17.5 feet below the surface at the time of the disaster.[15] H. B. Vehstedt, a naval architect employed by the city to examine the wreck and to prepare the plan of the position of the wreck in the river, estimated that at a point 26 feet east of La Salle Street, the keel of the *Eastland* during loading had been 10'-10" above the bottom of the river, and that the top of the smaller pile was 5'-1" below the nearest point on the hull. He estimated that when water began to flow into the ship through the gangways the ship lowered 1'-9" below her fully loaded draft and that this brought her no closer than 3'-4" from this piling. The larger piling, which was about 4'-6" high, was about 6 inches to 1 foot east of the east line of the starboard aft gangway through which the ship loaded. He estimated that the *Eastland* cleared this piling by about 10'-9".[16] In cross-examination, presented with the most extreme estimates of the effects of loading passengers and of inflow of water through the gangway, he estimated that the ship approached no closer than 1'-4" to the smaller piling and 1'-0" to the larger.[17] Darrow persisted with this argument, even sending down a diver, William Deneau, to cut off the tops of the two pilings to put in evidence.[18] Barbour put on the stand Henry E. Cordell, a consulting engineer, who, having observed

Robert Reid—the inspector who certified the *Eastland* for 2,500 passengers on July 2, 1915—was a Great Lakes captain of long experience, rather than a naval architect. (Library of Congress)

the disaster from a distance of 50 to 75 feet, concluded that the ship must have been resting on something, and thought he could observe a mark on the starboard side of the bottom of the hull left by a piling. He proved unable to identify it in a photograph of the wreck.[19] The *Tribune* actually reported a third piling in the area, but it was so loosely held in the mud that after the disaster Weckler had a gang of three men pull it out manually simply by putting a chain around it.[20] It was not at issue in the trial.

The alternative and less popular argument that the ship was resting on an obstruction was based on the collapse of a building in the vicinity an unspecified number of years earlier. This, it was alleged, had left a rubble of brick and concrete at the Chicago & South Haven wharf to which the starboard side of the ship might have descended. Dr. Evans, as foreman of the coroner's jury, reported that a man had phoned him to say he had heard that a scowload of material had once been dumped over the La Salle Street tunnel to close a leak, but Evans found no confirmation of this.[21] Scott, as harbormaster in 1911, had found some rubble down an estimated 11'-9" to 12'-9" below the surface, extending out about 5'-6" from the wharf.[22] Sylvester N. Howard, a surveyor, took soundings by a pole on November 3, 1915, finding at distances 5 to 6 feet out from the wharf depths of 14'-0" to 14'-8". He found no depths in immediate proximity to the wharf less than 12'-0".[23] The *Eastland*'s hull was either 2'-9" or 4'-0" out from the wharf, and her keel about 22 feet out. With her draft of about 14'-0", the ship should have cleared any debris by more than the distance by which she cleared the pilings.

In refutation of arguments that the *Eastland* was resting on an obstruction, it was pointed out that the *City of South Haven*, which used the wharf daily, drew between 11'-0" and 12'-0" forward and 14'-6" aft, more than the *Eastland* did.[24] The first ship to use the wharf after the wreck of the *Eastland* was cleared proved to be the freighter *Neptune*, which had passed through the Clark Street bridge upbound, but was then caught at Wells Street by the restriction on opening the bridges in rush hours. The *Neptune* drew 18 feet aft, but was moored immediately alongside the wharf without any difficulty.[25]

The collateral explanations that the tug pulled the *Eastland* over or that a shift of her passengers did so were also subject to refutation. As noted in Chapter IV, the *Kenosha* had taken a line thrown from the *Eastland* by deckhand William Flannigan while the tug's crew was having breakfast, at some unspecified time between 7:05 and 7:20; Flannigan then proceeded from the promenade deck down to the line room a deck below in the expectation of taking in the line when the tug cast it off near the mouth of the river. Apparently on the basis of the tension on the line, Flannigan assumed that the tug was pulling hard on it; he had no way of observing what was happening from the line room, which was entirely enclosed. Because the *Eastland* had not yet cast off her forward lines, he presumed this

caused a leverage that pulled the ship over.[26] Actually, the evidence is convincing that the tug never pulled on the line. O'Meara waited for Pedersen's command to take the *Eastland*'s bow out, but the command never came. O'Meara, who recognized the impending disaster much in advance of Pedersen, would almost certainly not have obeyed such a command, and he was specifically directed not to do so by Weckler. John Ryan, tender of the Clark Street bridge, who observed the event closely after noticing the serious list about 7:10, reported that the line to the tug remained slack throughout.[27] Arthur MacDonald, the *Kenosha*'s chief engineer, stated that the tug's engines were not even turning over at the time of the capsizing.[28]

The explanation that a shift of passengers was the proximate cause of the disaster has always had great popularity, but it has little factual support. The Chicago *Tribune*, in its initial account, stated that the St. Joseph–Chicago Steamship Company's first explanation of the capsizing was a rush of passengers to port to see a passing launch, but that survivors the newspaper had interviewed denied this interpretation.[29] This explanation was based on a statement of gauge tender John Elbert, who by his own testimony was at work in the engine room assisting Erickson in handling the ballast tanks. He told reporters that as soon as Erickson had corrected for the initial starboard list—which is to say at 6:51—the passing of a launch caused a shift of the passengers to port, initiating a list to port that brought the starboard intakes to the ballast system up out of the river, preventing admission of any

Joseph M. Erickson, chief engineer of the *Eastland*. (Library of Congress)

more water.[30] This interpretation is open to several objections. His statement that the list to port brought starboard intakes above the waterline could not have been correct because the only intake to the ballast system was on the port side. Because from his position in the engine room he could not possibly have witnessed a shift of passengers, either his statement was an assumption, like Erickson's at the same time that the passengers had moved, or it was hearsay gathered subsequently. Elbert was not a reliable witness, in any case. He purported to have been a crew member of the *Titanic*, but is not on any list.[31]

Any rush that occurred could have been concentrated among the passengers on the hurricane deck and possibly also the open portions of the promenade deck, but because of the rain, as has already been noted, this number was limited. Sladkey, whose jumping aboard the ship is established quite precisely at 7:18 by the drawing in of the gangplank, reported

Walter K. Greenebaum, general manager of the Indiana Transportation Company, was the dominant figure in the company's history, which dated from 1901. (Library of Congress)

that the principal concentration of passengers was still to starboard when he reached the promenade deck, probably at 7:19. At that time the ship was in the reversal of the listing to port that began at 7:18, immediately before the beginning of the continuation of the list to port. As mentioned in Chapter IV, David Durand observed from a vantage point diagonally above the ship and across the river that the resumption of the list to port after 7:20 caused a significant movement of passengers to starboard. If so, the concentration to starboard increased after Sladkey's observation. It is almost inevitable that there was some drift of passengers away from the starboard rail after the ship was loaded, either to get out of the rain, or because friends on the wharf moved off to the *Theodore Roosevelt* and *Petoskey*, or simply because the ship was leaving. As mentioned in Chapter IV, Theodore Soderstrom told reporters that just before the ship began to leave her mooring several hundred passengers who had been waving to people on the wharf came over to the port side, where passengers were already ten to twenty deep. He said this occurred shortly before the final plunge and immediately before the ship's final reversal of the list to port, which is to say about 7:24.[32] This was 33 minutes after Erickson and Elbert believed the passengers were shifting to port. There is a further problem that Soderstrom did not state where the movement took place. If the load of passengers on the hurricane deck was only 150 to 175, as several observers testified, there were not enough there for a movement of the size Soderstrom described. If Pedersen was correct that there were 175 passengers on the hurricane deck, a shift in their weight of about 12.25 tons should not have been enough to cause the ship to capsize unless her metacentric height had been reduced to zero or less.

Soderstrom, it should be noted, did not report that the movement to port was a rush. There is considerable direct evidence that no such rush took place. Passenger C. B. Hadley specifically denied that any rush to port took place, on the ground that the picnickers had been packed too closely together for any mass movement to occur.[33] For the passengers in the interior of the vessel this is indisputably true. Richard J. Moore, who made his way to the hurricane deck before the capsizing, denied in his testimony before the coroner's jury that there had been any surge.[34] McCreary, who observed the *Eastland* from the wharf immediately beside the aft gangway and also from the wharf beside the *Petoskey* on the west side of La Salle

Street, saw no surge of passengers.[35] Dr. Evans reported on the basis of

testimony before the coroner's jury, "It did not appear from the evidence that the passengers rushed or surged in any direction."[36] Harry Hansen, in his history of the Chicago River, in a short, nontechnical, but generally accurate chapter on the disaster, concluded, "There had been no sudden rush to port by the passengers, who jammed the decks but seemed well distributed."[37]

Dickerson N. Hoover, acting director of the Steamboat Inspection Service, requested a specific report on the alleged shift of passengers to port from Ira B. Mansfield and William Nicholas immediately after the disaster. Nicholas spent a morning interviewing men employed along the river who had viewed the disaster, and reported:

I am not at all satisfied that there was any sudden shift of weight on the vessel at the time the line was cast off. It was reported that a squad of mounted police passing over the bridge caused the crowd to surge to the rail. It was also reported that a motion picture machine in a launch caused this rush. I have fairly authentic information there was no rush.[38]

The evidence on the purported causes of a surge to port proves to be weak. Of these explanations, the most plausible, simply because of coincidence in time, is that passengers moved to port to watch the tug pass.

Harry Pedersen, captain of the *Eastland* (at right), giving his version of the disaster to assistant state's attorney M. F. Sullivan (at left). Between them is E. J. Fleming of Sullivan's staff. (Library of Congress)

William H. Hull, general manager of the St. Joseph–Chicago Steamship Company. (Library of Congress)

The *Kenosha* passed the port side of the *Eastland* about 7:00, or if one accepts MacDonald's chronology, as early as 6:45, a half hour to 45 minutes before the capsizing. If the tug passed by at 7:00, her movement approximately coincided with the beginning of the ship's second list to port, which caused Erickson to suppose that the passengers had shifted toward the river, and it is reasonable to presume that at least some people did so. After the accident none of the passengers provided any evidence of this, much less of a rush to port. The attribution of a shift to the passing of a fireboat is clearly incorrect. As noted in Chapter V, the fireboat *Graeme Stuart* was ordered out immediately after the disaster, but did not approach the *Eastland* for about ten minutes, either, as was alleged, because the captain feared a boiler explosion on the wreck or, as he stated, because the river was too clogged with people for him immediately to approach the wreck more closely than Wells Street. The other fireboat involved, the *D. J. Swenie*, was not in the immediate area, and arrived only along with the other rescue vessels well after the *Eastland* had come to rest. The most popular of these hypotheses, that a launch taking motion pictures went past, lacks substantiation. In summarizing the coroner's jury's findings Dr. Evans reported, "The street rumors that moving pictures were being taken from the river side, that a boat went by, were not corroborated." [39]

Similarly, there was no evidence brought forth of a fast-moving speedboat. The explanation that a whaleback steamer went past is demonstrably incorrect. The only whaleback steamer in the river was the *Christopher Columbus*, which was at the Goodrich wharf on the south bank just east of the Rush Street bridge awaiting her departure for Milwaukee at 9:30. The suggestion that one of the other steamers on the excursion left earlier and passed the *Eastland* from the west is wrong according to both literary and photographic evidence. The only ship chartered for the excursion with a berth to the west was the *Petoskey*, but she was not due out until 8:30, and photographs of the wreck show that she was still in her berth west of La Salle Street during the rescue operations immediately after the disaster. Because the picnic was canceled, the *Petoskey* not only failed to leave before the *Eastland* but never left on the excursion at all. Rather, she was moved later in the day to the Rush Street wharf for one of the Indiana Transportation Company's regular departures. There is no evidence of a troop of mounted policemen in the area.

The Sadler Evaluation

In an effort to establish the seaworthiness or lack of it of the *Eastland*, Clyne solicited an evaluation of the ship's stability by Professor Herbert Charles Sadler. Because this is the only professional analysis of the ship, and because it exists only in the form of testimony in an unpublished transcript, it is reproduced in this book as Appendix C, along with the comments on it of four naval architects. Sadler did not, as far as can be determined, prepare a written text of his evaluation.

Sadler went aboard the wreck as it lay in the river about a week after the disaster, and again about two weeks later after the hulk had been raised and moved to its mooring at the yard of the Chicago Ship Building Company on North Halsted Street on the North Branch. He took with him for the second inspection a set of plans of the ship showing her as built, and noted the changes made in her since construction. This meant that he did not consider the effect of the changes of July 2, 1915, in isolation from the numerous earlier changes in the ship. He calculated the metacenter directly from the plans and estimated the center of gravity by analogy to similar

Professor Herbert Charles Sadler in a photograph probably taken in Britain in the 1890's, well before he assumed his duties at the University of Michigan. (Michigan Historical Collections, Bentley Historical Library, University of Michigan)

ships with which he was familiar, combined with the information available to him on the loading of passengers and the admission of water to the ballast tanks. Necessarily, his calculations required several assumptions concerning the distribution of weight. He estimated that the passengers loaded over the course of half an hour at the rate to four to five tons per minute. He assumed that they distributed themselves so as to put 300 on the hurricane deck, 1,100 on the promenade deck, 1,100 on the 'tween decks, and remarkably, none on the main deck, even though there was abundant evidence that it was jammed with people. Sadler's basis for this assumption is particularly difficult to comprehend because, as he could hardly have been unaware, the principal concentration of bodies on the wreck had been on the main deck at the staircases leading upward. Sadler thought that his assumed distribution understated the number on the promenade deck. Partly because he estimated the number of passengers on the hurricane deck much higher than Pedersen, who put it at 175, or George Haber and Henry Vantak, who estimated 150, and partly because he assumed no passengers on the main deck, Sadler apparently estimated the center of gravity with respect to the passengers somewhat higher than it actually was. Sadler also was forced to make an assumption concerning the distribution of water in the ballast tanks. He assumed that at the time of capsizing, which he took as 7:30, the port No. 2 tank contained 10 tons, the starboard No. 2 tank 35 tons, and the starboard No. 3 tank 20 tons. Because the port tanks were submerged in the disaster and the starboard tanks exposed horizontally, it was impossible to know the content of the tanks from examination of the wreck. Erickson never estimated the amount of water he admitted to the ballast system. Accordingly, there appears no way of evaluating Sadler's estimates on the basis of the evidence. He assumed that the ship contained 60 tons of coal, which is considerably below any of the estimates of the officers except Pedersen, and even below the 75 to 80 tons of coal found in the wreck.

Because his calculations depended upon three assumptions, two of which contain apparent errors and one of which was unavoidably arbitrary, Sadler might have been expected to express his estimates as a range, but he did not do so. He estimated that the *Eastland*'s metacentric height when loading began was 1.75 feet. He developed a chart showing the decline in metacentric height during loading, ending with a metacentric height of only 0.15 feet as she was fully loaded. Under cross-examination by Clarence Darrow, he estimated that doubling his assumed amount of coal to 120 tons would have added only another 0.15 feet to her metacentric height when fully loaded. He estimated that the metacenter was 16.15 feet above the keel and the center of gravity only 16.0 feet. He had measured the aft port gangway on the hulk and ascertained that the half

doors were 4′-6″ high with a sill of 9 inches below them. He concluded
that a 15-degree list, which would be produced by a distribution of passengers centered 3 to 4 feet off of the center line, would bring water over the
half doors, flood the main deck, reduce the stability to negative, and cause
the ship to capsize. He stated that if the half doors were not watertight, the
situation would be accelerated. The Chicago *Tribune* specifically reported
that the half doors were not watertight.[40] As noted in Chapter IV, Lobdell
testified in Secretary Redfield's inquiry that the half doors to the aft port
gangway were open. Sadler's analysis implies that the ship was in a situation that would cause her to capsize possibly by 7:15, certainly by 7:20.
This is consistent with Erickson's first observation of water coming in
through the scuppers onto the main deck when the list to port resumed at
7:20. Water did not apparently begin coming through the gangways until
a few minutes later. Sadler's table, which has not survived in the file of the
case, led Sessions to conclude that the *Eastland* would have been ordinarily stable in the absence of ballast with a load of 1,250 passengers, a
conclusion with which Sadler agreed. Sadler stated that even under those
circumstances, the *Eastland* would have had a metacentric height only
about a third to half what is normal for an excursion steamer of her character, but he believed that an adequate margin of safety would have been
provided. Sadler estimated that a passenger steamer of her characteristics
should have had a metacentric height of two to three feet fully loaded. He
estimated that the *Eastland* would have been ordinarily stable if her No. 2
and 3 ballast tanks had been kept filled—a conclusion consistent with the
behavior of the Michigan Steamship Company after the event of July 17,
1904. He expressed a preference for a permanent ballast system of pig iron
or similar material on the ground that it is foolproof.

Sadler addressed himself to the question of the effect of the partly filled
ballast tanks on the stability of the ship. He showed the court a diagram of
the cross section of a ship—which has also not survived in the file of the
case—to demonstrate that in a partly filled tank at a slight degree of list
the water will take its effect on the center of gravity of the ship at a higher
level than the water itself. Specifically, he stated that the weight of the
water in the *Eastland*'s partly filled No. 3 starboard tank would have the
effect of the same weight, twenty tons, on the third deck up, which is to
say the promenade deck. This was presumably included in his calculations. In cross-examination by Darrow, he unambiguously denied that the
ship's alleged resting on a piling or on the river bottom would have contributed to her capsizing.[41]

Sadler's assumptions concerning the distribution of passengers, which
put them relatively high on the ship, and the weight of coal, which put a
low amount below the center of gravity, would lead one to believe that he

understated the actual metacentric height. There is no evidence, however, on the accuracy of his estimates for the weight of water in the ballast tanks. In particular, there seems no reason to accept his estimate that the No. 2 starboard tank held more water than the No. 3 starboard tank, which was considerably larger. Consequently, there is no presumption that his estimates are precisely accurate.

Apart from Sadler's other assumptions, he attributed the imbalance on the ship to the weight of the passengers being concentrated three to four feet off center to port.[42] He did not assign a time to this, but rather stated that the condition existed when the list to port reached 15 degrees, which would put it about 7:15. This does not accord with the historical evidence. As noted in Chapter IV, Sladkey found the principal concentration of passengers to starboard when he arrived on the promenade deck near the bow about 7:19, and Durand reported that the passengers moved to starboard when the list to port resumed at 7:20. As indicated previously, there is no credible evidence that any general drift of passengers away from the starboard side took place until the stern line was cast off and the stern began to swing out at 7:24. All allegations that such a shift occurred earlier, beginning with Erickson's, which put the shift at 7:00, after he first corrected for the list to port, and ending with Sadler's, are suppositions based on the ground that the behavior of the ship was consistent with such a shift's having taken place.

Although the initial list to starboard was discussed in the course of his interrogation, Sadler made no use of it in his calculations. Had he expressed his estimates of metacentric height as a range, rather than as specific numbers, he would almost certainly have had to consider the possibility that the ship's metacentric height was reduced to negative in the course of loading. The ship's behavior in first listing to starboard and immediately beginning to list more severely to port when Erickson attempted to correct for the initial list is more consistent with her metacentric height having turned negative before 7:00, possibly as early as 6:48, than with its having remained, as Sadler concluded, insignificantly positive until water began flowing through the scuppers onto the main deck about 7:20. The sequence of events starting at 6:48 is most consistent with a negative metacentric height with a strong free-surface effect from the partly filled ballast tanks. Sadler also took no notice of the reversals of direction in the course of the list to port.

Finally, Sadler did not consider the question whether the ship's asymmetry in ingesting water from port and pumping it out to starboard had played any role in the disaster. In the event of July 17, 1904, the more severe list to starboard that followed the initial list to port increased the angle of the intake pipe into the ballast system. Two of the serious problems reported during the *Eastland*'s service on Lake Erie involved primary lists to port. As mentioned in Chapter II, Frank Lee Stevenson, in his report on a list of the *Eastland* while loading an excursion of Sherwin-Williams employees at Cleveland, stated that the inclination was to port, but that movement of the passengers to starboard corrected for it. Robert O. Moyer was specific that on the excursion of the Maccabees out of Cleveland on July 1, 1912, the first list was to port and the second, which was the more severe, was to starboard. Erickson, even though he was dealing with a smaller concentration of weight on the hurricane deck than Eeles and Nack in the event of 1904, failed in his effort to right the ship when the initial list was to starboard and the secondary list was to port. As noted, he could not admit any significant amount of water after 7:16. Because the initial list was to starboard and the greater list was to port, the angle of the intake pipe became negative. Because the entire ballast system was below water level, it is not clear that this should have made any difference. Flatow, however, testified in 1932 that the *Eastland* "acted a whole lot different" when loading from the starboard side at the Chicago & South Haven wharf from the way she behaved when loading from the port side at her own berth at Rush Street.[43] She also loaded from the port side in St. Joseph. We are unlikely to advance upon Sadler's analysis, however, for the plans he used did not survive in the file of the case, and no plans beyond the outboard profile reproduced in this book are known.

Sessions delivered his decision on February 18, 1916, briefly stating that he could find no probable cause for believing that a conspiracy took place. He held the defendants not guilty and denied an application of the federal government for a writ of removal to extradite the defendants who were residents of Michigan to Illinois to stand trial on the indictments of the Cook County grand jury in Chicago.[44] Although the transcript of testimony and a limited number of exhibits were retained, many exhibits, including the plans and a model of the *Eastland*'s ballast system, were not, a loss that seriously reduces the possible documentation of the case.

It is difficult to find fault with Sessions's decision. As he found, there is no evidence of a criminal conspiracy among the defendants. Rather, they were all behaving as they habitually did, oblivious to the fact that a worldwide movement for increasing boat and raft capacity relative to passenger capacity would affect their ship as an outlier in a statistical distribution of ships ranked by stability, and in the process produce a catastrophe.

In two respects, however, Sessions's decision is unsatisfying. First, the testimony before him had refuted the explanation that the disaster followed from the *Eastland*'s resting on pilings about as thoroughly as legal evidence could do. He explicitly refrained from judgment on this point, however, on the ground that it was a matter of fact suitable for a jury's determination. Because he was hearing evidence as a commissioner and delivering his judgment in a case that had no jury, in conformity with admiralty procedure, he seems to have constrained himself unnecessarily.

Second, by basing his decision solely on the absence of evidence of a conspiracy, Sessions avoided making a judgment on whether the *Eastland* was seaworthy at the time of the disaster. There were two issues: whether the ship was unsafe and, if so, whether a conspiracy took place to operate her. He might easily have held, preliminary to finding the absence of a conspiracy, that the ship was unsafe, basing his opinion on Sadler's testimony. Sadler had testified, first, that a water ballast system of the sort the *Eastland* had was inherently unsafe in an excursion vessel because of the free movement of passengers on the decks and the risk of incorrect decisions by the officers operating the system. Second, Sadler told the court that the ship was dangerous unless tanks No. 2 and 3 were kept filled at all times. Either because of the ship's intrinsic characteristics or because of the company's practice of starting trips with the ballast tanks empty, the ship could have been held unseaworthy, even if Sessions, like Sadler, did not specifically consider the effect of the changes in her on July 2, 1915. Similarly, Dr. W. A. Evans's report as foreman of the Cook County coroner's jury was an official public document on which Sessions might have drawn. Evans had concluded that the *Eastland* was physically unfit for the voyage to Michigan City, and that she was negligently managed and operated.

The question of the ship's seaworthiness could not be avoided in the civil case, however. As a consequence of Sessions's failure to resolve the problems, both the issues whether the ship rested on pilings or other obstructions to the berth and whether the ship was seaworthy were unresolved. Both were to bulk large in the civil action.

The outcome of the federal criminal trial would probably have been more satisfactory if the prosecution had been carried on under the charges in the grand jury's indictments—conspiracy to defraud the government by interfering with execution of federal maritime laws and criminal carelessness—rather than the charge of conspiracy to operate an unsafe ship in Landis's bench warrant. The decision with respect to the alleged conspiracy would presumably have been the same, but the charge of criminal carelessness would have required determination of the seaworthiness of the ship and of the negligence or lack of it on the part of the accused. Because criminal carelessness was one of the charges of the Illinois indictments, along with manslaughter, these issues might have been determined in the state proceeding, but that too failed to accomplish what might reasonably have been expected of it.

At their meeting of September 22 Hoyne and Clyne purported only to establish federal primacy in the criminal actions, but as it proved, their agreement preempted criminal action for the federal authorities entirely. The files on the Illinois cases have been destroyed, but a British writer who investigated them states that the indictments had been dropped by 1920, those against Pedersen and Erickson with leave to reinstate, the rest outright. The indictments of Pedersen and Erickson were never reinstated.[45] Both Sessions's decision that the defendants in the criminal action were not guilty and his denial of the federal motion for a writ of extradition of the defendants to Illinois were strong disincentives to Hoyne to pursue the state action.

In the case of Erickson, the question became moot in 1919. He had joined the Army Transport Service and sailed in World War I as chief engineer on the transports *Buford* and *Peerless* as a lieutenant. His military experience had been favorable and he wanted to continue it, but he developed a heart condition. Following the war he was allowed to return to Grand Haven on a medical leave. He expected to return to his military service, but his physicians were pessimistic. He died at his home in Grand Haven of valvular heart disease on April 3, 1919, only five days after his thirty-seventh birthday.[46] His early death meant that he was able to testify on his actions only in the coroner's inquest and in the criminal trial, not in the civil trial.

If Erickson had survived to be prosecuted, the charges were of a character that Darrow should have been able to refute in his defense—although the nature of the defense he made for Erickson in Grand Rapids leads one to question whether he would actually have done so. As stated in the previous chapter, Erickson was charged with three counts: negligence in filling the ballast tanks, negligence in keeping the ballast tanks in repair, and negligence in failing to close the chock holes and gangways. The ballast tanks were in good repair and functioned as they always had. The intake may have been clogged after 7:16, but it had functioned perfectly well earlier, so that neither Erickson nor any other crew member could be said to have neglected its maintenance. Erickson did not have authority over the gangways and chock holes. Accordingly, the only charge on which he might reasonably have been found guilty was negligence in filling the ballast tanks. In this, he did only what he and his predecessors had done throughout the ship's history. If there was negligence involved, it was on the part of Hull or Pedersen in not informing him that the *Eastland* might now have to be handled as a ship of negative metacentric height because of the changes of July 2. Accordingly, Erickson should have been exonerated in the state action as well as the federal.

Similarly, the four officers of the firm indicted in Illinois—Hull, Arnold, Steele, and Davis—could probably have been exonerated on the five counts levied against them: that they knew the *Eastland* was unseaworthy and lacked stability; that they permitted 2,500 passengers aboard, which was in excess of the ship's capacity; that they were negligent in hiring an incompetent engineer; that the crew was too small; and that the ballast tanks were out of repair and not filled. The first count was rather the reverse of the charges that might properly have been laid against them. To judge from their testimony in Grand Rapids, they clearly did not know that the ship had stability problems and was therefore unseaworthy; rather, they were negligent in failing to ascertain the ship's history, which would have demonstrated abundantly that she had such problems. The 2,501 passengers were only 1 over her licensed capacity, and federal officers had counted the 2,500 aboard to assure compliance. Sladkey's boarding had the approval neither of the management nor of the federal inspectors. The size of the crew had also been certified by Reid when he assigned her the capacity of 2,500. Erickson's handling of the ship was competent relative to what he had been told. The management's negligence was not in hiring him but rather in failing to consider that the changes of July 2 might produce a negative metacentric height, and failing to inform him. As stated earlier, the ballast tanks were in the same state of repair they had always been and, until the mysterious occurrence that prevented their being filled after 7:16, were functioning normally. Accordingly, a case could be made for finding the management criminally negligent, but not on the counts of the Illinois indictment.

The case against Pedersen was also imperfect, but was much the strongest of the three indictments. On the first count, that he permitted boarding of a larger number of passengers than the ship could safely carry, he was only abiding by the recent federal licensure of the vessel. On the third and fourth counts, that he was negligent in assuring that the ballast tanks were in good repair and properly filled, he was doing only what his predecessors had all done—and what was customary on the Lakes—namely, leaving the ballast tanks to his chief engineer. On the fifth count, that he failed to keep the chock holes and gangways closed while the ship was boarding, the ship's usual practice was the standard one of keeping the lower portion of the half doors closed, but as photographic evidence indicates, she frequently operated with them open. Whether they should be opened or closed was the captain's responsibility, but there is no evidence that Pedersen took any action on this matter. When Lobdell testified that the port aft doors were entirely open, he did not say whose decision was responsible. Pedersen might be considered negligent for allowing the ship to board a load that he knew would fill her to her licensed capacity with the lower portions of the half doors open. The chock holes had no covers, and to have had them would not have been standard practice.

On the second count, that he failed to warn passengers to leave when it became apparent that the ship would overturn, Pedersen might easily have been found negligent. His perceptions of the listing of the ship had been erroneous until the instant of capsizing. Although he was not uniformly a truthful witness, there is no reason to question his testimony as to what he thought was the list at various times. He would not have rung "Stand by" at 7:24 unless, as he testified, he seriously underestimated the severity of the list throughout the event, relative to what Erickson was concluding by watching the pendulum indicator in the engine room. Weckler stated before the coroner's jury and in the criminal trial that Pedersen could have gotten the passengers off in the seventeen minutes the ship listed severely, and should have attempted to do so.[47] As noted in Chapter IV, William L. Nack, on the basis of his experience on the ship from 1904 to 1906, testified before Redfield's inquiry that with 2,500 passengers aboard, a list, and nearly empty ballast tanks, it was too late to correct the situation, and the passengers should have been ordered off.[48] This implies that the ship was in a hopeless condition by 7:10, exactly when Pedersen should have begun taking the passengers off according to Weckler's argument. By 7:28 or 7:29, when Pedersen finally recognized the ship was capsizing, his order came so late that only passengers in immediate proximity to the starboard gangways could jump off. Coroner's jury foreman Dr. W. A. Evans, in the passage quoted in the previous chapter summarizing his recommendations to the Cook County grand jury, concluded strongly that Pedersen had been negligent in failing to attempt to get the passengers off over the course of fifteen minutes when he could have done so. Evans also considered the management negligent for having hired Pedersen. These were issues that should have been placed before a jury.

Accordingly, in not pursuing the prosecution of Pedersen for criminal carelessness, the Illinois authorities prevented justice from being done in the criminal actions. Unfortunately, a worse miscarriage of justice was impending in the civil case.

CHAPTER SEVEN

The Civil Actions

A DISASTER that produced some 844 wrongful deaths assured long and acrimonious tort actions, even though one may question whether they should have endured for over 20 years. As stated in Chapter V, Judge Kenesaw Mountain Landis appointed James F. Bishop administrator of the estates of Kate Austin and the rest of the deceased, and Lewis F. Mason as commissioner. Bishop began his efforts by bringing suit in the form of a libel in the name of Earl H. Dawson and all other victims against the St. Joseph–Chicago Steamship Company, the Indiana Transportation Company, the Dunham Towing & Wrecking Company, the City of Chicago, the Chicago City Railways Company, the M. H. McGovern Company, M. H. McGovern himself, the Great Lakes Dredge & Dock Company, Cohen & Company, Ferdinand W. Peck, the Sanitary District of Chicago, and the Western Electric Company. Some of the defendants were obvious, but Bishop alleged that Dunham had negligently attached and operated the *Kenosha*, and that Chicago City Railways, with McGovern as its contractor, and Great Lakes Dredge & Dock had negligently allowed debris to remain after rebuilding the La Salle Street tunnel. Peck and Cohen & Company were owners of buildings along the Chicago & South Haven wharf, who, he alleged, had negligently allowed debris to accumulate. The Sanitary District was accused of not maintaining the level of the river at a safe figure. He accused Western Electric of negligence in providing the steamer.[1] The case was filed on August 21, 1915, but for reasons unclear, Bishop brought an essentially identical action in the name of Herman A. Ristow on June 14, 1916.[2] The cases were pursued jointly.

On July 24, 1916, Bishop received permission from Landis to add to the list of plaintiffs 373 additional libelants. The Indiana Transportation Company responded that it should not be called to answer additional libelants in an existing action. Landis overruled this objection, but directed Indiana Transportation's lawyers to respond within twenty days of his order, which was dated September 18, 1916. They petitioned the court on October 7 with the claim that it lacked jurisdiction with respect to the additional libelants, but they also petitioned the United States Supreme Court on October 25, 1916, for a writ of prohibition against expansion of the case. On June 11, 1917, Justice Oliver Wendell Holmes, Jr., issued the writ as requested, denying the 373 additional libelants the right to intervene.[3] This action did not literally estop the case, but did result in its not being pursued. As late as February 9, 1939, Judge James H. Wilkerson in Chicago agreed to hear argument on vacating the writ.[4] There is no indication that he took any action, nor even that he heard argument, but his document is the last known evidence of activity in the *Eastland* cases in the courts.

The Action to Limit Liability

Because Bishop's libel actions came to naught, the civil action was in fact fought out on the issue of the St. Joseph–Chicago Steamship Company's eligibility for a limitation of liability to the value of the hulk, adjusted for revenues pending and various claims. Because the St. Joseph–Chicago Steamship Company had already announced its intention to liquidate, this case would necessarily be an action between Bishop and the legal representatives of the insurers. The *Eastland* had been insured for sums between $120,000 and $150,000, depending upon circumstances, through Johnson & Higgins, insurance brokers.[5] The liability insurance was borne by members of Lloyd's of London. The case began with a petition on August 16, 1915, to the federal District Court at Chicago by the attorneys for the St. Joseph–Chicago Steamship Company for limitation of liability to the value of the hulk plus prospective revenues from the voyage, less the cost of salvage, outstanding obligations connected with the ship, and other prior claims.[6] Bishop responded on February 5, 1916, as administrator of the estates of 143 of the deceased. On July 22 he filed for an additional 359, and he later filed for 262 more.[7] Jesse Wilcox had filed as administrator for 80 between June 5 and July 8, 1915, and later filed for 2 additional.

Bishop and Wilcox between them represented 846 estates. Bishop's response of July 22 was also made in the name of 32 estates represented by relatives of the deceased or by independently appointed attorneys. This is a total of 878 estates, a number significantly larger than the 844 deaths in the highest report of the period immediately following the disaster. There was probably some degree of overlap in the submissions, and there were probably some fraudulent entries made in an effort to collect the $10,000 benefit. Bishop alleged 32 counts of negligence in operation of an unsafe steamer, acceptance of which by the court would have rendered the company ineligible for a limitation of liability.

The issue would be fought out within a framework of law unique to maritime issues.

The Framework of Law

The question of the St. Joseph–Chicago Steamship Company's eligibility for a limitation of liability had to be determined under a body of statute law dating in America from 1851. By the eighteenth century all major maritime nations except Britain had developed a doctrine that liability of a shipowner was limited to the value of the ship plus freights pending, which is to say the earnings of the voyage, if the ship were seaworthy and the negligent acts involved were committed without the knowledge and privity of the owner. Britain pursued an ordinary doctrine of *respondeat superior* whereby the owner bore the responsibility for tortious acts of the officers and crew of his ship. Britain began to conform with international practice when in 1734 it enacted a statute that limited liability to the value of the ship and freights pending in cases of embezzlement or malversion of masters or mariners.[8] In 1786 the limitation of liability was extended to losses in which the master and mariners had no part. Losses by fire were entirely excluded from the owner's responsibility, along with liability for gold and jewels unless the value was explicitly declared.[9] By an act of 1813 the limitation of liability was extended to negligence of masters and mariners, including damage to other ships and their cargoes in collisions.[10] Under this statute the value of the ship in the computation of its value and freights pending was taken as the worth before the injury to the ship.

The American statute of 1851, An Act to Limit the Liability of Ship Owners,[11] was, like its counterparts elsewhere, intended to increase the volume of capital committed to merchant shipping by providing a limitation of liability analogous to the limited liability of shareholders in corporations. Ships were expected to be owned by individuals or partnerships; corporate ownership, in the main, came later. The statute, which is brief, limited liability of owners to the value of the vessel and freights pending if the ship were seaworthy and the acts causing the damage were taken without the knowledge and privity of the owner. Remarkably, no use was made of the statute until 1866, when the steamer *City of Norwich* hit a schooner in Long Island Sound, sinking the schooner, setting herself on fire, and finally capsizing. Because it was unambiguous that the steamer was at fault, the owners petitioned for limitation of liability. The accident had brought forth a large number of actions by the owners of the schooner, shippers of freight on the steamer, and others. In a case of 1871, Norwich Co. v. Wright, the Supreme Court held that under the act of 1851 the owners were entitled to a limitation of liability in which the value of the vessel should be taken not as the value when she began the voyage but rather as the value of the hulk, which was $2,500.[12] This was a major difference from British practice. In 1875 it was held in the *City of Norwich* case that the surrender value of the ship should be her value when raised less the cost of raising her.[13] In the event of a total loss, the owner could be free of responsibility; Judge Erastus C. Benedict cited with approbation the continental precedent that the owner could discharge his liability by abandoning the wreck and the insurance money.[14] In one of the later cases arising from this accident, the Supreme Court held that proceeds of the insurance need not be turned over as part of the owner's equity.[15] It was later held, however, that an owner might be held for his outstanding contractual obligations, as for repair and supplies in his home port.[16]

The statutory authority for this policy was expanded in the 1880's. A statute of 1884 extended the limitation on liability to all claims except seamen's wages, and another of 1886 extended the policy to inland vessels.[17] Admiralty Rules 54, 55, 56, and 57, all of May 6, 1872, assigned exclusive jurisdiction to federal admiralty courts, assuring that the proceedings would be held without juries. Rule 55 specified that proof of claims must be submitted to a commissioner.[18] Mason had been appointed as that commissioner for the *Eastland*.

The limitation on liability was not absolute, but it was nearly so. The extent of it is best shown in the case of the *Annie Faxon*,[19] a decision of 1895 that stood in 1915 as the principal precedent for a case of the *Eastland*'s character. The vessel was a steamer on the Snake River in Idaho, owned by the Oregon Railway & Navigation Company and operated by an affiliate. She was inspected on December 12, 1892, and certificated to operate at 125 pounds pressure. In June 1893 the mud ring on the boiler was replaced and some minor changes were made. On August 14, 1893, proceeding downstream with 110 pounds pressure, her boiler exploded, killing 8 persons and injuring 15. The court found that the boiler was old, blistered, and patched. In the course of hammering incidental to installing the new mud ring, the iron became brittle, which condition caused the explosion. The court found that there was negligence on the part of some

servants of the owner in using such an old boiler, and also in not having
tested and inspected it after the last repairs. The law was found to have
been violated by the omission of inspection after the new ring was installed. There was no evidence that the managing officers had any knowledge of the weakness of the boiler, and thus they were entitled to the limitation of liability to the value of the hulk and freights pending, $3,520.

In the case of the *Eastland*, the changes of July 2, 1915, were made
with steamboat inspection, and the issue of how much Hull, the manager,
knew of them is ambiguous because he and Pedersen gave differing accounts of the decision to make the changes. There was no assurance which
account the court would accept, nor even any reason to believe that a court
would point to the changes of July 2 as the proximate cause of the disaster.

If applied to the *Eastland*, this body of law implied that if the ship were
seaworthy and the causes of the disaster were without the knowledge and
privity of the officers of the St. Joseph–Chicago Steamship Company, the
heirs of the deceased would at best get very little. The value of the hulk
was established by its sale at $46,000. Even if the heirs were held entitled
to the entire value of the hulk, they could expect barely more than $50
each. There were, however, extensive claims against the $46,000, so that
evaluating the claims and ascertaining the priority of the various claimants
had to be adjudicated.

Claims of the Great Lakes Towing
Company and the Life Salvors

Because their services were performed after the accident, the Great Lakes
Towing Company and the life salvors—the men who had dived into the
river to assist survivors to safety—had plausible prior claims on the value
of the hulk. Payment of the bill of the Great Lakes Towing Company for
clearing the wreck, if this expense were held a valid obligation of the
owner under the Act of 1899, could be enforced on penalty of the owner's
loss of his limitation of liability.[20] Because this bill under the contract approved by Hull amounted to $34,500, if the courts required payment, the
sum available to compensate the life salvors and the heirs of the deceased
in the event of the *Eastland*'s being held seaworthy would be only
$11,500. Given the magnitude of the disaster and the volume of claims in
prospect, the Towing Company could hardly have entered into its contract
to raise the *Eastland* without the expectation of a legal action to enforce
payment. It filed a claim with Sullivan on September 1, 1915, for a "pre-
ferred, paramount and first lien on said steamer." Landis denied the pre-
ferred claim on November 3, 1916, issuing an order against distributing

the $34,500 to the Towing Company. Landis assigned no reason for his denial; his decision merely states that after hearing the petition and considering the arguments of the rival claimants, he denied the claim.[21] The Towing Company immediately announced its intention to appeal the decision. The Circuit Court of Appeals found the raising of the *Eastland* a valid act of salvage under the Wreck Act, found no evidence of collusion, fraud, or duress, and reversed Landis's decision on August 22, 1918.[22] Bishop, who recognized that the decision greatly reduced the probability that the heirs would collect anything at all, appealed the case to the United States Supreme Court, but it declined to hear the action both on November 11, 1918, and on March 24, 1919.[23] The Pittsburgh Coal Company, which had a large claim of $1,997.70 for coal furnished before the disaster plus a note for $4,000 at 6 percent for coal furnished previously, also appealed the decision, but was rejected.[24] Consequently, on April 2, 1919, the Circuit Court directed the District Court to release the $34,500 to the Towing Company.[25]

The life salvors, who had been unsuccessful in opposing the Great Lakes Towing Company's prior lien, retained the right of recovery as a set of secondary claimants. They responded on April 24, 1919, by presenting a claim against the Towing Company's share. Their action was brought by Sherwood S. Mattocks on behalf of himself and eighteen other life salvors.[26] Their efforts also proved unsuccessful on this level. Judge George A. Carpenter of the Circuit Court ordered release of $41,883.98, the $34,500 plus accrued interest, to the Towing Company on December 23, 1919. He rejected the claims of the life salvors on the technical ground that they had not filed until March 29, 1919, beyond the two years after the accident provided by law.[27] This decision did not literally deny the life salvors their rights to pursue the action further as secondary claimants, but it actually ended their efforts. Their attorneys may have felt that the two-year limitation would apply to any later actions, or concluded that the claims against the remaining $11,500 were so great as to make recovery of anything very unlikely.

There were plenty of other claims. The largest was the Pittsburgh Coal Company's of about $6,000. Walter Scott made a claim of $500 for having gathered up fittings of the *Eastland* that had floated free from the wreck, which he evaluated at $8,214.77.[28] Claims of the Dunham Towing & Wrecking Company, the Chicago Ship Building Company, various suppliers and smaller claimants, plus survivors for personal damages and loss of property totaled $20,438.82.[29] Thus, the claims were enough to exhaust the residuum of the value of the hulk and the prospective revenue of the voyage of $500 nearly twice over. Consequently, if the ship were found seaworthy and if the causes of the disaster were beyond the knowledge and privity of the management, the heirs of the deceased would get nothing. If

the ship were found not seaworthy, the heirs would each receive $10,000 from the insurers, the State of Illinois's statutory compensation for a wrongful death. Accordingly, if the courts accepted all of the 878 claims for wrongful death brought before them, $8,780,000 was at issue in the question of the *Eastland*'s seaworthiness.

The Issue of Seaworthiness

Seaworthiness is an imprecise concept meaning nothing more specific than that the ship is reasonably fit for the voyage being undertaken.[30] Seaworthiness versus unseaworthiness is a concept analogous to sanity versus insanity in criminal law. Sanity is a concept in law rather than in psychiatry. Mental health professionals deal in evaluations of the question whether a person falls into a category of psychotic, psychopathic, psychoneurotic, or other accepted classification of mental illness; the judge or jury then decides on the basis of the evaluations and of other evidence whether the person is sane or insane. By analogy, expert witnesses such as Professor Sadler in the criminal action present evidence on the safety or lack of it in the engineering properties of the ship, on the basis of which the judge concludes whether the vessel was seaworthy. Notably, there was no precedent for seaworthiness with specific reference to the metacentric height of ships; a ship of negative metacentric height was not definitionally unseaworthy. More to the point, there was no precedent establishing that a ship was unseaworthy if she were of such marginal stability that the habitual or reasonable behavior of her officers would cause her to capsize.

Little progress was made in the case until November 26, 1928, when all parties were directed to submit their petitions to Mason.[31] Mason took testimony and drafted the report on which the civil decision was based. Unfortunately, neither the transcript of the testimony he gathered nor his report has survived in the file of the case. He heard testimony from the surviving major witnesses in the criminal case—Pedersen, Flatow, Lynn, Hull, Merwin S. Thompson, Ennes, Donaldson, and Steele—but also from Horatio M. Herriman, the naval architect who had approved the ship's design for the Great Lakes Register of the American Bureau of Shipping.[32] Erickson, as mentioned earlier, had died of natural causes in 1919, and Reid died in 1922.[33] Thus, neither was alive to testify, nor—more important—to defend his actions in the case.

Fortunately, briefs of both parties in the case have survived, allowing us to piece together the content of Mason's report and, to a more limited extent, the testimony on which he relied. The decision of the Circuit Court of Appeals quoted extensively from Mason's report in the course of adopting Mason's conclusions as the Court's own. In particular, the brief of the respondents, Bishop and the heirs of the deceased, urging the District Court to reject Mason's report makes 86 objections to it, covering what appear to be all of the major points in the document.[34]

As trustee for the estates of the deceased Bishop was represented by Harry W. Standidge and Justus Chancellor. They sought a jury trial, but Mason denied them.[35] The course of pleading that they chose is a strange one, and in retrospect one that could not have been successful. It was a three-pronged argument.

First, they asserted that the *Eastland* was unseaworthy, both when beginning to load with her tanks empty and when she capsized, but they did not document this with the design features that made her so. If they had presented the evidence available from the transcript of the criminal trial concerning the behavior of the ship in consideration of the modifications of July 2, 1915, they might have demonstrated successfully that the ship was a menace to her passengers.

Second, they argued that Hull and Flatow had knowingly and negligently sent the *Eastland* into a fouled berth. Intrinsic to this argument was the contention that Flatow, being solely responsible for the company's passenger business at Chicago, was an official of management within the scope of doctrine of knowledge and privity. They contended that Hull had been negligent in signing a contract with the Indiana Transportation Company that would put the ship in a fouled berth, and that Flatow had been negligent in not ordering a stop to loading after the ship was a fourth to three-fourths full, when he allegedly observed the ship in an unsafe situation. They argued that Flatow's negligence stemmed from Hull's telling him to get the *Eastland* out quickly when 2,500 people were loaded so as to have her back in Chicago for her 2:00 P.M. departure. The pilings that Darrow had used for his attempted demonstration had been removed by the time of the civil trial. There is no indication that Mason was familiar with the transcript of the criminal case, and considerable reason to believe that he was not, but the City of Chicago had so thoroughly refuted the argument that the berth was fouled that data were readily available to him to reject this pleading. It is anomalous that in the criminal trial the argument that the *Eastland* was resting on the bottom had been advanced by the defendants, who were endeavoring to demonstrate that the ship was seaworthy. Now the same thing was being argued by attorneys for the heirs of the deceased, who were attempting to show that the ship was not seaworthy.

Third and finally, Standidge and Chancellor argued that Erickson's handling of the ballast tanks had been negligent. This argument was derivative from the previous. They contended that he had a standing order to keep the tanks filled, but that was impractical given the obstructions on the starboard side in the berth in which she was loading. As a consequence, when he attempted to follow the standing order, the ship did not respond properly, and capsized to port.[36]

The St. Joseph–Chicago Steamship Company's interest was represented by Frederick L. Leckie and Robert Branard, Jr. They argued straightforwardly that the accident had been caused by Erickson's negligence in handling the ballast tanks, filling the port tanks and causing the ship to capsize. This, they argued, had been done without the knowledge and privity of the management. Necessarily, they denied that Flatow was anything more than an agent, and thus not a member of the management.[37]

Major items in the testimony survive in the briefs and in the printed decision. Flatow, who was presumably testifying for the steamship company, actually assisted in Standidge and Chancellor's line of argument by stating that he believed the ship was resting on mud at the bow, on concrete debris amidships, and on the pilings aft.[38] He also testified erroneously that the water level was 18 to 24 inches lower than normal; actually, it was only slightly more than an inch below.[39]

Pedersen's testimony is of most interest. He testified that the water level was about 8 inches below normal, which may represent faulty memory over the interval of more than 17 years.[40] Unfortunately, that cannot be said of some of his other testimony. Notably, he testified with respect to his orders to Erickson: "I didn't give him any orders on the morning of July 24, except the standing order to have the tanks full before he leaves the dock."[41] This was the basis for Leckie and Branard's argument that Erickson had been negligent, first in violating Pedersen's order and second in filling the port tanks in such a way as to cause the ship to capsize. At risk of euphemism, Pedersen's testimony may be said to have been tailored to the argument. It was, in fact, the reverse of what he well knew, that the company's practice was to start loading with the tanks empty. Immediately following the disaster he told a reporter for the Chicago *Examiner* that upon beginning to load, "There was no water ballast in the boat. We never use water ballast in the river."[42] In the criminal trial he had testified that he had assumed Erickson pumped out the tanks before coming up the river, that he habitually gave Erickson specific orders only to heel the ship in loading and unloading, and that he gave him a general order only to keep the ship steady.[43] His only specific order to Erickson immediately preceding the disaster had been exactly that, to keep the ship steady. This testimony of Pedersen's was not challenged. Because Standidge and Chancellor were arguing along lines only slightly different from Leckie and Branard's that Erickson had been negligent in dealing with the tanks, they explicitly accepted Pedersen's testimony.[44]

In his testimony in the civil case Pedersen also expressed the opinion that the *Eastland* had been resting on the bottom or on an obstruction, and had capsized because of it. He testified that he saw a circular mark on the hull, which he concluded had been caused by a piling, a cutting from which he had seen in Grand Rapids.[45] He had told State's Attorney Hoyne on July 26, 1915, that the ship was free of the bottom, and when confronted with that statement in the criminal trial he repeated his opinion that she was not on the bottom.[46] It is difficult to see what this change in view gained him except to conform to Leckie and Branard's argument, but possibly he may have felt that the change provided him with yet another opportunity for self-exculpation.

The testimony of Horatio M. Herriman would be of particular value, if only because he had not testified in the earlier actions, but there is relatively little record of it. His only competence was on the design of the ship, which he had approved for the American Bureau of Shipping. We know only that he testified against the hypothesis that the ship's resting on the bottom had helped cause the disaster.[47] Because he did not purport to have observed the events of the disaster, one presumes that his analysis was parallel to Sadler's in the criminal case, that given her design, resting on an obstruction would not have caused her to capsize.

The most influential witness proved to be Lynn. In the main, he testified concerning the event as he had done in 1915 and 1916, but he made some specific observations that greatly influenced Mason. Lynn testified that, upon sounding the area of the disaster, he found no obstructions less than 17 feet deep on which the ship could have rested; he estimated that she drew a maximum of 13'-4" aft.[48] In what may have been an offhand observation concerning his examination of the ship in the river, Lynn testified that starboard tanks of the wreck "had hardly any water and there was plenty in the opposite tanks."[49] This situation was inevitable because the disaster had submerged the port tanks and drained out the starboard. Lynn also stated that at the time of capsizing he observed few passengers at the starboard rail.[50] This is consistent with Soderstrom's observation of a drift of passengers away from the starboard rail after 7:24, but it ignores what had been occurring for well over half an hour previously, and makes no consideration of what Erickson was actually doing. By the time the passengers had moved to port, Erickson was trying desperately to admit water to the starboard tanks, but was failing to do so.

Mason put together the three foregoing statements of Lynn's to make his principal conclusion. Consistently with Lynn's first statement, he rejected the contention that the ship was resting on an obstruction. It was inevitable that Mason should come to this conclusion, even if he had not acquainted himself with the evidence on the point in the criminal

transcript. The evidence that the ship cleared any obstructions beneath her by about four feet was unambiguous. Mason proceeded to combine Lynn's two other
statements: "We have noted Lynn's testimony that the
port tanks had plenty of water and the starboard tanks
very little, and that there were very few passengers on her
starboard side. We know, too, that the tanks had been
pumped out the previous evening." [51] From this he concluded that the disaster had occurred because Erickson
had negligently mismanaged the ballast tanks, adding
water to the port tanks when the passengers were congregating on the port side. Mason, in fact, concluded that
improper operation of the ballast tanks was the only plausible explanation of the disaster.[52]

Joseph R. Lynn, assistant
harbormaster of the City
of Chicago.

It is difficult to see how Mason could have come to such a conclusion.
He was not newly come to the case; he had been appointed commissioner
less than four weeks after the disaster occurred, and must have had some
degree of familiarity with the entire proceedings. Even if he had never read
the transcript of the criminal case—and he seems not to have done so—
Erickson's log had been published on page 65 of *Investigation of Accident
to the Steamer "Eastland,"* the congressional document of testimony before Secretary of Commerce Redfield's inquiry. Consequently, it was a
matter of readily available record in a public document what Erickson had
actually been doing, and the evidence was unambiguous that it was not
what Mason concluded. Blaming Erickson was attractive, however, because both parties to the trial had alleged that his behavior had been negligent, and he was not alive to explain and defend his actions.

The judgment concerning Erickson's handling of the ballast tanks was
the first of Mason's five conclusions. Second was that Flatow was only the
agent of the company at Chicago and not a managing officer in the sense
that his knowledge and privity of the actions of the officers of the ship
would deprive the company of its limitation of liability. Third, he concluded "That on the morning of July 24, 1915, and at the time of the
disaster, the steamer *Eastland* was seaworthy in every respect, properly
equipped and manned and fit for the carriage of passengers if properly
handled." Fourth, he found that the negligence causing the disaster was
not within the knowledge and privity of the company. Finally, he concluded that the company was entitled to the limitation of liability it
sought.[53] Mason's report was accepted by the judge in the District Court,
John B. Barnes, who issued an order for the limitation of liability on December 21, 1933.[54]

Standidge and Chancellor considered Mason's report such an uneclectic acceptance of the steamship company's argument as to constitute a brief for their opponents. They had filed their 86 objections to it on November 20, 1933, and after Barnes's acceptance of it, filed 25 assignments of error on the basis of which they appealed Barnes's decision. The appellate justices—Evan A. Evans, William M. Sparks, and Louis FitzHenry— also rejected Standidge and Chancellor's principal argument that the ship had been resting on an obstruction, affirmed Barnes's decision on August 7, 1935, and with that affirmation made permanent Barnes's injunction against further efforts by Bishop and others to recover damages.[55] Standidge and Chancellor appealed the decision to the United States Supreme Court, which on January 20, 1936, denied a writ of certiorari, declining to hear the case.[56]

The Case of the *Edgar F. Coney*

The Supreme Court on a variety of grounds erred in denying certiorari. Apart from the fact that Mason's report had contained both factual errors and erroneous conclusions, the report was based on a legal tradition that was at best obsolescent. If the *Annie Faxon* case had provided the precedent for cases of the *Eastland*'s character in 1915, it should no longer have done so in 1935. The doctrine of knowledge and privity had been modified, and the limitation of liability no longer approached being absolute.[57] In particular, on July 17, 1934, the Circuit Court of Appeals for the Fifth Circuit, which is based in New Orleans, issued a decision in Sabine Tow-

The *Edgar F. Coney* of 1904 was a typical deep-sea tug of her time. The ship's original wooden superstructure, shown here, was replaced by a steel housing in her revisions of 1920. (T. H. Franklin collection, Steamship Historical Society of America)

ing Co., Inc., v. Brennan et al., a case concerning the sinking of the tug *Edgar F. Coney*, that should have provided a precedent for the *Eastland* case in the following year. The factual errors in the *Eastland* decision, consistently with the Supreme Court's practices, would not have caused it to hear the case, but the conflict in precedents between the cases of the *Annie Faxon* and the *Edgar F. Coney* should have caused it to do so. The fault was of Standidge and Chancellor, who apparently never found the case of the *Edgar F. Coney* and did not include it in their brief.

Like the *Eastland*, the *Edgar F. Coney* was stable as built, but was given a lateral stability problem by later modifications. To complete the analogy, she had her disaster shortly, but not immediately, after some additional modifications that added further weight to her. The *Edgar F. Coney* was built in 1904 by John H. Dialogue & Son of Camden, New Jersey, for the South Atlantic Towing Company of Brunswick, Georgia, and named for the president of the firm. She was a typical ocean tug, 102' × 20.8' × 10.6', with a cubic volume of 153 gross tons. She had no ballast system of any kind, but she had peak water tanks both fore and aft. The tug engaged in coastal towing for this owner generally uneventfully until she was sold to Philip Shore of Tampa, Florida, and his associates in February 1914.[58] The U.S. Navy chartered her on September 22, 1917, then nominally converted her to a mine sweeper by adding a one-pound gun forward and a tripod mast aft. The tug was based on Staten Island and used for towing in New York harbor for the duration of World War I. She was returned to Shore on July 5, 1919.[59]

Upon regaining the *Edgar F. Coney* Shore decided to convert her to oil burning, mainly to increase her range. Shore's tugs frequently made lengthy voyages with barges to points on the coast of Cuba. The coal bunker located forward of the boiler was replaced with an oil tank of 10,300-gallon capacity. A new oil tank with a capacity of 9,450 gallons was placed between the engine room and the aft peak water tank in an area not previously occupied. The changes replaced a bunker that could hold 30 tons of coal with tanks reportedly capable of holding 70.5 tons of oil.[60] The boiler was replaced with another secondhand from the passenger steamer *Olivette*, a foot longer and a foot greater in diameter than the original. The wooden superstructure of the tug was replaced with steel, and a housing was placed on the upper deck for the mate's quarters and a radio room.[61] The revisions increased the range of the tug between refuelings from four or five days to ten to twelve days, but in the process created several problems. The changes added an unspecified amount of weight to the ship and created a free-surface problem by replacing the coal with oil. To damp the free-surface effect, the tanks from the outset were fitted with longitudinal and transverse girder partitions, which the management called "swash plates."

The *Edgar F. Coney*'s former captain, Charles R. Wiebe, who retained an equity in the tug, rode her and reported that she had lost buoyancy both fore and aft. He reported that she tended to nose into oncoming waves rather than to ride over them. The new weight of the aft oil tank made her sluggish in response to the helm.[62] Her new captain, Frank Comforter, was shortly confronted with a more serious problem. The *Edgar F. Coney* began to manifest a dangerous lateral instability in beam winds—winds coming directly at one side or the other. The first of six such episodes occurred during a voyage to Philadelphia on October 9, 1920, when Comforter noted that the tug was diving into the oncoming sea. He decided to seek shelter at Tybee Island, Georgia, but before he could make port, a beam wind of only eighteen knots sent the tug over so badly to lee that water reached the upper deck and the lower edge of the pilothouse door. She recovered from that position, but continued to list seriously for about fifteen minutes.[63] Upon her return to Tampa, Shore had the Tampa Dock Company weld closed the holes in the swash plates in an attempt at greater lateral stability.[64] The effort proved unsuccessful. On December 16, 1920, when crossing the bar coming into Tampa, she listed seriously to starboard for more than two hours before she could be righted.[65] On January 27, 1921, while towing the barge *Mex Oil*, the *Edgar F. Coney* listed so heavily to port that she had to stop her engines for an unrecorded period before recovering.[66] When towing the *Mex Oil* into South Pass, Mississippi, on February 5, 1921, the tug listed to port until the engine room was flooded. She lay in that position with her engines stopped for ten to fifteen minutes before recovering.[67]

Both the management and the federal inspectors at Tampa had become alarmed by the tug's behavior. Shore, apparently voluntarily, but possibly at the suggestion of the inspectors, ordered the removal of the housing that had recently been added to the upper deck for the mate's quarters and the radio shack. The removal cut down a weight of 6,024 pounds from a high position on the vessel.[68] As a consequence of the *Eastland* disaster, the rules of the Steamboat Inspection Service had been modified to allow inspectors to order inclining tests, to be performed by the Service's own inspectors.[69] Shipowners were allowed to request this service, and Shore did so in a letter to inspectors John R. Blair and John W. Sullivan of Tampa.[70] The two inspectors made a formal request for the test in a memorandum of May 24, 1921,[71] but in the interim the *Edgar F. Coney* had two more episodes of serious instability on a trip to Key West. Upon entering the harbor on May 10, she listed heavily enough to bring water over the port rail. Going out to assist a vessel in distress on May 16 she listed so badly as to bring the sea more than a foot over the port rail. Wiebe, again captain, maneuvered her into a position where the wind could help right her, and brought her back into Key West.[72]

The inclining test was now a matter of urgency. The Steamboat Inspection Service sent a traveling inspector, Captain Fabian P. Noel of Portland, Maine, to Tampa, where he performed the test on June 16–17, 1921. He calculated the metacentric height at 1.34 feet in light condition, and 1.86 feet loaded. George Uhler, who remained supervising inspector, wrote to Shore that with such metacentric heights the tug was lacking in "reserve buoyancy." He ordered that the aft fuel tank, which extended to a height within 7 inches of the main deck, be cut down by 24 inches, that the tug's mean draft be limited to 10'-5", and that no additional weight be placed more than 7.9 feet above the keel.[73] Shore was unwilling to accept these terms because the reduction of the aft tank would cut fuel capacity by 15 tons, reducing the tug's range by some 2 days. He proposed that, instead, the aft peak tank, which held about 14 tons of water, be left empty.[74] Blair and Sullivan, the local inspectors, agreed to this, provided that no additional weight whatsoever be put upon the tug.[75] She had been operating with the aft water tank empty since August 17, 1921, but the inspectors sealed it off during February 1922.[76]

The handling of the *Edgar F. Coney* continued to be unsatisfactory because of the weight of the aft fuel tank. The Steamboat Inspection Service had told Shore in January 1922 that if he agreed to reduce the tank by 24 inches, the other restrictions placed on the tug would be lifted.[77] After some fruitless correspondence in search of a further compromise, in 1924 Shore agreed to the 24-inch reduction. The tank was cut down by the 24 inches in the summer of 1925, although the job was not completed until a new top was placed on the tank in April 1926.[78] Thereafter, the *Edgar F. Coney* had no reported problems of instability under Shore's management.

Shore died, however, and his executor put up the *Edgar F. Coney* for sale. Captain Munger T. Ball, head of the Sabine Towing Company of Port Arthur, Texas, considered the tug possibly suitable for his firm's operations, which were divided between the berthing of tankers in the Beaumont–Port Arthur area and deep-sea towing of barges along the Gulf Coast. He sent his vice president, R. P. Smith, and his port engineer, Charles H. Guy, to Tampa to inspect the tug. Along with a surveyor from the United States Salvage Association and an unidentified local inspector, they inspected the tug in dry dock, and concluded that she was in only fair condition, but suitable for acquisition. Sabine bought her about October 1, 1929, for $30,000, and with Smith, Guy, and a crew from Shore's firm, sailed her to Port Arthur. Smith and Guy had not inspected the tug's record at the Steamboat Inspection Service's Tampa office, and Ball later testified that his own inquiry into the ship was limited to looking her up in *Eads' Marine Journal*, a trade directory.[79]

Ball believed substantial revisions had to be made in the *Edgar F. Coney* to make her satisfactory for Sabine's operations, and allocated $20,000 for improvements. At the company's own yard in Port Arthur, Guy under-took to replace the tug's manual steering gear with a steam apparatus, to install a steam capstan, and to place a jacket on the stack to protect the crew from burns on accidental contact. Guy added a feedwater heater, along with some new pumps and evaporators. A large number of minor additions and revisions were also made. After the loss of the tug, it was computed that the new equipment had weighed 31,503 pounds, and the equipment removed weighed 17,747 pounds, for a net increase in weight of exactly 13,756 pounds, somewhat less than 7 tons.[80] For a vessel the size of the *Edgar F. Coney*, this was a substantial addition. Further, the new housing on the stack, which weighed 2,400 pounds, had its base 10 feet above the main deck and extended up to a point 27 feet above the keel. Because the center of gravity of the tug was computed as being 3.5 feet below the main deck, the new stack housing, in particular, was a potential source of instability.[81]

Following the work at Sabine's own facility, the vessel was taken to the yard of Pennsylvania Shipyards, Inc., in Beaumont for replacement of five or six rusted plates and some other work on her hull. She was then in-spected on December 9, 11, and 13 by federal inspectors Andrew A. Mir-anda and William H. Yant, from Galveston, who issued a new certificate for her on January 2, 1930.[82] She was immediately put to work berthing tankers, and on January 7 and 15 made trips to Galveston, 50 miles to the west, respectively to deliver the barge *Pure Fuel Oil* and to return it to Port Arthur.[83]

The *Edgar F. Coney*'s first long trip following the revisions was to be a tow of Sabine's whaleback barge *Pure Detonox* with a cargo of 21,213.5 barrels of gasoline from the Pure Oil Company's facility at Smith's Bluff in the Port Arthur area to Pensacola, Florida, after which the tug was to proceed to Mobile to pick up a tow, take it to Tampa, and return to Port Arthur. Captain William Brennan, who was only 37 years old, was in com-mand. The *Pure Detonox* had its own crew of 7, headed by Captain An-tonio Barrios. The tow left Smith's Bluff on January 27, but because of fog and a grounded tanker in Sabine Pass, did not venture out into the Gulf until the morning of the 28th. The tug was made fast to the side of the barge, but upon passing the Sabine Bar about 9:35 A.M., moved ahead and towed the barge by a hawser, a steel cable payed out for about 1,000 feet. The weather was calm, but about mid-day a storm appeared, with winds of a maximum of about 42 miles per hour. The weather conditions pro-duced a moderate sea. The tow proceeded normally, but about 10:00 P.M. the helmsman of the *Pure Detonox* told Barrios that the lights of the tug were disappearing intermittently. About 10:45 P.M. the lights disappeared completely, and the screams of the tug's crew members were heard in the water, but given the condition of the sea, the barge could not launch

The *Edgar F. Coney* on the ways, probably at Pennsylvania Shipyards in Beaumont after her modifications at Sabine Towing Company's own yard at Port Arthur. (National Archives and Records Administration, Southwest Center, Fort Worth)

its boat. The hawser had come free of the tug, and Barrios anchored the barge to ride out the storm. In the morning only the top of the masts of the *Edgar F. Coney* were visible from the barge, some 200 to 300 yards away. The tug was on the bottom on even keel in about 45 feet of water, 70 miles east of the mouth of the Sabine, approximately 10 miles off the Louisiana coast.[84]

All 14 members of the crew perished in the disaster, including Captain Brennan. Five bodies were picked up at sea, one on the beach.[85] The men had put on their life jackets, but otherwise there was every indication that the tug had sunk suddenly and unexpectedly. There had been no radio messages, and the lifeboat had not been launched. Rather, the lifeboat was found on February 4 floating keel up, with its canvas cover still in place, by the Gulf Refining Company's tug *Robert P. Clark* about 10 miles east of Sabine Pass.[86] Ball hired divers to inspect the wreck, but no evidence of an explosion or hitting an underwater obstruction was found. The tug was essentially intact. Federal inspectors at Mobile and Galveston held hearings and other investigations from February through April 1930, but were unable to assign a cause to the disaster.[87] For absence of evidence to the contrary, it is plausible to conclude that the *Edgar F. Coney* was simply swamped in a moderate sea and sank.

The legal action necessarily paralleled the *Eastland*'s. Sophia Brennan, widow of the captain, and heirs of the other victims filed suit against Sabine, beginning May 31, 1930.[88] On June 27, 1930, Sabine applied under the Act of 1851 for a limitation of liability to the value of the wreck and the freights pending for the Port Arthur–Pensacola segment of the voyage.[89] Title to the wreck had been vested in C. T. Duff of Beaumont as a trustee, and sold at auction for only $5. The tug was never salvaged. The towing fee pending from the Port Arthur–Pensacola segment of the voyage was $620.[90] Sophia Brennan and her fellow claimants alleged that the *Edgar F. Coney* was not seaworthy, and that Sabine was not entitled to a limitation of liability. Also at issue were whether Sabine's liability should extend to the *Edgar F. Coney*'s prospective revenues from the segments of the voyage beyond Pensacola, or to the *Pure Detonox*'s revenues, and whether Sabine should be required to post as bond the value of the *Pure Detonox* itself.

On several grounds, there was more reason to hold the *Edgar F. Coney* seaworthy than the *Eastland*. First, she had a well-documented inclining test made by the federal inspector, Fabian P. Noel, in 1921; the *Eastland* never had an inclining test at all. Sabine, in mounting its defense, hired Herbert Slade of the Todd Dry Dock & Engineering Company in New Orleans to update Noel's findings to the state of the *Edgar F. Coney* when she sailed on her final voyage. He computed that her metacentric height at that time was 1.392 feet.[91] No one even purported to know the *Eastland*'s metacentric height at the time of the disaster until Professor Sadler made his estimates in his testimony of February 1916, and as pointed out in Chapter VI, Sadler's estimates are open to very real question. Second, although the *Edgar F. Coney* had a history of lateral instability at least as well documented as the *Eastland*'s, the manifestations of it were narrowly limited to a period from October 1920 to May 1921, and the problem had been dealt with effectively by a mixture of private and federal action ending with the reduction in height of the aft fuel tank in 1925–26. None of the *Eastland*'s owners ever did more than temporize with her problem. Third, the *Edgar F. Coney* sank directly, and did not capsize. This was argued by Sabine's attorneys to show an absence of a problem of lateral instability. Finally, the *Edgar F. Coney*'s accident occurred in moderately heavy weather, whereas the *Eastland* capsized under calm conditions while still moored to the wharf.

Nonetheless, the *Edgar F. Coney* was held not seaworthy. Unlike the

Eastland's civil action, the case of the *Edgar F. Coney* was pursued with ordinary dispatch. Judge Randolph Bryant of the Federal District Court in Beaumont on July 13, 1933, issued his "Findings of Fact and Conclusions of Law," favorable to the claimants. He considered R. P. Smith and Charles H. Guy negligent as agents of Sabine in their trip to Tampa for failing to consult the records of Blair and Sullivan, the local inspectors. Guy, who had progressed from being an oiler to taking a license as a chief engineer, had no pretension to being a naval architect. Bryant found him incompetent in knowledge of stability and buoyancy, and held Sabine negligent both for failing to hire a naval architect and for placing Guy in his position of port engineer, where he had responsibility for the revisions in the tug. Bryant found Sabine negligent in sending out the *Edgar F. Coney* in unseaworthy condition, and concluded that this was the proximate cause of the disaster. He held that all of this had occurred with the knowledge and privity of the management. He considered the weather conditions in the Gulf of Mexico at the time of the sinking not unusual for January. He denied Sabine's application for limitation of liability, and allowed the claimants to recover full damages. His only holding in favor of Sabine was that the company's liability did not extend to the value of the *Pure Detonox*.[92]

Sabine appealed the decision to the Circuit Court of Appeals for the Fifth Circuit. The case was heard by a panel of three judges—Joseph C. Hutcheson, Jr.; Nathan P. Bryan; and Rufus E. Foster. Hutcheson delivered the decision favorable to the claimants, with which Bryan concurred. In its appeal Sabine had stressed the storm in which the sinking had occurred. Hutcheson held that, given the tug's history and the absence of an inclining test, weather conditions were insufficient to explain the accident:

When, however, the evidence of weather conditions is considered in light of the whole history of the tug, and of what was done to it by adding weight, and especially when it is considered that no inclining nor stability test was made on it, and the repairs and reconditioning were made without knowledge of or regard to its history of tenderness and crankiness, this weather evidence ceases to be explanatory of the loss as its cause. . . .

The inspection certificates on which appellant relies so strongly are of course evidence of due care, but they are not more. . . . They are certainly not evidence of the tug's stability when no tests were made. We think it quite clear that when an owner buys an old tug, licensed coastwise, and equips it for ocean going, it is negligence to send it out without knowing something of its stability, and especially to send it out without such tests, when as in this case its history and performance with regard to crankiness and tenderness is [*sic*] a matter of official record.[93]

Hutcheson found the tug unstable and lacking in buoyancy, considered the absence of an inclining test negligent, denied the limitation of liability, and affirmed the decision of the District Court. Foster dissented, considering Guy competent on the basis of his experience, construing the licensure of the tug as evidence of seaworthiness, and holding the adverse weather conditions significant in the disaster. He concluded that the precedent of the *Annie Faxon* should prevail, and that Sabine should be allowed its limitation of liability.[94]

Hutcheson's decision of July 17, 1934, proved final.[95] Sabine appealed the case, but on November 5, 1934, the Supreme Court denied certiorari.[96] By its refusal to hear the case, the Supreme Court expressed its acquiescence to Hutcheson's decision, and implicitly rejected Foster's dissent. Accordingly, it was inconsistent of the Supreme Court to refuse to hear the *Eastland* case in 1936, for the logic of the *Eastland* decision was consistent with Foster's dissent. The *Eastland* decision, however, contained factual errors in the account of Erickson's actions, whereas Foster's dissent was factually accurate.

By application of the precedent of the majority opinion in the case of the *Edgar F. Coney*, the *Eastland* should not have been found seaworthy, and the limitation of liability should not have been allowed. The *Eastland*'s tenderness or crankiness was a matter of record, but Hull, like Smith, Guy, and Ball, had made no effort to ascertain it. Even if Hull and the rest of the management were not held negligent on this score, they might have been held negligent on two specific counts: first, for having no inclining test by a naval architect before sending the ship out for the 1915 season after the addition of a considerable amount of concrete above the metacenter, and, second, for making no effort to ascertain, by inclining test or otherwise, the effects of the addition of boats and rafts on July 2, 1915. Hull and Pedersen, who were responsible for the alterations of July 2, 1915, had no more pretension to competence as naval architects than Guy did. The fact that the operator sought and secured certification in connection with those alterations should have been considered, as with the *Edgar F. Coney*, a demonstration only of "due care." Hutcheson's words concerning the *Edgar F. Coney*'s modifications might apply verbatim to both the *Eastland*'s addition of concrete flooring and the changes of July 2, 1915: "the repairs and reconditioning were made without knowledge of or regard to its history of tenderness and crankiness."

The *Eastland*'s civil case represented one of the last manifestations of the traditional doctrine of knowledge and privity in marine liability, as embodied in the case of the *Annie Faxon*. It is for this reason that, in spite of the magnitude of the disaster, the civil case concerning the *Eastland* has provided no major precedent in admiralty law. Later in August 1935, the month of the *Eastland*'s appellate decision, Congress enacted a requirement that a shipowner who was found at fault, but entitled to the limitation of liability, should supplement the fund for loss of life and bodily injury by $60 per gross ton of the ship.[97] The enactment was brought forth by the anticipated actions in the *Morro Castle* disaster of 1934 and the accident to the *Mohawk* early in 1935, rather than out of revulsion for the *Eastland* decision. The doctrine of knowledge and privity further declined with the growth in political power of the maritime unions after 1935.[98] With the Merchant Marine Act of 1936, the Roosevelt administration moved to the extensive use of general tax revenues to increase the capital devoted to merchant shipping. If it is desirable to attract more resources to the merchant marine than the market would allocate to it—which is at best highly questionable—the use of general tax revenues spreads the cost more in accord with the alleged benefits than denying tort remedies to the limited number of victims of marine disasters. Thus, among its other intellectual legacies, the *Eastland* disaster constitutes, in the resolution of its civil action, a last stand of an undesirable public policy after the onset of its decline.

CHAPTER EIGHT

The Wilmette

CAPTAIN Edward A. Evers's project of converting the *Eastland* into a training vessel for the Illinois Naval Reserve eventually came to fruition, but not over the course of the winter and spring months of 1916, as he had hoped. Neither the formal acquisition of the hulk nor the engineering process of conversion proved so simple as he had anticipated. As mentioned in Chapter V, on December 20, 1915, Evers had bid successfully for the hulk with a sum of $46,000, for which he had no appropriation. It was stated publicly only that he raised the funds from a group of Chicago businessmen who preferred to remain anonymous, of whom the utilities magnate Samuel Insull was rumored to be the most important.[1] The actual nature of the transaction was described by Frank J. Baker, vice president of Insull's Public Service Company of Northern Illinois, in a letter to the Secretary of the Navy at the time the transfer to the Navy was being arranged. Baker stated that he himself had conceived the conversion of the *Eastland* about the time the hulk had been delivered to the U.S. marshal, partly because he knew that Evers was seeking a ship for the Naval Militia, partly because he thought this the only service suitable for the ship in light of the disaster. Baker then identified the men who had put up the funds as Insull and twelve other prominent Chicago business figures, most of whom were residents of the Chicago north suburbs: J. Ogden Armour, William G. Beale, Charles Deering, Stanley Field, Chauncey Keep, Frank G. Logan, John J. Mitchell, Cyrus H. McCormick, James A. Patten, George M. Reynolds, Edward P. Russell, and Charles H.

Thorne.[2] They provided the money by their personal notes, and title to the hulk was vested in the hands of the Central Trust Company as trustee. At best, this could have been only a temporary measure while Evers secured a federal appropriation.

Evers began his work on the project almost immediately after acquisition of the hulk in December 1915. He developed his plans with the assistance of draftsman D. E. Charteroux. Construction was superintended by Lieutenant Commander Herman J. Elson. Correspondence indicates that a decision had been made by February 1, 1916, to name the training vessel *Wilmette*, after a Chicago north suburb.[3] The ship was designated only as S.S. 25, however. This was in the nature of a shop number for convenience in correspondence, rather than an official designation or enrollment. The Navy ordered an inclining test on the hulk, the first the ship is known to have had. The Bureau of Construction and Repair specified that 8 tons of weight be moved 12 feet off the center line to produce between 1 and 2 degrees of heel, and that readings be taken preferably with three pendulums, forward, amidships, and aft. All tanks were to be emptied or, if that were not possible, filled. The draft was to be measured and the hawsers made slack. All weights, including men and coal, were to be carefully measured. The test was performed on February 7, 1916. The ship was reported in very light condition; 150 tons of boats and permanent structures had already been removed from the upper decks. The metacentric height was found to be 2.8 feet.[4]

The first report of Evers's plans for the vessel dates from March 4, 1916. He proposed to cut away all of the superstructure above the promenade deck, and to remove the promenade deck itself abaft of frame 54, which was one frame behind the forward bulkhead of the boiler room. To the stern, what had been variously called the cabin deck and the 'tween decks of the *Eastland* would become an open deck, planked with teak. Evers proposed to erect a new bridge, chart and deck houses, handling gear for boats and other accoutrements standard for a small naval vessel. He planned berths for 244 crew and 21 officers. Recognizing that the price level was rising, he telegraphed the Bureau of Construction and Repair that it was urgent to start work.[5]

The House of Representatives Committee on Naval Affairs began considering an appropriation for acquisition of the ship. The chairman, Representative Lemuel P. Padgett, was leery of acquiring a ship of the *Eastland*'s reputation, and wrote to Rear Admiral David W. Taylor, chief of the Navy's Bureau of Construction and Repair, inquiring about the stability of the proposed training vessel. Taylor responded:

At the time she capsized with the excursionists aboard it is probable that she had a metacentric height of a few inches only, and it is understood that she had open cargo ports but a short distance above the water. The present owners intend to plate over solidly the openings referred to so as to give an intact side and thus greatly increase her range of stability. It is contemplated also to remove certain upper works, thus lowering the center of gravity of the vessel and greatly increasing the initial stability.

. . . Calculations based on the results of the [inclining] experiment [of February 7] indicate that after the alterations now contemplated, including the closing of the ports, . . . the ship will have a metacentric height of in the neighborhood of two feet instead of a few inches, as when she capsized, and a range of stability of more than 80 degrees, which is materially greater than that of a number of naval vessels now in service. . . . Even more stability could be provided if thought desirable, by installation of fixed ballast, but the Bureau would regard the installation of fixed ballast as unnecessary if the preliminary estimates above of metacentric height and range of stability are substantially verified.[6]

Taylor closed by assuring Padgett that the ship would be given the same sort of inclining experiments made upon all naval vessels. Reassured, the committee wrote an appropriation of $125,000 for purchase, repair, and alteration of an unnamed steamer for the Naval Militia of Illinois into a large omnibus naval appropriations bill, which was signed into law by President Wilson on August 29, 1916.[7] Evers treated the enactment as an indication to proceed with work on the hulk, which was still at its berth on the North Branch of the Chicago River. It was reportedly drydocked there on November 21, 1916.[8] His progress is not well documented, but on July 2, 1917, he received permission to replace the *Eastland*'s replaceable-blade screws with four-blade cast-iron propellers.[9]

In two respects, the enactment of August 29, 1916, was unsatisfactory for Evers's plan. First, it was inadequate to cover the $46,000 Evers had paid for the ship and the $100,000 that he initially estimated the conversion would require. Second, because the appropriation was not for a specific ship, the Navy decided it could only solicit an offer of a ship for the $125,000 provided in the statute. On October 27, 1916, the Department of the Navy issued a printed solicitation of bids for a steel ship of dimensions approximately 240′ × 40′ × 24′ and of 1,500 to 1,700 tons displacement, and a speed of not less than 14 knots—a ship both shorter and slower than the *Eastland*.[10] Announcement of the solicitation brought forth inquiries from three ship brokers in New York, A. H. Bull & Company, John O'Connor, and the Auten Engineering & Contracting Company, all of whom expressed interest in seeking ships to meet the specifications.[11] Bids were solicited for November 22, 1916, but the receiving officer, Solicitor Graham Edgerton, reported to Taylor, "This is the day set for the opening of proposals for the sale to the Government of a vessel for the use of the Illinois Naval Militia, but no proposals were received."[12]

The ship brokers, one presumes, did not respond because they found no suitable vessels, but Central Trust apparently did not do so because it be-

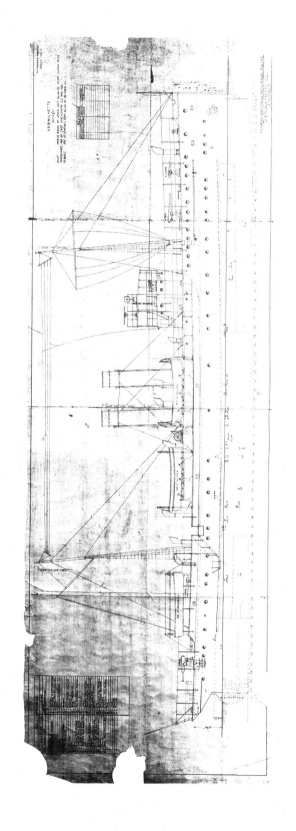

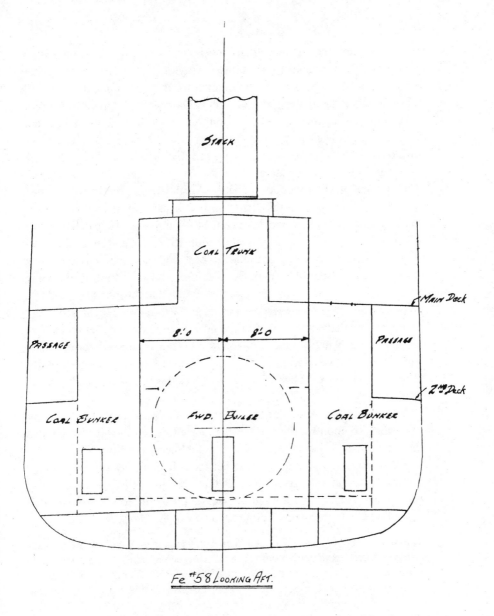

Fe #58 LOOKING AFT.

At left, an outboard profile of the *Wilmette* as originally projected by Captain William A. Evers and drawn by draftsman D. E. Charteroux. As noted in the text, the ship was not completed to this plan, but modified in the expectation that she would be a gunboat in World War I. In particular, the plan shows the ship with the *Eastland*'s unbalanced rudder, rather than with the balanced rudder working off a stock with which she was completed. Above is a cross section of the *Wilmette* drawn for the project of removing her forward port boiler and centering her forward starboard boiler. (Side elevation from a blueprint in the Institute for Great Lakes Research, Bowling Green State University, Perrysburg, Ohio; cross section from National Archives, Washington, D.C.)

lieved that the sum was inadequate for the purchase price and conversion expenses already made. Evers wrote to Taylor on March 22, 1917, that work on the ship could not be completed for the sum in hand, but stated that the Secretary of the Navy, Josephus Daniels, had agreed to support a request for another $50,000.[13] Congress appropriated the additional $50,000 in the Deficiency Appropriation Act of June 15, 1917. This allowed work to continue, but on August 10, Evers wrote to Taylor that the steamer could not be completed for the $175,000 already appropriated. The ship remained at the facility on the North Branch, but Evers reported that the yard had proved unreliable, in part because it had suffered a fire that had put many of its machines out of commission. He estimated that the work remaining to be done would require $18,310, and stated that Chicago Ship Building would guarantee to perform it for not over $22,000 at its main yard in South Chicago. Evers estimated that berths and plumbing would require an additional $10,000. He wrote that this would provide "a ship with hull and machinery in almost perfect condition" for $207,000, and observed that such a vessel could not be built new for over twice that. He urged the Navy to take over the ship in her unfinished form for the $175,000 already spent, and to complete her.[14] Central Trust responded with an offer on October 17, 1917, to sell the vessel to the Navy for $175,000.[15]

Because by this time the United States had been formally at war for more than six months, the Navy was more interested in ships for combat than in training vessels. Taylor wrote to the Secretary of the Navy on November 8 to raise the question whether the ship could legally be acquired for use as a gunboat, given the fact that the appropriations for her had been made specifically for a training vessel for the Illinois Naval Militia.[16] Franklin Delano Roosevelt, acting secretary of the Navy, responded:

This vessel if bought under the act authorizing its purchase would be the property of the Government notwithstanding the fact that the providing of it is declared by law to be for the use of the Naval Militia of Illinois, and if it had thus become the property of the Government there would be no obstacle to the conversion of it in the existing emergency to any use the public interest might dictate.

Therefore, and in view of the Government's urgent need of vessels for war purposes it is directed that the "Eastland" be bought and paid for in her present condition under the authorizing acts of Congress and be taken immediately for war uses and altered to meet the requirements thereof at the expense of appropriations for similar purposes on other vessels acquired by the Department.[17]

On November 26 and 27, before formally committing itself to acquiring the ship, the Navy subjected her to a material inspection. The ship, still known only as S.S. 25, had been moved to Chicago Ship Building's South Chicago yard by September 15, 1917. The inspection was performed there by an ad hoc Board of Inspection and Survey, headed by Captain W. A.

Gill. Evers was present for the inspection. Taylor had feared the hull might
lack the structural strength for deep-sea operation, but as always throughout the ship's history, the hull was found to be sound. The disaster had
done some damage to the mountings of the engines and, especially, to the
staybolts in the port boilers, which had been inundated, but the engines
and boilers themselves were in good condition. The Ellis and Eaves system
of induced draft had already been removed, but the board thought the ship
could run in satisfactory fashion on natural draft. The gangways and lower
portholes had already been riveted over. Almost all of the superstructure
had been removed, along with speaking tubes and most of the electrical
system. The board supervised an inclining experiment on November 26,
1917, in which the metacentric height was found to be a satisfactory
3.1 feet. The board concluded that the ship was suitable for conversion to
a saltwater gunboat for general naval service at a cost that would be "very
considerable, but not out of proportion to the value of the vessel."

Most of the specific proposals of the board were for fitting the ship
for deep-sea service. The board reported the coal capacity at 106 tons—
consistently with Vehstedt's estimate of 110 following the disaster—but
stated that this would give her a range of only 1,200 to 1,500 miles, which
was inadequate for a gunboat. To increase the coal capacity to 275 to 280
tons, the board recommended that the forward port boiler be removed,
and the forward starboard boiler be repositioned on the center line, with
the released space to be used to extend the wing portions of the bunkers.
This was estimated to give a range of 4,000 miles at 12 knots. Because the
ship had jet condensers that were inappropriate to salt water, the board
proposed installation of surface condensers outboard of the engines. The
Eastland's rudder—like the *Titanic*'s—was of an unbalanced, or hinged,
type, which the board thought could not take putting the ship over more
than 10 to 15 degrees at top speed. There is no indication that the board
even considered the design of the *Titanic*, but if the Navy thought a rudder
of this type unsafe for the projected *Wilmette*, we have corroborating evidence for the view of Colin Carmichael, summarized above in the prologue, that the *Titanic*'s rudder was grossly unsuitable for so large a vessel
and thus a major contributor to her disaster. The *Titanic* by measure of
gross tonnage was well over twenty times the size of the *Eastland*. The
board specifically recommended replacing the *Eastland*'s rudder with a
balanced rudder. Brass sleeves were required for the propeller shafts. The
board took a poor view of the drainage arrangements of the ballast system,
and suggested replacement of the 6″ piping with mains of 4″ and branches
of 2½″ to 3″ into each ballast tank, and also into the fore and aft peak tanks.
Because the ship as a gunboat would carry a smaller complement of men

than Evers had projected for a training vessel, the board proposed scaling down both the number of berths and the number of boats.

One of the principal problems in the conversion was to modify the ship to get out of the Great Lakes. The dimensions of the most restrictive lock of the Welland Canal were 261′ × 44′ × 14′-3″, but the ship was 275 feet long. The board concluded that it would be practical to cut off 15 feet of the bow at Buffalo to allow transit through the locks, and then to replace it on the Canadian side.[18]

When the board submitted its report of the inspection to the Bureau of Construction and Repair on December 31, 1917, the document was favorably received. On December 28, 1917, Baker had written to Taylor that the $175,000 would not cover the debt on the vessel with the principal and interest on the notes of the men who had advanced the funds for the acquisition.[19] Nonetheless, the parties proceeded with the transaction and Central Trust conveyed the title to the ship at South Chicago on January 17, 1918.[20] An auditor reported in 1923 that a payment for which he could find no specific authority had been made by a public bill dated March 23, 1918, with funds from an appropriation (No. 8501) for the Bureau of Construction and Repair for fiscal year 1917–18. He stated that the $125,000 in the original appropriation had never been expended and had reverted to the Treasury on June 30, 1919.[21]

On January 12, 1918, the Navy ordered Lieutenant T. W. Richards from the Philadelphia Navy Yard to temporary duty at South Chicago as superintending constructor for the ship. Richards's duties began on January 17, immediately upon the Navy's taking title to her.[22] Evers wrote to Washington on January 19 to request formally that the ship be named *Wilmette*, after the suburb in which he and "a number of gentlemen interested in the financing of the original purchase of the *Wilmette* reside."[23] The chief of naval operations approved the name on February 21.[24] Work on the ship began upon Richards's arrival; he reported that preparatory operations for removal of the forward port boiler were in progress on January 20.[25] Richards, who is shown by his correspondence to have been a very capable and conscientious officer, was not much impressed by what Evers had accomplished. He wrote on March 25:

It is my belief that the Bureau did not fully realize the extent of the work on this vessel, as there was practically nothing to her except the hull and some bulkheads. Therefore, the work of converting her into a typical gunboat is quite extensive and requires practically the installation of everything coming under the cognizance of the Bureau of Construction and Repair.[26]

The work proceeded along the lines of Evers's original plan as modified by the suggestions of the Board of Inspection and Survey of the previous November. The ship emerged with 225 berths for what was projected to

These two photographs show the ship at South Chicago in November 1917, after Captain Evers's preliminary efforts to convert the *Eastland* to a training vessel. She was in this state when Lt. T. W. Richards undertook her conversion to a gunboat for deep-sea service. At the time she was designated only as S.S. 25, although Evers had already determined to name her *Wilmette*. (National Archives)

be a normal complement of only 181 men, but with more ample accommodation in the superstructure for the officers. Two decks in the hull were allocated to berths for the crew, 143 on what was called the platform deck and 82 on the second deck. Petty officers were housed on the main deck and officers above.[27] The captain's quarters were aft, and 9 staterooms for other officers were placed forward.[28] The bridge was 27 feet above the waterline, and the mainmast 88 feet above the water. Accordingly, the superstructure was a low one that would present no stability problems.

Incidentally to removal of the boiler, the pressure was reduced to 150 pounds. In one of the few deviations from the board's recommendations, a forced-draft system with a blower on each furnace was installed. The changes reduced her speed to 15 miles per hour at 105 RPM; the ship had operated at 140 to 145 RPM in commercial service.[29] An auxiliary condenser was added, but never much used. The hull was left unchanged except that bilge keels were added to reduce rolling while under way.[30] Her normal draft was 14'-0", and her displacement 2,600 tons.

The Navy did not follow through with Evers's plan of replacing the *Eastland*'s tanks with fixed ballast, but several alterations were made in the system. The Navy referred to them uniformly as double bottoms, rather than as ballast tanks. Their height of 48 inches was unchanged. The forward peak tank was converted to a chain locker, designated A-101. A platform for storage of chains was fitted aft, replacing or covering the after peak tank. According to all the correspondence concerning the ship, the system had only eight tanks, rather than the ten on the *Eastland*. Instead of referring to tanks No. 1 through 5, port and starboard, as on the *Eastland*, the Navy personnel now wrote of tanks A-1 and A-2 through D-1 and D-2. Tanks A-1 and A-2 were lined with cement and used for potable water. Evers reported that these were small and did not affect the trim of the ship.[31] The largest tanks were B-1 and B-2, which together held about 39,000 gallons. They ran from frame 63 to frame 78, which put them, if the numbering of frames was unchanged from that shown on the outboard profile of the *Eastland* illustrated in this book, directly beneath the boiler room, where the *Eastland*'s No. 3 tanks had been. Tanks C-1 and C-2 together held about 26,000 gallons, and tapered from 32 feet wide forward to 27 feet wide aft over a 40-foot linear distance from frame 78 to frame 98; this put them exactly beneath the engine room, approximately where the *Eastland*'s No. 4 tanks had been. Tanks B-1, B-2, C-1, and C-2, which held the majority of the water, together had a capacity of about 269 tons, which implies that the system as modified was smaller than on the *Eastland*. Some of the tank capacity forward of the B tanks was apparently removed. It seems likely that this change amounted merely to dropping both tanks No. 2 from use, but there is no specific evidence of this. Tanks

D-1 and D-2 were immediately abaft tanks C-1 and C-2, but the surviving documents do not indicate their size. They were described as relatively small, however. The Navy retained the longitudinal girder partitions in the ballast tanks, but referred to them as auxiliary keelsons.

The fact that the tanks beneath the boiler and engine rooms were not much altered gave rise to the first evidence of survival on the *Wilmette* of some of the *Eastland*'s problems. Richards, who on September 20, 1918, had reported the work on the *Wilmette* 90 percent completed, wrote to the Bureau of Construction and Repair on September 28, requesting an inclining experiment before the ship left the yard. He wrote:

It has been observed the vessel is somewhat tender. . . . This is not to convey the impression that the Superintending Constructor entertains any doubt as to the vessel's stability, but owing to the previous accident to her (ex-*Eastland*), together with the facts as outlined above, it is considered desirable that this experiment be held under present conditions.[32]

On October 26, he was more explicit:

In connection with the inner bottoms of the *Wilmette*, it is believed that these compartments are so extensive that the slightest change in the contents thereof effects [*sic*] the vessel to a degree which is noticeable. It is therefore recommended that provision be made to sub-divide these tanks, particularly in the wake of the boiler and engine rooms, as it is believed that a tank of very much smaller capacity would meet the needs for reserve feed water.[33]

J. D. Beuret of the Bureau of Construction and Repair responded that the proposed division would be considered after the forthcoming inclining experiment;[34] but no modification was made.

Unfortunately, no full set of plans for the *Wilmette* is known to have survived to document the final arrangements. The file on the conversion of the vessel contains a blueprint of the engine, boiler rooms, and the coal bunker and a transverse section of the ship through the center-mounted boiler, but neither profiles nor hull lines.[35] Reverend Peter J. Van der Linden reports having seen the Navy's plans for conversion of the *Eastland* in the customs house at Port Huron at some time between 1959 and 1964, but believes that they were destroyed with a large amount of other material when the customs house was closed subsequently.[36]

Although some work remained to be done, the *Wilmette* was put in commission at the shipyard in South Chicago at noon on September 25, 1918.[37] Richards, in his report of September 20 that the work was 90 percent completed, had stated that the guns were yet to be installed.[38] The installation was probably finished early in October. The armament was as the board had recommended in November: "Four 4″ 50 Caliber Mark IX-5 guns, two forward, two aft. Two 3″ 50 Caliber-Mark X-2 antiaircraft guns, amidships. Two 1-pound saluting guns, position not stated." [39] The ship was given the hull number GX-13. The "G" denoted gunboat, and the "X" indicated that the number was arbitrarily issued for purposes of filing the documentary material regarding the ship, as distinct from a number issued officially by the Navy. Captain William B. Wells was appointed her first commander.

The problem of shortening the ship by somewhat more than 14 feet to traverse the locks on the Welland Canal remained to be solved. Cutting off her stern was impractical because the cut would have had to be forward of the stock of the new balanced rudder. The board had proposed that the 15 feet of the bow be cut off at the American Ship Building Company's yard at Buffalo in favor of a false bow, and then replaced at a Canadian yard on the St. Lawrence. On February 19, 1918, the Bureau of Construction and Repair approved a plan to cut the ship just forward of her collision bulkhead No. 16, which would have removed 31 feet of the bow and given her a length of 244 feet, short enough to present no problem in the locks. [40] By the time the ship was commissioned, the questions how large a cut from the bow should be made and which yard should make it had become urgent. The Navy wanted to bring the ship out through the St. Lawrence before ice closed the river for the winter, and then to take her to the Boston Navy Yard for installation of launching gear for depth charges and some other equipment. The Navy believed that this required a departure no later than November 15. By October 10 the Bureau of Construction and Repair was facing the impracticality of its plan. The yard at Buffalo was overburdened with work, and of the yards on the St. Lawrence equipped to do the restoration of the bow, the Montreal Shipbuilding Company and Canadian Vickers, Ltd., at Montreal were fully booked to the end of the navigation season. The Davie Shipbuilding & Repair Company of Levis, Quebec, did not even respond. [41]

Accordingly, the bureau decided to have the bow cut at South Chicago between the *Wilmette*'s frames 6 and 7, and to add a bulkhead and a short false bow to give her a length of 260 feet, only a foot shorter than the lock at the Welland Canal. This, it was hoped, would make her seaworthy for the trip to the Boston Navy Yard, where the bow would be restored. [42] The ship was drydocked at South Chicago, and Richards reported that work on cutting off the bow was begun on October 14. He hoped to have that and any other remaining work on the ship accomplished by October 28. [43] She was put back in the water with her new false bow only a day late, on October 29. On the 31st she was tied up at Navy Pier preparatory to departure, but she then had to be brought back to the yard at South Chicago. The Navy's Bureau of Construction and Repair was unwilling to send her forth without knowing her metacentric height and ordered the inclining test that Richards had requested in September. Richards performed the initial test at the shipyard on November 1. With 190 tons of coal on board, 60 tons of reserve boiler feedwater in the B tanks, and the A potable water tanks full, the metacentric height was calculated at 1.5 feet.[44] On November 4 she was moved to the Pugh Terminal on the north bank of the Michigan Canal to receive stores, supplies, electrical equipment, and a crew for the trip to Boston. The bureau, however, proved dissatisfied with the test on the ground that the readings from the port inclinations were erratic, consistent with seepage from a full starboard tank to a partly filled port tank.[45] Richards denied that the ship had this problem, but the bureau ordered a second test, which he performed at the Pugh Terminal on November 13. This time he assured that all of the tanks, including the potable water tanks, were dry, and the two aft boilers were drained. He used 4 weights of 1.25 tons each for the inclination. With 150 tons of coal and the same weight of stores and ammunition as before, the metacentric height was found to be 2.2 feet.[46] At the test she drew 13'-8½" and displaced 2,220 tons, less than what was expected to be normal for her, because she was restricted in draft as well as in length by her impending passage through the Welland Canal and the St. Lawrence River. In any event, the ship's stability was now well documented.

While the ship was being fitted out, and between the two inclining tests, the war ended. The chief of naval operations countermanded the *Wilmette*'s orders, and directed Wells to turn the vessel over to the commandant of the 9th Naval District for duty in training personnel.[47] The ship remained in her berth at the Pugh Terminal. On January 2, 1919, Wells was relieved of command and assigned to New York for duty concerned with returning servicemen. On January 8 command was turned over to Captain Evers for the Naval Reserve. To fit her out for use by the reserve unit, she was moved on May 6 to the Kraft shipyard in South Chicago, about half a mile away from Chicago Ship Building's yard. Kraft removed the false bow down to the waterline, but not having a dry dock large enough for the ship, he had to move her to Chicago Ship Building for replacement of her bow up to the waterline. She was returned to the Kraft yard on June 10 for completion of the job. On July 1 she was moved to the Reserve's facility at the foot of Randolph Street, where she would spend most of her remaining career. On July 9 she was placed in ordinary, or laid up, with a crew of ten. She remained in this status for nearly a year until June 29, 1920, when she was recommissioned. She was taken to the North Avenue turning basin on the North Branch, moored next to the U.S.S. *Yantic*, and fitted out for active duty. On July 5 she was towed out of the river and moored at a wharf of the Illinois Central Railroad at the foot of Randolph Street, where housings for lifeboats were removed, cabins were painted, and she was otherwise prepared for her duties as a training vessel.[48]

Officers and men assigned to the *Wilmette* began boarding her on August 1. On August 3, in her first active service since the disaster, the ship steamed out of Chicago and up to an anchorage off the Great Lakes Naval Training Station in the Chicago far-north suburbs. She left on August 4 for South Manitou Island, where she arrived on the following day. She proceeded to Harbor Springs, and left on August 13 for Milwaukee and Chicago. She made some shorter cruises in the late summer and was released from active duty on September 14. This was to be typical of her career as a training vessel, uneventful and satisfactory. On November 11 she was laid up for the winter at the Army Engineers' facility on the North Branch at Cherry Avenue and Weed Street.[49]

The *Wilmette* was towed back to Randolph Street on May 9, 1921, to begin a season that would include one of the few notable events of her naval career. After an early-season trip to Milwaukee and Detroit, she left Chicago on June 7 for an exercise in which she fired her guns for the first time, sinking the hulk of a German submarine, the *UC-97*, one of ten that had been turned over to the Allies at Harwich, England, under the terms of the Treaty of Versailles. By the treaty, the submarine had to be destroyed by July 1, 1921. The craft had sunk seven Allied ships during the war. She had been shown in Milwaukee in 1919, and then laid up for over a year in Chicago while she was stripped of all removable machinery and brass parts. The *Wilmette* left Chicago for the gunnery exercise early on

The *Wilmette* at the foot of Randolph Street, probably during the winter of 1920 as the ship was awaiting reconversion from a gunboat to a naval training vessel. (National Archives)

The *Wilmette* backing out from the slip at Randolph Street to begin a training cruise, probably in 1922. (National Archives)

June 7, steamed about 30 miles north, and rendezvoused at 10:20 A.M. at 42′10″ north and 87′20″ west with the patrol vessel *Hawk*, which had the *UC-97* in tow. The district commandant, with a party from the naval training station, came alongside at 11:35 on the submarine-chaser *No. 412*. At 11:45 the *Wilmette* opened fire on the submarine, sending thirteen rounds from her four-inch guns into the hulk. The submarine was reported in the press to have sunk within a minute. With the exercise over, the sub-chaser left about noon to return the commandant's party to the training station, and the *Wilmette* returned to Chicago.[50] She left the following day for a cruise to the Manitou Islands, and settled into what would be the routine of many summers. The sinking of the submarine was the only use of the four-inch guns in the *Wilmette*'s early history; as late as 1934 it was reported that they had not been fired again.[51]

The correspondence on the *Wilmette* does not indicate that any stability problems manifested themselves as long as the ship remained coal burning. The metacentric height was satisfactory, the ship carried no cargo, and she handled an average complement of 210 officers and men, with no reported load larger than 375 naval personnel. In fact, the board of officers who performed the material inspection of 1923 argued that Evers was overly cautious with respect to the ship's stability. The double bottoms were kept filled virtually at all times. The board found that this resulted in some rust and deterioration of the red lead with which the tanks were painted. The board showed considerable faith in the *Wilmette*'s stability:

Most of the double bottoms are ordinarily filled with water even in port. . . . The stability data examined by the board do not show this to be necessary. . . . It is practicable to empty and clean and care for the double bottom compartments in port and underway, at least part of the time. The *Wilmette*, formerly *Eastland*, has had upper works reduced and is now in a different condition from that when a passenger steamer.

The Commanding Officer should obtain stability data from the Bureau of Construction and Repair, and an excessive caution as to stability should not operate to prevent opening and cleaning and protecting structure within the double bottoms.[52]

The ship was to have several major changes in 1925. Probably incidentally to its moving to a more rational filing system, on February 21 the Navy changed the hull designation from GX-13 to IX-29. The Navy had filed material topically, an arrangement that made it virtually impossible to assure that one had found all the information on a given ship. In 1925 it went to a system in which it filed material by ship. The "I" designated the *Wilmette* as an unclassified auxiliary ship, and the "X" again indicated that the designation was only a filing code; it was made official, though still with the letter "X," on February 17, 1941.[53] More important, in 1925 the decision was made to convert the ship to oil burning. In February Evers wrote to the Navy's Bureau of Engineering requesting the conversion, principally on the ground that it would make the ship more attractive to engineering students in the Chicago area, whom he wanted to draw into the Naval Reserve. He planned to use the ship's existing ballast tanks for the fuel and estimated the cost of the conversion at only $6,000, which he thought would be compensated for in the savings of only a few years of operation.[54] The Navy approved,[55] and in November 1925 the *Wilmette* was drydocked for the conversion.

The conversion was to produce the only serious stability problems of the ship's history as the *Wilmette* and the only evidence from her naval career that conveys any direct implications with respect to the disaster. Two pairs of the ballast tanks were converted to use for oil, the D tanks to feed the burners directly and the C tanks as a reserve. This arrangement was an attempt at confining the inevitable variability of the content of fuel bunkers to the smaller D tanks. Except on long voyages, the C tanks could be kept full, thereby minimizing the free-surface effect. The B tanks were retained for water to feed the boilers, but the water was also used for stabilization. The transverse portion of the former coal bunker was converted into a pump room for the equipment used to pump oil or water between the tanks. The wing portions of the bunker were initially used for storage lockers for the engineers, and also to house small cylindrical fuel oil tanks, probably to serve the stoves in the galleys, which were also converted from coal to oil at this time.[56] In authorizing the alterations, the Bureau of Construction and Repair concluded on the basis of the 1918 inclining tests that the changes would result in a small reduction in displacement and stability. The chief of the bureau recommended adding 60 tons of permanent ballast in the wing-bunker area, 6 feet above the keel and 2 feet above the tanks, abreast of the boilers.[57] Evers, who had wanted permanent ballast since conceiving the idea of conversion of the ship to naval use, secured authority to buy 60 tons of pig iron, and installed it as directed.[58] The pig iron was piled to a height of about 2 feet, extending inboard from the hull for about 4 feet, immediately on top of tanks B from frame 64 of the hull to a watertight bulkhead at frame 78. Evers placed about 1.5 tons of grate bars, which had been removed from beneath the boilers in the conversion to oil, ahead of each of the stacks of pig iron.[59]

With the ship in this condition, the Bureau of Construction and Repair recomputed her metacentric height from the 1918 inclining test and concluded that fully loaded it was 2.24 feet, corrected for a free-surface effect of 1.41 feet.[60] This implies that the ship should have been quite stable with respect to weight distribution. Nonetheless, the revisions of 1926 produced a serious stability problem from an increased free-surface effect. It was no longer possible to keep the double bottoms filled. The potential problem of instability from the large tanks that Richards had warned of in 1918 had now manifested itself. In 1931 Evers wrote to the Bureau of Construction and Repair:

> The vessel has proven very satisfactory in every way except one, and that one is that it is impossible to keep her on an even keel due to too much free area in her double bottoms. As will be seen from the plans there are four pairs of double bottoms divided only by the keelson.
>
> The A and D bottoms are small and do not give any trouble, but the B and C bottoms contain so much water that it is necessary to keep them either completely filled or completely empty. The B bottoms are used for boiler feed make-up and, after a small quantity of water is taken out of either bottom, the ship takes a list, which seriously affects the compass . . . by four or five points, [and which] has been the cause of some very narrow escapes and could readily lead to a serious disaster.[61]

In other correspondence on this point, he estimated that each of the B tanks held 19,500 gallons of water.[62] The C tanks were difficult because they could not be filled with water until all of the oil had been pumped out. If the C tanks were empty or partly filled, it was necessary to keep the B tanks full because "when the fuel oil tanks are empty . . . the ship is very touchy unless they are filled."[63] Evers's proposed solution was to divide the B and C tanks into several smaller tanks by welding closed the openings in several of the transverse frames and in the auxiliary keelsons. The Bureau of Construction and Repair responded positively, stating that the calculated free-surface effect with only the keelson at the center line of the ship watertight was to reduce metacentric height by 0.47 feet. If the auxiliary keelsons were made watertight, this figure would be reduced to 0.13 feet. The bureau agreed with Evers that the principal problem was the B tanks, but held that only longitudinal division would be helpful on the ground that the moment of inertia varied as to the cube of the breadth of the water. Transverse subdivision, it said, would improve metacentric height only by providing smaller tanks that could more easily be kept either full or empty.[64] After considerable correspondence concerning the nature of the subdivision, the B tanks were divided longitudinally by welding shut the auxiliary keelsons and thus creating in each an inboard tank of 9,700 gallons and an outboard tank of 9,830 gallons. Each C tank was divided transversely into tanks of 8,000 and 5,000 gallons by welding closed frame 88.[65] All of the newly created small tanks had independent suction pipes, sounding tubes, and manholes. The changes were a success. The report of an inspection of September 21, 1933, stated: "the ship gave every indication of being entirely stable."[66] The only later problems Evers reported were a 6-degree list with 375 men and 766 rounds of 4-inch ammunition aboard in 1938, and similar listing in a beam wind. He reported that he dealt with the problem by emptying a water tank the ship carried on the main deck, and by rearranging her boats.[67]

This experience of the *Wilmette* with respect to her double bottoms tends to confirm the judgment expressed in Chapters IV and VI that the free-surface effect from the water in the partly filled ballast tanks No. 2 and 3 on the *Eastland* was a major force in the disaster. The *Wilmette*'s stability was now thoroughly documented, but the free-surface effect from the large expanses of water or oil in her tanks was enough to convince Evers that it constituted a potential for disaster. The *Eastland*, however, had a record of poor stability after the changes of the spring of 1904, was worsened by the application of concrete to her decks before the 1915 season, and was in a very dangerous condition after the changes of July 2, 1915. Her No. 2 and 3 tanks, which were used for stabilization leading to the disaster, were approximately of the same aggregate capacity as the B and C tanks on the *Wilmette*—271, as opposed to 269 tons—and we know with certainty that those tanks on the *Eastland* at the time of the disaster were only partly filled. Accordingly, the contribution of the free-surface effect to the disaster must have been considerable.

The *Wilmette* had a second major change in 1937. She had passed her approximately biennial inspections without difficulty until December 1, 1936, when the inspectors recommended her withdrawal because of the condition of her boilers. She was still powered by three of the *Eastland*'s original Scotch boilers, which were now well over 33 years old. Given the

The *Wilmette* in the St. Clair River in the early 1940's. A radar machine and some additional radio gear had been added, but otherwise her appearance had changed only slightly since 1922. (Rev. Peter J. Van der Linden collection)

age of the ship, the inspectors proposed that she be withdrawn, but stated that as an alternative, her boilers were still adequate to her use as a stationary floating adjunct to the naval armory.[68]

This proposal brought forth a show of opposition, which demonstrated that the ship had been quite satisfactory in her naval career. Evers, who could hardly have looked upon the *Wilmette* as other than his own creation, wrote to Washington that the ship was cruising with about 1,000 officers and men each year—she generally logged from 3,800 to 5,200 miles per season—and was extensively used for public functions throughout the Great Lakes when a naval vessel was required. The welcoming ceremony for General Italo Balbo in Chicago had been held aboard her on completion of his transatlantic flight of 24 seaplanes of the Italian air force to the Century of Progress Exposition of 1933.[69] Evers argued that the hull was excellent and that her interior had been upgraded or renovated from time to time, leaving her "particularly well suited for Naval Reserve training." [70] Hayne Ellis, commandant of the 9th Naval District, supported Evers, writing:

In many respects the ship is superior to the other ships assigned to the Naval Reserve organizations based on the Great Lakes. This is particularly true in respect to berthing accommodations for both officers and men. The Department is fully informed in respect of the difficulties occasioned by the non-availability of one of the five larger training ships on the Great Lakes in arranging cruising schedules.[71]

Evers and Ellis proposed that the ship be reboilered with four Babcock and Wilcox watertube boilers, three of which would be operated at any given time, with the fourth cold for cleaning, inspection, or use for instruction. The Navy quickly assented, and the ship was equipped with the four watertube boilers at a projected cost of $42,894 for the 1937 season. Two of the three Scotch boilers were removed in April, but the third, probably the center-mounted one, was not removed until November.[72] Evers sought to have the center boiler replaced with a fuel tank explicitly on the ground of stability, but was denied on the ground that the effect on metacentric height would be negligible.[73] The four watertube boilers were mounted on existing foundations athwartship between frames 67 and 78. At this time frame 67 was welded closed to subdivide the B tanks transversely. Thereafter, the portion below the new boilers was used only for feedwater, and ballast water was handled entirely in the portion between frames 53 and 67.[74] This implies that the maximum amount of water available for stabilization was only about 87.5 tons—further evidence that the *Wilmette* was looked upon by the Navy as quite stable. She had no reported stability problems after her reboilering. Use of her four-inch guns may have resumed in this period. The ship's material inspection of 1936 does not repeat what had been the regular statement that the guns had not again been fired,[75] and as noted, she was reported to be carrying a large amount of four-inch ammunition in 1938.

In spite of her recent reboilering, the ship would probably have been withdrawn from service in 1940 except for the prospect of American entrance into World War II. She was taken out of commission on February 15, 1940, but restored on February 17, 1941. The most noteworthy events of her later history occurred in 1943. She was overhauled in May, modified in appearance, and given considerable hull work. Most conspicuously, the two-stack configuration she had maintained since her days as the *Eastland* was replaced with a single stack. A military-style tripod mast replaced her two pole masts. In August she provided the marine portion of a fishing trip to the Manitoulin Island area of Ontario by President Franklin Delano Roosevelt for mixed recreation and war planning. The *Wilmette* left Chicago on July 29, calling at Great Lakes Naval Training Station to pick up eighteen additional crew members. She steamed north at a steady twelve miles per hour, passed through the Canadian Pacific Railway's swing bridge at Little Current, Ontario, at 4:00 P.M. on July 31, and anchored off Strawberry Island to await the president. He proceeded by train from Washington to Birch Island on the railway's Little Current branch, whence

In December 1944 the *Wilmette* was part of an exhibition of military and naval equipment on the Chicago lakefront as a promotion for war bonds. The ship, in the single-stack configuration to which she was converted in 1943, is at the center foreground of the upper photograph. Below, visitors to the exhibition were allowed to board the ship. The sign at right welcoming them makes no reference to her origin as the *Eastland*. The sign correctly states that the IX in her hull number designates her as an unclassified training vessel, but oddly refers to it as a roman numeral. (National Archives)

The *Wilmette* in her final state with a single stack after her revisions of 1943. Her boats removed, she was out of commission and awaiting sale for scrap. (Rev. Peter J. Van der Linden collection)

The *Wilmette* in the course of scrapping on the South Branch of the Chicago River in the winter of 1946–47. (Captain Frank E. Hamilton collection, Rutherford B. Hayes Memorial Library)

the *Wilmette* took him and his party cruising on McGregor and Whitefish
bays. His party included Admiral William D. Leahy, James F. Byrnes, and
Harry Hopkins, a passenger list indicating that the ship's accommodations
must have been considered, if not luxurious, at least comfortable.[76] After
an embarrassing grounding of two days on Magnetic Reef, the *Wilmette*
left the area on August 11, and returned to Chicago about 1:00 A.M. on
August 13.[77]

The ship's serious business in the war years was training gun crews at
Chicago for the defense of armed merchantmen. An Armed Guard School
was established in the naval armory on March 10, 1942, with facilities for
100 officers and 800 enlisted men, each of whom was given four weeks'
training, mainly on antiaircraft and machine guns. Similar schools were
established at Little Creek, Virginia, and San Diego, California. A sailor
who served on the *Wilmette* in this period, George R. Werthmann, reported that the ship was sent on short voyages to a designated area of sand
dunes on the east shore of Lake Michigan, where day-long gunnery practice was held, presumably with the four-inch guns.[78]

With the end of the war against Germany in the spring of 1945, the
Wilmette's role became unnecessary. She was decommissioned on November 28, and dropped from the Navy Register on December 19.[79] She
was offered for sale at her berth at the foot of Randolph Street, and sold
on October 31, 1946, to a prominent scrap dealer, the Hyman Michaels
Company. On November 1 she was slowly towed by the Great Lakes Towing Company's *Kansas* up the Chicago River past the point at which she
had capsized. The same company's *New Jersey* had a line on her stern.
She was towed to the wharf of William J. Howard on the South Branch
near 16th Street, where her superstructure and machinery were removed.
The hull was then towed to the Inland Steel Company's plant at East Chicago, Indiana, where what had been the *Eastland* was finally cut up early
in 1947.

Epilogue

THE *Eastland* in the form of the *Wilmette* outlasted most of the people involved in her history. Of the men who had brought her into being, John C. Pereue sold out his marine holdings in 1904, moved to South Carolina, and went into the lumber business. He and his wife moved to Maryland in 1914, but returned in 1929 to South Haven, where he died in April 1931.[1] His associate Patrick Noud died in Manistee in January 1925.[2] Robert R. Blacker retired to Pasadena, California, and died at his summer home in Santa Monica in September 1931.[3] Angus M. Carpenter, who had represented Jenks in the Michigan Steamship Company, died in New York while serving with the Shipping Board early in 1919.[4] Sidney G. Jenks, designer of the *Eastland*, became a manufacturer of engines and other automotive components in Port Huron after his shipyard closed in 1906.[5] In World War I he returned to naval architecture as a district officer of the Emergency Fleet Corporation. Following the war he joined the New York Shipbuilding Company, for which he rose to works manager of its yard in Camden, New Jersey. He died in retirement in Camden on December 13, 1965, at the age of 93.[6]

Of the men involved in the disaster, as mentioned in the text, chief engineer Erickson had died in 1919 and Reid, the inspector, in 1922. Fred Snow returned to the Pere Marquette Railway car ferries, and was serving as first assistant engineer on the *City of Saginaw 31*, when on December 16, 1929, walking from the ferry terminal to his home, he died suddenly on a sidewalk in Ludington.[7] Ray W. Davis became a prominent local figure at St. Joseph. He had served as secretary of the city's chamber

THE EASTLAND DISASTER

WHILE STILL PARTIALLY TIED TO ITS DOCK AT THE RIVER'S EDGE, THE EXCURSION STEAMER EASTLAND ROLLED OVER ON THE MORNING OF JULY 24, 1915. THE RESULT WAS ONE OF THE WORST MARITIME DISASTERS IN AMERICAN HISTORY. MORE THAN EIGHT HUNDRED PEOPLE LOST THEIR LIVES WITHIN A FEW FEET OF SHORE. THE EASTLAND WAS FILLED TO OVERFLOWING WITH PICNIC BOUND WESTERN ELECTRIC COMPANY EMPLOYEES AND THEIR FAMILIES WHEN THE TRAGEDY OCCURRED. INVESTIGATIONS FOLLOWING THE DISASTER RAISED QUESTIONS ABOUT THE SHIP'S SEAWORTHINESS AND INSPECTION OF GREAT LAKES STEAMERS IN GENERAL.

ERECTED BY THE ILLINOIS MATHEMATICS AND SCIENCE ACADEMY AND THE ILLINOIS STATE HISTORICAL SOCIETY, 1988

of commerce for twelve years, when on October 4, 1930, he suffered a
heart seizure at a football game, and died a few hours later at his home.[8]
William H. Hull became a banker, a director and chairman of the finance
committee of the Union Banking Company of St. Joseph. He was reportedly reluctant to leave the city out of fear of further prosecution in Chicago. He died in St. Joseph, also of a heart ailment, on September 21,
1933.[9] The most important figure, Captain Harry Pedersen, withdrew
from active service as a Great Lakes master to his farm at Millburg, Michigan, but he continued his consulting on compasses. He died of nephritis
in Cook County Hospital in Chicago on July 25, 1939, and was buried in
the cemetery at Millburg. His final lie was at least locally successful: the
St. Joseph *Herald-Press* stated in his obituary that the cause of the disaster
was the *Eastland*'s resting on a hidden spile.[10] The obituary noted that Del
Fisher, who became a police officer in St. Joseph, had already died.

Walter K. Greenebaum, after liquidating the Indiana Transportation
Company, set up an office as a ship broker in Chicago. During World
War I he represented the French government in maritime matters in Washington. Although he had administered the Indiana Transportation Company from Chicago, he had necessarily become thoroughly familiar with
Michigan City, and was convinced of the community's economic potential.
He moved there at the close of the war, and became the first secretary of
the Michigan City Chamber of Commerce. He devoted himself with great
success to the city's industrial and cultural development, while carrying
on his own business enterprises of a travel bureau and a real estate agency.
He spent most of the rest of his life in Michigan City and was made an
honorary citizen by the city council on November 7, 1958. He died at the
age of 81 at his home in the suburb of Pottawattamie Park on November 3,
1960, and was eulogized as one of the most revered figures in Michigan
City's recent history.[11]

Purser George Monger following the disaster became an accountant in
his home city of Kalamazoo. He died in Marshall, Michigan, on November 19, 1948, at the age of 77.[12] Radio officer Charles M. Dibbell remained
active with the Goodrich Line and the Pere Marquette Railway car ferries
until 1918, but then became a veterinarian in Allentown, Pennsylvania. He
retired from practice in 1964, became the city's inspector of meat and milk,
and died in the spring of 1982.[13] As far as is known, Dibbell, who had been
only 19 at the time of the capsizing, was the last survivor among the *Eastland*'s officers.

One of the strangest aspects of the aftermath of the disaster was the

Opposite: The Illinois Mathematics and Science Academy and the Illinois State
Historical Society jointly placed this plaque at the site of the disaster. The last line
of the plaque notwithstanding, the memorial was unveiled on June 4, 1989.

City of Chicago's failure to memorialize it. The Wacker Drive development of the 1920's obliterated the old produce market and lined the river with classical balustrades. At the site of the disaster was a small plaque noting that a large warehouse had stood on the site before the fire of 1871. The fiftieth anniversary of the disaster was duly noted in 1965, but no memorial was undertaken. Then, more than twenty years later, William Stepien and other faculty members of the Illinois Mathematics and Science Academy in Aurora, Illinois, became interested in the disaster as a research exercise for the honors students whom the academy had been established by the state to instruct. Partly with their contributions, and with the cooperation of the Illinois State Historical Society and the Chicago Maritime Society, a large aluminum plaque was struck giving a short but accurate account of the event. The text raised the questions of the ship's seaworthiness and of the adequacy of federal inspection, but did nothing to perpetuate the casual explanations of the disaster. The plaque was unveiled with a short ceremony on Sunday, June 4, 1989. Professor Ted Karamanski of Loyola University spoke on the disaster's role in the social history of Chicago, and Frank French, vice president for public relations of American Telephone & Telegraph, recounted Western Electric's relief efforts.[14]

At the time the plaque was erected there were believed to be four remaining survivors of the disaster: Marie Benes, 96; Willard Brown, 90; Borghild Carlson, 93; and Libby Hruby, 84. Of the four, only Libby Hruby was in a physical condition that allowed her to attend. As a 10-year-old girl, she had set out upon the excursion with her sister, whom she credited with having saved her from the river. Two other survivors then identified themselves, Mrs. Aida Woods Watson of Las Cruces, New Mexico, 77, and her brother, Robert Woods of New Port Richey, Florida, 79. As very young children, they had been members of a party of five, all of whom lived through the accident.[15] Another woman, Meta L. Otto, was identified as an *Eastland* survivor when she died on July 18, 1989, shortly after the ceremony. Marie Benes died in March 1991, and Borghild Carlson died on August 2, 1991.[16] Another survivor, Irene Zajic, died on August 4, 1992.[17] As far as is known, the rest remain alive at the present writing in 1992. Because the survivors were never well documented, and because some of them moved from the Chicago area, it is as impossible now as it ever was to be certain that they have all been identified. As a consequence, we are unlikely ever to know confidently when the last one has died.

Nonetheless, there is no prospect that the disaster will be forgotten. The great city takes its history seriously, and the event was so excruciating as to scar the collective memory of the metropolitan area far beyond the power of time to eradicate. Rather, the problem is that the casual explanations—the ship was resting on an obstruction, the tug pulled her over, the passengers surged to port—may continue indefinitely. They are now as old as the disaster itself, and although they never had factual support, they have the advantage of being simple in a situation that was actually quite complex. They are nontechnical, requiring no inquiry into the stability properties of ships. Perhaps more important, the casual explanations are nonincriminating in an event that in retrospect leaves almost no major figure appearing favorably save only the harbormaster, the tug captain, and the *Eastland*'s chief engineer—and it hardly need be repeated that the *Eastland*'s chief engineer was the man on whom the catastrophe was ultimately blamed.

Appendixes

Registry Data

Eastland. U.S. 200031. 1,961 gross tons. 1,218 net tons. Built 1903 by
  Jenks Ship Building Company, Port Huron, Michigan, hull no. 25.
Dimensions: 265' between perpendiculars, 275' overall × 38.2' × 19.5'.
Engines: Two triple-expansion, 21" + 34" + 56" × 30", built by Jenks.
Boilers: Four Scotch, 13.5' × 12', 200 pounds pressure, 3,500 horse-
  power, built by Jenks. Pressure later reported as 210 and 250 pounds.

Wilmette. GX-13 (1918–25). IX-29 (1925–45). 2,600 tons displacement.
Dimensions and engines unchanged from the *Eastland*.
Boilers: Three of the *Eastland*'s four Scotch boilers, 150 pounds pressure.
  Replaced by four Babcock and Wilcox watertube boilers, 1937.

Hull List, Jenks Ship Building Company

Hull No.	Name	Official No.	Gr. Tons	Dimensions	Year	Hull	Registry
1	*O. O. Carpenter*	155198	364	127.6 × 30 × 9.5	1891	Wood	Port Huron
2	*Desmond*	157350	456.14	149 × 30.5 × 9.5	1892	Wood	Port Huron
3	*C. D. Thompson* (tug)	126998	91.74	81 × 19.2 × 11	1893	Wood	Port Huron
4	*Lloyd S. Porter*	141264	536	159 × 30.6 × 10.7	1893	Wood	Port Huron
5	*H. E. Runnels*	96230	1,162	178 × 35 × 20.1	1893	Wood	Port Huron
6	*W. G. Harrow* (tug)	81434	84	85 × 19 × 9.2	1893	Wood	Chicago
7	*F. J. Haynes* (tug)	121004	27	50 × 14.2 × 7.5	1895	Wood	Port Huron
8	*B. B. Inman* (tug)	3561	89	81 × 19 × 10.6	1895	Wood	Port Huron
9	*Vigilant* (tug)	161767	372	128 × 24.5 × 12	1896	Wood	Port Huron
10	*Linden*	141370	894	206 × 35 × 12.6	1895	Wood	Port Huron
11	*Black Rock*	3721	1,646	237 × 43 × 16.5	1897	Wood	Port Huron
12	*W. G. Mason* (tug)	81617	99	84 × 20.5 × 10.5	1898	Wood	Port Huron
13	*Ravenscraig*	111284	2,402	243.5 × 43.2 × 23.8	1900	Steel	Providence
14	*Captain Thomas Wilson*	127469	4,917	420.5 × 50 × 24	1900	Steel	Cleveland
15	*Kennebec* (coaster)	161178	2,183	243.5 × 43.2 × 24	1901	Steel	New York
16	*Charles S. Neff* (cnl.)	127547	992	200 × 38 × 11.6	1901	Steel	Milwaukee
17	*Henry Steinbrenner*	96584	4,719	420 × 50 × 24	1901	Steel	Cleveland
18	*Kanawha* (coaster)	161199	2,182	243.5 × 43.4 × 23.5	1902	Steel	Belfast, ME
19	*John B. Cowle*	77559	4,731	420 × 50.2 × 24	1902	Steel	Cleveland
20	*T. F. Newman* (barge)	59589	855	165 × 36.3 × 14	1901	Steel	Duluth
21	*James R. Elliott* (fire)	77566	210	110 × 25 × 12	1902	Steel	Detroit
22	*Hyacinth* (buoy tender)	USLHS	677	150.7 × 28 × 14	1902	Steel	—
23	*Chesbrough Bros* (yacht)	—	8	50 × 9 × 4.3	1902	Steel	Bay City
24	Seven pontoon barges	USLS	—	—	—	Steel	—
25	*Eastland* (passenger)	200031	1,961	265 × 38.2 × 19.5	1903	Steel	Michigan City
26	*F. B. Squire*	200560	4,852	410 × 50.2 × 24	1903	Steel	Cleveland

SOURCE: Collections of the Rev. Edward J. Dowling, S.J., University of Detroit, and the Rev. Peter J. Van der Linden, Port Huron; *Merchant Vessels of the United States*; *Register of the American Bureau of Shipping*.

NOTE: Unless otherwise indicated, ships were Great Lakes bulk freighters. Fire = fire tug. Cnl. = canaller. USLHS = U.S. Lighthouse Service. USLS = U.S. Lake Survey.

Evaluation of the Eastland by
Professor Herbert Charles Sadler

This is an edited transcript of the direct testimony in the federal criminal trial U.S. v. Hull et al., from the typescript transcript of evidence at the National Archives and Records Administration, Great Lakes Center, Chicago, Record Group 21, CR #1628, boxes 358, 803, pages 1487–1543. As noted in the text, Sadler's is the only professional evaluation of the *Eastland* ever made by an academic naval architect. Sadler did not put a prepared paper in evidence, although he did show some tables that have not survived. The diagrams he presented have also not survived, but have been reconstructed from his testimony by Professor Harry Benford and drafted by Rodney L. Hill of Milan, Michigan. Unsuccessful objections, lawyer byplay, requests for repetitions, redundant questions, and other matters not germane to the substantive content have been removed. Obvious misspellings and confusion of the court reporter between words have been corrected. Punctuation and grammar have been modified at several points to present the testimony in complete sentences. Only the direct examination of Sadler is reproduced here. The cross-examination by Clarence Darrow and other defense attorneys, which was lengthy, did not cause Sadler to modify his estimates, and did not evoke any major additional information. Such relevant additional data as it did bring forth have been added as notations to the direct examination.

Questions attributed to "The Court" are those of Judge Clarence W. Sessions. The lawyers engaged in the trial were:

James J. Barbour, attorney for William H. Hull and Captain Harry Pedersen.
John D. Black, attorney for George T. Arnold.
Charles F. Clyne, U.S. District Attorney at Chicago.
Clarence Darrow, attorney for Chief Engineer Joseph M. Erickson.
Charles E. Kremer, counsel for the St. Joseph–Chicago Steamship

Company, George T. Arnold, William H. Hull, Robert Reid, and
Charles C. Eckliff.

Walter I. Lillie, attorney for Robert Reid and Charles C. Eckliff.

Myron H. Walker, a member of Clyne's staff.

Testimony

Herbert Charles Sadler, a witness, produced, sworn, and examined on behalf of the Government, testified as follows:

Direct examination by Mr. Clyne:

Q. Where do you live?

A. Ann Arbor, Michigan.

Q. What is your business?

A. I am professor of naval architecture and marine engineering at the University of Michigan.

Q. Doctor, where did you first receive your training and education concerning marine construction? Where did you get your early education and training, Doctor—I mean, generally speaking?

A. At Dulwich College, London.

Q. Graduate of the college?

A. Yes.

Q. After leaving there, where did you then go?

A. To Glasgow University. I received the Bachelor of Science degree in 1893 and Doctor of Science in 1903.

Q. What course did you follow at the University of Glasgow?

A. Naval architecture and marine engineering.

Q. And after, or during the time that you were attending that university, did you have any experience in shipbuilding?

A. Yes. I served a regular apprenticeship at all branches of practical shipbuilding on the Clyde.

Q. What kinds of boats were built there?

A. All kinds.

Q. Great and small?

A. Yes.

Q. After that experience there, then where did you go, Doctor? What work did you do?

A. In 1896 I was appointed assistant professor of naval architecture and marine engineering at the University of Glasgow.

Q. Now what other work at that time, or subsequently—immediately subsequent to that—were you engaged in, in the way of consulting in marine matters?

A. From 1896 to 1900 I was associated with Professor [J. H.] Biles [of the University of Glasgow] in consulting—general consulting practice.

Q. What lines had occasion to employ you?

A. The American and Red Star lines, and a number of railway companies.

Q. What railway companies?

A. The London & Southwestern.

Q. Do they operate boats? Where?

A. Between [England] and France.

Q. How long did you continue in the practice as consulting engineer for these railway companies and steamship—transatlantic steamship lines?

A. About four years.

Q. And then what did you do? Come to this country?

A. I was appointed professor at the University of Michigan.

Q. And you are the head of that department there, and engaged in teaching marine engineering in all its branches and departments?

A. Yes.

Q. I believe they have a large department there, have they not, at the University, [with] testing tanks and all equipment?

A. Yes.

Q. I believe, Doctor, that you were selected by the president of this country at the Safety at Sea Conference in London following the disaster of the *Titanic*?

A. Yes.

Q. Now, Doctor, did you ever see the steamer *Eastland*? Have you ever seen the boat? When or about when was the first time that you ever saw her?

A. About a week after the accident, in Chicago.

Q. And just describe, if you will, in a general way, what you saw on visiting the scene of the accident?

A. When I saw the vessel, she was over on her port side in the river, and there were several holes in her side where plates had been cut.

Q. Did you go upon the boat at that time [and] walk over its surface?

A. Yes.

Q. Did you have occasion to go into the interior at that time, down to where the water was?

A. Where the water was, yes, sir.

Q. When did you next see the boat after that time?

A. About two weeks after that, after she had been raised.

Q. Just describe, if you will, what you observed there at that time and on that visit?

A. I went all over the vessel in order to make myself thoroughly familiar with her construction, and also to see if she was substantially according to the construction plans. At the same time I took the original plans of the vessel and checked over those and marked on them where changes had been made in the way of removal of staterooms and so forth.

Q. That is to say, you took the plans and compared them by going through the boat at that time, and made some measurements?

A. Yes.

Q. At that time did you see the model of the *Eastland*?

A. I did.

Q. Now, Doctor, tell the Court, if you will, what was the occasion or purpose of your going to see the *Eastland* on your first visit? What did you come there for? What were you to do?

A. I was asked by Mr. Clyne to come and examine the vessel and try and determine what was the cause of the accident. As I recall the conversation, it was to the effect that they wanted to get to the truth of this matter.

Q. You proceeded, Doctor, with all the facts and information to get at the cause of the accident?

A. I did.

Q. Did you see the boat after the second visit, Doctor? As I understand you, you visited it twice. Did you see the boat after that time?

A. No, not since then.

Q. I wish you would—before taking up the boat—I want to have you explain some things. What do you mean—and what is meant by the "tonnage" of a boat?

A. The tonnage of the boat is obtained by taking the total tonnage capacity of the closed-in space and dividing the cubic feet by 100.

Q. Now, Doctor, assume that we have two boats of the same length, the same beam and the same depth, two boats that are known as sister boats, sister ships—is it possible for one of those boats to have a different tonnage than the other?

A. If one vessel is fitted with a permanent closed deck house in which cargo can be carried, that would be measured into the tonnage of the vessel, and although the dimensions would be the same in both cases, the vessel fitted with the deck house permanently closed would have the larger tonnage.

Q. So when you give the tonnage of a boat, that does not give you any information as to the—in considering length and breadth and width, unless you know how much of the upper structure is enclosed?

A. No.

Q. There is some evidence here, Doctor, that there is a boat known as the *Virginia* [of the Goodrich Line] that has about the same length, about the same beam and depth, but 300 tons less; that difference could be ex-

The *Virginia*, similar in size to the *Eastland*, served as the Goodrich Transit Company's principal night boat between Chicago and Milwaukee until World War I. After service on the English Channel, she was sold to the Wrigley family, which renamed her *Avalon* and ran her to Catalina Island off Los Angeles. (Rev. Peter J. Van der Linden collection)

plained, could it not, in the way that you have described, of including the upper portion of the enclosed part of the boat?

A. Yes, it is quite possible.

Q. Well, that is, as a matter of fact, if those figures are true, where the difference lies.

A. I am not familiar with the measurements of the *Virginia*.

Q. Doctor, what is meant by the term, a "water plane" of a boat?

A. That is the contour of the—or the area enclosed by the outside of the ship at the waterline.

Q. At the waterline. The curve or figure described in the water by the boat at the waterline?

A. Yes.

Q. Doctor, what do you mean by the "metacentric line" of a boat, explained in as simple terms as you can?

A. When a vessel is floating at a given waterline, the total displacement of the vessel may be assumed as concentrated at one point, known as the center of buoyancy. When the vessel is inclined to a small angle, that center of buoyancy, which represents the center of all the upward forces acting on the vessel, will move out towards the inclined side. The point of intersection between the lines through the center of buoyancy and those two positions is called the metacenter of the ship. Perhaps I could—

Q. Suppose you make your illustration, if you will, on this board.

(Witness makes drawing on board.) [The letters in Sadler's discussion are entirely consistent with Attwood's figures 45 and 46, reproduced on page 28 above.]

A. When the vessel is at first floating upright or at this waterline, W.L., her center of buoyancy will be in the center line, and at the center of displacement of the vessel—that is, at the point at which we get support for the ship—and she would remain in equilibrium. When the vessel in inclined to some small angle, the center of buoyancy will move out towards the inclined side, because we have put the buoyancy on that side and taken it off the other. The vertical forces now act through point B-1, whereas formerly they acted through B. This intersection of [a vertical line running straight up from B-1 with the center line of the ship] is called the metacenter. That is an important point in determining the stability of a ship. I may say that it can be calculated absolutely from the lines of the ship. Now, the point G represents the center of gravity of the ship or the center of all the weights on the vessel. [This has] nothing to do with the center of buoyancy, because that has to do entirely with water pressures, but [G] is the center of all the weights. The force of gravity acting on those weights acts downward through G. At any angle of inclination we have two forces acting on a vessel, one the weight acting through G, the other the buoyancy acting upwards through B. A couple is introduced, which is called the righting moment if it acts in the direction tending to bring the vessel back to the upright. The relative position of the center of gravity and the metacenter determines the stability of the ship. For small angles of heel, the distance GM is known as the metacentric height. It can be shown that if G gets higher until it coincides with M the stability is greatly reduced. If [G coincides] with M, we have the weight acting down in that direction and the buoyancy acting up in the other direction, and the vessel has no tendency one way or the other. She is then in neutral equilibrium, so that if she is put over to a certain point, she will stay there, and there is no couple. Then if the distance GM becomes nothing, G [coincides with the metacenter]. If G moves above M to some point there, then we have buoyancy acting upwards, and gravity acting downwards. Now the couple if the vessel was slightly inclined would tend to incline her still further, and the vessel would capsize.[1] I would be glad to answer any other question.

Q. Doctor, what do you mean by the term "small initial stability" of a boat?

A. That is the case where the distance between the center of gravity and the metacenter is small in amount.

Q. Doctor, what type or class, or whatever term you use, does this boat or the hull of the *Eastland* fall in?

A. What is known as the channel steamer type. It is generally a high-
speed type for comparatively short services, carrying a small number of
passengers in staterooms and small general cargo.

Q. Generally, how many decks does a channel steamer carry? What is
the type?

A. Generally, a two-decked type.

Q. Did you ever see any three-decked channel steamers?

A. No, two-deck and a light boat-deck, light superstructure is about the
usual type.

Q. From seeing this model here you would, I believe, describe it as a
channel steamer type?

A. Yes.

Q. In what particular, Doctor, do the lines of the hull of a channel
steamer differ from all other boats—generally speaking, I mean?

A. Well, they are vessels of fine form, built for high speed.

Q. That was the type of the hull of the *Eastland*?

A. Yes.

Q. Doctor, do you know of any boat that has been built—or do they
build—do you know of any plans that have been drawn that have used this
type of hull that you describe as a channel steamer type, in the excursion
business anywhere?

MR. BLACK: That we object to as immaterial, incompetent.

Q. Doctor, I believe you stated that you were connected with some railroad in England? Did that company operate any boats? How many boats
did they operate?

A. Oh, I forget the number now, quite a large fleet.

Q. A great fleet. What was the type and character of those boats in
general?

A. Channel steamer type.

Q. What capacity, or what relation did you bear to this company in
respect to these boats?

A. I prepared the plans, specifications, and designs as general consulting naval architect for the line.

Q. Doctor, have you seen boats on the Lakes? Have you seen excursion
boats?

A. I have. I am at present assisting consulting engineer for the Detroit,
Belle Isle & Windsor Ferry Company and the Detroit & Cleveland Navigation Company.

Q. In that capacity you have had occasion to see about all the boats on
the Lakes, haven't you?

A. Yes, I am familiar with their plans and designs and have experi-
mented with them.

The *Greyhound* was an excursion vessel operating mainly out of Toledo. She was built in 1902 and had a generally successful career until the Great Depression. (Steamship Historical Society of America)

Q. I want to ask you this question, Doctor: In the light of your experience building or preparing plans of channel steamers in England, and your knowledge of such hulls and your knowledge of Lake boats, excursion boats in this country, do you know of any boat at this time that is in operation engaged in the excursion business upon the Great Lakes that has a type of hull such as the *Eastland* had? Getting to this boat—

A. She is not of the type commonly known as the excursion steamer type.

Q. Explain if you will why this type of boat is not built or used for excursion purposes?

A. The average excursion steamer has not such a high side, the plating does not extend to such a high deck, the lines of the average excursion steamer are not so fine, and in general for carrying large loads of people, the proportions are different; the excursion steamers are wider.

Q. There has been some testimony here, Doctor, about a boat known as the *Greyhound*. Do you know that boat? Is that boat the same type of boat as the *Eastland*?

A. No. Entirely different.

Q. Just what is the marked distinction, the radical difference between the two boats?

A. She is a sidewheel boat, drawing about nine feet maximum draft, fitted with guards, and about fifteen feet deep. That is, the steel hull is fifteen feet deep, and above that the decks are a light wooden construction.

Q. Doctor, what relation or importance does the draft or does the depth of a boat bear to its stability?

A. In general, the height of the center of gravity is governed largely by the depth of the boat.

Q. I mean, comparing boats, one that has a nine-foot draft compared with one ten. I mean depth—I don't mean draft—I mean depth with respect to its stability.

A. I say, in general, the deeper the boat the higher the center of gravity.

Q. Less stability?

A. Yes, the higher the center of gravity is, accompanied with the increase in depth of a boat—. You didn't mean draft, did you?

Q. I mean depth. What relation to the stability of a boat has the beam of a boat?

A. The beam is the governing factor in the stability.

Q. It is the governing factor. Now, as that beam increases in length, what relation does it bear to the stability of a boat generally?

A. The height of the metacenter varies as the square of the beam.

Q. So, if the *Eastland* had a beam that was two feet longer than she had, what relation would it bear?

A. It would go up as the square of the difference.

Q. Doctor, they speak of the seagoing qualities of a boat; just explain, if you will, what that means?

A. In general, we understand by a good sea boat a boat that has a long period of roll; that is, for ocean-going vessels the long period of roll is accompanied by a moderate or small amount of metacentric height.

Q. Is that what we call an easy boat to ride in?

A. An easy boat, with a long period of roll and rather small initial stability.

Q. Is that a quality or a condition which is limited generally to ocean-going boats?

A. Yes, for any vessel that has to trade in rough seas, of course it is a desirable quality to have.

Q. Is that a desirable condition or element in an excursion boat upon the Great Lakes?

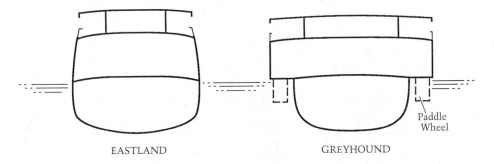

EASTLAND   GREYHOUND

A. It is not to my mind the primary consideration in an excursion steamer.

Q. What do you think is the primary consideration, or what do you consider to be the primary consideration?

A. Large initial stability.

Q. Why?

A. Because these vessels trade mostly in smooth water, and it is essential that the safety of the vessels should be the primary consideration.

Q. Doctor, as you increase the safety of the boat, do you decrease her riding qualities, or easy-going or seagoing qualities?

A. Only slightly. It varies inversely as the square root of the metacentric height. Put in this way, you could give a vessel four times the stability and only reduce her seagoing qualities one half.

Q. And that could be applied to this boat, the *Eastland*, could it?

A. That is perfectly true for all ships.

Q. Doctor, I want to ask you just one more question. Describe, if you will, in a general way what is the character of the waters and the sea that channel boats traverse in going from England to France?

A. It is at times rather choppy and rough. The water in the Channel varies a good deal; sometimes it is very rough.

Q. Generally some sea there?

A. Yes.

Q. Different than on the waters of the Great Lakes?

A. Yes.

Q. Now, Doctor, taking into account any given boat, considering her tonnage and her length and beam and depth, would that account or determine the stability of the boat entirely—or do they necessarily?

A. No, not necessarily.

Q. Well, what in your opinion, Doctor, is the real essential element in the determining of its stability?

A. It is the moment of inertia in the water plane.

Q. The water plane. And that is the figure described by a boat meeting the surface of the water?

A. Yes.

Q. Tell, if you will, briefly, and in a general way, what the draft of a boat is?

A. Usually, the draft is the distance from the bottom of the keel to the waterline.

Q. What relation does that bear to the stability of a boat?

A. As the draft increases or decreases, usually the stability increases with the decrease of draft.

Q. As the draft becomes less, the stability of the boat increases?

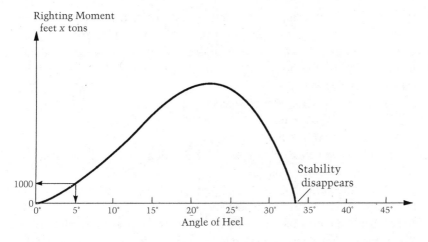

A. Yes.

Q. Doctor, will you tell us in a general way what the stability curve of any boat is—what you mean by "stability curve"?

A. That is a curve showing for each angle of inclination the righting moment or up-setting moment acting upon the vessel.

Q. Can a stability curve be prepared or calculated for any boat?

A. It can.

Q. Have you prepared a stability curve for the steamer *Eastland*?

A. Yes. For each angle of inclination of the vessel, 5, 10, 15, 20 degrees and so on, we can calculate what is called the righting moment of a vessel, or the tendency that that vessel has to get back to upright. And the length of the line represents to scale that tendency. That is, for instance, supposing the vessel weighed 2,000 tons, and the length of the lever arm [GZ] at 5 degrees list—you will recall the last diagram—if the length of lever arm was, say, one half of a foot—the distance between the lines or action between the buoyancy and gravity—then the moment tending to bring that vessel back to upright is 1,000 foot-tons. That represents the tendency, really, of the vessel to right itself at 5 degrees.

Mr. Darrow: Just tell us again what that means, that "2."

A. Two thousand multiplied by the length of the lever arm; that gives what is called a moment or a couple of value, a couple tending to bring the vessel back to upright.

Mr. Darrow: Well, a thousand foot-tons.

A. Yes. Now if you want to find how far the vessel will heel over—

Q. And you mean by that word "heel," tip?

A. Tip, yes.

Mr. Darrow: By "heel" you mean back, don't you?

A. No, if the vessel is upright and we want to know at any point how much weight it will take, moved a certain distance, to heel that vessel over, we can find it from this curve. For instance, if a weight of 100 tons on a vessel were moved 10 feet across the deck, we should have an upsetting moment of 1,000 foot-tons. And 1,000 foot-tons would then give the vessel a list of 5 degrees.

MR. LILLIE: Doctor, you have 2,000 multiplied by 5.

MR. CLYNE: Five-tenths.

MR. LILLIE: Well, I didn't see that.

A. So we can take every angle of the heel of a vessel and calculate the righting couple at each point.

Q. And the various figures, 5 degrees, 10 degrees, 20, and 25, denote the heeling angle or list of the boat?

A. Yes. Now at some angle [the] stability of a vessel may disappear. When she has been heeled over to a certain point the lines of action of the weight going downwards and the buoyancy going upwards come together; then there is no couple tending to bring her back to even keel from there. She comes to a point where her stability has disappeared. Of course, at that point the righting moment is zero. And after that point when we heel the vessel over still further, the righting couple becomes the opposite sign, or negative, and then the vessel will capsize. So that after this crosses the line the moments are reversed, or they are upsetting couples and the vessel capsizes.

Q. What does that upper line indicate, that dotted line?

A. In all vessels—in a good many vessels, at least—we have two conditions to consider: one is the possibility of the side of the vessel being intact or watertight up to a watertight deck; the other is where the side may be open and water may be allowed to come onto the first deck, as in the case of vessels with gangway doors or openings of any kind. We have two

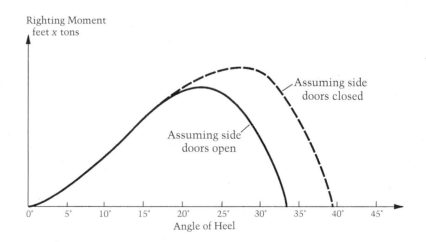

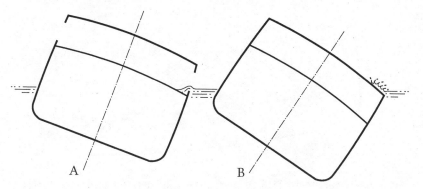

sets of conditions: one where the side is assumed to be intact or watertight, the other where water is assumed to be free to come on deck. The curve will take somewhat of this character in that connection. The upper curve would show the stability of the ship or the righting moment, assuming the side to be intact up to the deck. [The other] is assuming the stability not intact, with water free to come on this deck. At any point between the two decks if there is a place where water can come on we can determine the angle at which the water just begins to come through the ship's side. For example, supposing it was about 17 degrees there, the vessel would have a stability curve represented by the top curve at that point.

Q. Where the sides were closed?

A. Yes. After that the water would come over or through the opening and would drop down to this point and there[after] any stability curve would be on [the lower] line. If the side were intact all the way, this upper curve would hold.

Q. Now, with that explanation, Doctor, did you prepare such a curve for the *Eastland*, taking into account her measurements? Have you that curve here?

A. Yes.

Q. I just want to digress from that for a moment to illustrate one other point before passing on to the illustration of the stability curve of this boat. The *Eastland*, if I understand it, had ballast tanks for water in its bottoms?

A. Yes.

Q. In general, what influence or elements in the part of the stability of a boat do these tanks play, and what is the function of these tanks?

A. To help lower the center of gravity, and also to trim the vessel.

Q. And give it stability?

A. Stability.

Q. Is there any difference given to the stability of a boat where the tanks are entirely filled and where they are partially filled?

A. Yes, where the tanks are partially filled the virtual center of the wa-

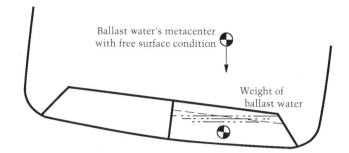

ter, or the point at which the water acts is considerably above the center of the water.

Q. Have you a diagram or illustration showing just what the influence of that condition is? Just explain, if you will, to the Court what you have there on that illustration.

A. This represents a vessel inclined to a small angle.

Q. That is a cross section of the boat?

A. A cross section of the boat at about midships. This line represents the top of the ballast tanks, and the W′L′ line the water. When the vessel takes a slight angle of heel and the water is free to move, instead of acting at the bottom of the vessel, it will act at some point higher up. That is, the effect of the water is the same as if you take the water in the bottom of the ship and place it up at this point.

Q. Well, Doctor, assume that the weight of the water that you have in the tank there to the right of this cross section weighs 150 tons, and with the quantity as shown there, do I understand that would have the effect of placing 150 tons up along that line there?

A. Yes.

Q. Where would that be at, Doctor?

A. Well, the height at that point depends upon the free surface of the water. The moment of inertia of the free surface of the water and the volume of the water in the tank, the one [divided] by the other, give us the position of that point, so that the tank in this particular case—

Q. No. 3 tank—this corresponds to the *Eastland*, does it?

A. Yes, at one-third filled with water, the center of the water would be at this point on the third deck up.

Q. That would be just the same as though the weight of the water were placed upon the third deck?

A. Yes.

MR. DARROW: You assume that this water is now in the bottom?

A. In the bottom of the ship.

Q. Well, but in the tanks?

MR. DARROW: In the tanks, in the bottom of a ship—you say the effect is just the same as though it had been placed up there above the water line?

A. Yes.

MR. BARBOUR: That is, if the tank is full?

A. If the tank is *not* full, the effect is the same as if it were placed—

MR. BARBOUR: It would raise it in every instance up above the water line?

A. Until the tank is filled.

MR. BARBOUR: Well, suppose it is nearly full, would it make any difference?

Q. Well, I think he will explain that if you will let him go ahead and let him explain each condition of the tank.

A. Well, if the tank has a small amount of water in it, and if the bottom is fairly flat, it has a large surface and a small body; consequently, the center is very high. As you proceed to fill that tank, the free surface increases slightly, probably, and the volume increases at a great rate. Consequently, the center goes down. And in this case, with the tanks half full the center would be some three or four feet above the main deck. When the tank is, say, seven-eighths full, it would come down lower still, and finally, when the tank was absolutely full of water, then it would be at the center of the water in the tank. It gradually drops.

MR. WALKER: Hadn't you better explain the principle on which that acts, why it results that way?

A. Well, it is just the same as if we assume the water to be a solid block.

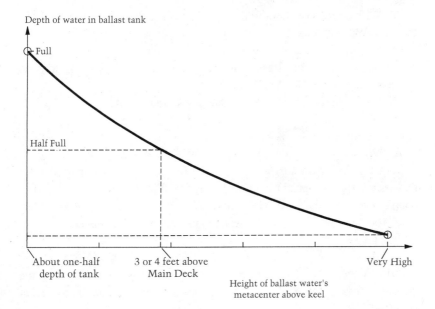

MR. DARROW: Frozen?

A. Pig iron, free to move on the least provocation. The very smallest angle that our block would be free to move out towards the side to which the vessel was heeled would be equivalent to suspending the block at the same point so that it would be perfectly free to move. In fact, it is equivalent to a pendulum. And we calculate that by finding the movement of this free water surface, divided by the volume of the water.

MR. DARROW: If the ship was on an even keel that would be true, would it?

A. This is true in an upright position, because in an angle the inclination is infinitely small, and the center would still be up there.

Q. Now, Doctor, while that condition is existing with tanks partially filled, what, if anything, has that to do with the stability of the boat?

A. If the center of the water is above the center of gravity of the ship, it will tend to reduce the stability. It would be equivalent to adding the weight above the center, consequently raising the center.

Q. Is that equivalent to what we call top-heaviness?

A. Yes, the same thing exactly.

Q. And the illustration which you have of the other tanks is the same thing, is it?

A. Yes.

THE COURT: Well, now suppose the No. 3 tank of the *Eastland* was a quarter full, would that tend to make her more or less top-heavy?

A. More.

Q. To what extent, Doctor?

A. With 20 tons of water in the tank, the center would be 25 feet above the keel. With 30 tons, 17.5 feet.

Q. Do you know, Doctor, what deck that would carry it onto?

MR. BARBOUR: May I ask a question right there: How many tons do you assume that the No. 3 tank holds?

Q. Well, I object to that. We haven't got to that point.

A. 165.

MR. BARBOUR: That is on one side?

A. No, altogether, on each side, I mean, 82.5 on each side.

THE COURT: Now just let me see if I understand you: assuming that the vessel is in an upright position and you fill both tanks, port and starboard, No. 3, evenly, and when the tanks are a quarter full you say she would be more top-heavy and unstable than she would if she had no water in the tank?

A. Yes.

THE COURT: At what point in the filling of the No. 3 tank would the weight of the water tend to make her less top-heavy and increase her stability?

A. Just—approximately—when the tanks were about—had about three feet of water in them, three or four feet deep, within a foot of the top. That tank itself is about three-fourths full.

MR. DARROW: Three-fourth inches deep?

THE COURT: As I remember, the testimony shows thus far they are about 40 inches.

MR. WALKER: The testimony was that they are 48 inches.

Q. Have you the measurements there of the tank, Doctor?

A. Four feet—48 inches.

THE COURT: You took that from the plans?

A. From the ship plan.

MR. BARBOUR: Let me ask one more question. What do you say is the capacity of No. 2 tank?

A. 106 tons.

MR. BARBOUR: That is on both sides?

A. Yes, 53 on a side.

THE COURT: Proceed, Mr. Clyne. I didn't mean to interrupt as much as I have.

Q. Now, is there anything else that you desire to explain in connection with this illustration, Doctor?

A. No, I think not.

Q. Now, starting from this stability curve which you describe, I will ask you whether you remember a stability curve with reference to the steamer *Eastland*. Have you that with you?

A. Yes.

THE COURT: Let me ask just one more question. This question of stability, in its increase or decrease by putting water in the tanks, depends upon the movement of the water rather than upon its weight, does it not— or on its being able to move?

A. Yes, being permitted to move.

THE COURT: Rather than its weight.

A. The weight, of course, also comes in.

THE COURT: Well, if it were [im]movable, of course, it would not make the vessel less stable, would it?

A. It would make her more stable.

THE COURT: But it is because it is movable that this element of instability arises?

A. Yes.

Q. Now describe, if you will, to the Court what you have there.

A. This diagram shows the changing in the metacentric height of the *Eastland* from 6:00 to 7:30.

MR. DARROW: What does he base that on?

Q. Well, let him explain that.

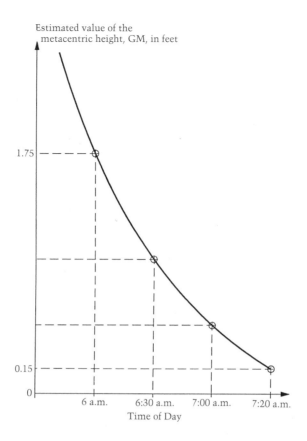

A. These are my heights obtained from my calculations of the vessel. The height of the metacenter is calculated directly from the plans, and the height of the center of gravity estimated. The time is based upon the evidence that I went over as to what was done at different times with regard to putting water ballast in, and also the average weight of people coming on board.

Q. Well, before we go into that, just describe in a general way, if you will, what those elements were, and the time of the people coming aboard.

A. From the number of people and the time which they took to go on board, they were going on at an average rate of from four to five tons a minute. Probably at the beginning it was a little greater. At different times, therefore, there were certain definite, but approximate, numbers of people on board the vessel, and their average positions were taken. At the same time, the vessel was gradually lowering in the water due to the extra weight of people, and that altered the height of the metacenter slightly. [Note: In redirect examination by Charles F. Clyne during cross-examination, Sadler stated that he estimated the ship would be lowered 8 inches by 2,500

passengers.] From the calculations from the lines of the vessel and the **261**
estimate of the position of the people at each time, this metacentric height *Evaluation*
was calculated. *of the*
Eastland

Q. Just a minute, Doctor: unless you are going to bring that in, will you describe at the point marked "6," six o'clock, you assume that she had no one on board?

A. Yes. Without the people on board. And as the people came on board the center of gravity rose owing to the people coming onto the upper decks.

Q. How did you distribute those people, Doctor?

A. At the different times I took what would be—what I considered to be—a fair average position for those people on the different decks. And also in all of those calculations, I think I have been conservative.

Q. How many people did she have on board, then, assuming—

A. Twenty-five hundred people. I assumed we distributed 300 on the boat deck, 1,100 on the next deck below, and 1,100 on the deck below that. And I took that average center [of gravity]. Probably there were more people on the deck below the boat deck, but I assumed that as a fair result.

Q. Would that vary the problem?

A. If there were more people, it would raise the center of gravity higher.

THE COURT: Well, you don't assume that there were any on the main deck?

A. On the first deck, no. I took them distributed as I say, 300 and 1,100 and 1,100.

Q. Doctor, had you finished the explaining on the other one—that at 7:30 her stability had disappeared?

A. Practically so. It was very small. Her metacentric height was a little over one-tenth of a foot.

MR. LILLIE: As I understood you this morning, Doctor, where the metacentric point and the center of gravity met, it was on a neutral equilibrium?

A. Neutral equilibrium. After that the center of gravity still rises.

Q. What did you find to be the metacentric height of this boat?

A. With the boat as she was before the people came on board, 1.75 feet.

Q. What are the elements upon which you base that or calculate that, Doctor?

A. The metacenter is calculated from the lines of the ship. The lines of the ship [lead to the estimate of the location of the metacenter], and the center of gravity [is] estimated. [Note: In cross-examination by Walter I. Lillie, Sadler stated that he made his estimate of the center of gravity by analogy to similar ships with which he had become familiar on the basis of inclining tests. He recognized that this involved what Lillie called "pure assumption."]

Q. Well, now, what as to the condition of the tanks with respect to water?

A. In the first case they were assumed empty [with] no people on board.

MR. WALKER: What weight above?

A. No weight.

MR. WALKER: Life rafts?

A. I took the vessel as a whole.

Q. Now, does the illustration labeled "Margin of Stability" take into account the letting in and excluding of water out of the water tanks between 6:00 and 7:30?

A. Yes, and the people coming on board.

Q. Now, what condition would you say, Doctor, the water tanks were in—based on the calculation—at 7:30 on the morning of the accident. What do you assume?

A. Port No. 2 tank, 10 tons; starboard No. 2 tank, 35 tons; and starboard No. 3 tank, 20 tons. This next diagram illustrates the vessel at about 15 degrees list to port.

Q. Would that be loaded or unloaded?

A. Just when everybody was on board.

Q. And all the stores and everything else aboard?

A. Final condition of the vessel just before she capsized.

Q. Have you taken these things into account, the stores and weights?

A. Yes. When the vessel is at 15 degrees list, from the stability curve I estimate that the people—the center of the people would have to be from 3 to 4 feet off the center of the ship in order to give her that list. At about 15 degrees, also, the water would begin to come over the gangway door aft, and thereafter the water would come onto the main deck. This is a stability curve similar to the one illustrated.

Q. And it applies to the *Eastland* at the time of the accident?

A. At the time of the accident. At about 14 or 15 degrees, on the assumption that the people—the center of the people was from 3 to 4 feet off the center of the ship, the gangway door would just be immersed—the top of the gangway door. Thereafter the vessel would lose the stability due to [loss of] the intactness of the side, and her stability at that point would become negative and she would capsize.

Q. So from these calculations, Doctor, and as shown on that illustration, taking into account the condition of the *Eastland* on the morning of the accident, at what point did you find that the boat would capsize?

A. About 15 degrees.

Q. Doctor, if a boat has its sides intact, is 15 degrees—will you say 15 degrees is a great list?

A. Not excessive.

Q. Then, in other words, the list which a boat takes depends—in other words, her ability to right herself will depend not only upon the degrees, but the condition of her sides with respect to being open or closed?

A. Yes.

Q. And you have taken into account in this illustration that the after gangway door was but half closed?

A. Yes.

Q. Do you know how high the sill of the after gangway was above the main deck?

A. I forget the figures now.

Q. Do you remember about how far—something, a few inches?

A. Oh, no, it was some feet.

Q. I mean above the first deck, the sill of the gangway?

A. About four feet six inches. [Note: Sadler apparently interpreted the question as an inquiry about the distance to the top of the lower portion of the gangway doors.]

THE COURT: He means one thing. He is talking about the sill.

A. The sill itself? About eight or nine inches—nine.

Q. And from that gangway to the one forward, [the one] known as the baggage gangway, is there some difference or sheer as they call it?

A. Yes. This point was taken at the lowest gangway, the one that would go into the water first.

Q. Do you know what the distance is of that gangway above the water under normal conditions?

A. I don't recall the distance now.

MR. BARBOUR: May I ask you one question? When you state the water coming over the gangway, you mean over the doors halfway up?

A. Yes.

MR. BARBOUR: This door closed?

A. Yes. And I have assumed that the side was watertight up to that point.

Q. Now, if the gangway door was not tight—in other words, if the gasket there did not make the door watertight and water came in or was permitted to come in, would that render the boat less stable?

A. Yes, that would be worse than my conditions show.

Q. And the same rule would apply to deadlights being open—in fact, anything that was open along the same line?

A. Yes.

Q. As the gangway doors. Now, Doctor, you have spoken of ballast.

Are there different kinds of ballast used in boats? And what are those different kinds?

A. Water or permanent ballast, in the form of pig iron.

Q. Pig iron ballast is used sometimes?

A. Yes.

Q. Doctor, [if you had] occasion to make any calculations as to the deck area of the boat *Eastland*, tell us, if you please, what was the result of those calculations.

A. The boat deck, about 1,330 square feet; promenade deck, 6,800; upper deck, 7,680; main deck, 2,040. Those were all taken from the plans, I might say.

Q. And what is the total of those decks, about?

A. About 17,860 square feet.

Q. If you were to place 2,500 people on that boat, and assuming that they occupied those decks, how much would it give to each person? I mean, how many square feet?

A. A little over 7 square feet for each person.

Q. Suppose you were to put 3,000 people on the boat, how much would it give to each individual?

MR. KREMER: We can figure that out ourselves.

A. 5.9.

Q. So, each person would be given 5 square feet of that boat?

A. About 5.9.

THE COURT: Nearly 6.

Q. Do you know, Doctor—have you any knowledge as to any rule or practice that is used in allotting [a] certain quantity of square feet of area to people being carried upon excursion boats?

A. I understand that it is the practice to allow between 8 and 10. Well, I should say about 8—something around there.

Q. Well, if you use 8 as the unit, what would be the maximum deck capacity of this boat?

A. About 2,230.

Q. And when you use that unit, that is merely a unit for convenience; that has nothing to do with the stability, has it?

A. That is just the amount of space that a person might want.

Q. Doctor, has it any relation to the qualities of the boat, the ability to carry people—those figures, that unit—I think he has answered the question. Doctor, taking into account the *Eastland* as she was originally constructed and launched, as a boat of the dimensions you know the *Eastland* to be, and considering that she had about 100 cabins in her, or staterooms, and lifesaving equipment to care for four or five hundred passengers, and considering that subsequent to that construction that I have described, the cabins were removed and the condition of the boat was as you saw it after

it was righted, would you say, or can you say as an expert that the whole
nature or condition for which the boat was used was changed?

A. It was.

Q. Now, assuming, Doctor, that the boat was in the condition which I
have described when it was launched, and it was desired to place this boat
in excursion service on the waters of Lake Michigan, what elements,
changes, or conditions would you think necessary to make in this boat,
taking into account her safety, to carry 2,500 persons in the excursion business? In other words, if the boat was submitted to you for your opinion,
considering her as you understand her to be when she was launched, and
it was desired to put her into the excursion business to carry 2,500 people,
what changes, if any, would you make in order to make her a safe, seaworthy boat?

A. As the service in which it was proposed to run the vessel was entirely different from that which the designer of the vessel had in view in
the first place, it would be necessary to look into these conditions carefully
to see how they differed from the original conditions, and if necessary to
so arrange the vessel by the addition of ballast, and so forth, so that she
would be safe under the new conditions, which were very different from
the old ones. I might say particularly in connection with crowds on board,
the crowd is free to move from one side to the other, and it is a very different set of conditions, carrying 2,500 people, as compared with carrying four or five hundred in staterooms where they are not likely to move
around quickly.

THE COURT: What he asked you was what changes you would have
made in the boat to make her an excursion boat to carry 2,500 people.

A. Well, I should have gone into the necessary calculations to find out
what her stability was and recommended the use of permanent ballast because it is foolproof. If you use water ballast for obtaining stability—
stability can be obtained by water ballast just as well as by pig iron—it
leaves the chance of having some of the water ballast pumped out through
the discretion perhaps of a captain or engineer who may not realize the
dangers that he is running into, especially when you take into account the
effect of half-filled tanks.

Q. And the pumping in and pumping out while a load is aboard?

A. Yes.

Q. Do they ever do that in boats, place permanent ballast in them?

A. I recommended it myself two years ago.

Q. Do they do it?

A. Yes.

THE COURT: You wouldn't say, would you, Doctor, that the con-

struction of a vessel for excursion purposes with water ballast and without permanent ballast was not recognized as good designing, a good
construction?

A. If you are changing a vessel as this was, I think I stated it was quite
possible to make her safe with the use of water ballast. If you were designing a new vessel, you probably wouldn't design her where her stability
depended solely on water ballast. She would be made of such proportions
that she would be safe without the use of water ballast; that is, the designer
would have in mind in designing that he had to carry large numbers of
people and load up on the vessel. He would design his hull accordingly.

Q. In other words, Doctor, would you have designed a boat such as the
Eastland with water ballast where it was to be used in excursion business
carrying 2,500 people?

MR. BARBOUR: In addition to the other objections—

THE COURT: I will sustain the objection. Of course, I presume that the
question is meant to be proper. It isn't a question of what this witness
would do or what he wouldn't do.

MR. LILLIE: The question is, what was the *Eastland*.

Q. Now, Doctor, taking into account the lines, shape, and proportion of
the hull of this vessel, and taking into account that she had been put into
the excursion business carrying 2,500 people on Lake Michigan, do you
consider the form of ballast that she had to be a safe or unsafe form of
ballast?

A. I think it is unsafe.

THE COURT: The question gets down to this: taking into consideration
the design and construction of the boat, in your judgment was she a safe
or an unsafe boat to be used in the passenger excursion trade and to carry
2,500 people.

A. I think she was unsafe without permanent ballast.

THE COURT: Would you call her under these conditions and under the
conditions that existed a seaworthy or unseaworthy boat in that trade?

A. Oh, she was a seaworthy boat. I want to make this point perfectly
clear, if I may.

THE COURT: That is the reason I am asking the question.

A. The *Eastland* could be made safe and stable with her tanks filled, or
even with tanks No. 2 and 3 filled; she would have stability and be, say, a
seaworthy boat.

THE COURT: Well, if those tanks were filled, that would be the same as
if she had permanent ballast?

A. Yes. The water would become [the equivalent of] permanent ballast,
but as that could be pumped out at the whim of anybody, the captain or the
engineer, I think there was an element of danger introduced there, leaving

the handling of the ballast to men who, perhaps, did not realize the dangers that they were running.

THE COURT: Suppose she had no water in her tanks at all, what would you say? Suppose the water ballast was not used at all?

A. Then she would be unsafe.

Q. What do you mean by the word "unseaworthy," as you understand it?

A. There are two elements coming in: first, the initial stability of the vessel, or her ability to carry heavy loads without large angles of heel, and then her seagoing qualities or safety, as represented by her range of stability. For instance, if a vessel's stability disappears at a small angle of heel, although she might be safe in the upright condition and in smooth water, she would not be a seaworthy boat.

Q. Doctor, when you say with tanks No. 2 and 3 filled, with this load she could operate, do you mean that she could operate with safety and without danger?

A. If No. 2 and 3 were full.

Q. All of the time?

A. All of the time, yes.

Q. And if they were not filled all of the time, have you an opinion as to whether it would be in a dangerous condition?

A. Yes, sir, certainly. Dangerous.

THE COURT: Let me ask another question: Suppose the tanks were not used, and there was no water in her at any time, would she be in your judgment a seaworthy craft to ply upon Lake Michigan with only her crew aboard?

A. Yes, with no passengers.

THE COURT: Then her seaworthiness under those conditions, without ballast, would depend upon her load, and the load might cause her to become unseaworthy?

A. Yes.

THE COURT: Under those same conditions and without ballast, in your opinion would she be a seaworthy boat in a storm, a severe storm, without a load of passengers and with only her crew aboard?

A. Yes.

THE COURT: I don't know whether you can answer this question or not, but I want to ask it: Can you give us approximately, according to your opinion and judgment, the number of people or passengers which she could carry safely and beyond which she would become unseaworthy?

MR. KREMER: With or without the water ballast?

THE COURT: Without any ballast in her?

A. I might say I haven't—

THE COURT: If you cannot do it conveniently—

A. I might put it this way, perhaps, that with half the number of people she would have a positive metacentric height, and half the number distributed as I have assumed them distributed before.

THE COURT: 1,250?

A. Yes, but comparing that with the metacentric height of typical excursion steamers, that is, about one-third, or one-half of the amount that they have, but still it would give the vessel a margin of stability.

THE COURT: If I understand you rightly, if her tanks No. 2 and 3 were filled and kept filled, she would carry 2,500 people in safety?

A. Yes.

THE COURT: So that the element of danger, as you believe, which enters into the problem is in filling and emptying of the tanks?

A. Exactly.

THE COURT: And in the—well, perhaps not altogether, but somewhat—in the skill of the engineer in filling and emptying them?

A. Yes.

THE COURT: In other words, the human element enters there?

A. Yes.

MR. DARROW: [May] I ask you what you assume was the amount of coal in the bins, if you made any allowance?

A. I assumed the same as before.

MR. DARROW: How much was that?

A. Sixty tons, I assumed.

MR. DARROW: Can you tell us how many extra passengers [would be the equivalent of] 60 tons? Figure what it would be for 120 or 150. How much more would a hundred tons do? Suppose there was a hundred there.

MR. CLYNE: Just a minute—to interrupt—they couldn't get that into the boat. We will show that.

MR. DARROW: We will show it was there.

THE COURT: I think, gentlemen, you had better wait to examine the witness when the time comes. I confess to have been at fault myself in interrupting the examination, which I ought not to have done.

MR. LILLIE: We are very glad you did.

THE COURT: Proceed, Mr. Clyne.

Q. Assuming, Doctor, that the steamer *Eastland* was tied at the dock at Clark Street—where you saw her in a capsized condition—and was loaded with 2,500 passengers ready to proceed on her voyage on the morning of July 24, and assuming that, as the passengers came aboard some half hour or so before 7:30, the boat took a list to starboard and after some little time recovered to an even keel, and then listed to port and capsized, is there anything in that statement of condition which I have given you from which you could form an opinion as to whether this boat, the *East-land*, was resting upon any obstacle or thing in the bottom of the river?

A. If there had been an obstacle between the center line of the ship and the dock—

Q. You mean the keel?

A. Yes, and the vessel heeled over towards the dock and touched that obstacle—a pile—and in heeling out towards the port side she would be still further away from it.

Q. Assuming that it did touch anything, would that contribute in any wise to its capsizing?

A. No.

MR. DARROW: Do you mean if she touched something when she went to starboard?

A. To starboard, yes.

Q. Taking the question that I asked you, Doctor, and eliminating the pile, if the boat was resting upon the ground or a portion of the bottom of the river, would it have been possible for this boat to have acted as she did? I mean by that, first listing to the starboard, then recovering to the upright, and then passing to the port?

MR. DARROW: You mean assuming that she was resting on the bottom before she listed to starboard, I take it?

A. She could list until her bottom touched the bottom of the river.

Q. You don't mean, of course, in this case. You mean, if it was physically possible for her to do that?

A. If she were aground on the center line, she could heel over until the bottom of the vessel touched the bottom of the river—the bottom of the vessel being sloped up on each side.

Q. Then recovering would take the same action as if she touched some spile—if it recovered, then, from that position?

A. Yes.

Q. If it did touch that, would that contribute at all to the boat capsizing, assuming the point of touching was between the keel and the dock?

A. No.

Q. If it was the practice and custom, Doctor, for the *Eastland* to come up to her dock and there receive a load of passengers, such as 2,500 people, and while the people were boarding the boat and being seated, the tanks were being filled, assuming that as the people came on, they were empty, have you an opinion as to whether that would render the boat in a dangerous condition.

A. Yes, there would be danger there, certainly.

Q. Doctor, it appears that in the construction of the ballast tanks of this boat that it was only possible—that the water was admitted through the seacock opening and into the manifold, and then into the tanks. That was the process of filling. That process couldn't be carried on while water was being expelled. Considering that condition, taking into account that this boat, the *Eastland*, was engaged in the excursion business—in the service in which she was employed, have you an opinion as to whether or not that is a good, safe kind of construction?

A. No, I think that a scheme where the ballast could be handled quickly or transferred quickly from one side to the other is preferable.

Q. Especially true, is that so, where water is being admitted and excluded from time to time?

A. Yes.

(Court here took a short recess.)

MR. BARBOUR: Your Honor, on behalf of my client, we have no cross-examination.

THE COURT: The [attorneys for the prosecution] desire to ask one or two more questions.

Redirect examination by Mr. Clyne:

Q. Doctor, I omitted to ask you this question: Assuming the *Eastland*, as you knew it from studying its plans and observations, and assuming that she was engaged in the passenger business carrying 2,500 people, have you an opinion as to what her metacentric height ought to be, to operate in a seaworthy and safe manner? How much should she have?

A. Oh, no definite rule, but about two or three feet.

Q. Now, assuming a load of 2,500 people with stores and other things aboard, as she was on the morning of the accident, from your calculation, what was the metacentric height of the *Eastland*?

A. With the passengers on board?

Q. Yes, loaded ready to—

A. .15 of a point. Fifteen-hundredths of a foot. [Note: During cross-examination by Lillie, Sadler amplified this estimate by stating that he calculated the metacenter at 16.15 feet above the keel and the center of gravity at 16 feet.]

MR. BARBOUR: Fifteen-hundredths of a foot on the morning of July 24, loaded?

A. Yes.

Q. Where would that, if you know, bring the waterline with respect to the aft gangway, assuming that you had tanks No. 2 and 3 filled?

A. I have forgotten the distance now. I don't remember.

Q. Would you consider it a safe practice to operate the *Eastland* with this load of 2,500 people where the metacentric height was but fifteen-hundredths of a foot?

A. No.

Q. It should be more than that?

A. Certainly.

Q. [When] the Judge asked you a question about when you were operating—as to whether you could operate safely with 2,500 people with tanks No. 2 and 3 filled, as I recall the question—did you in answering that take into account anything with respect to the sides of the boat, as to the openings being open or closed?

A. Well, the openings should be closed to make her perfectly safe.

Q. Yes, and if it was the practice to operate with the gangways partly open and the other openings in the side of the boat part open, would you regard that as safe?

A. No, it is not an advisable thing to do under those conditions.

THE COURT: Well, I suppose that you, in answering that question, considered the *Eastland* as she was?

A. Yes.

THE COURT: And that she was operated in a seamanlike manner?

A. Yes, certainly.

Q. And when you say tanks No. 2 and 3 filled, of course, you mean full to the top?

A. Completely full, yes, sir.

Q. Now, one more question: Assuming that the absence of adequate apparatus for ascertaining the quantity of water in the ballast tanks necessitated a practice of keeping them either full or empty, and that it was the custom, because it was necessary to the taking on of her load upon the main deck, for the officers to empty her ballast tanks when arriving at a dock, was not the *Eastland* unsafe and unseaworthy between the moment of her casting off and the moment when her ballast tanks No. 2 and 3 should be filled, she having 2,500 passengers aboard?

A. Yes, she was unsafe in those conditions.

Comments on Sadler's Testimony by Harry Benford
Professor Emeritus of Naval Architecture and
Marine Engineering, University of Michigan

Sadler's main point was that just before the ship capsized, the loading conditions were such that the initial transverse metacentric height was only 0.15 feet. A general move of the passengers to the port side had shifted the center of gravity 3 or 4 feet. With such a small degree of stability, such a modest shift would cause the ship to heel some 14 to 15 degrees, and that would be enough to immerse the top of the lower section of the aftermost sideport. Once that happened, the water poured in so that the vessel's righting moment changed from slightly positive to increasingly negative, and over she went.

There is one troublesome point in the foregoing. In Professor Hilton's careful step-by-step recapitulation of events leading up to the capsizing, there is no indication of any "general move of the passengers to the port side" such as Sadler presumed. I believe it more likely that what moved to port was the unconstrained water in the ballast tanks. As the passengers came aboard, and tended to congregate on the starboard side, the ship, with only a modest amount of inherent stability, listed to that side. That led the engineer to admit ballast water to tanks on the port side. The ship had already reached a condition of neutral or possibly slightly negative stability. The engineer continued adding water to the port side until it was enough to bring the ship upright. When she then began listing to port, he admitted water to the starboard side. But, by then the ship's metacentric height had all but disappeared, so that the unconstrained water in the tanks now surged to port, worsening the heeling moment and immersing the sideport. Thus, I believe it was the water, not the passengers, that shifted to port and triggered the capsizing. Because the evidence indicates that the aft sideport doors on the port side were entirely open, the water was free to flow onto the main deck at an even smaller angle than Sadler had estimated.

Sadler also concluded that with no passengers aboard she would have been seaworthy even if the ballast tanks were empty. With those 2,500 passengers, however, she would have been unseaworthy—i.e., only marginally stable—with empty tanks. If ballast tanks No. 2 and 3, port and starboard, had been full, she would have been seaworthy; but with them only partially full, as was the case, she was unseaworthy, and this caused the catastrophe.

I believe Sadler was essentially correct in his conclusion that those partially filled ballast tanks were the central culprits in the disaster. One could argue that the ship was doomed when the decision was made to start boarding passengers with the ballast tanks empty. Ballast was going to be needed, and while it was being added, free-surface effects would come into play. The engineer, in his haste to correct a list, compounded the mistake by adding water to more than one tank at a time. The captain should have urged the passengers to leave the ship until the ballast tanks could be completely filled. The captain and the chief engineer were apparently not communicating with each other.

Sadler criticized the design feature that prevented the engineer from transferring ballast water from side to side. Under the circumstances, I do not believe that possibility would have made much difference. The root of the problem was having too much free surface, and pumping from side to side would not have changed that. Indeed, it might have worsened the situation.

Sadler's estimate of the number of passengers on the various decks seems to me questionable. Judging from the various first-hand reports, I think there were fewer than he assumed on the uppermost decks. Some of this difference may arise from confusion about how the decks were identified.

Another possible source of error in Sadler's analysis was the all-but-impossible task of estimating accurately the position of the empty ship's vertical center of gravity. Sadler's chief tool was, presumably, the ship's original set of plans. I doubt that he had an accurate assessment of the many changes that had occurred over the intervening years. Overall, I suspect his estimate of the empty ship's vertical center of gravity was too low, but that any error in that figure was offset by an approximately equal and opposite error in his estimate of the passengers' center of gravity. In short, his total figure was probably about right.

For his part, the general manager, W. H. Hull, was more to blame than anyone else. In making major changes to the ship, such as adding lifeboats, he should have followed up by having a naval architect analyze the new stability characteristics, perhaps by an inclining experiment. Then, having found that the metacentric height was marginal, he should have done the prudent thing and had fixed ballast installed in the bottom. That would have minimized the possibility of the sort of errors in judgment that finally led to the catastrophe.

Comments of Walter C. Cowles
Naval Architect

It is with a good deal of trepidation that one presumes to comment on the testimony of a professional of Dr. Sadler's status long after the event. In addition, he had access to information no longer available, and we have access to some information not available to him, at least given the constraints of time and the format of the investigation. His testimony certainly would have been more meaningful had he been allowed to present it in a comprehensive manner with interrogation to follow, rather than having to respond to questioning by persons not only lacking in any technical background, but seeking to establish positions favorable to their clients. Due to the nature and sequence of questioning and the lack of technical competence on the part of the participants, much of the testimony is irrelevant, given that the purpose of that portion of the proceedings was to determine the relative seaworthiness of the vessel.

Professor Hilton has included considerable commentary in his text, particularly citing a number of inconsistencies between the testimony and the historical evidence.

Much of the preliminary proceedings deals with the doctor's qualifications. Sadler arrived in the United States about 1904, and thus had been associated with local practices, specifically concerning Great Lakes passenger vessels, for about nine years. Given his academic responsibilities, one might question how much exposure he really had to Great Lakes passenger ships. He does, of course, cite his connections with the Detroit & Cleveland Navigation Company and the Detroit, Belle Isle & Windsor Ferry Company, but ships operated by these companies were far different in configuration from the typical Lake Michigan passenger or passenger-and-freight vessel. Certainly the general arrangement of the *Eastland* as a three-deck vessel bears little resemblance to the two-deck ship that he describes as the typical channel steamer. By way of a local example, Canada Steamship Line's *Turbinia*, which had been built by the Hawthorne, Leslie Company in Scotland for Toronto-Hamilton service on Lake Ontario in 1904, bears much more resemblance to a channel steamer. Sadler is, however, rather specific in citing fine lines as being similar to the channel type. As a significant measure of hull fineness, the prismatic coefficient for cross-channel steamers ranges from 0.59 to 0.75.[2] The corresponding coefficient for Great Lakes passenger steamers of the era ranged from 0.640 to 0.677. It is interesting to note that the *Petoskey*, also chartered for the Western Electric excursion, had the relatively fine coefficient of 0.640.[3] Obviously, the higher value represents a fuller form. We do not have any original data on the hull form of the *Eastland*, but if Professor Beier's estimate from the hull form in Chapter I, derived from computer-assisted drafting, is even approximately correct that the prismatic coefficient of fineness was about 0.68, the ship did not have an exceptionally fine hull. Although Professor Sadler attributed the tenderness of the vessel to an unusually fine hull, it appears much more likely that it resulted from a higher than normal center of gravity. This was, of course, aggravated during the life of the vessel by the addition of significant topside weights. Finally, although it is quite evident that as the vessel loaded, the metacentric height became negative, the actual capsizing was not the result of inherent instability, but of downflooding of water through the gangways and air ports. Nowhere in these proceedings does there appear any consideration or discussion of this downflooding as the ultimate cause of the disaster.

The designer of the *Eastland* was faced with a very difficult set of requirements. The vessel was to have a relatively high speed and still be capable of operating at a restricted draft. The former required a ship of fine lines and high power; the latter prevented the use of permanent ballast. Although several reasons are cited in the text for the Michigan Steamship Company's specifying twin screws, it is most probable that from the designer's standpoint the driving motive was the need to transmit the required power with propeller diameter limited by draft. The resulting two triple-expansion engines resulted in a higher vertical center of gravity (VCG) for the machinery installation. The associated boiler installation probably also tended to raise the center of gravity.

The designer elected to extend the shell plating of the hull up to the promenade deck to allow portholes for the staterooms on the cabin deck. Although, as noted by Professor Hilton, ships designed for trading on Lake Superior were often configured in this manner, the arrangement was uncommon, though not unique, for ships intended primarily for Lake Michigan service. The *Manitou* was designed in this fashion, but because her route was a long one from Chicago to Mackinac Island, she had extensive stateroom space and an affluent clientele to whom an unobstructed view of the lake was desirable. The Georgian Bay Line, for its pair of cruise ships, the *North American* of 1913 and *South American* of 1914, both of which were originally intended to run to Duluth, specified plating of this sort. This use of the Lake Superior configuration on the *Eastland* was certainly a contributing factor to a higher center of gravity than would have resulted from the usual wood cabin construction.

Relative to Sadler's comments on the *Eastland* not being similar to the typical excursion steamer, while indeed much different from the excursion vessels on the Detroit River and western Lake Erie with which he was associated, she was typical in hull proportions to other Lake Michigan excursion ships. Her length-to-beam ratio of 6.94 is not markedly different from the *City of South Haven* at 6.15 and the *Theodore Roosevelt* at 6.89, as well as the *Turbinia* of Lake Ontario at 7.53. The *Cayuga*, which ran from Toronto to the Niagara River, was 8.36. Both were strictly excursion vessels, but the *Manitou* had a ratio of 6.51.[4]

Professor Sadler testified on February 3, 1916. Because he went aboard the wreck, we know that he had about six months of acquaintance with the *Eastland*, but we do not know how much time he had for his calculations after being invited to testify. He presumably had available the hydrostatic calculations prepared by the designer. Preparation of the righting moment curves represents a very time-consuming effort, certainly given the tools available to him at the time. In addition, he had to carry out his weight and centers calculations. It may well be that his testimony was less concise than it might have been had he more time to prepare. We also do not know how much time he spent in preparation for questions that were not asked.

As noted in Professor Hilton's text, it is most surprising that Sadler stated a precise value of GM, given the number of unknown and estimated values involved. It is very doubtful that the initial center of gravity was calculated at the time of construction. To carry out such a calculation from scratch is very arduous, and at best requires numerous assumptions and estimates. Normal practice is to determine an approximate value by reference to similar designs with an adjustment to reflect known differences. Whether or not it was customary to confirm this estimate by means of an inclining experiment at the time of building the *Eastland* is unknown. In any event, as Hilton has noted, this was not done in the case of the *Eastland*.

In retrospect, a fair approximation could have been made given the evidence that a zero to negative metacentric height had developed on the occasion of the near-capsizing of July 17, 1904. Apparently none of the principal figures involved in the ship's history noted the technical significance of this and similar events.

Sadler's discussion of the effects of free surface also seems somewhat exaggerated. In effect the VCG of the vessel must first be adjusted for the weight of ballast water, in this case lowering the VCG, then a correction made for the free surface. This correction—an effective raising of G or lowering of M—is equal to i/V, where i is the moment of inertia of the water in the tank and V is the immersed volume of the ship. In the case of double bottom tanks divided at the center line by a watertight keelson as in the ballast tanks of the *Eastland*, the value of i is relatively small. It would seem in the case of the *Eastland* that the addition of any significant water in the ballast tanks would almost certainly result in an *increase* in GM. This effect is implied in much of the testimony relating to the sequence of events. It might seem that Sadler's testimony regarding the adding of ballast was rather "top of the head," and if he had had an opportunity, or had anticipated the specific question, he would have made some calculations that almost certainly would have resulted in a different response.

In summary, though there were numerous inconsistencies in Sadler's testimony, and probably some erroneous or at least misleading comments, the overall tone was correct, though not helpful. The vessel would have been seaworthy for the allowable load if properly ballasted or for a reduced loading if unballasted. The unanswered question is who was responsible for assuring proper operation: the captain, chief engineer, general manager, inspector, or the regulatory bodies?

Finally, it is interesting to note that this disaster, in keeping with the other major marine disasters of the era, was never a topic for discussion at a meeting of the Society of Naval Architects and Marine Engineers, although Sadler was a frequent contributor to its publications. It is assumed that it would have been considered unethical if not illegal to discuss the matter while legal action was pending.

United States Navy, Retired; Formerly Officer in Charge of
Senior Engineering Courses, United States Naval Academy

Sadler's evaluation of the casualty, although basically correct, unfortunately was not a comprehensive analysis. Sadler appeared as an expert witness, according to his testimony, and analysis was restricted to answers to specific questions from lawyers for the prosecution and the defendants, who were trying to make their cases. His answers in direct and cross-examination depended on the motives, assumptions, and technical knowledge of the questioners. The answers to the questions were therefore made in piecemeal fashion. This did not provide him the opportunity to make a comprehensive analysis of the casualty, such as would have been done in a technical paper. Under these circumstances, it is indeed remarkable that Sadler was able to bring out the salient facts detailing the cause of the casualty.

His explanation of the principles of ship design was accurate and showed both in-depth academic knowledge and practical experience. He also put these complex subjects in terms that could be understood by laymen. His calculations based on the geometry and dimensions of the ship are undoubtedly correct, since he had access to the plans and design data of the ship as constructed. Thus, his calculations for the center of buoyancy and location of the metacenter can be considered accurate. However, his estimate of the center of gravity of the ship is just that, an estimate that cannot be proved since the ship had never been inclined. His technique of analyzing similar ships with known centers of gravity, examining the *Eastland* plans, and checking the actual ship for changes, combined with his practical experience, is considered as sound a basis for an estimate as could be made. Considering this, it is not possible to make a precise calculation for the ship's metacentric height, GM. His calculation of +0.15 feet for the metacentric height is of such small magnitude that under the variation of an estimate, it could just as well have been a small negative number. In fact, a negative GM is indicated, based on the ship's history of lolling from port to starboard in her previous instances of serious instability.

Sadler's testimony may not have considered other factors that contributed to the capsizing. Evidence from testimony by other witnesses to the casualty as described in the earlier chapters of this book was not discussed, or was at variance with his testimony. Discrepancies such as the sequences of flooding of the ballast tanks, the number of times the ship reversed her list, and the location and movement of passengers were not explained. Perhaps this was the result of the method of questioning, as discussed earlier, but it may indicate that he did not have knowledge of all the evidence. However, these other factors do not change the basic reason he gave for the capsizing—the inherent instability of the ship under her method of operation.

Based on the information provided in this book, and by Sadler, this instability can be attributed to the following:

a. The ship was not designed as an excursion vessel with a heavy top-side passenger load. Therefore her stability was less than it should have been for safe operation.

b. The center of gravity of the ship was raised by various changes to the original plan, decreasing her stability.

c. Operating the ship with ballast tanks neither empty nor completely full created a large free-surface effect that significantly raised the ship's center of gravity and decreased her stability.

d. The ballasting system was poorly designed. It could not be made to respond in a controlled manner to affect the list of the ship. This could have significantly reduced the stability of the ship by lagging behind or overcompensating for the intended corrective measures to correct list.

e. The gangway openings close to the waterline presented the danger of open communication to the sea, which would have a major effect in reducing the ship's stability. Since a list of only 15 degrees would admit water over the bottom half of the gangway door—the upper half was customarily left open—a dangerous situation was inherent. In addition, the gangway doors leaked and were sometimes left entirely open.

The measures taken by the U.S. Navy when it converted the *Eastland* to the *Wilmette* restored the ship's stability by reducing the above factors as follows:

a. The superstructure was removed, and the ship's passenger load was significantly reduced. The Navy's projected and actual use of the ship was more consistent with the *Eastland*'s original plan than use of the ship as an excursion vessel had been.

b. Although the Navy added light guns topside to the *Wilmette*, it removed much heavier weight, such as deck and structure, and the excess lifeboats and rafts.

c. The ship was operated with great care as related to loose water in her tanks. To reduce free-surface effects, the ballast tanks were kept full or empty. Later, tanks were subdivided to reduce further the free-surface effects when tanks were not full.

d. The ballast system was redesigned to make it more responsive and controllable.

e. The gangway openings were plated over to make the hull watertight, and thus to reduce the chances of reducing the ship's stability due to leak-

age through the openings.

The result of the above changes was to produce a positive metacentric height of over two feet, which coincides with Sadler's contention of what the *Eastland* should have had.

Comments of William duBarry Thomas
Naval Architect

Professor Herbert C. Sadler (1872–1948), a respected naval architect and academician, was active in his profession from the mid-1890's until his death. He became a member of the Society of Naval Architects and Marine Engineers (SNAME) in 1899. He served as a Member of Council from 1909 to 1928, became a vice president in 1929, and in the same year was elected an honorary vice president, an office he held until his death. By far his most important assignment in relation to the subject matter of the *Eastland* case was as a delegate to the 1913 International Conference on Safety of Life at Sea. Professor Sadler taught naval architecture at the University of Michigan from 1900 to 1937, when he retired because of ill health. He was the author or coauthor of fourteen papers before SNAME between 1901 and 1925.

I am puzzled by Professor Sadler's testimony—or perhaps by the way he responded to the lawyers' direct questions. I am not at all surprised that Sadler's responses were seemingly inconsistent. Having to answer direct questions from one or more novices in naval architecture was bound to obfuscate the real reason for the questions. I am sure those in the court thought they knew all about stability and free-surface effect and the idiosyncrasies of water ballast when they finished questioning Sadler, but I feel that the questioning meandered to such an extent that Sadler looked somewhat like a bumbling academic. The whole point of one important aspect of the testimony—that of the effect of free surface in ballast tanks on metacentric height and, accordingly, on the ability of a vessel to remain upright—was really not understood by the lawyers, as evidenced by the questions that they asked Sadler.

In terms of Sadler's testimony, the impact of his direct reply was lost because of the nature of the supporting questions. At no time during his testimony were the issue of weight added topside and other alterations to the vessel adequately covered. However, he did state at one point that he considered the vessel to be "unsafe" under a number of hypothetical operating conditions and that, if the ballast tanks were kept full all of the time, she would be a "seaworthy boat."

But the whole issue revolved unequivocally around the poor margin of stability of the vessel and the fact that, in 1915, this was a disaster waiting to happen. This is a difficult concept to explain to the layman, and Sadler was not very successful in making clear the basic principles of this vitally important aspect of naval architecture. In particular, his explanations of how the free surface of a liquid in a partially filled tank may drastically reduce the stability of a vessel that would be available if the tank were empty or completely full were not, strictly speaking, incorrect, but they suffered from a poorly organized set of questions.

Free-surface correction means reducing a ship's metacentric height by an amount equal to the transverse moment of inertia of the plane area of the liquid in a tank, divided by the volume of liquid. Because the moment of inertia of a rectangular tank is a function of the length of the tank times its breadth cubed, the correction may be significant in a tank having a large transverse dimension, such as a double-bottom tank. If a rectangular tank is subdivided by a center-line longitudinal bulkhead, making two smaller, identical tanks, the free-surface correction of each will be one-eighth of that of the large tank. It is for this reason that ballast tanks are generally configured to have small water-plane areas or are operated either completely filled or empty. The folly of using wide double-bottom tanks for ballasting an excursion vessel such as the *Eastland* is apparent, and was equally obvious to Sadler.

Sadler was a competent naval architect and an outstanding teacher, accustomed to preparing and delivering logically constructed lectures on complex subjects such as ship stability. However, when confronted with a battery of questions from a lawyer who, competent as he may have been in a general sense, was out of his depth in dealing with the subject of ship stability, the entire testimony was fragmented and unfocused. In this respect, Sadler cannot be faulted; Clyne and his staff certainly can be.

Professor Hilton, in the text, raises the question, which Sadler did not treat, whether the asymmetry of the ballast system—flooding water into the tanks from port and pumping it out to starboard—had any effect on the handling of the ship. This raises the question of what the relative filling rates of the various tanks were with the vessel listed to port or starboard. Although the filling rate of a given tank can, from a theoretical standpoint, be considered the same irrespective of the list of the vessel to port or starboard, it is possible that local constrictions within the piping system might result in somewhat different flow rates. We do not know the details of the system (including piping arrangement, diameter, types of valves, number and types of bends, and other attributes) by which the tanks were filled, nor do we know the system's condition after more than twelve years of service. It is, therefore, reasonable to assume that different filling rates might have been observed at individual tanks with the vessel listed to port relative to the corresponding rates while listed to starboard. It is by no means certain that this condition was present, but if so, it might explain why it may have been easier to correct a list to one side than to the other.

It did not matter what Sadler said, or what measures were taken in the attempt to correct for the wild excursions in list that accompanied the vessel's last moments prior to capsizing—a series of events that duplicated the vessel's near catastrophic experience of July 17, 1904. The effort to ballast the vessel was made in the best of faith by Erickson, the chief engineer, but with some degree of ignorance of the consequences. The metacentric height of the vessel was so small—even with bone-dry ballast tanks—that the good intentions of the chief engineer led him down a path from which there was no return, and, unfortunately, the point of no return had been reached before he started.

List of Victims

Victims Authenticated by Death Certificate

The following are deceased authenticated by Death Certificates, Cook County, Illinois; and Church of Jesus Christ of Latter Day Saints Family History Library, Salt Lake City, Utah, microfilm reels 1,287,523–31. These records of death certificates are not complete, particularly in entirely lacking names beginning with the letter "S." Accordingly, entries in this list beginning with "S" are from the manuscript Inquest Record, Coroner of Cook County, vol. 125, Office of the Medical Examiner, 2121 W. Harrison Street, Chicago. This volume is entirely devoted to *Eastland* victims. Cemeteries are as shown on the death certificates, but the Inquest Record does not show cemeteries. The cemeteries for victims from this source are from newspaper accounts, cemetery records, and the records of the St. Mary of Czestochowa Church, Cicero, Illinois. "WE" indicates a Western Electric employee. Names of the deceased are grouped by family, with the name of the head of the family first, followed by the children's names, indented. If the family members were siblings, the name of the oldest is first, followed by the others' names, indented. Cemeteries, unless otherwise identified, are in the Chicago metropolitan area. The Chicago *Tribune*'s Chicagoland map, issued biennially, shows locations of all major cemeteries.

Names in parentheses are other names the person is known to have used. Where there are rival spellings of the name, I have accepted, in order of credibility, the tombstone, the cemetery's records, the listing in the city directory, the death certificate, the coroner's inquest record, Western Electric's list of lost employees, and the final newspaper listing. The death certificates made out at the central morgue in the Second Regiment Armory were handwritten and, inevitably, give the impression of having been done under considerable emotional strain. They are not wholly accurate. Most of the deceased were young people who lived with their parents or in rented quarters such that they did not appear under their own names in city directories. Names in brackets are variant spellings I have been unable to reconcile. In such cases, I have shown the name on the cemetery record or, failing that, the name on the death certificate, followed by variants in newspapers and elsewhere. I have not attempted to reconcile variant spellings of Catherine, Eleanor, or Marie/Mary/May. Elizabeth Landaw of the UCLA Economics Department was most helpful in determining correct spellings of Slavic names.

Because of anglicization of names, use of names of stepparents, changes in names by marriage, gaps in the death certificates, conflict in sources, absence of any credible compilation of survivors, and the various other problems in assembling the list, it is unlikely to prove wholly accurate. I solicit corrections from descendants of the deceased and others. Any corrections received by December 31, 1995, and substantiated, I will incorporate in a typescript, which I will deposit in the Chicago Historical Society.

Adamkiewicz, Marya (Marie), 19, sister of Martha Adamkiewicz Darka, single, switchboard operator, WE. St. Adalbert's Cemetery.
Adler, Augusta, 29, married. Concordia Cemetery.
Affeld, Caroline Schroth, Mrs. Max, 36. Buried in Frankfort, Ill.
Albertz, Marie, 20, single, WE. St. Mary's Cemetery.
Albrecht, Lena, 17, single, shophand, WE. Waldheim Cemetery.
Allen, Kathryn G., 25, single, WE. Forest Home Cemetery.
Althaler, Hattie, 22, single, dry goods clerk. St. Boniface Cemetery.
Anderson, Alfred Edward, 36, shipping clerk, WE. Montrose Cemetery.
 Anderson, Anna Selina, Mrs. Alfred, 35.
 Anderson, Maurice Alfred George, 7.
Anderson, Allen, 4. Forest Home Cemetery.
Anderson, Anna, 26, single, forewoman, WE. Forest Home Cemetery.
Anderson, May C., Mrs. Gustav, 38, sister of Gertrud(e) Berg. Graceland Cemetery.
Anderson, Otto E., 43, married, blacksmith's helper, WE. Mt. Olive Cemetery.
Anderson, Robert Axel, 22, married, laborer, WE. Forest Home Cemetery.
Andren, Harold E., 19, single, drafting clerk, WE. Oak Ridge Cemetery.
Androvits, Susanna (Sunna), Mrs. Albert, 30. Resurrection Cemetery.
 Androvits, Amalia (Lusie, Amily), 6.
 Androvits, Emerentia, 3.
Austin, Kate, Mrs. Thomas E., 47, widow, cook, WE. Waldheim Cemetery.
Badalewska (Liska), Frances, 20, single, coding, WE. Resurrection Cemetery.

Baia, Harry, 16, single, laborer or chauffeur. Mt. Carmel Cemetery.

Bambasova, Emilie (Emma, Emily Bambas), 20, single, WE. St. Adalbert's Cemetery.

Bannach, Paul, 20, married, laborer. Resurrection Cemetery.
>   Bannach, Bessie Karvasek, Mrs. Paul, 19.

Bartlett, Edward S., 55, married, bartender. Montrose Cemetery.

Batruel, Anna, 21, single, WE. Mt. Olivet Cemetery.

Becker, Benjamin, 20, single, automobile repairman. St. Lucas Cemetery.

Becker, Margreth (Margaret), 18, single, cable dept., WE. St. Joseph Cemetery.

Beel, Jethro Richard, Jr., 27, married, salesman. Forest Home Cemetery.

Begitschke (Begitske), Florence, 18, single, inspector, WE. Concordia Cemetery.

Behrendt, Agnes, 22, single, cable tester, WE. St. Joseph Cemetery.
>   Behrendt, Gertrude, 15, sister of Agnes, single.

Belmonti (Belmont), William, 19, single, laborer, WE. Mt. Carmel Cemetery.

Belsky, Emma, 19, single. Bohemian National Cemetery.

Bender, Charles C., 22, single, grocery clerk. Oak Ridge Cemetery.

Benes, Anna, 20, single, worked for her brother in tailoring. Bohemian National Cemetery.

Benik (Bendick), Anna, 21, single. Bohemian National Cemetery.

Benn, Samuel, 37, married, tinsmith. Cemetery of the Progressive Order of the West; currently interred in Jewish Waldheim Cemetery.

Bennett, Leroy David, 21, single, shophand, WE. Forest Home Cemetery.

Benson, David G., 25, married, electrician, WE. Resurrection Cemetery.

Berg, Gertrud(e), Mrs. Gustav O., 35, sister of May Anderson. Mt. Olive Cemetery.
>   Berg, Irene, 1.

Berglund, Myrtle J., 12. Arlington Cemetery, Elmhurst, Ill.

Bergman, David A., 22, single, WE. Oak Ridge Cemetery.

Bergquist, Harry D., 15, schoolboy. Rosehill Cemetery.

Berlin, Ida May, Mrs. C. C., 42. Forest Home Cemetery.

Bertrand, Joseph B., 50, married, clerk, rooming house. Montrose Cemetery.

Betlack, Joseph W., 18, single, shipping clerk, WE. Bohemian National Cemetery.

Beutelspacher, Mathilda, 18, single, press operator or shop clerk, WE. Waldheim Cemetery.

Biehl, Frederick W., 26, married, gang boss, WE. Eden Cemetery.

Biel, Albert, 27, single, tinsmith, WE. St. Boniface Cemetery.

Bigalski, Anna, 23, single, wire inspector, WE. Mt. Carmel Cemetery.

Bilwachs, Louis, 19, single, bookkeeper, WE. Bohemian National Cemetery.

Binkley, James Frank, 20, single, clerk, ICRR. Mt. Auburn Cemetery.

Bizek, Mary, 19, single, mail stamper, Sears, Roebuck & Co. Bohemian National Cemetery.

> Bizek, Anna, 16, sister of Mary, single, employee, Bunte candy.

Blaich, John M., Jr., 24, single, receiving clerk, WE. Concordia Cemetery.

Bluch, Carl (Charles Block), 21, single, machinist, ICRR. Bethania Cemetery.

Bonga, Mathew J., 23, single, clerk. Mt. Carmel Cemetery.

Bosch, Elizabeth, 30, single, dressmaker. St. Boniface Cemetery.

Bosse, Louis George, 26, single, storekeeper. Waldheim Cemetery.

Bothun, Svend H., 30, single, electrician, WE. Central Freeborn Lutheran Church Cemetery, rural Albert Lea, Minn.

Bouffard, Oliver J., 25, single, clerk or foreman, WE. Mt. Olivet Cemetery.

Boult, Harry, 25, single, machinist. Forest Home Cemetery.

Boyle, Peter, 23, single, sailor on *Petoskey*. Mt. Carmel Cemetery.

Bradley, Frank J., 23, single, foreman, WE. Calvary Cemetery.

Brady, John, 23, single, attendant at Chicago State Tuberculosis Hospital. Mt. Carmel Cemetery.

Braitsch, John, 42, married, electrical toolmaker, WE. This family, of which only the mother, Mary Braitsch, survived, was buried in Jersey City, N.J.

> Braitsch, Anna, 17, single, clerk, WE.
> Braitsch, Frederick, 9.
> Braitsch, Gertrude, 11.
> Braitsch, Hattie, 7.
> Braitsch, Marie, 5 months, 16 days only.

Brennan, Joe, c. 35, deckhand on *Eastland*. Mt. Carmel Cemetery.

Brennan, Thomas F., 23, single, office worker, WE. Mt. Carmel Cemetery.

Brenner, Anna, 18, single, timekeeper, Belden Mfg. Co. St. Mary's Cemetery.

Brosche, Henry, 32, single, foreman, WE. Buried in Weehawken, N.J.

Bruesch, Sophia A., 48, single, wire insulator, WE. Rosehill Cemetery.

Brychta, Anton J., 37, married, cabinet maker, WE. St. Adalbert's Cemetery.

> Brychta, Joseph A., 31, brother of Anton, married, inspector, WE.

Brynacki, Anton, 30, married, WE. Resurrection Cemetery.

Buchholz, Mabel Deichmann, 21, married, designer. Mt. Olive Cemetery.

Buczkowski, George, 28, married, laborer, WE. St. Adalbert's Cemetery.

Budzinska, Yadwiga (Harriet, Hattie Budner), 18, single, WE. St. Adalbert's Cemetery.

Buege, Arthur, 19, single, WE. Concordia Cemetery.

Buelow, Herbert, 18, single, WE. Concordia Cemetery.

Buth, Anna, 20, single, pieceworker, WE. Oakwoods Cemetery.

Cajthaml (Cythamel), Josephine, 18, single, WE. Bohemian National Cemetery.

Capra, Andrew, 24, single, WE. Buried in St. Louis, Mo.

Caro, Jacomo (Jack Caros), 32, married, laborer, WE. Mt. Carmel Cemetery.

> Caro, Rose, Mrs. Jacomo, 30.
> Caro, Felicia, 5.

Carroll, Thomas Joseph, Jr., 20, single, WE. Mt. Carmel Cemetery.

Ceciorski, Marie, 24, single. St. Mary's Cemetery.

Cepak, Bessie, 19, single, laborer. Bohemian National Cemetery.

Ceranek, Mary, 17, single, WE. Resurrection Cemetery.

Cerney, Frank, 16, single, office clerk, WE. Bohemian National Cemetery.

Chamberlain, Michael Gallagher, 28, married, elevator operator, WE. Mt. Carmel Cemetery.

Chartoir (Charter), Katherine, 22, single, WE. Mt. Carmel Cemetery.

Chittuse, Pauline, 18, single, WE. Bohemian National Cemetery.

Cholke (Holke), George, 19, single, machinist, WE. St. Adalbert's Cemetery.

Christiansen, Frieda, 20, single, insulator, Belden Manufacturing Co. Waldheim Cemetery.

Cifrik, Josephine, 20, single, assembler, WE. St. Adalbert's Cemetery.

Cihak, Vaslav (James), 34, married, shipping clerk. Bohemian National Cemetery.

Clark, William, 20, WE. Mt. Carmel Cemetery.

> Clark, Alice B., 19, Mrs. William.
> Clark, Alice, 9 months only.

Clarke, Robert L., 33, assembler, WE. Cypress Hills Cemetery, Brooklyn, N.Y.; reinterred at Greenfield Cemetery, Hempstead, Long Island, N.Y., 1931.

> Clarke, Marie Eleanor Anderson, Mrs. Robert, 28.
> Clarke, Eleanor (Ella), 2.

Clausen, Anna Kerstina, Mrs. Claus, 31. Mt. Olive Cemetery.

> Clausen, Ella Kerstina, 7.

Cmucha, Rose Putz, Mrs. Joseph (Mrs. Joseph Smith), 27, probably sister-in-law of Mary Putz. Mt. Carmel Cemetery.

Columbik, Celia, Mrs. Frank, 24. Forest Home Cemetery.

Comerford, Anna, 18, single, telephone operator. Mt. Carmel Cemetery.

Cooney, Margaret Belle Quaine, Mrs. Matthew, c. 34, sister of Anna Quaine. Buried in Emmett, Mich.

> Cooney, Thomas F., 1.

Cox, Mildred S., 13. Mt. Auburn Cemetery.

Cullen, Rose Veronica, 21, single, stenographer, WE. Mt. Carmel Cemetery.

Curtin, Ruth, 22, single, office worker, WE. Forest Home Cemetery.

Daly, John J., 24, married, clerk, WE. St. Boniface Cemetery.

Daly, Agnes Forlop, Mrs. John J., 26, hand, WE.

Danda, Theresa, 19, single, WE. Bohemian National Cemetery.

Danda, Edward, 11, brother of Theresa.

Danek, Frantisek (Frank), 32, married, coil winder, WE. St. Adalbert's Cemetery.

Dankers, Frederick, Jr., 24, single, cable maker, WE. St. Joseph Cemetery.

Darka, Martha Adamkiewicz, 24, sister of Marya Adamkiewicz, married, WE[?]. St. Adalbert's Cemetery.

Davis, Lillian Schultz, 20, married, WE. Concordia Cemetery.

Dawson, Earl Harvey, 18, single, press feeder, WE. Oak Ridge Cemetery.

Debnar, John, 40, married, machinist, WE. Bohemian National Cemetery.

Dester, Howard John, 28, married, draftsman, WE. Waldheim Cemetery.

DeTamble, Caroline Mary, Mrs. John W., 26. Mt. Carmel Cemetery.

Dobberman, Frank A., 33, married, switchboard engineer, WE. Oakwoods Cemetery.

Dobek, George W., 19, single, case maker. Bohemian National Cemetery.

Dolejs, Anna, 20, single, WE. This group of four siblings is buried in Bohemian National Cemetery.

Dolejs, Joseph, 18, single, bookkeeper, WE.

Dolejs, Marie, 17, single, WE.

Dolejs, Rose, 19, single, WE.

Dolezal, Josephine, Mrs. Frank, 27. St. Adalbert's Cemetery.

Dolezal, Lillie, 9 months only.

Dolezal, Mary, 4.

Dolezal, Regina, 20, sister of Josephine Sindelar, single. Bohemian National Cemetery.

Dolgner, Paul H., 24, married, WE. St. Johannes Cemetery, location uncertain.

Doll, Robert, 21, single, WE. St. Joseph Cemetery.

Doll, Charles, 17, brother of Robert, single, messenger boy.

Dombkowski (Danskowski), Stanley, 30, single, painter, WE. Resurrection Cemetery.

Donajska (Doneske), Eleanore, 17, single, WE. St. Adalbert's Cemetery.

Drury, Florence T., 17, single, housework. Mt. Carmel Cemetery.

Dubek, Catherine (Kate), Mrs. Vincent, 38. Bohemian National Cemetery.

Dubek, Catherine (Katie), 16.

Dubek, Joseph, 11.

Dudek, John, 33, WE. Resurrection Cemetery.

Dudek, Mary Krzyzaniak, Mrs. John, 27.

Duggan, Charles James, 30, single, inspector, WE. Buried in Roanoke, Va.

Dulean, Victoria, 21, single, WE. Resurrection Cemetery.

Dunne, Rose, 25, married. Mt. Carmel Cemetery.

Dupke, Alexander, 21, single, assembler, WE. Concordia Cemetery.

Dvorak, Bessie, 21, single, Sears, Roebuck & Co. Bohemian National Cemetery.

Dziondziak, Marya (Minnie), 19, single, shop hand, WE. St. Adalbert's Cemetery.

Egan, Mary Helen, 15. Calvary Cemetery.

Ehrhardt, Fred J., 31, married, shipping clerk. Mt. Olive Cemetery.
    Ehrhardt, Clara C. Jensen, Mrs. Fred, 31.

Elecks (Illick), Nicholas, 45, single, WE. Resurrection Cemetery.

Elendt, Walter, 20, single, assembler, WE. Concordia Cemetery.

Engels, Lena, 23, single, WE. Oak Ridge Cemetery.

Engenhardt, Harry, 20, single, assembler, WE. Forest Home Cemetery.

Erickson, Jenny, 24, single, stenographer, WE. Elmwood Cemetery.

Erlandson, Carrie, 22, single, switchboard tester, WE. Mt. Olive Cemetery.

Etter, Alma, 21, single, dressmaker. Oak Ridge Cemetery.

Etzkorn, Angela, Mrs. Louis, 46. Oak Ridge Cemetery.

Evenhouse, Jennie, 26, single, WE. Forest Home Cemetery.
    Evenhouse, Anna B., 23, sister of Jennie, single, WE.

Farnara, Robert, 21, single, WE. St. Mary's Cemetery.

Farrell, Amelia, 19, single, WE. Concordia Cemetery.

Feehan, William Alexander, 39, single, assembler, WE. Buried in Joliet, Ill.

Fenik, James, 34, glazer, WE. Bohemian National Cemetery.
    Fenik, Mary, Mrs. James, 29.
    Fenik, Helen, 4.
    Fenik, William, 7.

Fick, Margaret (Marguerite), 19, single, assembler, WE. Mt. Olive Cemetery.

Fink, Alma F., 29, single, shop hand, WE. Evergreen Cemetery.

Fischer, Otto, 17, single, repair man, WE. Waldheim Cemetery.

Fisher, William, 21, single, WE. Bohemian National Cemetery.

Fitzgerald, Nellie, Mrs. John F., c. 27. Buried in Lansdowne, Pa.
    Fitzgerald, Dorothy, 3.

Fitzgerald, William L., 46, married, laborer, WE. Waldheim Cemetery.
    Fitzgerald, James, 9.

Fleischer, Caroline, 50, widow, housewife. Mt. Auburn Cemetery.

Fleming, Henry, 17, single, clerk in department store. St. Lucas Cemetery.

Flicek, Emil, 19, single, laborer, WE. Bohemian National Cemetery.

Fornero, Robert, 21, single, machinist. St. Mary's Cemetery.

Forst, Anna, 18, single, factory work, WE. Bohemian National Cemetery.

Forst, Anna Soukup, 17, probably sister of William Soukup, married. Bohemian National Cemetery.

Forst, Emelia (Emily Stirek), 23, single. [Not sister of Anna Forst.] Bohemian National Cemetery.

Foster, Harry L., 25, married, telephone assembler, WE. Forest Home Cemetery.

> Foster, Rachel, Mrs. Harry L., 25.

Fostle, Chester G., 18, single, WE. Bohemian National Cemetery.

Frackowiak (Francel[l]), Marya C., 21, Mrs. Albert J. Resurrection Cemetery.

Franzen, Anna, Mrs. Robert, 45. Forest Home Cemetery.

> Franzen, Arthur F., 19, single, WE.

> Franzen, Lillian, 22, single, dressmaker.

Freilich, Jan (John), WE. St. Adalbert's Cemetery.

> Freilich, Hattie (Yadwiga Frejlach), Mrs. John, 25.

Friedman, Carl, 24, single, electrician, WE. Forest Home Cemetery.

Frisina, Philippi (Philip), 21, single, clerk for ice cream co. Mt. Carmel Cemetery.

> Frisina, Anna, Mrs. Peter, 17, sister-in-law of Philippi.

Frydrych (Frederick), Alice, 17, single, WE. Resurrection Cemetery.

Fuchs, Catherine, 28, single, assembler, WE. St. Boniface Cemetery.

Fuka, Frank S. (Young Hanlon—name used as boxer), 19, single, assembler, WE. Bohemian National Cemetery.

Gabriel, Marie, 18, single, WE. Bethania Cemetery.

Gajicek, Henrietta, 17, single, WE. Bohemian National Cemetery.

Garner, Edward H., 38, married, draftsman, WE. Waldheim Cemetery.

Gatens, Edward J., 24, single, WE. Buried in New York, N.Y.

Geberbauer, Edwin, 19, single, WE. Montrose Cemetery.

Gecewicz, Wladyslaw (Walter), 20, single, draftsman, WE. St. Adalbert's Cemetery.

Genda, Emma (Emily Gonda), 35, married, seamstress, Hart, Schaffner & Marx. Bohemian National Cemetery.

Gibson, Mabel F., Mrs. N. E., 25. Mt. Olive Cemetery.

Ginsberg, Phillip L., 25, single, purchasing dept., WE. Oakwoods Cemetery.

Gorney, Clara, 19, single, inspector, WE. Buried in Lemont, Ill.

Goyette, Charles A., 16, single, office boy, WE. Buried in Burlington, Vt.

Gradert, Ellen Marie Sophia, 31, single, clerk. Mt. Olive Cemetery.

Graf, Raymond A., 16, single, clerk. Buried in Lemont, Ill.

Grajek, Frank, 19, single, WE. Resurrection Cemetery.

Grandt, Matilda (Tillie), 35, married, overlooker, WE. St. Mary's
Cemetery.
    Grandt, Clara, 12.
Greco, Leonardo, 36, married, laborer, WE. Mt. Carmel Cemetery.
Green, Arnold Martin, 51, married, cabinet maker, WE. Mt. Olive
Cemetery.
Grimms, Edward, 23, single, machine hand, WE. Concordia Cemetery.
Grochowska, Katarzyna (Kat, Kitty, Teddy), 17, single, candy factory.
St. Adalbert's Cemetery.
Grossman, Emma, 20, single, polisher, WE. Waldheim Cemetery.
Grzezkowiak, Helen, 19, single, WE. Resurrection Cemetery.
Guenther, William, c. 23, single, laborer. Arlington Cemetery.
Haertel, Benjamin F., 20, single, timekeeper, WE. Concordia Cemetery.
Haffer, William, 19, single. Concordia Cemetery.
Hajduk, Frank, 41, married, WE. St. Adalbert's Cemetery.
Hajek, Ladislav (William), 21, single, clerk. Bohemian National
Cemetery.
Hallas, Theodore, 25, single, drill press man, WE. Elmwood Cemetery.
Hamilton, Katherine Margaret, 18, single, Aluminum Products Co. Oak
Hill Cemetery.
Hammerstad, Inga L., 22, single, floor lady, WE. Oakwoods Cemetery.
Hansen, Harold, 35, WE. Mt. Olive Cemetery.
    Hansen, Gunvor Mary, Mrs. Harold, 33.
    Hansen, Margaret, 6.
    Hansen, Pearl, 4.
Hansen, Harold Hans, 20, single, drafting clerk, WE. Graceland Cemetery.
Hansen, Rose, 22, single, soldering, WE. Mt. Olive Cemetery.
    Hansen, Carrie, 14, sister of Rose.
Harke, Elizabeth, 21, single, WE. Bethania Cemetery.
Hawkins, John Frank, 22, single, clerk. Mt. Olivet Cemetery.
Hefferen, Mary, 40, single, floor lady, WE. Mt. Olivet Cemetery.
Heiden, Edwin, 18, single, odd work. St. Joseph Cemetery.
Heilemann, Rudolph Frank, 28, married, foreman, WE. Forest Home
Cemetery.
Helfenbein, Jan (John), 22, single, electrician, WE. Bohemian National
Cemetery.
Hengels, Barbara Elizabeth, 18, single. Mt. Carmel Cemetery.
Hennings, Edward, 18, single, WE. Concordia Cemetery.
Henzlik, Ruzena (Rose) M., 17, single, typist, WE. Bohemian National
Cemetery.
Herries, James, 29, single, WE. Arlington Cemetery.
Herzfeldt, Fred, 32, married, millwright, WE. Forest Home Cemetery.

Hill, Emily Georgia, Mrs. Harry, 41. [Not wife of Henry Hill.] Montrose Cemetery.

Hill, Henry, 35, single, tinner. Mt. Carmel Cemetery.

Hill, Mary, 23, sister of Henry, single, bench work.

Hillman, Anna M., 22, single, telephone operator, WE. Buried in Hoboken, N.J.

Hinczewski, Vijcenty (William), 21, single, assembler, WE. St. Adalbert's Cemetery.

Hipple, Cora May, Mrs. John, 41, daughter of Anna N. Stamm. Waldheim Cemetery.

Hipple, Clifford Edward, 7.

Hipple, Hazel Marie, 13.

Hoffman, Joseph M., 41, married. Arlington Cemetery.

Hoffman, Martha A., Mrs. Joseph, 37.

Hoffman, Marie, 19, single, WE. St. Adalbert's Cemetery.

Holcombe, John Ralph, 22, single, millwright's helper, WE. Buried in Asheville, N.C.

Holdsworth, James William, 68, widower, machinist, WE. Rosehill Cemetery.

Holstedt, Oscar J., 26, single, switchboard operator, WE. Montrose Cemetery.

Holtz, William, 21, single, grocery clerk, ex-WE. Forest Home Cemetery.

Holub, Vercinc (Vincent), 26, married, laborer, WE. St. Adalbert's Cemetery.

Homola, Sophia Strobo, Mrs. John, 27. Resurrection Cemetery.

Homola, Vlasta, 2.

Homolka, Caroline S., 16, single, clerk, WE. Bohemian National Cemetery.

Horazdovsky, Ella, 18, single. Bohemian National Cemetery.

Horazdovsky, Emma, 17, sister of Ella, single, WE.

Hosman, Amalie (Emily), single, elec. work. Bohemian National Cemetery.

Hrebout (Kral), Anna Stella, 23, single, WE. Bohemian National Cemetery.

Hrivnak, Emma, 16, single, WE[?]. Mt. Auburn Cemetery.

Hubbard, Ruth E., 22, single, clerk, WE. Mt. Auburn Cemetery.

Humpal, Jan (John), 23, single, WE. St. Adalbert's Cemetery.

Hunt, Joel B., 45, married, foreman, WE. Oak Ridge Cemetery.

Hurt, Lillian, 19, single, housework. Bohemian National Cemetery.

Hutchinson, Joseph L., 20, single, clerk, AT&SF Ry. Mt. Carmel Cemetery.

Ignasiak (Miller), Antonett, 21, single, WE. Resurrection Cemetery.

    Ignasiak (Miller), Anna, 17, sister of Antonett, single, WE.

Illig, William, Jr., 18, single. Montrose Cemetery.

Immel, Albert J. 25, motorcycle repairman. St. Boniface Cemetery.

Inciardi, Antoinetta, Mrs. Henry, 37. Mt. Carmel Cemetery.

Ivanecky, Katerina (Kathryn), 19, single, stenographer, WE. Bohemian National Cemetery.

Jackson, Mary E., 24, single, clerk, WE. Mt. Auburn Cemetery.

Jacobsen, Oscar I., 27, married, inspector, WE. Mt. Olive Cemetery.

Jagoda, Stanislaus (Stanley), 18, single, WE. Resurrection Cemetery.

Jahnke, Paul, 30, married, electrician, WE. Buried in New Hampton, Iowa.

    Jahnke, Louise, Mrs. Paul, 29.

Jakubowski, Ignatz (I. L. Jackson), 16, single, laborer, WE. Resurrection Cemetery.

Jannisch, Anna F., Mrs. Fred, 20. Bethania Cemetery.

Jarzembowska, Antoinette, 19, single, WE. Resurrection Cemetery.

Jaszka, Emilia (Emma Joschko), 18, single, punchpresser, WE. St. Adalbert's Cemetery.

Jaworski, Martha, 21, single, packer, candy factory. St. Adalbert's Cemetery.

    Jaworski, Julia, 16, sister of Martha, single, dipper, candy factory.

Jelen, Wladuslawa (Lottie), 18, single, WE. St. Adalbert's Cemetery.

Jelinek, Blanka (Blanche), 18, single, clothing sales lady. Bohemian National Cemetery.

Jilek, Josef, 24, single, tailor, Kriha Bros. Resurrection Cemetery.

Johnson, Edward, 19, single, machine shop, WE. Forest Home Cemetery.

Johnson, Elizabeth, Mrs. J. N., 27. Mt. Carmel Cemetery.

Johnson, Elna V., 21, single, WE. Forest Home Cemetery.

    Johnson, Eva, 19, sister of Elna, single, WE.

Johnson, Gustaf Ander, 36, married, pattern maker, WE. Forest Home Cemetery.

Johnson, Harry B., 23, single, WE. Arlington Cemetery.

Johnson, Louis H., 42, married, machinist, Illinois Glass Co. Mt. Olive Cemetery.

    Johnson, Ida K., Mrs. Louis, 33.

    Johnson, Esther Randine, 3.

Johnson, Nels Peter, 60, married, blacksmith, WE. Graceland Cemetery.

Johnson, Thomas, 53, married, cabinet maker, WE. Mt. Olive Cemetery.

Jonas (Jones), Joseph, 26, single, cabinet maker, WE. Buried in South Bend, Ind.

Jost, George W., 17, single, clerk, WE. Waldheim Cemetery.

Judge, Martin R., 27, married, clerk, WE. Buried in New York, N.Y.

Judge, Martin R., Jr., 2.

Jungwirth, Lillie, 17, single, bookkeeper, WE. Bohemian National Cemetery.

Jungwirth, Mamie, 16, sister of Lillie, single, snuff factory.

Justin, James C., Jr., 20, single, inspector, WE. Concordia Cemetery.

Kain, Frederick, 36, married, WE. Buried in Newburgh, N.Y.

Kalal, Marie, 19, single, WE. St. Adalbert's Cemetery.

Kalder, Rosalia (Rose), 17, single, hours keeper. St. Adalbert's Cemetery.

Kallal, Blanche, 17, single, counter, WE. Bohemian National Cemetery.

Kannberg, Frieda, 39, single, forelady, WE. Eden Cemetery.

Kapoun, Edward, 19, single, draftsman, WE. Bohemian National Cemetery.

Karner, Paul J., 23, single, stock keeper, Western Felt Co. Buried in Stevens Point, Wis.

Kasparaite, Kotrina (Kathryn Casper), 18, single, typist, WE. St. Casimir's Cemetery.

Kasperski, Agnes, 18, single, WE. Resurrection Cemetery.

Kasprszak (Kasper, Casper), Nellie, 18, single, WE. Resurrection Cemetery.

Kaszuba, Mary, 24, single, Novelty Candy Co. Resurrection Cemetery.

Kech, Catharine (Katherine Keck), 25, single, timekeeper. Eden Cemetery.

Keenan, Mary, 27, single, WE. Mt. Carmel Cemetery.

Keenan, Margaret, 21, sister of Mary, single, WE.

Kennedy, Albert J., 24, clerk, WE. Calvary Cemetery.

Ketschke, Rose, 11. Buried in New York, N.Y.

Ketschke, Josephine, 9, sister of Rose.

Kirkwood, Anne MacDonald, Mrs. John J., 35. Elmwood Cemetery.

Klefbohm, Ernest George, 27, married, WE. Rosehill Cemetery.

Kleifges, Sebastian J., 36, married, stockkeeper, WE. St. Boniface Cemetery.

Klemkowski, Helen, 19, single, WE. Resurrection Cemetery.

Kluczynska, Lucy, 19, single, canvas maker, McCormick Harvester. Resurrection Cemetery.

Kluczynski, Aloysius, 8, brother of Lucy.

Knoff, Carl (Clark), 19, single, electrician, WE. Mt. Carmel Cemetery.

Knopik, Anna, 18, single, telephone operator, WE. Resurrection Cemetery.

Koch (Cook), Emma, 21, single, clerk, WE. St. Boniface Cemetery.

Kodidek, Joseph, 35, married, WE. Bohemian National Cemetery.

Kolar, Anna, Mrs. Jerome, 25. Bohemian National Cemetery.

Kolar, Julia, 25, single, wire work, WE. St. Adalbert's Cemetery.

Kommer, Margaret, Mrs. Peter, 44. Mt. Olive Cemetery.

Komorous, Emma, 21, single, telephone tester, WE. Bohemian National Cemetery.

Korn, Hattie E., 24, single, WE. Concordia Cemetery.

Kotovsky, Ruzina (Rose), 20, single, covered wire, WE. St. Adalbert's Cemetery.

    Kotovsky, Johanna (Jennie), 18, sister of Ruzina, single, knitted neckware.

Kouba, Steve, 29, single, WE. St. Adalbert's Cemetery.

Koukl, Anna, 21, single, WE. Bohemian National Cemetery.

Kowalska, Anna, 18, single, WE[?]. Resurrection Cemetery.

Kowalska, Julia, 18, single, WE. Buried in Spring Valley, Ill.

Kozel, Carrie, 21, single, laboress, WE. Bohemian National Cemetery.

Krajnik, Walter, 17, single, office boy, Montgomery Ward. Resurrection Cemetery.

Krause, Emma, 20, single, solderer, WE. Concordia Cemetery.

Krch, Fred, 12, newsboy. Bohemian National Cemetery.

Krebel, Marie Catherine, 23, single. Bohemian National Cemetery.

Krejca, Joseph G., 21, single, laborer, WE. Bohemian National Cemetery.

Krich, George M., 30, married, belt man, WE. St. Lucas Cemetery.

Kriz, Joseph, 25, single, clerk. Bohemian National Cemetery.

Krueger, Erich (Ernest) W. C., 22, married, musician on ship. Montrose Cemetery.

Kruse, Louis, 29, married, WE. Mt. Carmel Cemetery.

Krzewinski, Wladyslaw (Walter; Mike Bloom), 46, married, millwright, WE. Resurrection Cemetery.

    Krzewinski (Bloom), Helen, 21, daughter of Wladyslaw, single, WE.

Kubiak, Anna, 17, single, WE. Resurrection Cemetery.

Kubicki, Wladyslaw (Walter Owens), 30, single, electrician, WE. St. Adalbert's Cemetery.

Kudrna, John, 21, single, printer. Bohemian National Cemetery.

Kupkowski, Tadeusz (Frank), 21, single, WE. Resurrection Cemetery.

Kupski (Cooper), Mary A., 22, single, WE. Resurrection Cemetery.

Kurvanek, John James, 19, single, picture frame feeder. St. Adalbert's Cemetery.

Kuzma, Lillian, 18, single, packer, WE. St. Adalbert's Cemetery.

Kwak, Antoni (Anton), Jr., 18, single, compositor, WE. Resurrection Cemetery.

LaCorzia, Joseph, 28, married, musician. Mt. Carmel Cemetery.

Laline, Casper, Jr., 25, single, scrap dept., WE. Buried in New York, N.Y.

Landsiedel, Mary, Mrs. George, 32. Buried in Philadelphia, Pa.

    Landsiedel, Naomi, 6.

Lane, Ada, 20, single, inspector. Buried in Grand Rapids, Mich.

Lange, Ladislaus (Walter), 19, single, WE. Resurrection Cemetery.

Larskowski, Anna (Annie Lorek), 16, single, WE. Resurrection Cemetery.

Larson, John Lambert, 23, single, insurance. Graceland Cemetery.

Latowski (Summit), Nellie, 26, single, WE. Resurrection Cemetery.

    Latowski (Summit), Walter, 24, brother of Nellie, single, WE.

Laurinaciute, Petronele (Hattie Laurainitis, Lorenat), 17, single, WE. St. Casimir's Cemetery.

La Valle, Margaret, Mrs. O. E., 31. Mt. Carmel Cemetery.

Lazzara, Rose, Mrs. George, 25. Mt. Carmel Cemetery.

Leff, Frank, 37, married, foreman. Bohemian National Cemetery.

    Leff, Edward, 9.

    Leff, Frank, Jr., 12.

Lemke, Elizabeth, 23, single, WE. St. Lucas Cemetery.

    Lemke, Emily, 18, sister of Elizabeth, single, WE.

    Lemke, Wilhelmine (Minnie), 21, sister of Elizabeth, single, WE.

Leonarczyk, Ignatius, 19, single. Resurrection Cemetery.

Lepine, Joseph, 37, single, clerk, WE. Mt. Carmel Cemetery.

LeRoy, Edgar, 29, single, machinist, WE. Mt. Carmel Cemetery.

Leu, Edward, 21, single, WE. Concordia Cemetery.

Lewandowska, Walewja (Viola, Violet), 18, single, machine hand, WE. St. Adalbert's Cemetery.

Lewitzki (Lewicki), Leo, 34, married, WE. St. Adalbert's Cemetery.

    Lewitzki, Ottilia [Leokadya] (Ophelia Lewicki; Tillie Leurtzke), Mrs. Leo, 30.

    Lewitzki, Jan (John Lewicki), 4.

Liening (Rivy), Elisabeth, 20, single, laborer, WE. Concordia Cemetery.

Locke, Adolph M., 19, single, electrician, WE. Mt. Olive Cemetery.

Lockey, John W., 22, single, switchboard mechanic, WE. Mt. Carmel Cemetery.

Loftgren, Esther, 19, single, clerk, WE. Elmwood Cemetery.

Lohr, Frances, 32, single, cable wire worker, WE. Bohemian National Cemetery.

Lukens, Barbara, Mrs. William T., Jr., 32. Buried in Fullersburg, Ill.

Lungerschausen, Lillian, 22, single, machine operator, WE. Forest Home Cemetery.

Lynch, John E., 23, single, switchboard inspector, WE. Mt. Carmel Cemetery.

Lyons, John J., 37, married, foreman, WE. Buried in Northampton, Mass.

    Lyons, Thomas, 3.

Maciejewski, Angela (Nellie), 17, single, does housework. Resurrection Cemetery.

Magnuson, Sigrid, Mrs. Edward, 28. Rosehill Cemetery.

    Magnuson, Irene E., 3.

    Magnuson, Robert C., 4.

Mahr, Josephine, 19, single, WE. St. Adalbert's Cemetery.

Malecha, Julia C., 19, single, time clerk, WE. Bohemian National Cemetery.

Malik, Mary, 21, single, WE. Resurrection Cemetery.

    Malik, Stella, 17, sister of Mary, single, WE.

Maniak, Anton, 19, single, laborer, WE. St. Adalbert's Cemetery.

Mankowski, Jan (John), 61, male, married, laborer. St. Adalbert's Cemetery.

Mann, Margaret Anna, 17, single, clerk, WE. Forest Home Cemetery.

Manthey, Mary, 22, single, dressmaker. Concordia Cemetery.

Maranz, Louis, 21, single, WE. Forest Home Cemetery.

Mares, Otto, 20, single, baker. Bohemian National Cemetery.

Markowski, Josephine, 20, single, WE. St. Adalbert's Cemetery.

Marsik, Emma, 19, single, winder, WE. Bohemian National Cemetery.

Martin, Mary, Mrs. Louis, 40. Forest Home Cemetery.

Marton, Paul, 37, married, cabinet maker, WE. Bohemian National Cemetery.

    Marton, Paul, Jr., 12.

Marvin, Emma, 19, single, accountant, WE. St. Adalbert's Cemetery.

Mathieson, Isabella C., 23, single, cable dept., WE. Oak Ridge Cemetery.

Mayer, Emma, 21, single, machinist's helper, WE. Bohemian National Cemetery.

Mayer, George, 29, married, machinist, WE. Mt. Auburn Cemetery.

    Mayer, Muriel, 5.

McCrory, Edna, 5, niece of Agnes J. Olsen. Mt. Olive Cemetery.

    McCrory, Mildred, 3, sister of Edna.

McGinley, Richard G., 40, married, WE. Wheaton Cemetery.

McGlynn, Marie, 22, single, stenographer, WE. Buried in New York, N.Y.

McKenna, Mary, 19, single, clerk, WE[?]. Mt. Carmel Cemetery.

McLaren, Mary, 22, single, clerk, WE. Calvary Cemetery.

McMahon, John Joseph, 18, single, electrician, WE. Mt.Carmel Cemetery.

Medrzycki (Mendriski), Stanislaus J., 30, electrician, WE. Resurrection Cemetery.

Meicke, Anna, 21, single, clerk, WE. Concordia Cemetery.

Menges, Charles W., 40, married, electrician, WE. Buried in Milwaukee, Wis.

Menth, Joseph, 55, elevator operator. Resurrection Cemetery.

    Menth, Katherine, Mrs. Joseph, 53.

Mertz, Lillian, 18, single, tailoring. Bohemian National Cemetery.

Meyer, Emma, 21, single, clerk in candy factory. Oak Ridge Cemetery.

Meyer, Harold L., 22, single, machinist, WE. Mt. Olive Cemetery.

Michaelis (Mitchell), Edna, 18, single, file clerk, WE. Concordia Cemetery.

Michalska, Stanislawa (Stella), 19, single, coil winder, WE. St. Adalbert's Cemetery.

Mielczarski, Hedwig (Edith), 20, single, WE. St. Joseph Cemetery.

Mietlicka, Johanna (Anna), 35, married, WE. St. Adalbert's Cemetery.

Mohn, Inga, Mrs. Finn, 54. Mt. Olive Cemetery.

Moldt, Rose Frances, 17, single, insulating lamps, WE. St. Joseph Cemetery.

Montgomery, Eva Elizabeth, 26, single, WE. Oak Hill Cemetery.

Mootz, Joseph, 20, single, shipping clerk in shoe factory. St. Boniface Cemetery.

Moran, Catherine, 22, single, clerk, WE. Mt. Carmel Cemetery.

    Moran, Nellie, 18, sister of Catherine, single, messenger, WE.

Moreau, Edward, 20, single, electric wireman, WE. Mt. Carmel Cemetery.

Morgan, Margaret N., 18, single, file clerk, WE. Oak Ridge Cemetery.

Morizmeier, Edward, 17, single, messenger boy, WE. Concordia Cemetery.

Mosna, Katerina, Mrs. Jan, 50. Bohemian National Cemetery.

    Mosna, Bohumil, 17, single, WE.

    Mosna, Rose, 21, single, WE.

Moynihan, Catherine, 31, single, WE. Mt. Olivet Cemetery.

    Moynihan, Hanora (Norah), 25, sister of Catherine, single, WE.

Mueller, William R., 32, married, clerk, WE. Concordia Cemetery.

Muense, Rose, 17, single, worked at home. Eden Cemetery.

Mulac, Julia, 24, single, book binder. Bohemian National Cemetery.

    Mulac, Lillian, 21, sister of Julia, single, clerk, WE.

Murawski, John, 24, single, asst. foreman, WE. Resurrection Cemetery.

Murphy, David M., 25, electrician, WE. Mt. Olivet Cemetery.

    Murphy, Mary, Mrs. David M., 22, cable dept., WE.

Myszkowska, Anna, 17, single, WE. Resurrection Cemetery.

Nadenik, Ervan, 18, single, boilermaker, contractor. Bohemian National Cemetery.

Nagel, Elsie, 22, single, counting room, WE. Waldheim Cemetery.

Nagel (Lipsky), Irwin, 20, single, WE. Concordia Cemetery.

    Nagel, Margaret, 17, sister of Irwin, single, WE.

Nelson, August, 37, single, electrician, WE. Rosehill Cemetery.

Nelson, Emil, 23, single, WE. Mt. Auburn Cemetery.

Nepras, Mildred, 23, single, tailor, Kadlec & Son. Bohemian National Cemetery.

Neumann, Lillian (Lillie), 21, single, embroidery, WE. Oak Ridge Cemetery.

Nosek, Vlasta, 22, single. Bohemian National Cemetery.

Novak, Anton J., 20, single, plumber. Bohemian National Cemetery.

Novotny, James, 33, married, cabinet maker, WE. Bohemian National Cemetery.

> Novotny, Agnes, Mrs. James, 35.
>
> Novotny, Mamie, 9.
>
> Novotny, William, 7.

Nowaczyk, Eva, 21, single, WE. Resurrection Cemetery.

Nowak, Francisza (Frances), 19, single, WE. St. Adalbert's Cemetery.

> Nowak, Floryan (Florian), 15, brother of Francisza, employee of Henry Friend.

Nowakowski, Piotr (Peter Waszko), 40, married, machinist, WE. St. Adalbert's Cemetery.

Nyka, Angelina, 20, single, examiner of cords, WE. Resurrection Cemetery.

O'Donnell, Catherine, 20, single, office. Mt. Carmel Cemetery.

Oerter, Rose Brenner, 28, widow, electric spools, WE. St. Boniface Cemetery.

Olbinski, Clara Miller, Mrs. John, 26, WE. All Saints Parish Cemetery.

Olsen, Agnes J., 24, aunt of Edna and Mildred McCrory, single, comptometer operator, WE. Mt. Olive Cemetery.

Olson, John Gotfried (Godfrey), 51, married, blacksmith, WE. Graceland Cemetery.

Olson, Margaret, 24, single, inspector, WE. Forest Home Cemetery.

O'Neill, Margaret, 22, single, clerk. Mt. Carmel Cemetery.

Orbes, Eleanor, 16, single, WE. Free Sons of Israel Cemetery.

O'Reilly, Patrick J., 20, single, laborer, WE. Calvary Cemetery.

Osen, Pearl, 21, single, WE. Mt. Auburn Cemetery.

> Osen, Ethel, 18, sister of Pearl, single, typist, WE.

O'Shaughnessy, Margaret E., 20, single, WE. Mt. Carmel Cemetery.

Ostrowski, Martha, 18, single, Leffer Candy Co. Bethania Cemetery.

Padrta (Paderta), James, 23, single, cab driver. Bohemian National Cemetery.

Palacz, Frank, 29, single, WE. Resurrection Cemetery.

Pansegrau, Ewald A., 19, single, clerk, Acme Steel. Bethania Cemetery.

Parkowski, Piotr (Peter Weth), 40, married, WE. St. Adalbert's Cemetery.

Parminter, Thomas W., 50, WE. Mt. Auburn Cemetery.

> Parminter, Anna, 16, daughter of Thomas W.

Parucka, Caroline M., 22, single, inspector, WE. Resurrection Cemetery.

Patnoe, Raymond H., 23, single, day superintendent, WE. Mt. Carmel Cemetery.

Patrunky, Anna, 22, single, WE. Waldheim Cemetery.

> Patrunky, Martha, 20, sister of Anna, single.

Pavletich, Joseph J., 24, single, plumber. Forest Home Cemetery.

> Pavletich, Marion, 17, sister of Joseph, single, stenographer.

Payne, James H., Jr., 21, single, boxmaker. Calvary Cemetery.

Pecha, Albert, Jr., 20, laborer, WE. Bohemian National Cemetery.

Pelmar, Mary, 17, single. St. Adalbert's Cemetery.

Perich, Thomas, 36, married, WE. Resurrection Cemetery.

Pesch, Anna, 21, single, WE. St. Boniface Cemetery.

Pesek, Martha, 20, single, WE. Bohemian National Cemetery.

Peternell, Joseph, 28, single, inspector, WE. St. Joseph Cemetery.

Petersen, Charles Andrew, Jr., 11. Mt. Olive Cemetery.

Petersen, Niels (Nelson) Rasmus, 46, married, foreman, WE. Oak Ridge Cemetery.

> Petersen, Viola Harriet, Mrs. Niels.

> Petersen, Royal, 4.

Peterson, Martha K., 22, single, tester, WE. Forest Home Cemetery.

Peterson, Ruta (Ruth), 8. Graceland Cemetery.

Petrik, Joseph L., 24, single, printer. Bohemian National Cemetery.

Petrik, Karel (Charles) L., 16, single, plaster contractor. St. Adalbert's Cemetery.

Pfeiffer, Martha, 19, single, servant. Bethania Cemetery.

Picard, Gildia Marie, Mrs. S. J., 28, machine operator, WE. Mt. Carmel Cemetery.

Pichas, Amelie, 19, single, WE. Bohemian National Cemetery.

Pierce, Charles F., 46, married, electrician, foreman, WE. Mt. Olive Cemetery.

Pierson, Albert, 37, married, steamfitter, WE. Oak Ridge Cemetery. [This man's death certificate is made out for Alexander Pearson. The cemetery record and all other sources show him as Albert Pierson.]

Pilarski, Jan (Thomas), 23, single, machinist, WE. St. Adalbert's Cemetery.

Pinkall, Edna Will, 16, married. Concordia Cemetery.

Piotrowski, Walter, 31, married, electrician, WE. St. Adalbert's Cemetery.

Pisano, Martino, 23, married, stock keeper, WE. Mt. Carmel Cemetery.

Pittelkow, Helen, 21, single, laborer. Concordia Cemetery.

Pivko, Mathes (Mike), 40, married, janitor, WE. Bohemian National Cemetery.

Plachitka, William, 18, single, clerk, WE. St. Adalbert's Cemetery.

Placzek, Wladislawa (Lottie; Lucy Fillips), 21, single, electrician, WE. St. Adalbert's Cemetery.

Plamondon, Susan Byrne, Mrs. Edwin K., 42. Mt. Carmel Cemetery.

Plocharczyk, Joseph, 30, single, WE. Resurrection Cemetery.

Poch, May, 19, single, WE. Resurrection Cemetery.

Poleta, Frank J., 25, married, foreman, WE. Bohemian National Cemetery.

Potter, Bessie, 29, single, manicurist. Buried in Carlyle, Ill.

Powlowski, Martin, 41, married, gas dept., WE. Resurrection Cemetery.

Pozesky, Martha, 17, single. Mt. Auburn Cemetery.

Prochniewski (Pronesky), Helen, 15, single, bookkeeper, WE. Concordia Cemetery.

Prochnow, Lillian, 18, cousin of Alma Zielske, single, laundress. Concordia Cemetery.

Prugert, Robert J., 26, single, musician. Oak Ridge Cemetery.

Psynko, Michael, 41, married, WE. Resurrection Cemetery.

Punicka, Marya (Mamie Ponicki), 18, single, office worker, Sears, Roebuck & Co. St. Adalbert's Cemetery.

Putz, Mary, Mrs. Joseph, 35, probably sister-in-law of Rose Cmucha. Mt. Carmel Cemetery.

Quaine, Anna, 18, sister of Margaret Belle Cooney, single, clerk, mail order house. Buried in Emmett, Mich.

Quinn, Anna E., 22, single, clerk, WE. Mt. Carmel Cemetery.

Quwas, Martha, 19, single, WE. Concordia Cemetery.

Rackow, Elizabeth, 8, granddaughter of Augusta Wieser. Concordia Cemetery.

Radoll, Louise M., 25, covering wire, WE. Concordia Cemetery.

Rakowski, Wladyslaw (Frank), 46, married, janitor, WE. Resurrection Cemetery.

Redlich, Adolph, 18, single, clerk, WE. Wunders Cemetery.

Rehak, Blanche, 20, stenographer, WE. Bohemian National Cemetery.

Rehor, Frank, 20, single, clerk, WE. Bohemian National Cemetery.

Reidl, Mary, 21, single, WE. Bohemian National Cemetery.

Reidl, Ruzena (Rose), 19, sister of Mary, single, WE.

Reinhardt, Elsie, 18, single, WE. Concordia Cemetery.

Reis, Sophia, 20, single, spooling. St. Joseph Cemetery.

Reitinger, Anna, 15, clerk, WE. St. Mary's Cemetery.

Remy, Ella, 27, single. Buried in Grovers Mills, N.J.

Remy, Florence, 19, sister of Ella, single, clerk, WE.

Richten, George P., 29, single, WE. Buried in Fairview, N.J.

Riker, Robert J. T., 13. Mt. Auburn Cemetery.

Rimnac, Ladislaw (Laddy, Jerry) [Lang Rinnar], 22, single, plugs, WE. Resurrection Cemetery.

Ristow, William F., 30, married, WE. Waldheim Cemetery.

Ristow, Herman A., Jr., 25, brother of William F., single, WE.

Robel, Morris W., 20, single, foreman, WE. Graceland Cemetery.

Robinson, Thomas, 22, single, machinist, WE. Mt. Carmel Cemetery.

Roche, William David, 25, single, steamfitter's helper. Mt. Carmel Cemetery.

Roglin, Mary E., 20, single, stenographer, WE. Mt. Carmel Cemetery.

Rohn, Clara, 19, single, WE. Concordia Cemetery.

    Rohn, Lydia, 16, sister of Clara, single, examiner, tailor shop.

Rohse, Lillian, 21, bench hand, WE. Oak Ridge Cemetery.

    Rohse, Ella A. W., 19, sister of Lillian, single, waitress.

Roser, Minnie Engelbrecht, Mrs. George W., 44. Concordia Cemetery.

Rossow, Ralph A., 19, single, dry goods clerk. Concordia Cemetery.

Rossow, William A., 38, married, foreman, WE. Concordia Cemetery.

    Rossow, Mamie, Mrs. William A., 36.

    Rossow, Ruth, 14.

    Rossow, William A., Jr., 6.

Roth, Ella, 19, single, WE. Bohemian National Cemetery.

Rozycka, Monika, 23, single, operated candy store. St. Adalbert's Cemetery.

Rucinskaite, Juozefa (Josephine Roshinski), 18, single, WE. St. Casimir's Cemetery.

Rudczka, Bronislawa (Blanche Rudcki), 20, single, ex-WE. Resurrection Cemetery.

Rudin, Fern Lee Garland, Mrs. Oliver Wendell, 23. Buried in Lafayette, Ind.

Rudolph (Kourim), Anna, 26, single, telephone operator, WE. Bohemian National Cemetery.

Rupp, William J., 25, single, clerk, WE. Buried in Elizabeth, N.J.

Rusch, Elsie, 22, single, WE. Waldheim Cemetery.

Rutvki, Bronislawa, 20, single, WE. Resurrection Cemetery.

Rylands, Minnie Miller, Mrs. James, 27. Forest Home Cemetery.

Rynarzewski, Rozalia (Rose Rynar), 21, single, seamstress, Hart, Schaffner & Marx. Resurrection Cemetery.

Sagenbrecht, Frank, 22, single, Armour & Co. Waldheim Cemetery.

Salak, Fannie, Mrs. John. Resurrection Cemetery.

Sallmann, Ella, 16, single. Concordia Cemetery.

Sallwasser, John R., 47, married. Mt. Auburn Cemetery.

Samec, Marie. St. Adalbert's Cemetery.

Samek, Emma, 17, fiancée of William Sherry, single, WE. Bohemian National Cemetery.

Schaefer, Edwin M., 17, single, WE. Calvary Cemetery.

Schank, Gustav, Jr., 24, single, assembler, WE. Forest Home Cemetery.

Schiff, Ludwig, 16, single, machine hand, WE. Mt. Auburn Cemetery.

Schlentz, Gabrielle (Ella), 20, single, accountant, WE. St. Joseph Cemetery.

Schmelz, Edward J., single. Oakwoods Cemetery.

Schmidt, George E., 22, single, Canadian. Buried in Baden, Ontario.

Schmidt, Louise, 19, fiancée of Edward Selig, single, WE. Concordia Cemetery.

Schmidt (Smith), Myrtle, single. Rosehill Cemetery.

Schmidt (Smith), Sophia, 28, single, WE. St. Joseph Cemetery.

Schneider, George C., 42, married, WE. Buried in New York, N.Y.

    Schneider, Emma [Anna], Mrs. George.

    Schneider, Leslie, 9.

Schnell, Carolina (Carrie), single, WE. St. Boniface Cemetery.

Schnorr, Nellie, Mrs. John, 32, widow, boarding house keeper. Cemetery not reported.

Schoenholz, Adolphina, Mrs. William, 55. Waldheim Cemetery.

Schoenke, Alma, 25, single. Concordia Cemetery.

Schreiber, Joseph, 48, single, painter, WE. Mt. Carmel Cemetery.

Schroeder, Antoinette (Nettie) Octzel, Mrs. Charles. Mt. Olivet Cemetery.

    Schroeder, Carl A., infant son of Antoinette.

Schroll, Julius, 32, WE. Bohemian National Cemetery.

    Schroll, Emma Staker, Mrs. Julius, 30, sister of Anna and Pauline Staker, WE.

Schroth, Dora, 23, sister of Caroline Affeld, single, polisher, WE. Buried in Frankfort, Ill.

Schuette, Henry, 28, WE. Concordia Cemetery.

Schultz, John S., 23, Chicago City Railways conductor. St. Adalbert's Cemetery.

    Schultz, Veronika (Verna), Mrs. John S., 25.

    Schultz, Edward J., 17 months only.

Schultz, Sabina Melvin, Mrs. Joseph, 20. Mt. Carmel Cemetery.

Sedlacek, Bessie, 17, single, WE. Cemetery not reported.

Seip, Helena E. (Lena), 16, single, winding coils, WE. Cemetery not reported.

Selig, Bertha, 45, married or widow. Concordia Cemetery.

    Selig, Edward, 19, fiancé of Louise Schmidt, single, WE.

    Selig, Frank, 26, single.

Shannon, Nannie, 33, single, WE. Oak Ridge Cemetery.

Sheridan, Catherine, 21, single, WE. Cemetery not reported.

Sherlock, Nellie Carney. Cemetery not reported.

Sherry, William, 22, fiancé of Emma Samek, single, Metropolitan Elevated trainman. Bohemian National Cemetery.

Sieczkarski [Sieczkowski] (Sarkarska, Sager), Josephine, 21, single. St. Adalbert's Cemetery.

Siedlecka, Frances. Cemetery not reported.

Siegmann, Wilhelm (William) M., 25, single. St. Joseph Cemetery.

Sierazek, Joseph, 28, single, cabinet maker, WE. Eden Cemetery.

Sierazek, Mary, Mrs. Theodore, 28, sister-in-law of Joseph.

Silha, Lillian (Belle), Mrs. Jacob, 23. Bohemian National Cemetery.

Simmons, Leslie Elliot, 20, photographer, WE. Cemetery not reported.

Sims, Neville George, 31, foreman, WE. Waldheim Cemetery.

Sims, Estella (Stella), Mrs. Neville George, 23.

Sindelar, George Albert, married, WE. Bohemian National Cemetery.

Sindelar, Josephine, Mrs. George, sister of Regina Dolezal.

Sindelar, Adella.

Sindelar, Albert.

Sindelar, George, Jr.

Sindelar, Sylvia.

Sindelar, William, Jr.

Sivickis, Boleslovas, 40, married, WE. St. Casimir's Cemetery.

Skala, Bertha, Mrs. Edward, 38. Cemetery not reported.

Skala, Edwin, 9.

Skala, Helen, 17.

Sklenicka, Jaroslav (Jerry), 40, foreman, WE. Cemetery not reported.

Sladek, Bessie, 20, single, WE. Cemetery not reported.

Sladek, Mamie, 18, sister of Bessie, single, WE.

Slowinski, Roman, 26, single, WE. Resurrection Cemetery.

Smith, Margaret, 20, single. Forest Home Cemetery.

Smola, Frank, 44, married, supt. of maintenance, WE. Bohemian National Cemetery.

Soderstrom, Minnie, Mrs. Theodore A., 33. Oakwoods Cemetery.

Soderstrom, Stanley, 10.

Sosnowska (Keeran), Hattie, 23, single. Resurrection Cemetery.

Soukup, William, 18, probably brother of Anna Soukup Forst, single. Bohemian National Cemetery.

Squillace, Ernest, 17, single, cabinetmaker, WE. Cemetery not reported.

Sramek, Bosina (Bessie), 19, single, typist, WE. Cemetery not reported.

Stack, Marie, 24, single, WE. Mt. Carmel Cemetery.

Stahlik, Karol (Charles), 24, single, WE. Cemetery not reported.

Staker, Anna, 22, sister of Emma Schroll, single, WE. Bohemian National Cemetery.

Staker, Pauline, 19, sister of Anna, single, WE.

Stamm, Anna N., Mrs. Edward, 63, mother of Cora May Hipple. Waldheim Cemetery.

Steffen, Hattie, 25, single, WE. Concordia Cemetery.

Stejskal, Josephine, 16, single, timekeeper, WE. Cemetery not reported.

Stekelon, Helena, 22. Resurrection Cemetery.

Stender, Martha, 19, single. Waldheim Cemetery.

Stenson, James, 21, single, asst. purser, *Eastland*. Mt. Carmel Cemetery.

Stephenson, Willis F., 12. Arlington Cemetery.

Stevens, Grace W., 24, single, WE. Buried in Rockton, Ill.

Stork, Gertrude, 15, single. Waldheim Cemetery.

Straan, Grace, 15. Resurrection Cemetery.

Stranc, Katarzyna (Kate), 22, single, WE. St. Adalbert's Cemetery.

Strauss, Lottie, 19, fiancée of Fred Wittforth, single. Resurrection Cemetery.

Streit, Jenny, 24, single. Bohemian National Cemetery.

Struszyna, Victor, 21, single, WE. Cemetery not reported.

Stump, Mary. Cemetery not reported.

Suchwalko, Jacob, 19, single, WE. Cemetery not reported.

Suerth, Nicholas H., 42, married, WE. St. Boniface Cemetery.

Sullivan (Scully), Mary Elizabeth, 23, single, WE. Cemetery not reported.

Sulzman, Catherine, Mrs. Arthur. Buried in New York, N.Y.

Swanson, Arthur J., 24, single, planning dept., WE. Mt. Olivet Cemetery.

Swedin, John, 47, married, foreman, WE. Montrose Cemetery.

Switala, Benedicta (Bessie), 24, stepsister of Eva Wodtke, single. Cemetery not reported.

Sykes, William T., 35, married, WE. Mt. Auburn Cemetery.

    Sykes, Harry D., 10.

    Sykes, Margaret, 6.

Szalacinski, Mieczyslaw (Matthew), 17, single, office boy, WE. Resurrection Cemetery.

Szymanska, Josephine, 17, single, WE. St. Adalbert's Cemetery.

Taube, Herbert, 24, single, WE. Concordia Cemetery.

Techajar, Albert, 20, single. Bohemian National Cemetery.

Teichmiller, Clara, 18, single, clerk, WE. Buried in Muscatine, Iowa.

Tempinska, Anna, 20, single, winding coils, WE. St. Adalbert's Cemetery.

Theede, George, 16, single, apprentice, WE. Concordia Cemetery.

Theis, Klara (Clara), 22, single, WE. St. Adalbert's Cemetery.

    Theis, Agnieszka (Agnes), 17, sister of Klara, single.

Thiel, Louise R., Mrs. Roy C., 28. Mt. Olive Cemetery.

Thomas, Rose, 21, single, inspector, WE. St. Joseph Cemetery.

Thommen, Caroline (Lena), 20, single, saleslady. Bethania Cemetery.

    Thommen, Emma, 16, sister of Caroline, single, WE.

Thompson, Louise M., 19, single, cashier of Racklio's Restaurant, WE. Concordia Cemetery.

Thoresen, Leif Edward, 18, single, clerk, WE. Mt. Olive Cemetery.

Thyer, Henry H., 36, married, clerk, WE. Forest Home Cemetery.

    Thyer, Helen M., 9.

Tiedemann, Emily, Mrs. Henry, 42. Bethania Cemetery.

    Tiedemann, Arthur, 17, single, WE.

Tismer, Elizabeth, 24, single, examiner, WE. These four siblings were buried in St. Lucas Cemetery.

    Tismer, Ernest, 18, single, bookkeeper.

    Tismer, Herbert, 14.

    Tismer, Minnie, 16, single, trimmer, tailor shop.

Toellet, Herman, 23, single, electrician, WE. Oakwoods Cemetery.

Toman, Bessie, 17, single, operator, WE. Bohemian National Cemetery.

Tonnesen, George Livingston, 24, single, clerk, WE. Graceland Cemetery.

Tranckitella, Frank, musician on *Eastland*. Mt. Carmel Cemetery. [This man's death certificate reads "Franckitella," an apparent error.]

Traznik, Ella, 20, single, WE. Bohemian National Cemetery.

Trh, Bertha, 24, single. Bohemian National Cemetery.

Trogg, Charles W., 46, married, assembler, WE. Concordia Cemetery.

    Trogg, Katherine, Mrs. Charles W., 31.

Tseuko, Michael, 42, married, laborer, WE. Resurrection Cemetery.

Turek, Albert, 31, single, bench hand, WE. Bohemian National Cemetery.

Turek, John E., 34, married, machinist, WE. Resurrection Cemetery.

    Turek, Alma, 10.

    Turek, Edna, 8.

Uebel, John, 38, married, cabinet maker, WE. Montrose Cemetery.

Uldrych, Jan (John), 19, single, WE. Bohemian National Cemetery.

Urban (Nat), Anna, 19, single, laborer, WE. Bohemian National Cemetery.

Urbanowicz, Zigmund (Sigmund Urban), 18, single, WE. St. Adalbert's Cemetery.

Uren, Philip, 19, single, electrical worker, WE. Forest Home Cemetery.

Valchar, Joseph, 44, married, wood finisher, WE. Bohemian National Cemetery.

Valentine, Estella (Estelle Decker), 20, single, embroiderer. Mt. Olive Cemetery.

Varela, Sylvia Eva, 14. Mt. Auburn Cemetery.

Vavra, Frank, 20, single, clerk, WE. Bohemian National Cemetery.

Velan, Frank, Jr., 24, single, machinist, ex-WE. Bohemian National Cemetery.

    Velan, Ella, 15, sister of Frank.

Vlasak, Josef F., 21, single, inspector, WE. St. Adalbert's Cemetery.

Vlasak, Mary, 24, single, WE. Bohemian National Cemetery.

Vogel, Christian, 25, single, WE. Mt. Greenwood Cemetery.

Volsonsky, Frank, 22, single, machinist, WE. Bohemian National
Cemetery.
Wahl (Graebner), Emily H., 33, single, clerk, WE. Mt. Olive Cemetery.
Warren, Theresa, Mrs. Edward, 22. Mt. Auburn Cemetery.
> Warren, Viola, 3.
Warren, Thomas F., 19, single, WE. Mt. Carmel Cemetery.
Wastak, Jan (John), 28, single, WE. St. Adalbert's Cemetery.
Weichbrodt, Albert Z., 19, single, switchboard dept., WE. Concordia
Cemetery.
Weinesfelder, Hattie, Mrs. William, 45. Mt. Auburn Cemetery.
Weinschenk, Edward, 49, married, trimmer, WE. Eden Cemetery.
Wellestat, Lydia C., 21, single, clerk, WE. Mt. Hope Cemetery.
Wesemann, Carie A., 18, single, WE. St. Lucas Cemetery.
Wichtendahl, Walter W., 24, married, special police. Concordia Cemetery.
Widran, Samuel E., 29, married, auditor, WE. Forest Home Cemetery.
Wielgosz, Thomasz (Thomas Wielgos), 17, single, WE. St. Adalbert's
Cemetery.
Wieser, Augusta, 65, grandmother of Elizabeth Rackow, widow. Concor-
dia Cemetery.
Wilkens, John Henry, 42, married, cabinet maker, WE. Elmwood
Cemetery.
Wilkinson, John Edward, 24, married, clerk, WE. Mt. Carmel Cemetery.
Will, Clara, 18, single, WE. Concordia Cemetery.
Winski, Leonard, 22, single, bookkeeper, Chicago *Examiner*. Buried in
Spring Valley, Ill.
Wittforth, Fred, Jr., 21, fiancé of Lottie Strauss, single, electrician, WE.
Bethania Cemetery.
Wodtke, Eva, 26, stepsister of Benedicta Switala, printing shop. St. Adal-
bert's Cemetery.
Wolf, Lulu Clerer, Mrs. Charles, 32. Jewish Waldheim Cemetery.
Woller, Henry C., 17, single, WE. Forest Home Cemetery.
Wood, Catherine (Kitty) E., Mrs. George John, 22. Mt. Carmel Cemetery.
> Wood, George John, Jr.
Wrobel, Thomasz (Thomas), 23, married, punch presser, WE. St. Adal-
bert's Cemetery.
Wroblewski, Jacob, 34, married, machinist, WE. Buried in Lemont, Ill.
> Wroblewska, Marie, 4.
Zajicek, George, 24, single, timekeeper, WE. Bohemian National
Cemetery.
Zak, Emil T. (Edward T. Zack), 37, married, clerk, WE. Bohemian Na-
tional Cemetery.
Zastera, Marie, 23, single, factory worker, WE. These three sisters were
buried in Bohemian National Cemetery.

Zastera, Antonie (Antonette), 20, single, factory worker, WE.

Zastera, Julie, 18, single, factory worker, WE.

Zdrojewska, Frances, 19, single, WE. Resurrection Cemetery.

Zeiss, Henry (Harry), 18, single, Chicago *Tribune*. Concordia Cemetery.

Zezerski, Mary, 23, single, bakery saleslady. St. Mary's Cemetery.

Zielske, Alma (Anna), 21, cousin of Lillian Prochnow, single, spring operator, WE. Concordia Cemetery.

Ziervogel, Emil, 30, married, storekeeper, WE. Concordia Cemetery.

Zimma, Josefa (Josephine), 17, single. St. Adalbert's Cemetery.

Zintak, Apolonia (Pauline Vantak, Mrs. Henry), 43. Resurrection Cemetery.

    Zintak, Helen (Leona Vantak), 15.

Zitt, Charles H., 23, single, machinist, WE. Mt. Olivet Cemetery.

Zobac, Edward J., 25, married, machinist, WE. Bohemian National Cemetery.

    Zobac, Anna, Mrs. Edward J., 24.

Zopke, Metha (Meta, Mayetta), 23, single. Concordia Cemetery.

    Zopke, Hedwig (Hattie), 20, sister of Metha, single, laborer.

Zuchowski, Klemens (Clements), 20, single, WE. St. Adalbert's Cemetery.

Victims Found in Cemetery Records

Fischer, Frederick George, 9 months. St. Mary's Cemetery.

Gustafson, Theodore, 27, single. Cremated at Graceland Cemetery.

Guziolek, Marya (Maryanna). Probably invalid; probably an error in the cemetery's interment record. St. Adalbert's Cemetery.

Jamieson, Charles. Rosehill Cemetery.

Roach, Thomas, 2. Mt. Carmel Cemetery.

Rudel, Stanislaw. St. Adalbert's Cemetery.

Slominski, Salomea (apparently her variant of Slowinski). Resurrection Cemetery.

Employees of Western Electric and Members of Their Families Reported Lost

These are names in Western Electric's list of employees and their families who died on the *Eastland* which are not included in the foregoing list, and not identifiable as variants of names of other deceased. They have been verified, if possible, in cemetery records. Western Electric's list is published in *Western Electric News*, 4, no. 6 (Aug. 1915), pp. 9–15.

Brady, Patrick, father of John Brady. Mt. Carmel Cemetery.

Carney, Nellie, 20, single, WE. Mt. Carmel Cemetery.

Cox, Bethel, single, sister of Mildred Cox, WE. Mt. Auburn Cemetery.

Fanret (Kesel), Mary, 19, single. St. Adalbert's Cemetery.

Gembora [Gembara], Anna, WE. Cemetery not reported.

Hipple, Ada W. Member of family of Cora May Hipple; exact relation unreported. Waldheim Cemetery.

Marecks, Mary, WE. [Address is that of Josephine Markowski.] Cemetery not reported.

Mejka, Josie Lipinski, Mrs. Adam, 23, WE. Resurrection Cemetery.

Streit, Ella, 18, single, sister of Jennie Streit. Bohemian National Cemetery.

   Streit, Emma, 17, sister of Jennie and Ella Streit, single, WE.

Wolf, John, WE. Cemetery not reported.

Zoumis, Peter, WE. Cemetery not reported.

Names Appearing Only as Estates

The following names appear in James F. Bishop's submission to the federal court in the civil case on July 22, 1916, as administrator of the estates of the deceased, and in the list of estates in Illinois House Bill 237 of 1917, but neither in the death certificates nor in any list of the dead following the disaster. The names may not be valid additions to the list of deceased for several reasons: they might be variants of names of authenticated deceased or names of assignees of the heirs of victims, or they may represent fraudulent efforts at collecting the death benefit. On the other hand they may be valid—they might be the names of persons who died subsequently of causes related to the disaster, or who belong on the list for other valid reasons.

Baldwin, Morris W. [May be Morris W. Robel.]

Clarke, Signa Sheelen. [Probably a relative of Marie E. Clarke, whose mother was Signa Johnson Anderson. There is no evidence of a person of this name in the disaster.]

Ignasiak, Agnes. [Mother of Anna and Antonett Ignasiak; reported survivor.]

Meicke, Edna. [May be Anna Meicke. Edna not identifiable.]

Poppas, Eleanora, Mrs. Tom. [Not identifiable with disaster.]

Names Reported in Newspapers
with a High Probability of Validity

The following, with the exception of Mrs. Albert Unterich and her son, Robert, are based on biographical accounts of the deceased in "In Memoriam: *Eastland* Victims," Chicago *Tribune*, July 31, 1915, pp. 13–17.

Mrs. Unterich and her son are included on the basis of an account in the Milwaukee *Journal*, July 25, 1915. Where possible, these names have been verified in cemetery records.

Betrich (Betrik), John, 20. Bohemian National Cemetery.

Foreman, Henry W., widower, WE. Cemetery not reported.

Hilles, John. Cemetery not reported, probably not in Chicago area.

Ingenzo, Antonette, 27, married. Cemetery not reported.

Meyer, Nellie, 17, single, medical-dental assistant. Resurrection Cemetery.

Schnierle, Mamie, 23, single. Mt. Hope Cemetery.

Smarzk, Mary. Cemetery not reported.

Unterich, Mrs. Albert, 29. Cemetery not reported, probably in Milwaukee, Wis.

Unterich, Robert.

Questionable Identifications

Mainly in newspaper lists published immediately after the disaster are a large number of names of victims that cannot be substantiated by death certificate, entry in the Coroner's Inquest Record, cemetery records, or other credible sources, but that cannot be rejected as duplicative of the names of actual deceased. The newspapers from which they are drawn are the Chicago *Tribune, Examiner*, and *Evening Post*, the Detroit *News* and *Free Press*, the Milwaukee *Journal*, and the New York *Times*, all between July 24 and 29, 1915. Some names may be of actual victims which were not picked up in other lists. Some are probably alternate or garbled versions of the names of actual victims, and others are probably of people who were originally reported dead but who actually survived. Several people who appear in early newspaper lists of victims are known to have survived: Edward Arko, Mary Gunderlock, Eddie Gunderson, Cecelia Leline, Otto Leu, William Menth, Mary Muzarawski, and George J. Wood, Sr. Because less than half the survivors reported themselves to the police, it is highly likely that others are in this category. Because I have endeavored to err on the side of exclusion from the list of probable victims in newspaper accounts immediately above, some of the names in this list are probably valid.

Adams, George. [Probably the late father of Kathryn Allen.]

Adams, K., female, single. [Probably Kathryn Allen.]

Adams, Martha.

Adams, Mary.

Alexander,—, male, WE.

Anderson, Albert.

Anderson, Catherine.

Anderson, Ida.

Larson, Ella, 19.

Leaks, Jack.

Lemtage, Emily. [Probably Emily Lemke.]

Lo, Georgine.

Lomlewicz, Mamie.

Lovett,—. [Probably Petronele Laurinaciute.]

Maloney, Thomas, 44.

Mayer, Morris. [Probably Muriel.]

Mejka, Grace. [Probably Josie.]

Menth, William.

Miller, John.

Montgomery, Alexander.

Nusckofski, Anna. [Probably Anna Myszkowska.]

Ocea, L.

Offerin, Mrs. C. W.

O'Reilly, Catharine.

Osterhott, Iona, 22.

Praznick, Walter.

Press, Martha.

Reidl, Paul, 19.

Robel, Minnie. [Probably Morris W. Robel.]

Rominski, Maurice.

Rose, Edna.

Rose, Thomas, 28. [Probably Rose Thomas.]

Roser, Philip.

Rowells, Michael, 54.

Sage, H. A., 10.

Saxe, A. J., 26.

Schaeffer, Mabel.

Schintz, J. [Probably John S. Schultz.]

Schollo, Frank, WE. [Probably Schroll.]

Schollo, Mrs. Frank. [Probably Schroll.]

Schriezyer [Shriezyn, Spriezyn, Shriodyn], Frank, 28.

Schwartz, Mrs. John. [Probably Veronika Schultz.]

Seidl, Rose. [Probably Rose Reidl.]

Semocsin [Semoism], William.

Sevecski, William.

Sheldon, Hattie, married.

Sinkow, Marie. [The *Tribune* published a photograph of this woman as one of the deceased on July 26, 1915. She has no other documentation.]

Slieck, M. O. [May be Emil Flicek.]

Smith, D. Ray.

Smith, Mary.

Stranc, Simon.

Strogl, Jule. [Probably Schroll.]

Strogl, Mrs. Jule. [Probably Schroll.]

Swanson, Margaret [Mary], 18.

Tannor, Mrs.—.

Timmel, A. J.

Thomas, Ella.

Thomas, Eva.

Vasenowski,—, female.

Vasenowski, J.

Verilla, Anna, 20, married.

Wertel, Anna, 24.

Yokushetz, Agnes.

Zwoclan [Gezosolg], Alma.

Thomas E. Golembiewski on the basis of search of the Chicago Polish-language press has ascertained that Walter Praznick, above, was Waclaw Prajnik, 17, a *bona fide* victim of the disaster. Cemetery not reported.

Notes

Prologue

1. Colin Carmichael, "Was *Titanic* Unsafe at Any Speed?" *Steamboat Bill: Journal of the Steamship Historical Society of America*, no. 121 (1972): 5–10.

2. John P. Eaton and Charles A. Haas, *"Titanic": Triumph and Tragedy* (New York: W. W. Norton & Co., 1986), p. 137.

3. This is the view of Wyn Craig Wade in his *The "Titanic": End of a Dream* (New York: Penguin Books, 1980), p. 253.

4. On the inappropriateness of Murdoch's command, see Carmichael, "Was *Titanic* Unsafe at Any Speed?"; K. C. Barnaby, O.B.E., *Some Ship Disasters and Their Causes* (South Brunswick, N.J.: A. S. Barnes & Co., 1970), pp. 102–21; Wade, *The "Titanic,"* p. 253.

5. Barnaby, *Some Ship Disasters and Their Causes*, p. 102. Charles Haas and John P. Eaton believe on the basis of their research on the *Titanic* that the watertight bulkheads were higher than this. By the specification sheets under which she was built, the bulkheads rose 42 feet from the bottom of the hull. This would have brought them to seven or eight feet above the waterline. Letter from John P. Eaton to the author, Oct. 3, 1992.

6. Barnaby, *Some Ship Disasters and Their Causes*, pp. 105–7, 116; Sir Westcott Abell, K.B.E., *The Safe Sea* (Liverpool: The Journal of Commerce, 1932), p. 196.

7. Abell, *The Safe Sea*, p. 196.

8. Ibid., pp. 193–94.

9. "The *Titanic* Judgement and the Advisory Committee's Report," *Marine Engineer and Naval Architect*, 35 (1912–13): 35–36.

10. Data from John P. Eaton, Appendix 3 in A *"Titanic" Time Line* (unpub-

lished; copyright 1991 by John P. Eaton; all rights reserved). Cf. Barnaby, *Some Ship Disasters and Their Causes*, p. 114.

11. Abell, *The Safe Sea*, p. 195.

12. Ibid., p. 194.

13. John Carroll Carrothers, "The *Titanic* Disaster," *United States Naval Institute Proceedings*, 88, no. 4 (Apr. 1962): 57.

14. Barnaby, *Some Ship Disasters and Their Causes*, p. 116.

15. Wreck Commissioner's Court, *Formal Investigation of the Loss of the S.S. "Titanic,"* Evidence, appendixes, and index (London: His Majesty's Stationery Office, 1912), Q. 23,075, p. 599.

16. Ibid., Q. 23,081, p. 600.

17. *Syren & Shipping Illustrated*, 63 (1912): 90.

18. "White Star Liner *Olympic*: Structural Alterations," *Marine Engineer and Naval Architect*, 35 (1912–13): 382–83.

19. See obituary of Herbert Charles Sadler, *Society of Naval Architects and Marine Engineers, Transactions*, 56 (1948): 591.

20. See Robert M. La Follette, "Andrew Furuseth and His Great Work," *La Follette's Weekly*, 6, no. 4 (Apr. 1915): 2. For a favorable evaluation of Furuseth's lifework, see Hyman Weintraub, *Andrew Furuseth, Emancipator of the Seamen* (Berkeley and Los Angeles: University of California Press, 1959).

21. *A Bill to Abolish Involuntary Servitude Imposed upon Seamen in the Merchant Marine of the United States While in Foreign Ports and the Involuntary Servitude Imposed upon the Merchant Marine of Foreign Countries While in Ports of the United States, to Prevent Unskilled Manning of American Vessels, to Encourage the Training of Boys in the American Merchant Marine, for the Further Protection of Life at Sea, and to Amend the Laws Relative to Seamen, H.R. 23673,* 62nd Cong., 2nd sess., May 15, 1912.

22. New York *Times*, Oct. 24, 1913, p. 7.

23. *International Conference on Safety of Life at Sea* [London, 1913–14]: *Messages of the President of the United States Transmitting an Authenticated Copy of the International Convention Relating to Safety of Life at Sea . . . Signed at London, January 20, 1914* (Washington: Government Printing Office, 1914), pp. 10–21, 91.

24. The regulation was more complicated than Furuseth stated in his public utterances against it. The directive nominally required boats for all, but provided exceptions for ships of various categories, ultimately specifying boatage and raftage for 70 to 80 percent of the people aboard in most cases. See *Merchant Shipping (Life-Saving Appliances). Rules Made by the Board of Trade Under Section 427 of the Merchant Shipping Act, 1894. Pursuant to Act 57 & 58 Vict., Cap. 60, S. 427 (2)* (ordered by the House of Commons to be printed, 8th May 1914), no. 219.

25. Letter of Andrew Furuseth to President Woodrow Wilson, Jan. 12, 1914, in *International Conference on Safety of Life at Sea*, pp. 131–42.

26. New York *Times*, Jan. 6, 1914, p. 5.

27. United Kingdom, *Hansard Parliamentary Debates*, 5th series, vol. 37 (1912), col. 519.

28. *Syren & Shipping Illustrated*, 63 (1912): 67.

29. "The *Titanic* Enquiry," *Marine Engineer and Naval Architect*, 34 (1911–12): 461–62.

30. Estimates from James Croall, *Fourteen Minutes: The Last Voyage of the "Empress of Ireland"* (New York: Stein and Day, 1979), pp. 16, 26, 30, 76, 147, and passim. See also Logan Marshall, *The Tragic Story of the "Empress of Ireland"* (1914; London: Patrick Stephens, 1972), and Edward E. Suarez, Jr., "Empress of Ireland," *Grist* (newsletter of the Millbrook Society, Hatboro, Penn.), 6, no. 3 (Fall 1990): n.p.

31. *Syren & Shipping Illustrated*, 71 (1914): 503.

32. A. A. Hoehling and Mary Hoehling, *The Last Voyage of the "Lusitania"* (New York: Henry Holt & Co., 1956), pp. 19, 83, 171, 227. On the experience of the ship's lifeboats, see Colin Simpson, *Lusitania* (London: Penguin Books, 1983), pp. 157–67.

33. Telegram to Senator James P. Clarke, Sept. 9, 1914, from E. A. Dustin, Ashley & Dustin Line; W. E. Campbell, Detroit Steamer Line; John Stevenson, Star-Cole Line; and C. F. Bielman, White Star Line, in U.S. Senate, Committee on Commerce, *The Seamen's Bill: Hearings on S. 136, an Act to Promote the Welfare of American Seamen in the Merchant Marine of the United States, September 14, 1914*, 63rd Cong., 2nd sess. (Washington: Government Printing Office, 1914), p. 3.

34. New York *Times*, Apr. 14, 1914, p. 8.

35. "Able Seamen," New York *Times*, Jan. 13, 1914, p. 8.

36. This point is particularly identified with Friedrich August von Hayek. See, e.g., his discussion of the consequences of rent control in his *The Constitution of Liberty* (Chicago: University of Chicago Press, 1960), pp. 343–46.

37. Senate Committee on Commerce, *The Seamen's Bill*, p. 4.

38. This was argued editorially by the New York *Times* in "The Marine Full Crew Law," Mar. 6, 1915, p. 10.

39. New York *Times*, Sept. 1, 1914, p. 16. See also Dec. 4, 1913, p. 3.

40. *Congressional Record*, vol. 48, pt. 9, p. 9429.

41. New York *Times*, Dec. 14, 1914, p. 12.

42. *An Act to Promote the Welfare of American Seamen in the Merchant Marine of the United States; to Abolish Arrest and Imprisonment as a Penalty for Desertion and to Secure the Abrogation of Treaty Provisions in Relation Thereto; and to Promote Safety at Sea*, Public Law 302, 63rd Cong., 3rd sess., chap. 153 (1915), *U.S. Statutes at Large*, vol. 38, pt. 1, pp. 1164–85.

43. "The American Sailor a Free Man," New York *Times*, Mar. 22, 1915, p. 8.

44. *Marine Review*, 45 (1915): 284; New York *Times*, Mar. 5, 1915, p. 7.

45. "Safety at Sea," New York *Times*, Dec. 16, 1914, p. 14.

46. "Ruinous Competition Encouraged," *Marine Journal*, July 24, 1915, p. 3.

Chapter 1

1. *Marine Review*, Mar. 27, 1902, p. 16.

2. On Blacker, see *American Lumbermen* (Chicago: The American Lumberman, 1905), 1: 207–9.

3. Typescript notes of Captain Frank E. Hamilton, *Eastland* file, Frank E. Hamilton collection, Rutherford B. Hayes Memorial Library, Fremont, Ohio.

4. *Biennial Report of the Secretary of State of Indiana, for the Two Years Ending October 31, 1902* (Indianapolis: Secretary of the State of Indiana, 1902), p. 140.

5. South Haven *Daily Tribune*, Dec. 22, 1902.

6. Ibid., Oct. 13, 1902.

7. Ibid., Jan. 26, 1903.

8. Ibid., Mar. 25, 1903.

9. Ibid., Jan. 21, 1903.

10. Ibid., Apr. 25, 1903.

11. U.S. v. William H. Hull, George T. Arnold, Harry Pedersen, Joseph M. Erickson, Robert Reid, and Charles Eckliff, tried in the U.S. District Court, Western District of Michigan before the Hon. Clarence W. Sessions, typescript transcript of evidence, 4 vols. (pages numbered sequentially), National Archives and Records Administration, Great Lakes Center, Chicago, Record Group 21, CR 1628, file 358,803 (3 boxes). Hereinafter cited as "criminal transcript." Testimony of Herbert Charles Sadler, p. 1494.

12. South Haven *Daily Tribune*, Nov. 29, 1902. Great Lakes ships are rated by miles per hour, not knots.

13. Testimony of Captain Harry Pedersen, criminal transcript, p. 930.

14. Testimony of Captain Frank A. Dority, criminal transcript, p. 63.

15. Chicago *Tribune*, July 25, 1915, p. 7.

16. *Ordinances, Rules and Regulations, Harbor, Harbor Master, Bridges, Wharves and Vessels, of the City of Chicago*, 2nd ed. (Chicago: City Department of Public Works, 1913), chap. 36, art. 3, sec. 1124, p. 5; South Haven *Daily Tribune*, June 14, 1907; June 17, 1909.

17. Robert Reid, "Hull Inspector's Report" (handwritten entries in a codex with printed queries and blanks to be filled), report of June 7, 1915, p. 15, in file of U.S. v. Hull et al.

18. For reasons to be treated below, plans of the *Eastland* have not survived except for the outboard profile published in the Port Huron *Times*, Mar. 12, 1903, and reproduced below in this book. The description given here is based on that profile and the account of the finished ship, ibid., May 6, 1903.

19. Testimony of Nils B. Nelson, supervising inspector at Cleveland, in U.S. House of Representatives, Committee on the Merchant Marine and Fisheries, *Investigation of Accident to the Steamer "Eastland," Chicago, Ill., July 24, 1915*, 64th Cong., 1st sess. (Washington: Government Printing Office, 1916), p. 154. The hearings recorded in this volume were chaired by Secretary of Commerce William C. Redfield at the request of President Wilson.

20. "Contract for *Eastland*," typescript articles of agreement, Oct. 7, 1902, in file of U.S. v. Hull et al.

21. One example of such commentary is this: "The *Eastland* was a tender ship from the day she slid down the ways, and her reputation as a difficult vessel to manage became legend all over the lakes." Dwight Boyer, *True Tales of the Great Lakes* (New York: Dodd, Mead & Co., 1977), p. 51.

22. Rev. Peter J. Van der Linden, "The Jenks Ship Building Company of Port Huron," *Telescope*, 25 (1967): 91–97, 115–20. See also the short history of the

firm in the Port Huron *Times*, Oct. 3, 1902, and the obituary of William S. Jenks, ibid., Dec. 13, 1902.

23. Letter from George R. McDermott, in *Investigation of Accident to the Steamer "Eastland,"* pp. 229–30.

24. Edward L. Attwood, O.B.E., *Theoretical Naval Architecture* (London: Longmans, Green & Co., 1922), pp. 94, 96, with accompanying text.

25. Testimony of James L. Ackerson, naval architect, in *Investigation of Accident to the Steamer "Eastland,"* p. 314.

26. Testimony of William J. Wood before federal grand jury, Chicago *Tribune*, Aug. 1, 1915, p. 4.

27. Chicago *Tribune*, Aug. 5, 1915, p. 5. Evans's calculation was presumably that the change reduced buoyancy and as a consequence lowered the metacenter.

28. Letter from McDermott, in *Investigation of Accident to the Steamer "Eastland,"* pp. 229–30.

29. Chicago *Tribune*, July 27, 1915, p. 2.

30. For a detailed description of the process, see Thomas Walton, *Know Your Own Ship* (London: Charles Griffin & Co., 1896), pp. 128–47; more briefly in Harry Benford, *Naval Architecture for Non-Naval Architects* (Jersey City, N.J.: The Society of Naval Architects and Marine Engineers, 1991), pp. 67–69.

31. Testimony of Sidney G. Jenks, criminal transcript, pp. 463–65.

32. Port Huron *Times*, May 6, 1903. By coincidence the stream on which she was built at Port Huron and that out of which she was to operate at South Haven bore the same name, Black River.

33. Dorothy Marie Mitts, *That Noble Country: The Romance of the St. Clair River Region* (Philadelphia: Dorrance & Co., 1968), pp. 132–43.

34. Testimony of Sidney G. Jenks, criminal transcript, p. 465.

35. Ibid.

36. South Haven *Daily Tribune*, May 6, 1903. This account states that the system was intended to change her draft from 10′-6″ to 16′-0″, but this would be impossible for tanks only 48 inches high.

37. On the nature of the Kingston valve, see Rene de Kerchove, *International Maritime Dictionary*, 2nd ed. (New York: Van Nostrand Reinhold Co., 1961), p. 422.

38. Testimony of Joseph M. Erickson, criminal transcript, p. 1112.

39. The calculation of the angle of descent is based on the intake as a mean 7′-0″ below the waterline. The ship's draft, as planned, was about 14′-0″ and her beam 38′-0″. The tanks amidship were 4′-0″ high and the manifold 1′-2″.

40. The description of the ballast system is based on testimony of the ship's engineers: William L. Nack, in *Investigation of Accident to the Steamer "Eastland,"* pp. 204–28, and in criminal transcript, pp. 199–264; Grant Donaldson, criminal transcript, pp. 265–89; William P. Eeles, in *Investigation of Accident to the Steamer "Eastland,"* pp. 317–27; Fred G. Snow, criminal transcript, pp. 847–66; Erickson, criminal transcript, pp. 1062–1152; "Interrogation of Joseph M. Erickson by Superintendent of Police, July 25, 1915," file of U.S. v. Hull et al. See also testimony of Frank A. Dority, in *Investigation of Accident to the Steamer "Eastland,"* pp. 176–200, and in criminal transcript, pp. 12–81; Robert Reid,

criminal transcript, pp. 745–825; H. B. Vehstedt, ibid., pp. 1331–35; Conrad Whiting, ibid., p. 1285. The capacities of the No. 2 and 3 tanks are from the testimony of Sadler, ibid., pp. 1507–8.

41. Testimony of Dority, in *Investigation of Accident to the Steamer "Eastland,"* p. 182.

42. Port Huron *Times*, July 9, 13, 15, 16, 1903; Port Huron *Daily Herald*, July 13, 15, 16, 1903.

43. Port Huron *Times*, July 16, 1903; South Haven *Daily Tribune*, July 18, 1903.

44. Port Huron *Times*, July 13, 1903.

45. South Haven *Daily Tribune*, July 15, 1903.

46. Ibid., July 18, 1903.

47. Ibid., July 18, July 21, 1903.

48. Interview with W. J. Wood, Chicago *Tribune*, July 25, 1915, p. 7.

49. South Haven *Daily Tribune*, July 22, July 27, Aug. 1, 1903; Port Huron *Times*, Aug. 29, 1903.

50. *Annual Report of the U.S. Life-Saving Service for the Fiscal Year Ending June 30, 1904* (Washington, D.C.: Government Printing Office, 1905), p. 66.

51. Manistee *Daily News*, Aug. 28, 1903. On Dority, see *History of the Great Lakes* (Chicago: J. H. Beers & Co., 1899), 2: 937.

52. South Haven *Messenger*, Dec. 11, 1903.

53. Manistee *Daily News*, Sept. 22, 1903.

54. South Haven *Daily Tribune*, Sept. 21, 1903.

55. *Marine Review*, 29, no. 21 (May 26, 1904): 32.

56. Advertisement in *Engineering*, Dec. 25, 1896, p. 47.

57. "The Atlas Works, Sheffield: Messrs John Brown & Co., Limited," *Marine Engineer*, 20 (1898): 179–83, diagram at p. 181.

58. See also F. Gross, "Recent Experience with Cylindrical Boilers and the Ellis and Eaves Suction Draft," *Marine Engineer*, 16 (1894): 232–34.

59. This version of the McCreery system is registered under U.S. patent number 586,363 (1897).

60. *Marine Review*, 29, no. 21 (May 26, 1904): 32.

61. Chicago *Tribune*, July 25, 1915.

62. Port Huron *Times*, Oct. 28, Nov. 13, 1903, Mar. 9, Apr. 6, Apr. 20, May 3, 1904. See also interview with Wood, Chicago *Tribune*, July 25, 1915, p. 7.

63. Testimony of Albert R. Jefferson, criminal transcript, p. 164.

64. Testimony of William H. Cochrane, former general passenger agent of Michigan Steamship Co., criminal transcript, p. 683.

65. Manistee *Daily News*, Aug. 4, 1904.

66. The *Tribune* did not state the authority for this, but it was apparently either Wood or another naval architect interviewed for the issue, John Devereux York. Chicago *Tribune*, July 27, 1915, p. 2.

67. Technical Board on Vessel Safety, "Report of Stability Test, *City of South Haven*, No. 127,731, Performed September 3, 1915, Chicago River at Kinzie Street," typescript in file of U.S. v. Hull et al.

68. Testimony of Eeles, in *Investigation of Accident to the Steamer "Eastland,"* p. 321.

69. Testimony of Dority, in *Investigation of Accident to the Steamer "Eastland,"* p. 200.

70. Merwin S. Thompson, "Just What Was the Cause of the Steamer *Eastland* Disaster?" *Inland Seas*, 15 (1959): 200–206.

71. Typescript notes of Hamilton, *Eastland* file, Hamilton collection. Captain Hamilton's notes are based on his own experiences as a master on Lake Erie, on research, and on a long period of discussions with other officers. They are highly credible.

72. Testimony of Edward C. Gillette, superintendent of naval construction, U.S. Lighthouse Service, in *Investigation of Accident to the Steamer "Eastland,"* p. 303.

73. Ibid. In technical terms, the forward motion may have increased the polar moments of the ship. That is, the action of the propellers may have acted like a flywheel as a force for stability.

74. Testimony of Dority, criminal transcript, p. 32.

75. Testimony of Nack, criminal transcript, pp. 215–22.

76. Testimony of Sadler, criminal transcript, p. 1539.

77. Testimony of Nack, criminal transcript, pp. 229–34.

78. Testimony of Dority, in *Investigation of Accident to the Steamer "Eastland,"* p. 179.

79. Testimony of Ira B. Mansfield, in *Investigation of Accident to the Steamer "Eastland,"* p. 252.

80. Testimony of George Hale, criminal transcript, p. 1177.

81. Testimony of Dority, criminal transcript, p. 27.

82. Testimony of Cochrane, criminal transcript, p. 698.

83. The weight of the lifeboats is estimated by a calculation based on the weight of lifesaving equipment taken off the wreck in 1915, to be discussed in Chapter III, below. As noted below, the lifeboats added in 1915 were smaller than the original six, and the weight on the hurricane deck in the event of July 17, 1904, is understated.

84. Letter of Dr. P. S. Staines, an observer of the departure, in *Investigation of Accident to the Steamer "Eastland,"* p. 251.

85. Testimony of Nack, criminal transcript, pp. 223–26.

86. Testimony of Henry J. Welch, criminal transcript, p. 1200.

87. On the way in which such a new equilibrium could be reached, see note 1 to the transcript of Professor Sadler's testimony in Appendix C, below.

88. Testimony of Dority, criminal transcript, pp. 27–29.

89. *Marine Review and Marine Record*, 30, no. 3 (July 21, 1904): 27; testimony of Dority, criminal transcript, p. 62.

90. Testimony of Nack, criminal transcript, p. 222.

91. Testimony of Dority, criminal transcript, pp. 47–48.

92. Ibid.; *Marine Review and Marine Record*, 30, no. 3 (July 21, 1904): 27.

93. Testimony of Eeles, in *Investigation of Accident to the Steamer "Eastland,"* p. 323.

94. Testimony of Dority, criminal transcript, p. 49.

95. Testimony of Nack, in *Investigation of Accident to the Steamer "Eastland,"* p. 215.

96. Ibid., pp. 235–38.

97. Testimony of Dority, in *Investigation of Accident to the Steamer "East-land,"* p. 30.

98. Testimony of Eeles, in *Investigation of Accident to the Steamer "East-land,"* p. 322.

99. MS Drydock record, *Eastland* file, Hamilton collection.

100. *Nautical Gazette*, 67 (1904): 169.

101. South Haven *Tribune*, May 26, 1905.

102. A photograph of the *Eastland* in South Haven dated June 1905, in the *Eastland* file, Hamilton collection, shows the lifeboats in place. See the photograph of the ship in her 1906 livery in Rev. Peter J. Van der Linden, ed., *Great Lakes Ships We Remember* (Cleveland: Freshwater Press, 1979), p. 170, bottom. The South Haven *Tribune*, May 15, 1906, was explicit that no changes were made in her for the 1906 season.

103. R. Reid, "Hull Inspector's Report" of June 7, 1915, p. 15.

104. Armstrong Cork Co. v. Steamer "Eastland," libel action filed Nov. 15, 1905, in U.S. District Court, Northern District of Illinois, National Archives and Records Administration, Great Lakes Center, Chicago, USDC/NO I, record group 21, CR 9706, file 368,373. This is the only file of the three libel actions to survive.

105. Detroit *Free Press*, Oct. 19, 1904. The *Free Press* stated, apparently erroneously, that this was the bill of the Chicago Ship Building Company.

106. *Marine Review and Marine Record*, 32 (1905): 33.

107. *Biennial Report of the Secretary of State of Indiana for the Two Years Ending October 31, 1906* (Indianapolis: Secretary of the State of Indiana, 1906), p. 98.

108. Testimony of Cochrane, criminal transcript, p. 686.

109. Testimony of George T. Arnold, criminal transcript, p. 1052.

110. Letter of George E. Foulkes, in *Investigation of Accident to the Steamer "Eastland,"* p. 231. Because July 23, 1905, was a Tuesday, and her weekday loads usually presented no problem, this date may be in error.

111. Testimony of Nack, in *Investigation of Accident to the Steamer "East-land,"* p. 208.

Chapter 2

1. Typescript notes of Captain Frank E. Hamilton, *Eastland* file, Frank E. Hamilton collection, Rutherford B. Hayes Memorial Library, Fremont, Ohio.

2. Testimony of William H. Cochrane, criminal transcript, pp. 684–85.

3. Cleveland *Plain Dealer*, June 7, 1907; Cleveland *Leader*, June 7, 1907.

4. Typescript notes of Hamilton, *Eastland* file, Hamilton collection.

5. Ibid.; Cleveland *Plain Dealer*, July 27, 1915, p. 3. Hull testified (criminal transcript, p. 1004) that the Eastland Navigation Co. paid $275,000 for her, but he was probably confusing her price in this transaction with her price when she was new, which was exactly that.

6. This use of the term differed from deep-seas usage. On an ocean steamship, the 'tween decks was typically the deck below the main deck. What was called the 'tween decks on the *Eastland* would have been known on an ocean vessel as the shelter deck.

7. Sandusky *Register*, June 9, 1907.

8. Ibid., Sept. 5, 1909, July 19, 1912. I am indebted to Gordon Wendt for these references.

9. Ibid., July 27, 1912.

10. Frank Lee Stevenson, *The "Eastland" Disaster* (Chicago: Hansen & Stevenson, [1915]), p. 5.

11. Chicago *Evening Post*, July 24, 1915.

12. Testimony of Robert O. Moyer, criminal transcript, pp. 1153–68.

13. Testimony of J. Grant Snyder, criminal transcript, pp. 1168–70.

14. Cleveland *Plain Dealer*, Aug. 9, 1910, p. 10; Cleveland *Leader*, August 9, 1910, p. 3.

15. Testimony of Merwin S. Thompson, criminal transcript, p. 104.

16. Testimony of Nils B. Nelson, in U.S. House of Representatives, Committee on the Merchant Marine and Fisheries, *Investigation of Accident to the Steamer "Eastland," Chicago, Ill., July 24, 1915*, 64th Cong., 1st sess. (Washington: Government Printing Office, 1916), pp. 82–88.

17. Robert W. Poole, Jr., "Is This Any Way to Run an Airway?" *Reason*, 10, no. 9 (Jan. 1979): 18–32.

18. U.S. Dept. of Commerce, Steamboat Inspection Service, *General Rules and Regulations Respecting Bays, Rivers and Sounds* (1914), Rule 3, p. 178. Put in evidence by Merwin S. Thompson, in criminal transcript, pp. 136–37. Rule 3 is the codification of the circular letter.

19. See Table 1, above in Chapter 1. Testimony of Grant Donaldson, criminal transcript, p. 271.

20. This is the interpretation of Captain Frank E. Hamilton, in his typescript notes, *Eastland* file, Hamilton collection.

Chapter 3

1. Benton Harbor *News-Palladium*, Apr. 15, 1913.

2. Testimony of William H. Hull, criminal transcript, pp. 987–88; Chicago *Tribune*, July 25, 1915, p. 12.

3. "Corporate Record of St. Joseph–Chicago Steamship Company," p. 11, in file of U.S. v. William H. Hull, George T. Arnold, Harry Pedersen, Joseph M. Erickson, Robert Reid, and Charles Eckliff, National Archives and Records Administration, Great Lakes Center, Chicago.

4. Testimony of George T. Arnold, criminal transcript, pp. 1048–49.

5. Testimony of Hull, criminal transcript, pp. 988–89.

6. Ibid., p. 1003; testimony of Arnold, ibid., pp. 1052–58.

7. Chicago *Tribune*, July 28, 1915.

8. Testimony of Hull, criminal transcript, pp. 989–90; testimony of Walter C. Steele, ibid., pp. 377–81. Scott's report was put in evidence in U.S. v. Hull et al. (ibid., p. 991), but is not in the surviving file of the case.

9. Testimony of Hull, criminal transcript, p. 991.

10. Testimony of Arnold, criminal transcript, p. 1059; testimony of Claude M. Ennes, ibid., p. 194.

11. St. Joseph *Daily Press*, June 5, 1914; Benton Harbor *News-Palladium*, June 5, 1914.

12. Testimony of Robert Reid, criminal transcript, pp. 746–47.

13. Testimony of Charles C. Eckliff, criminal transcript, pp. 875–76.

14. Testimony of Reid, criminal transcript, pp. 794–95.

15. Ibid., p. 823.

16. Testimony of Hull, criminal transcript, p. 1020.

17. Testimony of Ennes, criminal transcript, p. 186.

18. Benton Harbor *News-Palladium*, June 13, 1914; St. Joseph *Daily Press*, June 13, 1914.

19. Testimony of Harry Pedersen, criminal transcript, pp. 892–94, 934.

20. Ibid., p. 897.

21. Ibid., p. 898.

22. Ibid., p. 978.

23. Chicago *Evening Post*, July 27, 1915, p. 4.

24. Testimony of Hull, criminal transcript, p. 995; signature of Robertson on *Eastland*'s reinspection certificate of Aug. 25, 1914, in file of U.S. v. Hull et al.

25. Benton Harbor *News-Palladium*, Apr. 21, 1913.

26. "Number of Passengers Carried on Steamer *Eastland*," typescript certified statement of R. H. McCreary, deputy collector of customs, Chicago, Jan. 31, 1916, in file of U.S. v. Hull et al.

27. Chicago *Tribune*, July 25, 1915.

28. Chicago *Tribune*, July 27, 1915, p.1.

29. Testimony of Arthur D. MacDonald, criminal transcript, p. 1268.

30. *Ordinances, Rules and Regulations, Harbor, Harbor Master, Bridges, Wharves and Vessels, of the City of Chicago*, 2nd ed. (Chicago: City Department of Public Works, 1913), art. 6, par. 1140.

31. Michigan City *News*, July 29, 1914.

32. Testimony of Pedersen, criminal transcript, p. 929.

33. Testimony of Reid, criminal transcript, pp. 791–92.

34. The weight of concrete is estimated by Randolph W. Chalfant, architect, of Baltimore.

35. Testimony of Pedersen, criminal transcript, p. 929.

36. Testimony of Reid, criminal transcript, p. 764.

37. Ibid., p. 766.

38. Testimony of Robert Reid, in U.S. House of Representatives, Committee on the Merchant Marine and Fisheries, *Investigation of Accident to the Steamer "Eastland," Chicago, Ill., July 24, 1915*, 64th Cong., 1st sess. (Washington: Government Printing Office, 1916), pp. 114–15.

39. Grand Haven *Daily Tribune*, Dec. 26, 1914. The bride recognized the maritime associations of the marriage by wearing a blue sailor suit.

40. Testimony of Joseph M. Erickson, criminal transcript, pp. 1062–71.

41. Testimony of Reid, criminal transcript, pp. 812, 822.

42. Testimony of Joseph M. Erickson, criminal transcript, p. 1079. References to "Erickson" in absence of first name will continue to be to Joseph M. Erickson.

43. Ibid., p. 1069.

44. On the subject generally, see George W. Hilton, *The Great Lakes Car Ferries* (Berkeley, Calif.: Howell-North Books, 1962).

45. Testimony of Hull, criminal transcript, p. 996.

46. Testimony of Grant Donaldson, criminal transcript, p. 276. Hull denied making these statements. Testimony of Hull, ibid., p. 998.

47. Testimony of Erickson, criminal transcript, p. 1085.

48. Testimony of Fred G. Snow, criminal transcript, p. 847.

49. Testimony of Erickson, criminal transcript, p. 1086.

50. Ibid., p. 1084. Erickson did not specify the date of the crossing.

51. Testimony of Donaldson, criminal transcript, pp. 266-67.

52. Typescript letter from W. K. Greenebaum to Charles J. Malmros, Central Committee, Hawthorne Club, n.d., in "Transcript of Testimony, Inquest on the Bodies of Kate Austin *et al.*, July 24-29, 1915, Peter M. Hoffman, Cook County Coroner," typescript, Office of the Medical Examiner of Cook County, 2121 W. Harrison St., Chicago. There is also a published version of this transcript: *Transcript of Testimony Before the Coroner's Jury, July 24, 25, 26, 27, 28, 29, on the Body of Kate Austin and All Others Lost by Overturning of the Excursion Steamer "Eastland" While Tied to the Dock at Clark and S. Water Street in the City of Chicago, July 24, 1915* (Chicago: City of Chicago, 1915). The published version gives every evidence of having been printed hurriedly, with a great many typographical errors. The typescript is superior.

53. Chicago *Tribune*, July 27, 1915, p. 1.

54. Ibid.

55. See the statements of Frank Baubles and Frank Frisina, survivors, in the Chicago *Tribune*, July 25, 1915, p. 3.

56. "Number of Passengers Carried on Steamer 'Eastland,' Season 1915," Treasury Department, U.S. Customs Service, Chicago, Jan. 28, 1916, in file of U.S. v. Hull et al.

57. Typescript letter from W. H. Hull to William C. Redfield, secretary of commerce, June 30, 1915, carbon copy in file of U.S. v. Hull et al.

58. Testimony of Hull, criminal transcript, p. 1019.

59. Hull's estimate, ibid., p. 997.

60. *Transcript of Testimony Before the Coroner's Jury*, p. 147.

61. Testimony of Hull, criminal transcript, pp. 997, 1014.

62. Testimony of Pedersen, criminal transcript, pp. 945-47.

63. Ibid., p. 946.

64. Indeed, Pedersen's response can be interpreted as saying that he was incapable of doing simple arithmetic:

Q. You don't know how to figure?

A. No.

(Criminal transcript, p. 947). Such an interpretation seems hardly consistent with the general competence in navigation that he must have shown in his licensure examinations, and with his specialization in calibration of compasses.

65. Letter from Hull to Redfield.

66. Testimony of Reid, criminal transcript, p. 815.

67. Ibid., pp. 817-18.

68. Ibid., p. 818.

69. Testimony of Hull, criminal transcript, p. 1020; testimony of Pedersen, ibid., p. 948.

70. Robert Reid, "Hull Inspector's Report" (handwritten entries in a codex

with printed queries and blanks to be filled), June 7, 1915, in file of U.S. v. Hull et al. Because these boats were not added until July 2, Reid's entries for them may have been inserted later.

71. Negative PB 238, Mariners Museum, Newport News, Va.

72. Estimate of Reid, criminal transcript, p. 798.

73. Testimony of Reid, criminal transcript, p. 766.

74. Ibid., p. 772.

75. Ibid., p. 936.

76. Testimony of Walter Scott, criminal transcript, p. 415. Captain Scott had gone on the payroll of the St. Joseph–Chicago Steamship Company in June 1914 to do purchasing and maintenance on the firm's two steamers, but had been discharged in mid-July 1915 as a cost-reduction measure. (Ibid., p. 384.)

77. Detroit *Free Press*, July 31, 1915, p. 8.

78. Testimony of H. B. Vehstedt, criminal transcript, p. 1331.

79. The reason for the ambiguity is that, as will be noted below, one boat floated free in the disaster, and it is not clear whether its weight was included in the figure of 62 tons. If it was not, the average weight of a lifeboat was about 3.96 tons instead of 3.62, and the weight of the equipment added on July 2 was about a ton greater.

80. Testimony of Reid, criminal transcript, pp. 797, 824.

81. Detroit *Free Press*, July 31, 1915, p. 8.

82. Testimony of Reid, criminal transcript, p. 807.

83. Milwaukee *Evening Wisconsin*, July 24, 1915.

84. Testimony of Hull, criminal transcript, p. 1018.

85. Testimony of Erickson, criminal transcript, p. 1089.

86. Typescript letter from James P. McAllister to W. C. Redfield, secretary of commerce, July 31, 1915, Bureau of Marine Inspection and Navigation, Steamboat Inspection Service, Numerical Correspondence, 1905–23, box 545A, no. 71330, National Archives, Washington, D.C.

87. Chicago *Examiner*, July 30, 1915, p. 2.

88. Treasury Dept., "Number of Passengers Carried on Steamer 'Eastland,' Season 1915."

89. "Interrogation of Joseph M. Erickson by Superintendent of Police, July 25, 1915," p. 5, in file of U.S. v. Hull et al.

90. Testimony of Martin Flatow, criminal transcript, pp. 1024–26; testimony of Del Fisher, ibid., p. 670.

Chapter 4

1. The MS letter to the United States Local Inspectors, Chicago, July 25, 1915, survives in the National Archives, Washington, D.C., Record Group 41, Bureau of Marine Inspection and Navigation, Steamboat Inspection Service, Numerical Correspondence, 1905–23, no. 71330, box 546. The letter is published in U.S. House of Representatives, Committee on the Merchant Marine and Fisheries, *Investigation of Accident to the Steamer "Eastland,"* p. 65, with the erroneous signature "James Erickson." Hereinafter cited as Erickson log.

2. Testimony of Harry Pedersen, criminal transcript, p. 926.

3. Testimony of Joseph M. Erickson, criminal transcript, p. 1093. Earlier

(p. 1090) he stated that he had watched the clock closely only until 7:10 A.M., but he corrected himself. The rest of his testimony is more consistent with his having watched the clock after 7:10.

4. Typescript letter from W. H. Hull to Harry Pedersen, July 16, 1915, carbon copy in file of U.S. v. William H. Hull, George T. Arnold, Harry Pedersen, Joseph M. Erickson, Robert Reid, and Charles Eckliff, National Archives and Records Administration, Great Lakes Center, Chicago.

5. Testimony of Erickson, criminal transcript, p. 1088.

6. Testimony of Pedersen, criminal transcript, p. 943.

7. Testimony of Erickson, criminal transcript, pp. 1134–35.

8. Testimony of H. B. Vehstedt, criminal transcript, p. 1354.

9. Chicago *Tribune*, Aug. 1, 1915, p. 2.

10. Testimony of Vehstedt, criminal transcript, p. 1331; testimony of H. G. Clabaugh, ibid., p. 1372.

11. Testimony of Pedersen, criminal transcript, p. 914; Chicago *Examiner*, July 25, 1915.

12. Erickson estimated 3:45 A.M., in "Interrogation of Joseph M. Erickson by Superintendent of Police, July 25, 1915," p. 1, in file of U.S. v. Hull et al. In the criminal transcript he estimated 3:55 (p. 1090), and Pedersen estimated 4:00 (p. 958).

13. Testimony of Martin Flatow, criminal transcript, p. 1026.

14. Typescript report of Edward Morville, gauge keeper, in file of U.S. v. Hull et al.

15. Testimony of Pedersen, criminal transcript, p. 921.

16. Testimony of Flatow, criminal transcript, p. 1027; testimony of Joseph R. Lynn, ibid., pp. 702–3; testimony of Pedersen, ibid., pp. 922–23, 944.

17. Testimony of Lynn, criminal transcript, p. 703.

18. Vehstedt stated 2′-9″; criminal transcript, p. 1366. The appellee's brief in the civil action stated 4′-0″; "Brief for Appellee, Frederick L. Leckie and Robert Branard, Jr., Proctors for Appellee," p. 17, In the U.S. Circuit Court of Appeals for the Seventh Circuit, In re Petition of the St. Joseph–Chicago Steamship Co. for Limitation of Liability, docket no. 5257, October term, 1934. Copy in Law Library, Library of Congress.

19. Testimony of Del Fisher, first mate, *Transcript of Testimony Before the Coroner's Jury, July 24, 25, 26, 27, 28, 29, on the Body of Kate Austin and All Others Lost by Overturning of the Excursion Steamer "Eastland" While Tied to the Dock at Clark and S. Water Street in the City of Chicago, July 24, 1915* (Chicago: City of Chicago, 1915), p. 128.

20. Testimony of Flatow, criminal transcript, p. 1036.

21. Testimony of Lynn, criminal transcript, p. 703; "Brief for Appellee," p. 17.

22. Testimony of Lynn, criminal transcript, pp. 704–6; testimony of Flatow, ibid., p. 1031.

23. Finding of coroner's jury, reported in Chicago *Tribune*, Aug. 4, 1915.

24. Chicago *Daily News*, July 27, 1915, p. 3. The charter of the *Maywood* was confirmed by Mildred Anderson, an officer of the Hawthorne Club who survived the disaster; Chicago *Evening Post*, July 24, 1915, p. 1.

25. Chicago *Tribune*, July 25, 1915.

26. The description of the relative positions of the ships is based on a sketch map by Rev. Edward J. Dowling, S.J., and modified on the basis of newspaper accounts.

27. Testimony of Fred G. Snow, criminal transcript, p. 848; "Interrogation of Erickson by Superintendent of Police," p. 3.

28. "Interrogation of Erickson by Superintendent of Police," p. 2.

29. Testimony of Pedersen, criminal transcript, p. 962.

30. Ibid., p. 912.

31. Ibid., p. 962.

32. Toledo *Blade*, July 26, 1915, p. 2.

33. Testimony of Robert H. McCreary, in *Investigation of Accident to the Steamer "Eastland,"* pp. 13–14; testimony of Luman A. Lobdell, ibid., p. 30; testimony of Curtis J. Oakley, ibid., pp. 40–41. Spelling of Monger's name varies between "Monger" and "Munger" in newspaper accounts of the disaster. "Monger" is used here on the basis of the entry for him in *Kalamazoo City and County Directory*, 1914, p. 718, and 1916, p. 692.

34. Testimony of McCreary, in *Investigation of Accident to the Steamer "Eastland,"* p. 14.

35. *"Eastland" Disaster Relief: American Red Cross 1915–1918: After the Capsizing of the Steamer "Eastland" in the Chicago River, July 24, 1915, to Completion of Relief Work*, final report of the *Eastland* Disaster Relief Committee (Chicago: Chicago Chapter, American Red Cross, 1918), p. 186.

36. Ibid., p. 184.

37. Fisher's first name is somewhat in doubt. The published version of the transcript of testimony for the coroner's inquest shows it as "Adelbert" (*Transcript of Testimony Before the Coroner's Jury*, p. 126), but the criminal transcript shows it as "Delbert" (p. 648). St. Joseph newspapers reported it as "Delwin" (St. Joseph *Evening Herald*, July 24, 1915; St. Joseph *Daily Press*, July 24, 1915, July 24, 1916). The certificate of Fisher's license was lost in the disaster. He applied for a replacement under the name of "Delwin," which is presumably the correct one. Typescript letter from C. H. Metcalf, U.S. supervising inspector at Detroit, Sept. 8, 1915, Bureau of Marine Inspection and Navigation, Steamboat Inspection Service, Numerical Correspondence, 1905–23, no. 71330, box 545A, National Archives, Washington, D.C.

38. Testimony of Fisher, criminal transcript, p. 663. In the hearings before the commissioner in the civil case in 1932, Joseph R. Lynn stated that the list to starboard was of six to seven minutes' duration ("Respondents' Reply Brief" [typescript], filed Nov. 20, 1933, p. 21, U.S. District Court, Northern District of Illinois, Eastern Division, In re Petition of the St. Joseph–Chicago Steamship Co. for Limitation of Liability, no. 32,231, Record Group 21, National Archives, Great Lakes Center, Chicago). Because in his testimony of 1916 Lynn stated that he did not arrive until 7:18, this statement appears to be derivative from Del Fisher's testimony.

39. Testimony of Lobdell, in *Investigation of Accident to the Steamer "Eastland,"* p. 31; testimony of Oakley, ibid., p. 41; testimony of Flatow, criminal transcript, p. 1029.

40. Testimony of Oakley, in *Investigation of Accident to the Steamer "East-land,"* p. 41.

41. Detroit *News*, July 25, 1915, p. 3.

42. Erickson log.

43. Ibid.

44. Testimony of Fred M. Reed, criminal transcript, p. 1182.

45. Erickson log.

46. Testimony of Snow, criminal transcript, p. 857.

47. Testimony of Reed, criminal transcript, p. 1190.

48. This time sequence is given both by Erickson in his log and by John H. O'Meara in his testimony before the coroner's jury (*Transcript of Testimony Before the Coroner's Jury*, p. 53). The *Kenosha*'s chief engineer, Arthur D. MacDonald, placed the tug's arrival earlier, about 6:45, and estimated the *Eastland*'s list at 10 to 15 degrees to starboard (criminal transcript, pp. 1270, 1273). MacDonald's estimate of the arrival time and the *Eastland*'s degree of list are consistent, but he probably was able to observe the *Eastland* from the tug's position in the river west of Wells Street well before the tug arrived at the ship.

49. Testimony of O'Meara, *Transcript of Testimony Before the Coroner's Jury*, p. 54. Identification of Flannigan from Chicago *Daily News*, July 24, 1915, p. 1. The Detroit *News*, July 25, 1915, p. 1, identifies him as James Flannigan.

50. Detroit *News*, July 25, 1915, p. 1.

51. Testimony of McCreary, in *Investigation of Accident to the Steamer "East-land,"* p. 29.

52. Testimony of Lobdell, in *Investigation of Accident to the Steamer "East-land,"* pp. 30–33; testimony of Oakley, ibid., p. 43. These figures, especially the latter, seem low relative to the time the ship became fully loaded. The preponderance of evidence is that the ship was fully loaded well before 7:15. See below.

53. Estimate of Lobdell, in *Investigation of Accident to the Steamer "East-land,"* p. 30.

54. Erickson log.

55. Ibid.

56. Testimony of Erickson, criminal transcript, p. 1109.

57. Testimony of Snow, criminal transcript, p. 851.

58. Chicago *Tribune*, July 28, 1915.

59. Testimony of Adam F. Weckler before the coroner's jury, reported in Chicago *Tribune*, July 28, 1915.

60. Testimony of Adam F. Weckler, criminal transcript, pp. 1433–34.

61. Testimony of Flatow, criminal transcript, p. 1040.

62. Testimony of Luman A. Lobdell, *Transcript of Testimony Before the Coroner's Jury*, p. 30.

63. Testimony of Robert H. McCreary, *Transcript of Testimony Before the Coroner's Jury*, p. 14.

64. Testimony of McCreary, in *Investigation of Accident to the Steamer "East-land,"* p. 20.

65. "The S.S. *Eastland* Catastrophe," *Sparks Journal* (Society of Wireless Pioneers), 7, no. 1 (Oct. 1984): 32, reprinted photographically from *The Marconigraph*, Aug. 1915. I have been unable to locate the original of this periodical.

66. Testimony of Pedersen, criminal transcript, p. 962.

67. Ibid., p. 924.

68. Chicago *Evening Post*, July 24, 1915, p. 1.

69. Testimony of Del Fisher, criminal transcript, p. 658.

70. Testimony of Martin Flatow, *Transcript of Testimony Before the Coroner's Jury*, p. 88.

71. "The *Eastland*, Pride of the City Toppled over One Year Ago Today: Delwin Fisher Tells of Disaster," St. Joseph *Daily Press*, July 24, 1916.

72. "Interrogation of Erickson by Superintendent of Police," p. 3.

73. Erickson log.

74. Testimony of Erickson, criminal transcript, p. 1116.

75. Testimony of H. F. Bangs, a marine engineer who worked on righting the wreck, criminal transcript, p. 826,

76. Article by Dr. William A. Evans, foreman of the coroner's jury, Chicago *Tribune*, Aug. 2, 1915, p. 1. The maximum time the effort to fill the starboard tanks could have occupied was fourteen minutes, if Erickson's chronology of his opening of the valves and the time of final capsizing is correct.

77. Report of Dr. W. A. Evans, Chicago *Tribune*, Aug. 1, 1915, p. 1.

78. "Respondents' Reply Brief" (1933), p. 20.

79. Testimony of William L. Nack, in *Investigation of Accident to the Steamer "Eastland,"* p. 214.

80. Testimony of Peter Erickson, *Transcript of Testimony Before the Coroner's Jury*, p. 125.

81. Testimony of Nack, in *Investigation of Accident to the Steamer "Eastland,"* p. 288.

82. Erickson log.

83. Testimony of Peter Erickson, *Transcript of Testimony Before the Coroner's Jury*, p. 122.

84. Erickson log.

85. "Respondents' Reply Brief" (1933), p. 23.

86. *"Eastland" Disaster Relief*, p. 9.

87. Testimony of Snow, criminal transcript, p. 852.

88. Testimony of Lynn, criminal transcript, p. 707.

89. Testimony of O'Meara, *Transcript of Testimony Before the Coroner's Jury*, p. 54.

90. Testimony of Joseph R. Lynn, *Transcript of Testimony Before the Coroner's Jury*, pp. 702–3.

91. Testimony of McCreary, in *Investigation of Accident to the Steamer "Eastland,"* p. 29.

92. Detroit *Free Press*, July 25, 1915, pp. 1–2. Spelling of his name varies between "Sladkey" and "Shadkey" in newspaper accounts.

93. Testimony of McCreary, in *Investigation of Accident to the Steamer "Eastland,"* p. 14.

94. Chicago *Daily News*, July 24, 1915.

95. Testimony of Lobdell, in *Investigation of Accident to the Steamer "Eastland,"* p. 34.

96. Detroit *Free Press*, July 25, 1915, p. 1.

97. Flatow testified that it remained in place and simply went slack (criminal transcript, p. 1035). Lynn testified that four lines were in place when the order to cast off came, one of which was the aft breast line to a cleat just aft the gangway (criminal transcript, p. 705). This appears to imply that the stern line had been thrown off earlier, but Lynn may have been confused either in terminology or in memory. A photograph of the wreck taken from the Clark Street bridge immediately following the disaster, while survivors were still climbing off, shows the starboard side clearly without showing this line either in place or lying slack on the hull (Chicago *Tribune*, July 25, 1915, p. 7). A photograph of the immediate area published in this book shows it in place and taut, being used as a vehicle for escape by survivors on the hull. A later photograph taken during removal of the bodies shows the line in place, but affixed to a spile, not, as Lynn said, a cleat (Chicago *Evening Post*, July 24, 1915, p. 16). It had presumably been replaced to assist survivors in climbing off the hull or to prevent the wreck from moving. It is shown clearly in a later photograph of the wreck in *Shipping Illustrated*, 52 (1915): 99.

Dr. W. A. Evans, in his summary of the findings of the coroner's jury, appears to corroborate Lobdell: "The main stern line had been loosed . . . [and] taken in. . . . One stem line running back from the stern was not even taut" (Chicago *Tribune*, Aug. 4, 1915, p. 4). This is consistent with the observations of George Haber, who stood on the wharf about 100 feet west of the *Eastland*. He stated that he had seen some men on the ship loosening one of the lines, but seven or eight minutes before the capsizing he observed one heavy line still fast to the stern (Chicago *Evening Post*, July 24, 1915, p. 1). The Coast Guard stated in its casualty report, "One of the stern lines had been hauled in board" (U.S. Coast Guard, Wreck Report No. 129, received by Collector of Customs, Grand Haven, Mich., Aug. 20, 1915, microfilm reel T925-2, National Archives, Washington, D.C.). The conclusion most consistent with the evidence is that the aft breast line was thrown off when Lobdell and Sladkey stated, taken in, restored in the course of the rescue effort, and kept in place throughout the salvage operation.

98. Chicago *Tribune*, July 25, 1915, p. 9; Sept. 29, 1915, p. 5.

99. Detroit *News*, July 25, 1915, p. 3.

100. Erickson log; testimony of Erickson, criminal transcript, p. 1131.

101. Chicago *Tribune*, July 28, 1915; testimony of Richard J. Moore, "Transcript of Testimony, Inquest on the Bodies of Kate Austin *et al.*, July 24–29, 1915, Peter M. Hoffman, Cook County Coroner," typescript, Office of the Medical Examiner of Cook County, 2121 W. Harrison St., Chicago, pp. 6–7. The Red Cross accepted Moore's supposition that what he heard was the falling of the refrigerator, and also his chronology, but stated that the event caused panic among the passengers (*"Eastland" Disaster Relief*, p. 9). Moore's supposition and chronology, however, appear to be incorrect. Most other observations are more consistent with the refrigerator's toppling immediately before the capsizing, about six minutes later than Moore said, and initiating the panic at that moment. If the Red Cross was even near correct in asserting that the ship had returned almost to an even keel in the reversal of 7:18 to 7:20, it is unlikely that she could have reached a degree of list by 7:22 that could have caused the toppling of the refrigerator. What Moore heard may have been a case of beer sliding off the bar, or some similar premonitory

event. No account by a survivor indicates that panic came before about 7:28; this is consistent with placing the fall of the refrigerator at that time. We have specific evidence, noted below, that panic had not broken out by 7:23, and more general descriptions of the passengers' behavior to indicate that it had not done so by 7:27.

102. Chicago *Tribune*, July 25, 1915, p. 3.

103. Testimony of Pedersen, criminal transcript, pp. 915, 969. There is some evidence that Pedersen was told of the ship's perilous state at this time or shortly afterward. Fireman James O'Dowd stated to reporters that about five minutes before the vessel went into the water he sent his assistant up to the bridge to tell Pedersen that the ship was about to capsize, and shortly went up there himself. He said that Pedersen had told them, "Mind your own business and get back to the engine room." (Chicago *Examiner*, July 26, 1915, p. 2; Detroit *News*, July 26, 1915, p. 1.) O'Dowd's story is highly questionable; there is no corroboration of it in the testimony in the legal actions.

104. Testimony of Lobdell, in *Investigation of Accident to the Steamer "East-land,"* p. 38.

105. Testimony of McCreary, in *Investigation of Accident to the Steamer "Eastland,"* p. 21.

106. Erickson log.

107. Testimony of Frederick W. Willard, *Transcript of Testimony Before the Coroner's Jury*, p. 105.

108. Testimony of Joe Conrad, criminal transcript, p. 1287.

109. Testimony of Lobdell, in *Investigation of Accident to the Steamer "East-land,"* p. 37. See the letter from Admiral David W. Taylor to Congressman Lemuel P. Padgett, quoted below in Chapter VIII, which also states that the gangways, which the admiral called cargo ports, were open.

110. Letter from Fred G. Snow to his wife, published in the Ludington *Daily News*, July 27, 1915.

111. Erickson log.

112. Testimony of Pedersen, criminal transcript, p. 969.

113. Ibid., pp. 969, 980.

114. Testimony of Lynn, criminal transcript, p. 708.

115. Testimony of Weckler to coroner's jury, reported in Chicago *Tribune*, July 28, 1915; testimony of Lynn, criminal transcript, p. 707.

116. "The harbor master was on the dock. He shouted, 'Are you ready, captain?' He wanted to throw the lines out. I didn't start." Chicago *Tribune*, July 25, 1915, p. 2.

117. Testimony of Lynn, criminal transcript, pp. 707–8.

118. Interview with Pedersen, Chicago *Tribune*, July 25, 1915, p. 2.

119. Testimony of Pedersen, criminal transcript, p. 916.

120. Owing to the ambiguity about the casting off of the aft breast line, this cannot be stated with certainty. Lasser did not give times in his account of casting off one stern line and waiting for orders to cast off the other. If Flatow was correct that the aft breast line had not been cast off earlier but had merely been allowed to go slack, Lasser now cast that off, too; the photographic evidence cited previously reveals that it was not on the hull immediately following the capsizing.

The preponderance of evidence indicates that Lasser threw off only one line, the stern line out aft, at this time. Reed testified that the hand on the wharf cast off the stern line and went directly forward to the three lines from the bow (criminal transcript, p. 1183). Conrad, who was in full view of the wharf from the forward gangway, testified that the man took the stern line off a spile with some difficulty and threw it into the river before running up to deal with the forward lines (criminal transcript, pp. 1288–89).

121. Testimony of Del Fisher, criminal transcript, p. 655.

122. Detroit *News*, July 25, 1915, p. 3.

123. "The S.S. *Eastland* Catastrophe."

124. Testimony of Pedersen, criminal transcript, pp. 919–21.

125. Testimony of O'Meara, *Transcript of Testimony Before the Coroner's Jury*, p. 54.

126. Testimony of MacDonald, criminal transcript, p. 1274.

127. Willard Brown, one of the four survivors identified as still living at the time of dedication of a plaque at the site of the disaster on June 4, 1989 (he was 90 at this time), correctly stated that the ship made three tips, or reversals, in capsizing toward the river, but he also said she made three such tips when listing to the wharf earlier. If so, they are not noted in any of the immediate accounts of the disaster. Karen Dillon, "Remembering the *Eastland*: Plaque Honors Victims, Heroes of Maritime Tragedy," Chicago *Tribune*, June 5, 1989, pt. 2, p. 1.

128. Erickson log.

129. Testimony of Pedersen, criminal transcript, p. 916.

130. Ibid.

131. Testimony of Erickson, criminal transcript, p. 1095.

132. Testimony of an unidentified witness before the federal grand jury, reported in the Chicago *Evening Post*, Aug. 6, 1915, p. 1.

133. Erickson log.

134. Testimony of Reed, criminal transcript, p. 1184.

135. Testimony of Oakley, in *Investigation of Accident to the Steamer "Eastland,"* pp. 41–42.

136. Chicago *Evening Post*, July 26, 1915, p. 12.

137. Chicago *Tribune*, July 25, 1915, p. 3.

138. San Francisco *Chronicle*, July 25, 1915, p. 30.

139. Chicago *Examiner*, July 26, 1915, p. 5.

140. This account is corroborated by, for example, the report of a survivor, J. Peterson: "The first thing I heard was something like beer cases falling over. I dropped my cane and it went slipping across the deck toward the cable. I leaned over to reach for it, but before I could grab it I was kicking about in the water." Chicago *Tribune*, July 25, 1915, p. 11.

141. The New York *Times*, July 26, 1915, p. 2, stated that the refrigerator wedged one woman beneath it. The late Dwight Boyer, in his *True Tales of the Great Lakes* (New York: Dodd, Mead & Co., 1977), p. 38, stated that the refrigerator hit Agnes Kasperski and Stella Michalska, both of whom are well documented as victims. Most other writers on the disaster concluded that the refrigerator fell at this time, rather than earlier, as Richard J. Moore believed. See A. A.

Hoehling, *Disaster: Major American Catastrophes* (New York: Hawthorn Books, 1973), p. 49; Harriet K. Nye, "Tragic Queen of the Lakes," in Ben Kartman and Leonard Brown, eds., *Disaster!* (New York: Pellegrini & Cudahy, 1948), p. 172.

142. Chicago *Tribune*, Aug. 14, 1915, p. 1; July 25, 1915, p. 1.

143. Testimony of Peter Erickson, *Transcript of Testimony Before the Coroner's Jury*, p. 120.

144. Testimony of Flatow in the civil case, quoted in "Brief for Appellee," p. 82.

145. Pedersen testified (criminal transcript, p. 916) that he shouted down to Lynn, but according to Lynn's own testimony (ibid., p. 708) Lynn had returned to the Clark Street bridge to speak to Weckler, and then went to a telephone. Pedersen also stated that his order resulted in the gangways being opened, but Flatow stated that the ship went over before this could be done (ibid., pp. 708, 916).

146. Chicago *Evening Post*, July 27, 1915, p. 4.

147. Testimony of Del Fisher, criminal transcript, p. 655. Lynn testified that the head and spring lines also held, ibid., p. 710, but this is apparently in error. Flatow testified that only the breast line was in place after the disaster, ibid., p. 1042.

148. Blueprint, "Soundings of Chicago River Between Clark and La Salle Streets," July 29, 1915, City of Chicago, Department of Public Works, Bureau of Engineering, Division of Bridges and Harbors, drawing no. 1726, in file of U.S. v. Hull et al.

149. Testimony of Lynn, criminal transcript, p. 732.

150. Chicago *Daily Journal*, July 24, 1915, p. 4.

151. Chicago *Tribune*, July 25, 1915, p. 1.

152. Ibid.

153. Testimony of Pedersen, criminal transcript, pp. 916, 923, 984.

154. Statement of John V. Elbert, the *Eastland*'s gauge tender, Chicago *Tribune*, July 25, 1915, p. 11.

155. Erickson log.

156. Testimony of Conrad, criminal transcript, p. 1288.

157. "The S.S. *Eastland* Catastrophe."

Chapter 5

1. Testimony of Joseph R. Lynn, criminal transcript, p. 733.

2. Chicago *Evening Post*, July 27, 1915, p. 4.

3. *Annual Report of the Coast Guard*, 1916, p. 7.

4. "The Experiences of a Hawthorne Nurse," *Western Electric News*, 4, no. 6 (Aug. 1915): 19.

5. Detroit *News*, July 25, 1915, p. 1.

6. Statement of John Parotto seeking status as a life salvor, Apr. 29, 1919, in file of U.S. District Court, Northern District of Illinois, Eastern Division, In re Petition of the St. Joseph–Chicago Steamship Co. for Limitation of Liability, no. 32,231, Record Group 21, National Archives, Great Lakes Center, Chicago. Hereinafter cited as civil case, District Court file. Because the statements of the life salvors were made in the course of seeking a legal status in which they had a

claim against the owners of the *Eastland*, one should bear in mind a possible bias toward overstating their contributions to the saving of life.

7. Statement of Frank Actobowski seeking status as a life salvor, Nov. 30, 1918, civil case, District Court file.

8. Accusation of J. W. Fuhrmann, a passenger on a Wells Street car, reported in Chicago *Tribune*, July 26, 1915, p. 10.

9. Ibid., July 27, 1915, p. 4.

10. New York *Times*, July 25, 1915, p. 2.

11. Statement of Walter C. Rost seeking status as a life salvor, May 5, 1919, civil case, District Court file.

12. Statement of William P. Kearney seeking status as a life salvor, May 2, 1919, civil case, District Court file.

13. Statement of Sherwood S. Mattocks seeking status as a life salvor, Nov. 27, 1918, civil case, District Court file.

14. Statement of Charles Nicholas Klein seeking status as a life salvor, Apr. 24, 1916, civil case, District Court file.

15. New York *Times*, July 26, 1915, p. 1.

16. Ibid.

17. Statement of Edward Johnson seeking status as a life salvor, n.d., civil case, District Court file.

18. Much the best account of the rescue effort is Rev. Edward J. Dowling, S.J., "Tragedy at Clark Street Bridge," *Steamboat Bill: Journal of the Steamship Historical Society of America*, no. 94 (1965): 43–49. Identification of the vessels involved is from his comprehensive collection of photographs of the disaster.

19. Milwaukee *Sentinel*, July 25, 1915, p. 1.

20. William Ratigan, *Great Lakes Shipwrecks and Survivals* (Grand Rapids: William B. Eerdmans Publishing Co., 1960), pp. 65–66, apparently based on an interview with Bright.

21. Detroit *Free Press*, July 25, 1915, pp. 1–2.

22. Chicago *Examiner*, July 25, 1915, p. 7.

23. Chicago *Evening Post*, July 24, 1915, p. 1.

24. Detroit *News*, July 25, 1915, p. 3.

25. Chicago *Evening Post*, p. 1.

26. Detroit *Free Press*, July 25, 1915, p. 2.

27. Chicago *Tribune*, July 25, 1915, p. 3.

28. Ibid., July 31, 1915, pp. 13–17.

29. Chicago *Daily Journal*, July 24, 1915, p. 4.

30. The Chicago *Evening Post* (July 24, 1915, p. 7) reported that she had been killed. On the following morning the Chicago *Examiner* (July 25, 1915, p. 6) stated that she had been rescued.

31. Chicago *Tribune*, July 25, 1915, p. 3.

32. "In Memoriam: *Eastland* Victims," Chicago *Tribune*, July 31, 1915, pp. 13–17.

33. Detroit *News*, July 29, 1915, p. 16.

34. Ibid., July 27, 1915, p. 9.

35. Grand Haven *Daily Tribune*, July 26, 1915.

36. Ibid., Aug. 4, 1915.

37. Obituary of Ray W. Davis, St. Joseph *Herald-Press*, Oct. 6, 1930, p. 2.

38. New York *Times*, July 26, 1915, p. 2.

39. Detroit *News*, July 25, 1915, p. 3.

40. Chicago *Tribune*, July 31, 1915, pp. 13–17.

41. Ibid., July 25, 1915, p. 3.

42. Detroit *News*, July 25, 1915, p. 3.

43. Chicago *Examiner*, July 25, 1915, pp. 2, 11; Detroit *News*, July 25, 1915, p. 1.

44. Chicago *Daily Journal*, July 24, 1915, p. 3.

45. "In Memoriam: *Eastland* Victims," Chicago *Tribune*, July 31, 1915, pp. 13–17.

46. Chicago *Evening Post*, July 27, 1915, p. 4.

47. Dowling, "Tragedy at Clark Street Bridge," p. 47.

48. "The Experiences of a Hawthorne Nurse," p. 19.

49. New York *Times*, July 26, 1915, p. 1.

50. *"Eastland" Disaster Relief: American Red Cross 1915–1918: After the Capsizing of the Steamer "Eastland" in the Chicago River, July 24, 1915, to Completion of Relief Work*, final report of the *Eastland* Disaster Relief Committee (Chicago: Chicago Chapter, American Red Cross, 1918), pp. 11–12; Detroit *News*, July 25, 1915, p. 3.

51. *"Eastland" Disaster Relief*, p. 13.

52. Chicago *Tribune*, July 25, 1915, p. 1.

53. Ibid.; Chicago Sunday *Herald*, July 25, 1915.

54. Chicago Sunday *Herald*, July 25, 1915.

55. Statement of Klein as life salvor, civil case, District Court file.

56. Chicago *Tribune*, July 15, 1915, p. 8.

57. "The *Eastland*, Pride of the City Toppled over One Year Ago Today: Delwin Fisher Tells of Disaster," St. Joseph *Daily Press*, July 24, 1916.

58. Chicago *Tribune*, July 25, 1915, p. 1; testimony of Harry Pedersen, criminal transcript, pp. 917–18.

59. Chicago *Tribune*, July 25, 1915, p. 1.

60. Statement of Otto J. Blaha seeking status as a life salvor, Dec. 6, 1918, civil case, District Court file.

61. Statement of Daniel P. Brazill seeking status as a life salvor, May 13, 1919, civil case, District Court file.

62. Milwaukee *Journal*, July 24, 1915, p. 2; Detroit *Free Press*, July 25, 1915, p. 2.

63. "The Experiences of a Hawthorne Nurse," p. 19.

64. Ibid., p. 20.

65. New York *Times*, July 25, 1915, p. 1.

66. Chicago *Tribune*, July 25–31, 1915, passim.

67. Ibid., July 25, 1915, pt. 2, p. 1.

68. "In Memoriam: *Eastland* Victims," pp. 13–17.

69. Michigan City *Evening Dispatch*, July 23, 1915; Michigan City *News*, July 28, 1915.

70. St. Joseph *Evening Herald*, July 24, 1915.

71. Chicago *Tribune*, July 28, 1915, p. 1.

72. Chicago *Daily Journal*, July 27, 1915, p. 1.

73. Chicago *Examiner*, July 26, 1915, p. 10.

74. Chicago *Tribune,* July 25, 1915, p. 7.

75. Ibid., p. 8.

76. "Chicago's Affliction," New York *Times*, July 26, 1915, p. 8.

77. New York *Times*, July 27, 1915, p. 2.

78. Ibid., July 25, 1915, p. 10.

79. Testimony of Joseph M. Erickson, criminal transcript, p. 1132.

80. Testimony of Harry Halvorson, criminal transcript, p. 1409.

81. Chicago *Tribune*, July 25, 1915, pp. 2, 11.

82. Hull presented the combined explanation in conversation with William F. Sweet, assistant to William C. Redfield, secretary of commerce, at the opening of the Grand Army of the Republic Hall in St. Joseph. Typescript letter from William C. Redfield to Colonel William V. Judson, Corps of Engineers, U.S. Army, Chicago, Sept. 20, 1915, Bureau of Marine Inspection and Navigation, Steamboat Inspection Service, Numerical Correspondence, 1905–23, no. 71330, box 545A, National Archives, Washington, D.C.

83. "The Expected Happened," Chicago *Tribune*, editorial, July 27, 1915, p. 8.

84. *La Follette's Weekly*, 7, no. 8 (Aug. 1915): 1.

85. Detroit *News*, July 27, 1915, p. 1.

86. "The Story of July Twenty-fourth," *Western Electric News*, 4, no. 6 (Aug. 1915): 3–4; Ernest P. Bicknell, "The *Eastland* Disaster: An Incredible Tragedy in the Heart of Chicago," *The American Red Cross Magazine*, 10 (1915): 305–9.

87. "Thirty-four Hours at the Switchboard," *Western Electric News*, 4, no. 6 (Aug. 1915): 21.

88. "The Experiences of a Hawthorne Nurse," p. 20.

89. "In Memoriam: *Eastland* Victims" pp. 13–15.

90. Chicago *Tribune*, Aug. 1, 1915, p. 3.

91. Ibid., July 28–29, 1915, passim.

92. Chicago *Evening Post*, July 28, 1915, p. 2.

93. Ibid., July 29, 1915, p. 2.

94. "Hawthorne's Automobile Fleet," *Western Electric News*, 4, no. 6 (Aug. 1915): 17.

95. Chicago *Tribune*, July 28, 1915, p. 5.

96. Ibid.

97. New York *Times*, July 28, 1915, p. 7; July 29, 1915, p. 5.

98. Chicago *Evening Post*, July 26, 1915, p. 1; July 27, 1915, p. 1.

99. Chicago *Tribune*, July 25, 1915, p. 1.

100. Chicago *Evening Post*, July 27, 1915, p. 3.

101. Chicago *Tribune*, July 30, 1915, p. 5.

102. Chicago *Examiner*, July 25, 1915, p. 1.

103. One such person, Marie Clinehart Benes, recorded her experience. She was uninjured, and merely proceeded to an Elevated station and took the train home. Tape in collection of her son, Louis Benes, Des Plaines, Ill.

104. Chicago *Tribune*, Aug. 15, 1915.

105. U.S. Coast Guard, Wreck Report no. 129, received by Collector of Customs, Grand Haven, Mich., Aug. 20, 1915, microfilm reel T925-2, National Archives, Washington, D.C.

106. Chicago *Tribune*, Sept. 3, 1915, p. 5.

107. *"Eastland" Disaster Relief*, pp. 10, 185.

108. Microfilmed death certificates, Cook County, Ill., Church of Jesus Christ of Latter Day Saints Family History Library, Salt Lake City, Utah, reels 1,287,523–31. The absence of names beginning with S is an apparent oversight of the camera operator in the transition from reel 1,287,529 to reel 1,287,530.

109. MS Inquest Record, vol. 125, Office of the Medical Examiner, 2121 W. Harrison Street, Chicago.

110. Typescript answer of James F. Bishop, administrator of estates, civil case, District Court file.

111. Chicago *Tribune*, July 25, 1915, p. 1; July 26, 1915, pp. 6–7; July 31, 1915, pp. 13–17.

112. "The Dead," *Western Electric News*, 4, no. 6 (Aug. 1915): 9–15.

113. MS interment records, Resurrection Cemetery, Justice, Ill. I am greatly indebted to Mr. Gregg Szelung, of the cemetery's staff, for search of these records.

114. Chicago *Examiner*, accounts of funerals, July 28, 1915; MS interment record, Rosehill Cemetery, Chicago.

115. Chicago *Tribune*, July 31, 1915, p. 13. Oscar Dahl of Albert Lea verified the cemetery as that of the Central Freeborn Lutheran Church.

116. *"Eastland" Disaster Relief*, p. 10.

117. "In Memoriam: *Eastland* Victims," pp. 13–17. It might be noted that the disaster produced two additional known suicide attempts. Casper Laline survived along with his daughter Anna, but upon learning of the death of his son, Casper, Jr., he threatened suicide so vigorously that he had to be restrained forcibly by the police (Chicago *Daily Journal*, July 24, 1915, p. 3). Elmer Scott, one of the morbidly curious, made a suicide attempt after viewing the wreck and then visiting the morgue in the armory (Chicago *Evening Post*, July 26, 1915, p. 12).

118. Chicago *Evening Post*, July 28, 1915, p. 2.

119. "In Memoriam: *Eastland* Victims," pp. 13–17.

120. Death certificate of Joe Brennan, microfilmed death certificates, Cook County, Ill., reel 1,287,523, Church of Jesus Christ of Latter Day Saints Family History Library, Salt Lake City, Utah.

121. U.S. Coast Guard, "Wreck Report, *Petoskey*, July 24, 1915," microfilm reel T925-2, report no. illegible, National Archives, Washington, D.C.

122. Chicago *Tribune*, July 29, 1915, p. 2

123. New York *Times*, July 26, 1915, p. 2. The *Times* incorrectly stated Schroll's name as "Jule Strogl."

124. Chicago *Tribune*, July 31, 1915, p. 13.

125. Ibid., July 30, 1915, p. 4.

126. *"Eastland" Disaster Relief*, pp. 183–87.

127. Detroit *News*, July 26, 1915, p. 1; Ralph Lutz, "Worst Disaster on Lakes Recalled by Sawyer Man," Benton Harbor *News-Palladium*, July 22, 1970.

128. "In Memoriam: *Eastland* Victims," pp. 13–17.

129. Ibid.

130. Ibid.

131. Ibid. This man's name was subject to the largest variety of angliciza-
tions of any of the victims' names. The spelling shown is that of the records of
St. Casimir's Cemetery, Chicago.

132. "In Memoriam: *Eastland* Victims," pp. 13–17.

133. Ibid.

134. Ibid.

135. Ibid.

136. Chicago *Tribune*, July 26, 1915, p. 11.

137. "In Memoriam: *Eastland* Victims," pp. 13–17.

138. St. Joseph *Daily Press*, July 28, 1915.

139. Ibid., July 29, 1915.

140. Office of the Circuit Court of Cook County, Probate Division, Room
1202, Richard J. Daley Center, Chicago. The files must be ordered individually by
the name of the deceased.

141. *"Eastland" Disaster Relief*, pp. 29–31; "The Story of July Twenty-
fourth," pp. 3–8 passim; "How the Hawthorne Hospital Staff Worked," *Western
Electric News*, 4, no. 6 (Aug. 1915): 18.

142. *"Eastland" Disaster Relief*, p. 15.

143. Ibid., pp. 15–20, 32, 187 and passim.

144. *A Bill for Relief of Victims of the "Eastland" Disaster*, 64th Cong., 1st
sess. Sabath introduced this measure four times as a bill and once as a joint reso-
lution, all between May 11 and Aug. 15, 1916: H.R. 15581, May 11, 1916; H.R.
15653, May 13, 1916; H.R. 17264, July 29, 1916; H.R. 17482, Aug. 15, 1916;
H.R. J. Res. 223, May 12, 1916.

145. *A Bill for an Act to Adjudicate the Claims of the Surviving Husbands,
Widows and Next of Kin of the Various Deceased Persons, Arising out of the
"Eastland" Disaster*, House Bill 237, Feb. 6, 1917, with typescript report of
the Committee on the Judiciary (R. E. Church, W. N. Dieterick, and John L.
Cooper), Illinois State Archive, Springfield.

146. *Ordinance: Appropriating $20,000 for Use of Commissioner of Public
Works for Expenditures Growing out of "Eastland" Disaster*, doc. no. 221,392,
July 26, 1915, approved by William Hale Thompson, mayor, Aug. 9, 1915, Chi-
cago City Council proceedings files, Illinois State Archives, Regional Depository,
Northeastern Illinois University, Chicago.

147. *An Act Making Appropriations for the Construction, Repair and Preservation of Certain Public Works on Rivers and Harbors and for Other Purposes*,
55th Cong., 3rd sess., chap. 425, *U.S. Statutes at Large*, vol. 30 (1899), pp. 1121–
61, sec. 19 at p. 1154.

148. See George W. Hilton, *The Great Lakes Car Ferries* (Berkeley, Calif.:
Howell-North Books, 1962), pp. 83–85, 261.

149. Typescript letter from W. C. Steele to Captain Robert Young, Dunham
Towing & Wrecking Co., July 25, 1915; typescript letter from Alexander Cunning
to W. C. Steele, July 26, 1915; typescript letter from William H. Hull to A. G.
Lange, Chicago; typescript letter from A. G. Lange to Alexander Cunning, exhibits 1–4, civil case, District Court file, box 1 of 3.

150. Chicago *Tribune*, July 29, 1915.

151. Typescript examination of Captain Alexander Cunning, p. 12, civil case, District Court file.

152. The account of the salvage process is based on the examination of Alexander Cunning, pp. 9–36 passim; "Righting *Eastland* a Difficult Task," *Marine Review*, 40 (1915): 379–80; Chicago *Tribune*, July 29–Aug. 17, 1915; Chicago *Daily News*, Aug. 12–14, 1915; Chicago *Evening Post*, July 27–Aug. 14, 1915.

153. Chicago *Daily News*, Aug. 17, 1915.

154. Chicago *Tribune*, Aug. 17, 1915, p. 1; Aug. 18, 1915, p. 12.

155. Lake Carriers' Association, *Annual Report* (1915), pp. 59–60.

156. *Transcript of Testimony Before the Coroner's Jury, July 24, 25, 26, 27, 28, 29, on the Body of Kate Austin and All Others Lost by Overturning of the Excursion Steamer "Eastland" While Tied to the Dock at Clark and S. Water Street in the City of Chicago, July 24, 1915* (Chicago: City of Chicago, 1915).

157. Chicago *Tribune*, Aug. 1, 1915, p. 2; Aug. 3, 1915, p. 3; Aug. 4, 1915, p. 4.

158. Ibid., Aug. 1, 1915, p. 1.

159. Ibid., Aug. 3, 1915, p. 3.

160. Ibid., p. 4.

161. *Transcript of Testimony Before the Coroner's Jury*, p. 137; Chicago *Tribune*, July 29, 1915.

162. State of Illinois v. George T. Arnold et al., Case 6,824, Circuit Court, Chicago, Aug. 1915, microfiche docket of cases, Criminal Courts Building, 26th Street and California Avenue, Chicago.

163. State of Illinois v. Harry Pedersen and Joseph M. Erickson, Cases 6,825–26, Circuit Court, Chicago, Aug. 1915, microfiche docket of cases, Criminal Courts Building, 26th Street and California Avenue, Chicago.

164. Summary of indictments from Chicago *Evening Post*, Aug. 11, 1915, p. 1.

165. Ibid.

166. Chicago *Evening Post*, Aug. 13, 1915, pp. 1–2.

167. Ibid., Aug. 27, 1915, p. 1; State of Illinois v. Walter K. Greenebaum, Case 6,832, Circuit Court, Chicago, Aug. 1915, microfiche docket of cases, Criminal Courts Building, 26th Street and California Avenue, Chicago.

168. Chicago *Evening Post*, Aug. 27, 1915, p. 1.

169. Typescript letter from William C. Redfield, secretary of commerce, to Woodrow Wilson, Aug. 10, 1915, Bureau of Marine Inspection and Navigation, Steamboat Inspection Service, Numerical Correspondence, 1905–23, nos. 71, 308–30, box 545A, National Archives, Washington, D.C.

170. Ibid.; typescript report of the Board of Inquiry, Aug. 5, 1915, Bureau of Marine Inspection and Navigation, Steamboat Inspection Service, Numerical Correspondence, 1905–23, nos. 71,308–30, box 545A, National Archives, Washington, D.C.

171. Letter from Redfield to Woodrow Wilson, Aug. 10, 1915.

172. Chicago *Evening Post*, Aug. 3, 1915, p. 1.

173. Ibid., July 27, 1915, p. 1.

174. Ibid., July 31, 1915, p. 1.

175. Ibid., Aug. 2, 1915, p. 2; Chicago *Tribune*, Aug. 24, 1915, p. 5. The com-

mittee consisted of William J. Wood; Adam F. Weckler; Henry A. Allen, a mechanical engineer in the employ of the city; William A. Nelson, identified as an MIT graduate; and F. H. Avery, assistant city bridge engineer.

176. Testimony of Harry Pedersen and Joseph M. Erickson, "Transcript of Testimony, Inquest on the Bodies of Kate Austin *et al.*, July 24–28, 1915, Peter M. Hoffman, Cook County Coroner," typescript, Office of the Medical Examiner of Cook County, Chicago, pp. 291–92.

177. Chicago *Evening Post*, July 30, 1915.

178. Chicago *Tribune*, Sept. 29, 1915, p. 5.

179. Chicago *Evening Post*, Aug. 10, 1915.

180. Chicago *Tribune*, Sept. 23, 1915, p. 7.

181. Ibid., Sept. 29, 1915, p. 5.

182. The indictments were for violation of Section 282 and other sections of the criminal code. See Chapter VI, below. Criminal transcript, p. 2.

183. Typescript report of Board of Inquiry, Aug. 5, 1915; U.S. House of Representatives, Committee on the Merchant Marine and Fisheries, *Investigation of Accident to the Steamer "Eastland," Chicago, Ill., July 24, 1915*, 64th Cong., 1st sess. (Washington: Government Printing Office, 1916), pp. 337–44.

184. *A Bill to Provide for a Board of Naval Architects in the Department of Commerce and for Other Purposes*, 64th Cong., 1st sess., S. 1221, Dec. 10, 1915; H.R. 4787, Dec. 14, 1915.

185. "Proceedings of the Meeting of the Special Committee of Supervising Inspectors of Steam Vessels Held at Detroit, Mich., September 22 to October 5, 1915," typescript, pp. 9–10, Bureau of Marine Inspection and Navigation, Steamboat Inspection Service, Numerical Correspondence, 1905–23, no. 71330, box 545A, National Archives, Washington, D.C.

186. Ibid., pp. 20–31.

187. Chicago *Tribune*, Aug. 6, 1915. See also James L. Elliott, *Red Stacks over the Horizon: The Story of the Goodrich Steamboat Line* (Grand Rapids, Mich.: William B. Eerdmans Publishing Co., 1967), pp. 158–59.

188. Chicago *Tribune*, Aug. 15, 1915, p. 1.

189. Ibid., Aug. 17, 1915, p. 9.

190. Ibid., Aug. 18, 1915, p. 12.

191. Chicago *Evening Post*, Aug. 19, 1915, p. 12.

192. Chicago *Tribune*, Dec. 19, 1915, p. 12.

193. Edwin L. Dunbaugh, *The Era of the Joy Line* (Westport, Conn.: Greenwood Press, 1982), pp. 278–79, 285–88, 296, 299 and passim.

194. Chicago *Daily News*, Dec. 20, 1915, p. 1.

195. Robert D. Long, "The *Eastland* Story," unpublished typescript (n.d.), Manitowoc Maritime Museum Library, Manitowoc, Wis.

196. Chicago *Herald*, Dec. 21, 1915, p. 9; Chicago *Daily News*, Dec. 20, 1915, p. 1.

197. MS docket book, vol. 42, p. 181, U.S. District Court, Northern District of Illinois, Eastern Division, In re Petition of St. Joseph–Chicago Steamship Co., Owner of Steamer *Eastland* for Limitation of Liability, no. 32,231, National Archives, Great Lakes Region, Chicago. Hereinafter cited "Civil case, docket book."

198. Ibid.

199. "Privity" means private or internal information of the management.

200. Civil case, docket book, p. 181.

201. Chicago *Tribune*, Aug. 18, 1915, p. 12.

202. Ibid., Dec. 19, 1915, p. 12.

203. Ibid., July 25, 1915.

204. Milwaukee *Sentinel*, July 25, 1915, p. 1.

205. New York *Times*, July 26, 1915, p. 2.

206. Elliott, *Red Stacks over the Horizon*, pp. 213, 215–22, 274–77.

207. William R. Childs, *Trucking and the Public Interest* (Knoxville: University of Tennessee Press, 1985), p. 21.

208. Elliott, *Red Stacks over the Horizon*, pp. 264, 279–82.

Chapter 6

1. Chicago *Tribune*, Sept. 23, 1915, p. 7.

2. Ibid. The indictments were for violations of Sections 282 and 37 of the Criminal Code, and also of Section 77, par. 4561, which is Section 11 of the Act of December 21, 1898. The judge to whom the case was assigned considered the indictments other than under Section 282 probably extraneous. (Criminal transcript, p. 2.)

3. Charles F. Clyne, criminal transcript, pp. 10–11.

4. James J. Barbour, criminal transcript, p. 11.

5. Testimony of Joseph R. Lynn, criminal transcript, pp. 711–18, 735.

6. For example, a passenger, Dr. J. G. Barnsdale of Superior, Wisconsin, attributed the disaster to the tug's having pulled her over while she rested on the bottom (Chicago *Tribune*, July 27, 1915, p. 7). The Chicago *Daily News* (July 24, 1915) advanced the explanation that the tug had pulled on the *Eastland* while the ship was still moored at the bow, producing a leverage that pulled her over.

7. Robert A. Freeman, "The Epitaph of the *Eastland*," *The Chicago Fire Fighter*, Sept. 1966, pp. 9, 11; Ben Hecht, *Gaily, Gaily* (Garden City, N.Y.: Doubleday, 1963), p. 186. Hecht stated that 900 passengers rushed to starboard to watch the tug.

8. George Spencer, a health officer working on the wreck, stated that he had heard this explanation (St. Joseph *Daily Press*, July 26, 1915).

9. T. L. Witz, "The *Eastland* Disaster," *Sparks Journal*, 7, no. 1 (Oct. 1984): 7, 32, based on an interview with Radio Officer Charles M. Dibbell in an unidentified newspaper in Allentown, Penn. Dibbell's retrospective presentation of his role in the disaster in this interview differs radically from his account in *The Marconigraph* of August 1915, cited above in Chapter IV. In the interview in which he presented the speedboat hypothesis, he said that he was shaving in his quarters on the hurricane deck at the time of the capsizing, and had his face half lathered. If so, he presumably did not observe the alleged passing of the speedboat, which he attributed to the time of the capsizing, viz., about 7:28, rather than to the early stages of the list to port, about 7:00, when Erickson surmised a movement of the passengers to port had taken place.

10. This was argued retrospectively by the surviving crew member Robert Burns in his "Revisiting the Scene," Chicago *Sun-Times*, July 20, 1969.

11. James P. Barry, *Ships of the Great Lakes* (Berkeley: Howell-North Books, 1973), p. 190.

12. Interpretation of Joseph J. Paluch, a survivor, in "Survivor Relives River Tragedy," Detroit *News*, July 23, 1965.

13. Chicago *Examiner*, July 26, 1915, p. 2.

14. William Ratigan, *Great Lakes Shipwrecks and Survivals* (Grand Rapids: William B. Eerdmans Publishing Co., 1960), p. 64.

15. Testimony of Percy R. Hynes, criminal transcript, pp. 1304–6; Chicago *Tribune*, Feb. 2, 1916. Note that Hynes presumed the river was 0.2 feet below normal, rather than the 0.1 feet stated in the report of Morville, the gauge keeper, cited earlier.

16. Testimony of H. B. Vehstedt, criminal transcript, pp. 1321–28.

17. Ibid., pp. 1348, 1366.

18. Testimony of William Deneau, criminal transcript, pp. 532–37.

19. Testimony of Henry E. Cordell, criminal transcript, pp. 290–95.

20. Chicago *Tribune*, Sept. 23, 1915, p. 9.

21. Chicago *Tribune*, Aug. 4, 1915, p. 4.

22. Testimony of Captain Walter Scott, criminal transcript, pp. 342–43.

23. Testimony of Sylvester N. Howard, criminal transcript, pp. 516–17, 524.

24. Testimony of Fred M. Avery, engineer in charge of bridge construction and repair for the City of Chicago, criminal transcript, p. 1244.

25. Testimony of Adam F. Weckler, criminal transcript, pp. 1441–42.

26. Detroit *News*, July 25, 1915, p. 1.

27. Chicago *Tribune*, July 29, 1915, p. 2.

28. St. Joseph *Daily Press*, July 26, 1915.

29. Chicago *Tribune*, July 25, 1915, p. 1.

30. Detroit *News*, July 25, 1915, p. 3; Chicago *Tribune*, July 25, 1915, p. 11.

31. Chicago *Tribune*, July 25, 1915, p. 11. Charles Haas and John P. Eaton were kind enough to search the list of crew in the United States Senate's investigation of the *Titanic* disaster, and the Board of Trade's crew agreement list for the vessel; they were, however, unable to find Elbert's name or anything approximating it. Letter to the author from Charles Haas, July 11, 1992.

32. Detroit *News*, July 25, 1915, p. 1.

33. Chicago *Tribune*, July 27, 1915, p. 3.

34. "Q.: No running from one side to the other? A.: No. They jumped from one seat to another." Testimony of Richard J. Moore, "Transcript of Testimony, Inquest on the Bodies of Kate Austin *et al.*, July 24–28, 1915, Peter M. Hoffman, Cook County Coroner," typescript, Office of the Medical Examiner of Cook County, Chicago, p. 13.

35. Testimony of Robert H. McCreary, in U.S. House of Representatives, Committee on the Merchant Marine and Fisheries, *Investigation of Accident to the Steamer "Eastland," Chicago, Ill., July 24, 1915*, 64th Cong., 1st sess. (Washington: Government Printing Office, 1916), p. 21.

36. Chicago *Tribune*, Aug. 3, 1915, p. 3.

37. Harry Hansen, *The Chicago*, Rivers of America Series (New York: Farrar and Rinehart, 1942), p. 251.

38. Chicago *Examiner*, July 26, 1915, p. 2. The actual report has apparently not survived.

39. Chicago *Tribune*, Aug. 3, 1915, p. 3.

40. Ibid., July 25, 1915, p. 7.

41. Testimony of Professor Herbert Charles Sadler, criminal transcript, pp. 1487–1543, reproduced in full, edited, in Appendix C, below.

42. Ibid., p. 1538.

43. "Objections of James F. Bishop, Administrator of the Estate of Marie Adamkiewicz, deceased, et al., Respondents, to the Report of the Honorable Lewis F. Mason, Special Commission, Filed June 26, 1933," p. 4, civil case, District Court file.

44. *Decision of Justice Sessions in Case of Steamship "Eastland," Letter from the Secretary of Commerce Transmitting Transcript of the Decision of Justice Sessions of the District Court of the United States for the Western District of Michigan, Southern Division, in Case Relating to Steamship "Eastland,"* 64th Cong., 1st sess., House of Representatives, document 814 (1916).

45. Lawrence Webley, *Across the Atlantic* (London: Stevens & Sons, 1960), p. 119. Chap. 4 of Webley's book is devoted to the *Eastland* cases.

46. "Death Claims Young Officer Last Night," Grand Haven *Daily Tribune*, Apr. 4, 1919; microfilmed death records, office of the Clerk of the Ottawa County Court, Grand Haven, Mich.

47. Chicago *Tribune*, July 28, 1915; testimony of Weckler, criminal transcript, p. 1474.

48. Testimony of William L. Nack, in *Investigation of Accident to the Steamer "Eastland,"* p. 288.

Chapter 7

1. In the District Court of the U.S. for the Northern District of Illinois, Eastern Division in Admiralty, James F. Bishop, Administrator of the Estate of Earl H. Dawson, Deceased, et al., Libelants, v. St. Joseph–Chicago Steamship Co. et al., Respondents, Case 32,236, filed July 24, 1915, Record Group 21, 345/369, 411, box D593A, National Archives, Great Lakes Center, Chicago.

2. In the District Court of the U.S. for the Northern District of Illinois, Eastern Division in Admiralty, James F. Bishop, Administrator of the Estate of Herman A. Ristow, Deceased, et al., Libelants, v. St. Joseph–Chicago Steamship Co. et al., Respondents, Case 32,237, filed June 14, 1916, Record Group 21, 345/369, 411, box D593A, National Archives, Great Lakes Center, Chicago.

3. Petition of Indiana Transportation Company for a Writ of Prohibition, Supreme Court of the U.S., no. 25, original, October Term, 1916, June 17, 1917.

4. Ibid.

5. Chicago *Examiner*, July 26, 1915.

6. U.S. District Court, Northern District of Illinois, Eastern Division, In re Petition of St. Joseph–Chicago Steamship Co., Owner of Steamer *Eastland*, for Limitation of Liability, no. 32,231, Record Group 21, National Archives, Great Lakes Center, Chicago.

7. "Response of Lewis F. Mason to K. M. Landis," n.d., civil case, District Court file.

8. George II, chap. 15 (1734).

9. George III, chap. 86 (1786).

10. George III, chap. 159 (1813).

11. *An Act to Limit the Liability of Ship Owners, and for Other Purposes*, 31st Cong., 2nd sess., chap. 43, *U.S. Statutes at Large*, vol. 9 (1851), pp. 635–36.

12. Norwich Co. v. Wright, 80 U.S. 104 (1871) at 127.

13. Petition of Norwich & New York Transportation Co., 8 Ben. 312 (1875).

14. Ibid., pp. 116–17.

15. The *City of Norwich*: Place and Others v. Norwich & New York Transportation Co., 105 U.S. 24 (1881).

16. Richardson v. Harmon, 222 U.S. 96 (1911).

17. *An Act to Remove Certain Burdens on the American Merchant Marine and Encourage the American Foreign Carrying Trade and for Other Purposes*, 49th Cong., 1st sess., chap. 121, *U.S. Statutes at Large*, vol. 23 (1884), p. 53, sec. 18, at pp. 57–58; *An Act to Abolish Certain Fees for Official Services to American Vessels, and to Amend the Laws Relative to Shipping Commissioners, Seamen, and Owners of Vessels and for Other Purposes*, 49th Cong., 1st sess., chap. 421, *U.S. Statutes at Large*, vol. 24 (1886), p. 79, sec. 4289, at pp. 80–81.

18. Erastus C. Benedict, *The American Admiralty: Its Jurisdiction and Practice*, 4th ed. (Albany, N.Y.: Banks & Co., 1910), p. 378.

19. In re *Annie Faxon*, 66 F. 575 (1895).

20. *An Act Making Provisions for the Construction, Repair and Preservation of Certain Public Works on Rivers and Harbors, and for Other Purposes*, in *U.S. Statutes at Large*, vol. 30, p. 1121, sec. 15, pp. 1152–53.

21. Decree of K. M. Landis, Nov. 3, 1916, filed Jan. 26, 1917, in *Transcript of Record in the U.S. Circuit Court of Appeals for Seventh Circuit, October Term, 1916, No. 2465, Great Lakes Towing Company, Appellant, v. St. Joseph–Chicago Steamship Company et al., Appellees*. Printed record.

22. Great Lakes Towing Co. v. St. Joseph–Chicago Steamship Co., 253 F. 635 (1918).

23. James F. Bishop, Administrator, etc., v. Great Lakes Towing Co., 248 U.S. 578 (1918); 249 U.S. 609 (1919).

24. Pittsburgh Coal Co. of Illinois v. Great Lakes Towing Co., 248 U.S. 579 (1918).

25. Great Lakes Towing Co. v. St. Joseph–Chicago Steamship Co., 253 F. 635 (1918); opinion of J. Carpenter, case 32,231, Dec. 23, 1919, civil case, District Court file.

26. John W. Hipple, William Raphael, Albert Johnson, John Parotto, James Huml, Edward A. Aitken, Walter C. Rost, Louis N. Schoenick, William P. Kearney, David P. Brazill, Louis Rochetta, Edward K. Plamondon, William Doderlein, John J. Aman, Edward Johnson, Frank Actobowski, Albert P. Actobowski, and Otto J. Blaha. "Exceptions of Great Lakes Towing Co. to Claims of Sherwood S. Mattocks and Others for Services as Salvors of Human Life," n.d., civil case, District Court file. Harry H. Braun made a separate claim as a life salvor for throwing five chicken coops into the river, then with others pulling at least 10 people to safety with ropes. "Claim of Harry H. Braun," July 30, 1915, civil case, District Court file.

27. In re St. Joseph–Chicago Steamship Co., the *Eastland*, 262 F. 535 (1919).

28. "Exceptions of Great Lakes Towing Co. to Claims of Mattocks and Others."

29. Report of Lewis F. Mason under monition of Aug. 21, 1915, filed Jan. 20, 1917, civil case, District Court file, box 0592A.

30. "Seaworthiness [means] reasonable fitness for the voyage" (The *Millie B.*

Bohannon: Hewlett et al. v. the *Millie B. Bohannon*, 64 F. 883 [1894] at 884). "By seaworthiness is meant 'that the ship shall be in a fit state as to repair, equipment, crew, and in all other respects, to encounter the *ordinary perils* of the contemplated voyage' " (The *Titania*, 19 F. 101 [1883] at 105).

31. Civil case, docket book, p. 293.

32. Although neither the minutes of evidence nor the report has survived, the table of contents to the minutes of evidence survives in a file marked "Report of Lewis F. Mason, U.S. Commissioner," civil case, District Court file.

33. "Veteran Lake Captain Dies at Home Here," Grand Haven *Daily Tribune*, Jan. 12, 1922, p. 1.

34. "Respondents' Reply Brief," case 32,231, filed Nov. 20, 1933, submitted by Harry W. Standidge and Justus Chancellor, proctors for respondents, in civil case, District Court file.

35. "Objections of James F. Bishop, Administrator of the Estate of Marie Adamkiewicz, Deceased, et al., Respondents, to the Report of the Honorable Lewis F. Mason, Special Commissioner, Heretofore Filed Herein. Filed June 26, 1933," p. 1, civil case, District Court file.

36. "Respondents' Reply Brief," Nov. 20, 1933, pp. 13–14.

37. "Brief for Appellee, Frederick L. Leckie and Robert Branard, Jr., Proctors for Appellee," passim, In the U.S. Circuit Court of Appeals for the Seventh Circuit, In re Petition of the St. Joseph–Chicago Steamship Co. for Limitation of Liability, docket no. 5257, October Term, 1934. Copy in Law Library, Library of Congress.

38. Ibid., p. 83, citing testimony of Flatow.

39. Ibid., p. 85, citing testimony of Flatow.

40. Ibid., p. 85, citing testimony of Pedersen, pp. 129–30.

41. "Brief for Respondents," filed Oct. 30, 1933, citing testimony, pp. 278–80, civil case, District Court file; corroborated in "Respondents Reply Brief," Nov. 20, 1933, p. 4, citing testimony, p. 267, and Mason's report, p. 44.

42. Chicago *Examiner*, July 25, 1915, p. 8.

43. Testimony of Harry Pedersen, criminal transcript, p. 941.

44. Objections of James F. Bishop to the report of Lewis F. Mason, June 26, 1933, p. 5, civil case, District Court file.

45. "Respondents' Reply Brief," Nov. 20, 1933, pp. 19, 32, citing Mason's report, pp. 42–44, 46, 56; citing Pedersen's testimony, pp. 262, 264–67, 298–99.

46. Testimony of Pedersen, criminal transcript, p. 972.

47. "Brief for Appellee," p. 92.

48. Ibid., p. 15, citing testimony of Lynn.

49. Ibid., p. 70, citing testimony of Lynn, p. 495.

50. Ibid., p. 75, citing testimony of Lynn, p. 483.

51. Ibid., p. 75, citing testimony of Lynn, p. 483. Actually, the tanks had been pumped out on the morning of the disaster, but this error is not intrinsic to the argument.

52. The *Eastland*: James F. Bishop et al., Appellants, v. St. Joseph–Chicago Steamship Company, Appellee, 78 F. 2d 984 (1935) at 986; "Brief for Appellee," p. 11.

53. "Brief for Appellee," p. 11.

54. "Final Decree in the Matter of the Petition of the St. Joseph–Chicago Steamship Co. for Limitation of Liability," typescript, in civil case, District Court file.

55. Trustees of the Estate of Kate Austin v. St. Joseph–Chicago Steamship Co., 78 F. 2d 984 (1935).

56. James F. Bishop, Administrator, et al. v. St. Joseph–Chicago Steamship Co., 297 U.S. 703 (1936). The file of the case consists of a single card recording the addresses of the lawyers for the petitioner and respondent, and a notation of the date of the denial of certiorari. It has no factual material and no indication of the reason for the denial. Certiorari cards, Record Group 267, no. 633, October Term, 1935, National Archives, Washington, D.C.

57. An excellent hostile evaluation of the doctrine with an account of its decline is Richard C. Angino, "Limitation of Liability in Admiralty: An Anachronism from the Days of Privity," *Villanova Law Review*, 10 (1965): 721.

58. Enrollments of *Edgar F. Coney*, Bureau of Marine Inspection and Navigation, Steamboat Inspection Service, Numerical Correspondence, 1905–23, no. 71330, box 3451, file 201,104, National Archives, Washington, D.C. Shore owned the ship in partnership with Charles R. Wiebe, the tug's captain, and Raymond Hodgson. Shore held a one-half share, the others one-fourth each. (Consolidated Certificate of Enrollment and License, *Edgar F. Coney*, May 10, 1915, Record Group 1, box 54, National Archives and Records Administration, Southwest Region, Fort Worth, Tex. This set is the file of the Federal District Court at Beaumont, Tex., hereinafter cited as Sabine file.)

59. *Transcript of Record in the United States Circuit Court of Appeals, Fifth Circuit, No. 7267, Sabine Towing Company, Inc., Appellant, v. Sophia Brennan, Administratrix, et al., Appellee*, appeal from the U.S. District Court, Eastern District of Texas (printed, two vols., numbered consecutively). Records of the Circuit Court of Appeals, case files 1891, 7264–67, box 1921E, National Archives and Records Administration, Southwest Region, Fort Worth, Tex. Hereinafter cited as Sabine transcript. File *Edgar F. Coney* S.P. 346, Ships Histories Section, Naval History Center, Washington Navy Yard, Washington, D.C.

60. Sabine transcript, testimony of Capt. Munger T. Ball, p. 115; deposition of John W. Sullivan, p. 488; deposition of Douglas F. Gillette, p. 665; deposition of Dickerson N. Hoover, p. 925; deposition of Fabian P. Noel, p. 1071. Because Shore burned a heavy bunker C fuel oil, the reported weight of 70.5 tons is probably an understatement. At a weight of 8.331 pounds per gallon, the tanks should have been able to accommodate about 82 tons.

61. Sabine transcript, testimony of Charles R. Wiebe, p. 246; testimony of William H. Yant, p. 309; deposition of John W. Sullivan, p. 486; deposition of Fabian P. Noel, p. 1284.

62. Sabine transcript, p. 253; photostat of typescript letter from Charles R. Wiebe to Philip Shore, July 20, 1921, loose document, Sabine file, box 54.

63. Testimony of A. Amanda Parsons, chief engineer during the event, Sabine transcript, p. 880.

64. Ibid., p. 891.

65. Deposition of John W. Sullivan, boiler inspector, Sabine transcript, p. 528.

66. Ibid., p. 529.

67. Ibid.

68. Deposition of Will Cook Disbrow, Jr., Sabine transcript, p. 640.

69. Rule 7, sec. 16, U.S. Department of Commerce, Steamboat Inspection Service, *General Rules and Regulations Prescribed by the Board of Supervising Inspectors, Ocean and Coastwise*, Mar. 27, 1927, p. 162.

70. Letter from Shore to John R. Blair and John W. Sullivan [1921], Sabine transcript, p. 934.

71. Memorandum of John R. Blair and John W. Sullivan, May 24, 1921, Sabine transcript, pp. 1366–67.

72. Deposition of John W. Sullivan, Sabine transcript, pp. 529–30.

73. Text of order of General George Uhler, July 9, 1921, Sabine transcript, pp. 1325–26.

74. Letter from Philip Shore to local inspectors, Tampa, Dec. 20, 1921, Sabine transcript, pp. 570–71.

75. Letter from John R. Blair and John W. Sullivan to Philip Shore, Feb. 10, 1922, Sabine transcript, pp. 920, 1345–46.

76. Sabine transcript, deposition of John W. Sullivan, p. 575; testimony of John R. Blair, p. 620.

77. Letter from Cecil Bean, Steamboat Inspection Service, Washington, D.C., to Shore, Jan. 27, 1922, Sabine transcript, p. 1164.

78. Testimony of William F. Brown, superintendent of the Florida Machine & Engineering Company, Sabine transcript, p. 644; deposition of Douglas F. Gillette, chief engineer of the *Edgar F. Coney*, ibid., p. 662.

79. Testimony of Ball, Sabine transcript, pp. 67–73. There is no record of a publication of this title. Ball almost certainly meant *Johnson's Steam Vessels and Motor Ships Annual: A Directory of American-owned Self-propelled Craft* (New York: Eads Johnson, M.E., Inc., 1916–54). Douglas L. Haverly, chief library officer of the Steamship Historical Society of America, recognized Ball's reference as a corruption of this title, and Ann C. House, the Society's librarian, located for me an incomplete set, which includes the volume for 1930. This publication could have provided Ball with only basic registry data on the tug.

80. Exhibits P-13 and P-14, Sabine transcript, pp. 698–700.

81. Testimony of Ball, Sabine transcript, p. 138; testimony of Charles H. Guy, ibid., p. 224.

82. Testimony of Andrew A. Miranda, Sabine transcript, pp. 274, 99, 266. The certificate of Jan. 2, 1930, is in the Sabine file, box 54.

83. Sabine transcript, pp. 144–46.

84. Sabine transcript, pp. 2–7, 85–88, 368–81 and passim; accounts of the disaster in New Orleans *Times-Picayune* and Mobile *Register*, Feb. 1, 1930, p. 1 in each instance. Position of the wreck is from Sabine's advertisement for bids for salvage, New Orleans *Times-Picayune*, Feb. 14, 1930, p. 30, col. 2.

85. Sabine transcript, pp. 4–5.

86. Typescript testimony of J. B. Bodden, second mate, and A. L. Urie, master of the *Robert P. Clark*, Sabine file, box 53.

87. Typescript report of federal inspectors at Galveston, Apr. 30, 1930, Sabine file, box 53.

88. Sabine transcript, statement of facts of the case, p. 824.

89. Sabine transcript, preliminary material, p. 12.

90. Sabine transcript, preliminary material, pp. 7, 12; testimony of Ball, p. 88; statement of facts of the case, p. 1431.

91. Testimony of Herbert Slade, Sabine transcript, p. 328. This figure is not entirely comparable to Noel's figures of 1.34 feet empty and 1.86 feet loaded. Slade concluded that Noel had calculated the center of buoyancy too high, thereby erring on the position of the metacenter and understating the metacentric height. Brennan and the other applicants hired J. A. Laing, a marine surveyor of New Orleans, to comment on the calculations of Noel and Slade. Laing concluded that Noel had been approximately correct (testimony of J. A. Laing, ibid., pp. 793–820).

92. Findings of Fact and Conclusions of Law, Sophia Brennan et al. v. Sabine Towing Co., Case 334 in Admiralty, by Randolph Bryant, District Judge, U.S. District Court, Eastern District of Texas, July 13, 1933, printed in full in Sabine transcript, pp. 1380–84.

93. Sabine Towing Co., Inc., v. Sophia Brennan et al., 72 F. 2d 490 (1934).

94. *Sabine Towing Co., Inc., v. Sophia Brennan et al.*, no. 7267 (July 17, 1934), printed decision, pp. 11–19. Loose document filed with Sabine transcript.

95. To fill out the account, Louisiana law provided penalties for wrongful deaths based on the present value of lost income streams, rather than a flat sum as Illinois did. The next round in the proceedings was determination of the sums. Commissioner Samuel C. Lipscomb, on Feb. 2, 1935, awarded a total of $92,200 to the claimants, ranging from $21,000 to the widow of Captain Brennan to $700 to the heirs of Edward C. Van Beeck, the second mate. (Typescript volume of hearings before Samuel C. Lipscomb, Esq., Commissioner, at Beaumont, Tex., Feb. 2, 1935, Sabine file, box 53.) Sabine appealed the awards, but they were affirmed in circuit court on Aug. 14, 1936. (In the Matter of the Petition of Sabine Towing Co., Inc., Owner of the Tug *Edgar F. Coney*, Praying for Exoneration of or Limitation of Liability, no. 334 A.D., final decree, Sabine file, box 53.)

96. Sabine Towing Co. v. Sophia Brennan, Administratrix, et al., 293 U.S. 611 (1934). Sabine's petition for a rehearing was denied on Dec. 3, in 193 U.S. 632 (1934).

97. *An Act Relative to Limitation of Shipowners' Liability*, 74th Cong., 1st sess., chap. 804, Public Law No. 391, *U.S. Statutes at Large*, vol. 49 (1935), pp. 960–61.

98. See Angino, "Limitation of Liability in Admiralty."

Chapter 8

1. Robert D. Long, "The *Eastland* Story," typescript (n.d.), in Manitowoc Maritime Museum Library, Manitowoc, Wis.

2. Letter from Frank J. Baker to Secretary of the Navy, Oct. 19, 1917, in Report no. 1976-A272, vol. 2, Bureau of Construction and Repair, General Correspondence, 1912–25, Record Group 19, National Archives, Washington, D.C. Vols. 1 and 2 are in box 349, vol. 3 in box 350, along with unbound correspondence. Baker did not list himself among the contributors, which may have been an act of modesty.

3. Memorandum from J. L. Ackerson to Edward A. Evers, Feb. 1, 1916, Report

no. 1976-A272, vol 1. Ackerson refers to the ship as the *Ouilmette*, a spelling that was repeated as late as Oct. 16, 1917, in a memorandum of W. A. Moffett, commandant of the Naval Training Station at Great Lakes, Ill., ibid.

4. Memorandum from Rear Admiral David W. Taylor, chief, Bureau of Construction and Repair, to Evers, Mar. 4, 1916, Report no. 1976-A272, vol. 1.

5. Ibid.; telegram from Evers to Bureau of Construction and Repair, Mar. 4, 1916; memorandum from Taylor to Division of Naval Militia Affairs, Sept. 18, 1916, both in Report no. 1976-A272, vol. 1.

6. Letter from Taylor to Hon. Lemuel P. Padgett, chairman, Committee on Naval Affairs, U.S. House of Representatives, May 9, 1916, Report no. 1976-A272, vol. 1.

7. *An Act Making Appropriations for the Naval Service for the Fiscal Year Ending June 30, 1917*, H.R. 15947, Public Law no. 241, 64th Cong., 1st sess., chap. 417, approved Aug. 29, 1916, *U.S. Statutes at Large*, vol. 39, pt. 1, pp. 556–619, at p. 559.

8. The chronology of the ship's transfer and conversion is based on the typescript history in the folder "*Wilmette* (IX-29)," Ships Histories Section, Naval History Center, Washington Navy Yard, Washington, D.C.; *Eastland* file, Frank E. Hamilton collection, Rutherford B. Hayes Memorial Library, Fremont, Ohio; and Report no. 1976-A272.

9. Memorandum from Taylor to Bureau of Steam Engineering, July 2, 1917, Report no. 1976-A272, vol. 1.

10. Printed solicitation of bids, signed by Acting Secretary of the Navy W. S. Benson, Oct. 27, 1916, Bureau of Construction and Repair, General Correspondence, 1912–25, Record Group 19, box 350.

11. Letters of A. H. Bull & Company, John O'Connor, and Auten Engineering & Contracting Company, New York, Bureau of Construction and Repair, General Correspondence, 1912–25, Record Group 19, box 350.

12. Memorandum from Graham Edgerton to Bureau of Construction and Repair, November 22, 1916, Bureau of Construction and Repair, General Correspondence, 1912–25, Record Group 19, box 350.

13. Memorandum from Evers to Taylor, Mar. 22, 1917, Report no. 1976-A272, vol. 1.

14. Memorandum from Evers to Taylor, Aug. 10, 1917, Report no. 1976-A272, vol. 1.

15. Letter from W. T. Abbott, vice president of the Central Trust Company, to the Secretary of the Navy, Oct. 17, 1917, Report no. 1976-A272, vol. 1.

16. Memorandum from Taylor to the Secretary of the Navy, Nov. 8, 1917, Report no. 1976-A272, vol. 1.

17. Memorandum 8028-49:20, from Franklin D. Roosevelt, acting secretary of the Navy, to Taylor, Nov. 17, 1917, Report no. 1976-A272, vol. 1.

18. "Report of Inspection of 'Eastland,' " inspection conducted Nov. 26–27, 1917, in South Chicago, by Board of Inspection and Survey, Captain W. A. Gill, Naval Constructor W. P. Roberts, Lieutenant Commander F. D. Karns, and Lieutenant C. S. Joyce, Report no. 1976-A272, vol. 1.

19. Letter from Baker to Taylor, Dec. 28, 1917, Report no. 1976-A272, vol. 1.

20. Memorandum from William N. McMinn, assistant commandant, 9th, 10th,

and 11th Naval Districts, Chicago, to Bureau of Construction and Repair, Jan. 17, 1918; letter from Lloyd R. Steere, estate officer, Central Trust Company, Chicago, to Franklin D. Roosevelt, Jan. 17, 1918, both in Report no. 1976-A272, vol. 2.

21. Memorandum from McCall Pate to Chief, Bureau of Construction and Repair, Jan. 17, 1923, Report no. 1976-A272, vol. 3.

22. Memorandum from Taylor to Commandant, 9th, 10th, and 11th Naval Districts, Jan. 9, 1918, Report no. 1976-A272, vol. 2.

23. Memorandum from Evers to the Bureau of Construction and Repair, Jan. 19, 1918, Report no. 1976-A272, vol. 2. The usual explanation that "Wilmette" was chosen because the village had distinguished itself in a war-bond drive lacks substantiation. A less common attribution that the name was chosen in memory of victims of the disaster who lived there is clearly incorrect. None lived within miles of it.

24. Memorandum from Taylor to Richards, Feb. 21, 1918, Report no. 1976-A272, vol. 2.

25. Memorandum from Richards to Bureau of Construction and Repair, Jan. 20, 1918, Report no. 1976-A272, vol. 2.

26. Memorandum from Richards to Construction Officer, Navy Yard, New York, Mar. 25, 1918, Report no. 1976-A272, vol. 2.

27. Memorandum from Senior Medical Officer, U.S.S. *Wilmette*, to Bureau of Medicine and Surgery, Jan. 1, 1921, Bureau of Construction and Repair, Correspondence Re Ships, 1916–25, Record Group 19, box 673, file 3-GX-13-5, p. 1.

28. Memorandum from Bureau of Construction and Repair to Bureau of Navigation, July 31, 1918, Report no. 1976-A272, vol. 3.

29. "Report of Material Inspection of U.S.S. *Wilmette*," Jan. 3, Feb. 28, and Mar. 7, 1934, Sub-Board of Inspection and Survey, Bureau of Construction and Repair, General Correspondence, 1925–40, Record Group 19, 6-24-46 (hereinafter cited as *Wilmette* file), box 2911, IX 29/FS, vol. 1, p. 41.

30. "Material Inspection of U.S.S. *Wilmette*," Apr. 7, 1930, p. 7, *Wilmette* file, box 2911.

31. Memorandum from Evers to Bureau of Construction and Repair, Apr. 22, 1931, *Wilmette* file, box 2910.

32. Memorandum from Richards to Bureau of Construction and Repair, Sept. 28, 1918, Report no. 1976-A272, vol. 3.

33. Memorandum from Richards to Bureau of Construction and Repair, Oct. 26, 1918, Report no. 1976-A272, vol. 3.

34. Memorandum from J. D. Beuret to Richards, Nov. 4, 1918, Report no. 1976-A272, vol. 3.

35. Report no. 1976-A272, vol. 2.

36. Letter to the author, Mar. 10, 1992.

37. Memorandum from Richards to Bureau of Construction and Repair, Sept. 30, 1918, Report no. 1976-A272, vol. 3.

38. Memorandum from Richards to Bureau of Construction and Repair, Sept. 20, 1918, Report no. 1976-A272, vol. 3.

39. *Wilmette* file, box 2911, vol. 1, p. 41.

40. Memorandum from R. Stocker to Richards, Feb. 19, 1918, Report no. 1976-A272, vol 2.

41. Memorandum from Chief of Naval Operations to Bureau of Construction and Repair, Oct. 19, 1918; memorandum from H. C. Richardson, superintending constructor of aircraft, U.S. Navy, Buffalo, to Bureau of Construction and Repair, Oct. 17, 1918, both in Report no. 1976-A272, vol. 3.

42. Memorandum from Bureau of Construction and Repair to Richards, Oct. 11, 1918; memorandum from Bureau of Construction and Repair to Chief of Naval Operations, Oct. 14, 1918, both in Report no. 1976-A272, vol. 3.

43. Memorandum from Richards to Bureau of Construction and Repair, Oct. 20, 1918, Report no. 1976-A272, vol. 3.

44. Telegram from Richards to Bureau of Construction and Repair, Nov. 2, 1918, Bureau of Construction and Repair, Record Group 19, box 1336, file 39-GX-13.

45. Typescript despatch, Bureau of Construction and Repair to Richards, Nov. 9, 1918, Bureau of Construction and Repair, Record Group 19, box 1336, file 39-GX-13.

46. Telegram from Richards to Bureau of Construction and Repair, Nov. 13, 1918, Bureau of Construction and Repair, Record Group 19, box 1336, file 39-GX-13.

47. Despatch 09012 from the Chief of Naval Operations, cited in memorandum from T. S. O'Leary, Boston Navy Yard, to Bureau of Supplies and Accounts, Report no. 1976-A272, vol. 3.

48. Folder "*Wilmette* (IX-29)," Naval History Center; *Eastland* file, Hamilton collection.

49. From chronology in *Eastland* file, Hamilton collection.

50. Chicago *Tribune*, June 8, 1921, p. 3; Milwaukee *Journal*, June 7, 1921, p. 1; *Eastland* file, Hamilton collection.

51. "Material Inspection of U.S.S. *Wilmette*," Jan. 3, Feb. 28, Mar. 7, 1934, *Wilmette* file, box 2911.

52. "Report of Material Inspection of U.S.S. *Wilmette*," Oct. 23–24, 1923, Bureau of Construction and Repair, Record Group 19, box 351, file 1-GX-13-3.

53. "Wilmette," *Dictionary of American Naval Fighting Ships*, vol. 8 (1981), p. 387.

54. Memorandum from Evers to Bureau of Engineering, Feb. 17, 1925, Bureau of Construction and Repair, Record Group 19, box 673, file 3-GX-13-9.

55. Memorandum from W. G. DuBose to Commandant, 9th Naval District, May 29, 1925, *Wilmette* file, box 2911.

56. "Report of Material Inspection of U.S.S. *Wilmette*," Nov. 29, 1926, *Wilmette* file, box 2911.

57. Memorandum from W. G. DuBose, chief, Bureau of Construction and Repair, to Commandant, 9th Naval District, May 29, 1925, *Wilmette* file, box 2911.

58. Memorandum from Evers to Bureau of Construction and Repair, June 5, 1925, *Wilmette* file, box 2911.

59. Memorandum from Evers to Bureau of Construction and Repair, Apr. 22, 1931, *Wilmette* file, box 2911.

60. Memorandum from Henry Williams, Bureau of Construction and Repair to Commandant, 9th Naval District, Apr. 4, 1931, *Wilmette* file, box 2911.

61. Memorandum from Evers to Bureau of Construction and Repair, Mar. 5, 1931, *Wilmette* file, box 2911. Captain John F. Kalina pointed out in the course of

reading this manuscript that this passage presents a problem. The Navy's magnetic compasses of the time were mounted in gimbals, with the compass cards floating in alcohol, an arrangement that should have protected them from error—particularly from an error of this large magnitude. Captain Kalina notes that Evers's letter is consistent with Pedersen's remark to Erickson outside the officers' mess immediately before the disaster that list of the ship biased his compass. It is more probable that the compass erred for some other reason, but there is no presumption that the Navy was using the same magnetic compass the *Eastland* had.

62. Memorandum from Evers, Mar. 11, 1931, *Wilmette* file, box 2911.

63. Memorandum from Evers, Apr. 22, 1931, *Wilmette* file, box 2911.

64. Memorandum from Henry Williams, Bureau of Construction and Repair, to Evers, Apr. 4, 1931, *Wilmette* file, box 2911.

65. Diagram of tanks, enclosed with memorandum from Evers to Bureau of Construction and Repair, June 27, 1938, *Wilmette* file, box 2912.

66. "Material Inspection of U.S.S. *Wilmette*," Dec. 1, 1936, p. 5, *Wilmette* file, box 2912.

67. Memorandum Evers to Bureau of Construction and Repair, Sept. 23, 1938, *Wilmette* file, box 2912.

68. "Material Inspection of the *Wilmette*," Dec. 1, 1936, p. 49, *Wilmette* file, box 2912.

69. New York *Times*, July 16, 1933, p. 1.

70. Memorandum from Evers to Chief, Bureau of Navigation, Feb. 10, 1937, *Wilmette* file, box 2912.

71. Memorandum from Hayne Ellis, commandant, 9th Naval District, to Chief, Bureau of Navigation, Feb. 11, 1937, *Wilmette* file, box 2912.

72. Memorandum from Evers to Bureau of Construction and Repair, Nov. 15, 1937, *Wilmette* file, box 2912.

73. Memorandum from Bureau of Construction and Repair to Bureau of Navigation, Nov. 9, 1938, *Wilmette* file, box 2912.

74. Memorandum from Evers to Bureau of Construction and Repair, June 27, 1938, *Wilmette* file, box 2912.

75. "Material Inspection of U.S.S. *Wilmette*," Dec. 1, 1936, *Wilmette* file, box 2912.

76. New York *Times*, Aug. 10, 1943, p. 1; Washington *Post*, Aug. 10, 1943, p. 1.

77. Log of the U.S.S. *Wilmette*, volumes for January 1–July 31, 1943, and Aug. 1–Dec. 31, 1943, Record Group 24, National Archives, Washington, D.C.; George R. Werthmann, "The Night the *Wilmette* Went Ashore," *Telescope*, 23, no. 4 (July–Aug. 1974): 94–99.

78. Werthmann, "The Night the *Wilmette* Went Ashore," p. 95. Werthmann, who was explicit that he was writing from memory, stated that the ship carried 4.50″ shells. This is in error according to all surviving records of the ship.

79. "Wilmette," *Dictionary of American Naval Fighting Ships*, vol. 8 (1981), p. 387.

Epilogue

1. Obituary of J. C. Pereue, South Haven *Daily Tribune*, Apr. 23, 1931.

2. Manistee *Daily News*, Jan. 20, 1925.

3. Ludington *Daily News*, Sept. 18, 1931, p. 1.

4. Port Huron *Times-Herald*, Jan. 7, 1919.

5. Testimony of S. G. Jenks, criminal transcript, p. 417.

6. Obituary in Camden *Courier-Post*, Dec. 14, 1965, p. 43. For direction to information on Jenks's later career and death, I am indebted to Gould P. Coleman, archivist, Cornell University, who searched alumni records.

7. Ludington *Daily News*, Dec. 17, 1929.

8. St. Joseph *Herald-Press*, Oct. 6, 1930.

9. St. Joseph *Herald-Press*, Sept. 22, 1933.

10. St. Joseph *Herald-Press*, July 26, 1939.

11. *Marine Review*, 46 (1916): 442; obituary in Michigan City *News-Dispatch*, Nov. 3, 1960, pp. 1, 6. The community changed its name to Pottawatomie Park in 1970.

12. Kalamazoo *Gazette*, Nov. 20, 1948.

13. T. L. Witz, "The *Eastland* Disaster," *Sparks Journal*, 7, no. 1 (Oct. 1984): 7, 32.

14. Karen Dillon, "Remembering the *Eastland*: Plaque Honors Victims, Heroes of Maritime Tragedy," Chicago *Tribune*, June 5, 1989, pt. 2, p. 1.

15. Letter to the author from Mrs. Francis P. Watson, May 11, 1992.

16. Chicago *Tribune*, obituaries, July 22, 1989; Aug. 3, 1991.

17. Chicago *Tribune*, Aug. 5, 1992.

Appendix C

1. For Sadler's purpose in elucidating the *Eastland* disaster, this statement was adequate, but it is not universally true. An initially unstable ship in the course of inclining may reach a new point of stable equilibrium if the underwater hull form creates a new center of buoyancy in the same vertical line as the center of gravity. This is presumably why the list to starboard stopped at 20 to 25 degrees in the *Eastland*'s near capsizing of July 17, 1904. See Edward L. Attwood, O.B.E., *Theoretical Naval Architecture* (London: Longmans, Green & Co., 1922), pp. 184–85.

2. The prismatic coefficient of fineness is the ratio of the volume of displacement of a vessel up to a given waterline to the volume of a solid having a length equal to the load waterline and a constant cross-section area equal to that of the vessel's midships section up to the given waterline. See Society of Naval Architects and Marine Engineers, *Principles of Naval Architecture*, vol. 1 (1941), p. 54.

3. Great Lakes Historic Ships Research Project (Kingston, Ontario: Marine Museum of the Great Lakes, 1989), n.p.

4. Rev. Peter J. Van der Linden, ed., *Great Lakes Ships We Remember* (Cleveland: Freshwater Press, Inc., 1979), pp. 21, 74, 133, 170, 267, 345, 380.

Index

In this index an "f" after a number indicates a separate reference on the next page, and an "ff" indicates separate references on the next two pages. A continuous discussion over two or more pages is indicated by a span of page numbers, e.g., "pp. 57–58." *Passim* is used for a cluster of references in close but not continuous sequence.

Because of limitations of space, this index includes references only to the deceased who appear in the text and footnotes. Readers seeking names of individuals should begin by consulting the lists of victims in Appendix D, pp. 283–312. Similarly, readers seeking information on ships built by Jenks should first consult the hull list in Appendix B, p. 241.

Library of Congress Cataloging-in-Publication Data

Hilton, George Woodman.
    Eastland, legacy of the Titanic / George W. Hilton.
        p.   cm.
    Includes bibliographical references and index.
    ISBN 0-8047-2291-9 (cl.) : ISBN 0-8047-2801-1 (pbk.)
    1. Eastland (Ship)   2. Titanic (Steamship)
    3. Shipwrecks—Illinois—Chicago River.
    4. Shipwrecks—North Atlantic Ocean.
    I. Title.
    G530.E18H55   1995
    977.3'11—dc20   93-33883
                                                    CIP

ⓧ This book is printed on acid-free paper.

Original printing 1995
Last figure below indicates year of this printing:
05   04   03   02   01   00   99   98   97   96

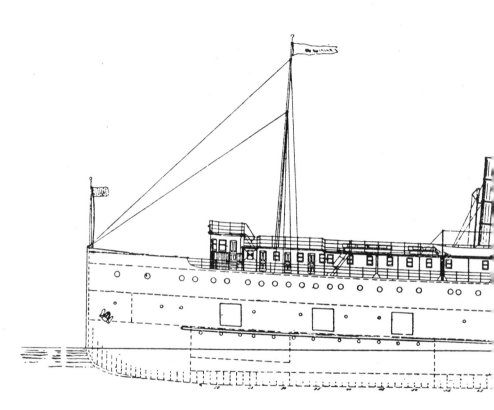

New Twin-Screw Passenger and